THE CLASSICS
OF **WESTERN**
SPIRITUALITY

THE CLASSICS OF WESTERN SPIRITUALITY
A Library of the Great Spiritual Masters

President and Publisher
Lawrence Boadt, C.S.P.

EDITORIAL BOARD

Maria Maddalena de' Pazzi

TRANSLATED AND INTRODUCED BY
ARMANDO MAGGI

PREFACE BY
E. ANN MATTER

PAULIST PRESS
NEW YORK • MAHWAH

These translations were made by the permission of Nardini Editore from *Tutte le Opere* (7 vols., eds. Bruno Nardini, Bruno Visentin, Carlo Catena, and Giulio Agresti [Florence: Nardini, 1960–66]).
Some material in the translator's introduction has been reprinted from *Uttering the Word* by Armando Maggi by permission of the State University of New York Press. © 1998, State University of New York. All rights reserved.

Library of Congress Cataloging-in-Publication Data

De' Pazzi, Maria Maddalena, Saint, 1566–1607.
   [Selections. English 2000]
   Maria Maddalena De' Pazzi : selected revelations / [translated] by Armando Maggi.
    p. cm. — (The classics of Western spirituality ; #97)
   ISBN 0-8091-3923-5; ISBN 0-8091-0509-8 (alk. paper)
   1. Mysticism—Catholic Church. I. Maggi, Armando. II. Title. III. Series.
BV5080 .D562 2000
248.2′2′092—dc21
                                            99-088285
                                              CIP

Published by Paulist Press
997 Macarthur Boulevard
Mahwah, New Jersey 07430

www.paulistpress.com

Printed and bound in the
United States of America

Contents

Translator of this Volume

ARMANDO MAGGI is Associate Professor of Romance Languages and Literatures at the University of Chicago. A specialist of Renaissance culture, he received his Ph.D. from the University of Chicago. He has published several essays on female mysticism, Renaissance theories on visuality, Neoplatonic treatises on love, seventeenth-century books on demonology, and Portuguese literature. He is the author of *Identita e impresa rinascimentale* (Ravenna: Longo, 1998), *Uttering the Word: The Mystical Performances of Maria Maddalena de' Pazzi, a Renaissance Visionary* (Albany: State University of New York Press, 1998), and *Satan's Rhetoric, a Study of Renaissance Demonology* (Chicago: University of Chicago Press, forthcoming).

Author of the Preface

E. ANN MATTER is R. Jean Brownlee Term Professor of Religious Studies at the University of Pennsylvania. She did her undergraduate work in religion at Oberlin College and received her Ph.D. in Religious Studies from Yale University. Her teaching and publishing centers on medieval and early modern Christianity, especially biblical interpretation, visionary and mystical literature, and women in the Christian tradition. She is currently completing a book on the Italian visionary Maria Domitilla Galluzzi (d. 1671) and has edited, with Armando Maggi and Maiju Lehmijoki-Gardner, a series of unpublished visions by Lucia Brocadelli da Narni (d. 1545), the Court Prophet of Ferrara.

Acknowledgments

I want to thank above all Bernard McGinn. Without his precious suggestions and fine remarks, this volume would not exist. Bernard McGinn has always supported and enlightened my research on Maria Maddalena de' Pazzi. I am also grateful to Alvises Svejkovsky, professor of Comparative Studies at the University of Chicago, for his brilliant insights concerning the linguistic aspects of de' Pazzi's mysticism.

I am particularly grateful to E. Ann Matter, professor in the department of Religious Studies at the University of Pennsylvania. Prof. Matter has read and commented both on my translation and on my introduction to this volume.

I am also grateful to Dr. Grazia Visintainer of the Kunsthistorisches Institut in Florence for her friendly help in choosing the cover of this volume.

A special thanks to the students of my seminar on women mystics at the University of Pennsylvania (Spring 1998). In particular, Franz Matzner and Dara Lovitz have had insightful suggestions concerning this translation. A final thanks to Kathleen Walsh for her invaluable help in editing and correcting my work.

Preface

In 1851, St. John Neumann, Bishop of Philadelphia was approached by a group of Italian immigrants who asked him to establish a parish church for their community. Neumann agreed to the project and appointed a pastor, Father Gaetano Mariani, an Italian priest then teaching sacred music at St. Charles Borromeo Seminary. Mariani was a native of Florence, and so, when the cornerstone was laid in 1854, the new church was dedicated to a Florentine mystic, Maria Maddalena de' Pazzi.[1] This was the first ethnic Italian parish in the United States. The parish church of St. Mary Magdalen de Pazzi still stands on a quiet side street just off of Philadelphia's bustling Italian Market. Every May, the saint's statue is paraded through the streets of the neighborhood, but hardly anyone in that community, nor anyone in the United States at all, knows much about the woman this parish honors.

Maria Maddalena de' Pazzi has been curiously neglected by scholars of Christian history and Italian literature alike. In his introduction to this splendid first English translation of her works, Armando Maggi suggests that this situation is partly the result of a systematic exclusion of mystical writings from the modern canon of Italian literature. This is certainly true, but it is not the whole story. After all, a number of mystics of the Italian language, including Catherine of Siena, Catherine of Genoa, and Jacopone da Todi, have appeared in English translation several times, including in this series.[2] Why, then, not Maria Maddalena de' Pazzi?

Surely, part of the reason why this woman mystic has been so dramatically overlooked has to do with the fact that she had no public persona in her own age. Unlike Catherine of Siena who moved

1

from Tuscany to Avignon and back again to Rome, teaching and preaching, or Catherine of Genoa who served the sick and unfortunate of her community, Maria Maddalena de' Pazzi spent all of her adult years, from the age of 16 until her death at 41, in strict enclosure in the convent of Santa Maria degli Angeli in Florence. There she was immersed in the extravagantly interiorized spirituality developed by the Jesuit, Dominican, and Carmelite orders during the Catholic Reforms of the sixteenth century.

Unlike the public mystics of her age, the women whom Gabriella Zarri has dubbed "living saints" *("sante vive"),*[3] Maria Maddalena's spirituality was intensely private. She never wanted her raptures to be recorded or read by anyone in the outside world. Had it not been for the teams of her sister nuns who were assigned to record her words (and the acts that accompanied them) in detail, we would not even have the records from which these translations have been made. The transcriptions made by her companions did not circulate widely; even though they were written down in her lifetime, Maria Maddalena's visions were not edited for publication until the middle of the twentieth century and have been the object of very few critical studies. It is very easy to get the feeling that scholars have rather been avoiding Maria Maddalena de' Pazzi.

Indeed, when one turns to the visions ascribed to her, it is not hard to see why she has inspired such neglect. The few historians who have written on Maria Maddalena de' Pazzi's spirituality all comment on the intensely oral quality of her texts and the performative quality of what is ascribed to her. One cannot even say that she "wrote" these visions in any real way, not even in the secondarily dictated form of much medieval women's visionary writing such as the "works" of Elisabeth of Schönau or Angela of Foligno.[4] Instead, what we have here is a type of sacred eavesdropping. Consequently, what emerges is rather messy, at least from the point of view of a systematic mysticism.

Nevertheless, these are fascinating and powerful texts. Giovanni Pozzi describes the experience of grappling with the visionary world of Maria Maddalena de' Pazzi as a series of conflicting emotions:

Prolixity, discontinuity, disorder, interruption, digressions, symbolic monstrosities, fallacies, continually stalk the steps of the reader on this itinerary; on the other hand, the reader is consoled by lyrical effusions, rushes of vehement and eternal passion, ardent speculation, abysmal descent into the core of the human soul, elevations to the threshold of the sublime.[5]

In other words, this is not easy reading, neither the soaring cosmologies of Hildegard of Bingen nor the practical spirituality of Catherine of Siena, but Maria Maddalena's words do offer a gripping experience of Christian spirituality. Furthermore, as Antonio Riccardi has pointed out, the discourses of Maria Maddalena de' Pazzi, precisely because of their performative theatricality, give important testimony to the role of language and the body in early modern Catholic piety. This interpretation places Maria Maddalena's language in the middle of the sixteenth-century Catholic struggle with the "Babel" of Protestantism, a quest for authenticity in spiritual language in which the wounds of the crucified Christ are increasingly incorporated into mystical discourse. As the body became more and more the "privileged space" of mystical discourse, embodied spirituality (stigmata, eucharistic piety) became more and more central to early modern Catholic religious language.[6]

This perspective turns our attention away from the concrete representation of words to the sighs, mumblings, silences that frame and (as Maggi demonstrates in his introduction) give meaning to Maria Maddalena's mystical vocabulary. Interpreting this "unlinguistic" language will present the greatest challenge to the twentieth-century scholar. This timely contribution to the Classics of Western Spirituality series brings the visionary world of Maria Maddalena de' Pazzi into the mainstream of the history of Christian thought right at the moment when that history is opening to serious study of mystical experience as never before.[7] For, as foreign as they might seem, with all their discontinuities and silences, the raptures of Maria Maddalena de' Pazzi are in a direct line of Christian spiritual language, a tradition that moves from the visions of medieval mystics to the glossolalia of modern Pentecostals.

NOTES

1. Alfred M. Natalia, *Saint Mary Magdalen De Pazzi Parish* (Philadelphia, 1991); Dorothy Noyes, *Uses of Tradition: Arts of Italian Americans in Philadelphia* (Philadelphia: Philadelphia Folklore Project, Samuel S. Fleisher Art Memorial, 1989), pp. 6, 15.

2. Catherine of Siena, *The Dialogues*, translated by Suzanne Noffke (New York: Paulist Press, 1980); Catherine of Genoa, *Purgation and Purgatory, The Spiritual Dialogue*, translated by Serge Hughes (New York: Paulist Press, 1979); Jacopone da Todi, *The Lauds*, translated by Serge and Elizabeth Hughes (New York: Paulist Press, 1982).

3. Gabriella Zarri, *Le sante vive: profezie di corte e devozione femminile tra '400 e '500* (Turin: Rosenberg & Sellier, 1990).

4. See Anne L. Clark, *Elisabeth of Schönau: A Twelfth-Century Visionary* (Philadelphia: University of Pennsylvania Press, 1992); Angela of Foligno, *Complete Works*, translated by Paul Lachance (New York: Paulist Press, 1993).

5. Giovanni Pozzi, "Introduzione," in Maria Maddalena de' Pazzi, *Le parole dell'estasi* (Milano: Adelphi, 1984), p. 21.

6. Antonio Riccardi, "The Mystic Humanism of Maria Maddalena de' Pazzi (1556–1607)" in E. Ann Matter and John Coakley, ed., *Creative Women in Medieval and Early Modern Italy: A Religious and Artistic Renaissance* (Philadelphia: University of Pennsylvania Press, 1994), p. 215.

7. See, for example, the multivolume study by Bernard McGinn, *The Presence of God: A History of Western Christian Mysticism*: vol. 1, *The Foundations of Western Mysticism* (New York: Crossroad, 1991), vol. 2, *The Growth of Mysticism* (New York: Crossroad, 1994), vol. 3, *The Flowering of Western Mysticism* (New York: Crossroad, 1998).

Introduction

Maria Maddalena de' Pazzi and Teresa of Avila are the two most significant female mystics of the late Renaissance. However, unlike Teresa of Avila, the Italian saint has not received the recognition that she deserves. This is primarily due to the fact that Italian scholars have traditionally excluded mystical literature from the canon of their national literature. Except for Catherine of Siena, no other female mystic is taught in the Italian schools and cultural institutions. For that matter, the case of Angela of Foligno is paradigmatic. Her powerful books were reevaluated after being translated into French. When George Bataille stated that Angela's disturbing mysticism had highly influenced his writing, her texts were granted a renewed interest in Italy.

Maria Maddalena de' Pazzi's mysticism follows a similar pattern. Although a group of religious scholars had published a complete, albeit rather inaccurate, edition of her work in the early sixties, no academic study was written on her texts until the mid-eighties when Giovanni Pozzi, an eminent student of Italian literature, focused his research on the overlooked phenomenon of Italian female mysticism. Pozzi's and Leonardi's seminal *Scrittrice mistiche italiane* (Genoa, 1988), a groundbreaking anthology of Italian female mysticism, and *Le parole dell'estasi* (Milan, 1984), a modest but fascinating selection of de' Pazzi's texts, founded a new area of academic research.

Like every anthology, my selection of de' Pazzi's texts is inevitably partial and personal. I have based my choice on two fundamental premises. First, I selected those visions that highlight de' Pazzi's original interpretation of mystical language. As I will explain in this introduction, I believe that de' Pazzi's most relevant contribution to Renaissance mysticism has a strong linguistic connotation. Second, I have chosen to offer a selection from the whole corpus of de' Pazzi's visions. Although some of her most interesting raptures are quite long (in some cases more than seventy pages), I thought it was important to present each vision in its complete version. Given their essentially oral structure, the raptures of Maria Maddalena de' Pazzi defy a strictly logical interpretation. As a consequence, any attempt to edit these texts would be in error.

The following introduction is divided into three parts: First, a brief biography of the mystic and a description of the convent where she spent most of her life; second, an analysis of de' Pazzi's mystical experience; third, a brief study of the terms *blood (sangue)*, *contemplation (risguardo)*, and *love (amore)*, three key terms in de' Pazzi's mysticism.

I. LIFE AND WRITING

Maria Maddalena de' Pazzi was born on April 2, 1566, into the noble de' Pazzi Florentine family. She was baptized Caterina but took the name of Maria Maddalena when she became a nun. Her deeply religious family raised Maria Maddalena according to Jesuit teachings. When she was still a child, the Jesuits introduced her to their meditation techniques and to some of their basic writings. At the age of eight she had already contemplated embracing the religious life, and she joined the convent Santa Maria degli Angeli when she was sixteen (August 1582), taking the veil the following year. She chose this convent because it was known to be particularly rigorous, and it gave her the opportunity to have communion more often than in other convents. This convent was, however, very crowded (it had more than eighty nuns) and was dominated by the severe sister Vangelista del Giocondo (1534–1625), who strongly wished to have a "blessed soul" in her convent. The mother superior tried to merge the active and practical teachings of the Jesuits with the intellectual piety of the Dominicans. In addition to the

Jesuits and the Dominicans, the Carmelites, who had ruled the convent in the past, still influenced it through their strict discipline.

The daily life in the convent reflected the standardized rules introduced in the Carmelite institutions. Apart from the usual recital of the breviary, one of the most important activities was manual work. The nuns worked together in the so-called *sala di lavoro* (workroom). While they attended to their specific tasks, the nuns recited psalms and listened to passages from the Gospel. One of the older sisters was allowed to comment on the passage read. Often this extemporaneous exegesis resulted in a lively discussion among the nuns. The practice of meditation was also a collective and oral activity, but private prayer, exercised in total silence, was important as well. As we shall see later, orality and silence play a crucial role in de' Pazzi's mysticism.

Very soon after entering the convent, Maria Maddalena had intense mystical experiences that led her to a mysterious and almost fatal disease. As in the case of other mystics, for Maria Maddalena this disease represents a turning point in her life. Indeed, when she recovered from this illness Maria Maddalena began to have daily visions during which she spoke to the Trinity, and in particular to Christ, whom she generally refers to as the Word. Despite the extraordinary intensity of her raptures, Maria Maddalena never had a special role within her convent. Her sisters succeeded in keeping her mystical experiences secret, informing only their immediate male superiors. During the last years of her life, when Maria Maddalena felt urged to communicate with the external world and thus wrote letters to bishops, priests, even to the pope in the attempt to influence the moral and religious life of her time, her letters almost never left the convent. Unlike St. Catherine of Siena, Maria Maddalena's mystical message remained within the walls of her convent. She died years after her visions ended, at the age of 41. Maria Maddalena de' Pazzi was canonized in 1669 after a long "trial" where more than fifty nuns were asked to testify.

The sources of Maria Maddalena's mysticism are primarily well-known manuals of meditations: *Instrutione et avertimenti per meditare la passione di Cristo nostro redentore, con alcune meditationi intorno ad esse* (Rome, 1571), a devotional book on the Savior's passion and death written in Italian by the Spanish Jesuit Gaspar Loarte. The saint's convent still has two copies of this book, which was Maria Maddalena's very first reading. Other works she had access to include Fulvio Androtio's *Meditatione della vita e morte del nostro Salvatore Gesù Cristo* (Milan, 1579); the Pseudo Augustine's *Le meditazioni, il manuale e i soliloqui* (Venice, 1574), an anthology of twelfth-century religious texts; Antonio Gagliardi's *Compendio della perfetione cristiana* (Venice, 1572), a mystical text highly influenced by German mysticism; and Luigi Granata's *Della introdutione al simbolo della fede* (Venice, 1587), an Italian anthology of German mystics, including Tauler and Meister Eckhart. In her *Renovatione della Chiesa (Renewal of the Church)*, the last volume of her writings, Maria Maddalena de' Pazzi directly refers to Tauler's crucial concept of *Gelassenheit* (abandonment), which she translates as *"relassatione."* Citing Tauler, Maria Maddalena stresses that the final step in the soul's process of purification entails the soul's total abandonment to God.[1] For Maria Maddalena other crucial references were Catherine of Siena's *Letters* and Augustine's *Confessions* and *The City of God*. Both Catherine and Augustine are recurrent presences in her visions. Also very influential were the numerous sermons that both the Dominicans and the Jesuits delivered in the convent of Santa Maria degli Angeli. The library of the convent still has the transcriptions of the homilies by Agostino Campi and Alessandro Capocchi, which were particularly important to her thought.

The saint's visions have been preserved in several manuscripts. Between 1960 and 1966 Francesco Nardini, Bruno Visentin, Carlo Catena, and Giorgio Agresti published her writings in seven volumes. Not a critical edition, these scholars have simply transcribed the nuns' manuscripts without even correcting their most apparent linguistic mistakes. The titles of the volumes are the following: *I quaranta giorni (The Forty Days)*, the mystic's visions from May 27, 1584, to July 4 of the same year. Its title, not present in the manuscript itself, has been chosen because the text actually covers a period of forty days. *I colloqui (The Dialogues)*, two volumes; this contains her raptures from Christmas of 1584 to June 4, 1585. The title refers to the fact that, after their transcriptions, the nuns asked the saint questions in order to clarify some of the unclear points of their text. *Rivelatione e intelligentie (Revelations and Knowledge)*, the visions Maria Maddalena had interruptedly during eight days beginning on June 8, 1585. *Probatione (Probation)*, two volumes that report the Saint's most painful mystical experiences, from June 16, 1585, to June 10, 1590. In this text the nuns tend to summarize the content of her raptures, rather than report her actual words. Finally, *Renovatione della Chiesa (Renovation of the Church)*, a miscellany of works of different nature. Its title is a quotation from the text: a four-day rapture (August 11–15, 1586), twelve letters written by the saint herself, as well as some other secondary texts, such as meditations and prayers.

II. MARIA MADDALENA'S ORAL MYSTICISM

Maria Maddalena's visions have a distinctly oral nature. Indeed, unlike any other mystical book of the Western tradition, most of the texts attributed to the Florentine mystic are not the narrative reportage of the ecstatic encounters between the divinity and a "blessed soul." Maria Maddalena de' Pazzi did not intend to communicate anything to us. Not only did she not care for any form of audience or readership, but she did not even want "her" books to be written. Indeed, to approach her texts correctly, two essential elements must be borne in mind: First, Maria Maddalena's oral discourses had a specific goal—the expression of the Word. The mystic believed that through oral language she might be able to evoke the Word's being. Her raptures revolve around her reiterated attempts to fulfill her task. Let us clarify this essential point with three brief quotations:

> [Y]our idea, your might, your goodness, everything is a language in the Word's God...the Word proceeding from the Word communicates us the Word and unites him with us...(*The Dialogues* 1:345); the voice of the creatures is nothing but a little sound that one hears, and then it vanishes. But the voice of Jesus is eternal, so that Truth is God's being and his voice...(1:172–173); I will belch forth, I mean, I will pronounce the good word, the good Word, my Jesus, since I hold you in my heart (1:152).

Second, with the exception of short passages from *The Forty Days* and *Renovation of the Church,* her texts were not written by Maria Maddalena de' Pazzi herself. Her sisters transcribed, corrected, edited, and censored her monologues. As soon as the mystic entered a rapture, the nuns took pen and paper and jotted down as much as they could of her spoken words. When she whispered, screamed, cried, mumbled, Maria Maddalena was not speaking to her sisters. She spoke exclusively because the Word wanted her to summon his being. Some critics, accustomed to more traditional mystical works, regret that the Saint did not write down the raptures herself: They would have rather had clear, rationally developed descriptions of her private religious experiences. Let us read, for example, what Ermanno del S.S. Sacramento, who first described the mystic's manuscripts, says about the transcriptions of Maria Maddalena's visions:

> If, instead of dictated reports of her raptures, we had a systematic book about her rich spiritual experience, without a doubt we would have a much bigger, and probably more important one than that which actually remains, given the subtlety and depth of her thought. In the present text she does not hint at the many problems she must have faced and solved in her visions.[2]

For Ermanno del S.S. Sacramento a mystical text can be only a written description of a previous experience. The fundamental element of Maria Maddalena's discourse, its orality, is seen by Ermanno del S.S. Sacramento as a major flaw, one that prevents the reader from following the development of a rational meditation.

Thought, according to Ermanno del S.S. Sacramento, seems to have nothing to do with orality. "To speak one's mind" in fact does not seem to mean "to speak one's thought." Orality, for traditional students of any form of literacy, is what a thought is not. However, the mystic's fellow sisters embrace a quite different ideology. They decided to write down her spoken words when they realized that *Maria Maddalena's orality was saying something.* Over time, their method of transcription changed. They first limited themselves to composing a resumé of the saint's raptures, choosing to quote only some of her spoken words. Later, the nuns perceived that the overall meaning of her discourses could not be easily summarized, and thus they developed a complex method of *live* reportage. When the mystic entered a rapture, they sat around her in a group, and each of them wrote only a short section of her discourse. In other words, the first nun transcribed the mystic's first utterances, then the second took over and wrote down the second part of her speech, and so on.

Through her voice the mystic endeavored to give a body to the Word; she attempted to embody him in the physicality of her voice. As a consequence, Maria Maddalena could not help but despise her sisters' transcriptions. Left alone with one of her sisters' manuscripts, she burned it, provoking the rage of her confessor. The written word is of no use in her task. The Word does not reside in the written page; his being is as impalpable and transient as the oral word. A page from the *Probation* synthesizes the complex problem of the mystic's authorship:

> [S]he happened to find those notebooks where we had written everything that had occurred during the first and most of the second year of her probation. When she realized that those notebooks concerned her, without even reading them through, she threw them into the fire and burned them. According to what she told us, she did not do that out of arrogance or conceit. Indeed, she has often told me that when she hears someone read her raptures and communications from God,…she feels as if she were reading some other spiritual book…But, her superiors having forbidden her to do such a thing, from then on she has not touched anything. (*Probation*, 1:32–33)

Maria Maddalena took part in the editing of her sisters' transcriptions only when her confessor forced her to do so. In fact, she despised the nuns' work. She believed that the act of writing is a betrayal. We might say that for Maria Maddalena to write means to betray or to deny the Word, who can only be summoned on the oral level of language.

In her raptures the Word constantly reminds Maria Maddalena of his request. We may define the *opera omnia* of Maria Maddalena de' Pazzi as the narration of an excruciating obsession. Maria

Maddalena is actually persecuted by the Word. As the nuns point out at the beginning of each of their transcriptions, a few lines from the Gospel read during the morning mass or the sudden memory of a passage of a Psalm remind the mystic of the absence of the Word and thus of her still unfulfilled task. Although they are not the Word's being, the sacred texts contain his request to the mystic. When Maria Maddalena perceives the Word's request, so to speak, she starts to speak. Her words express her obsession for the Word. She neither speaks to the Word, nor does she speak with the Word; *she attempts to speak the Word.* The Word is a "verbal body" devoid of being; he is a signifier without signified. The mystic's voice both articulates her anxiety, triggered by the absence of the Savior, and her attempt to fill that void. Maria Maddalena's voice echoes the absence of the second Person of the Trinity.

It is necessary to clarify two important points of Maria Maddalena's mysticism: the nature of her oral mystical language and the relationship between her monologues and her listeners/readers. As far as the first point is concerned, we have pointed out that the mystic knew most of St. Augustine's books and often invoked him in her visions.

Indeed, following St. Augustine's *On Christian Doctrine*, Maria Maddalena believes that words and things share some characteristics; both things and words can be seen as *signs*, that is, both things and words signify something. In his work Augustine defines a *sign* as follows: "A sign is a thing which causes us to think of something beyond the impression the thing itself makes upon the senses...[there is no] other reason for signifying, or for giving signs, except for bringing forth and transferring to another mind the action of the mind in the person who makes the sign."[3] A sign, says Augustine, is essentially something that makes us think about something else.

Augustine further develops this concept of sign by introducing a distinction between *use* and *enjoyment*. Because things are similar to signs as both are signifiers, there are things/signs that exist in order to be used and things that can only be enjoyed:

INTRODUCTION

> It is to be asked whether man is to be loved by man for his own sake or for the sake of something else. If for his own sake, we enjoy him; if for the sake of something else, we use him. But I think that man is to be loved for the sake of something else. In that which is to be loved for its own sake the blessed life resides; and if we do not have it for the present, the hope is for it to console us.[4]

As is well known, for Augustine the only "thing" that can be enjoyed is God because everything else, both words and things, have no existence in themselves. They, rather, "refer to" something else, the divinity himself. Reality is empty, so to speak, whereas the ultimate signified is the divinity, for Maria Maddalena the Word himself. It is the Word that grants reality its being. By attempting to conjure up the Word through language, the mystic's monologues aim to evoke the Word's being.

Maria Maddalena's mystical language is intrinsically related to Augustine's theory. If everything, words and the world, is nothing but a sign of God, everything, language included, somehow "participates" in the divinity. The unique aspect of Maria Maddalena's visions is that the saint comes into contact with the divinity through language and, more importantly, in language; in her rapture she tries to convert language into the Word's body, the "thing" that can only be enjoyed but never used.

There is another central element to point out, namely that Maria Maddalena's oral discourses are never directed to us, the readers. When the mystic converses with the Savior, the transcribers can hear her voice but not that of her divine interlocutor. In other words, her convent sisters and thus all of us, the readers of their manuscripts, "overhear" a conversation that does not concern us. Paradoxically, the Word's voice can be perceived only by the speaker who articulates his, the Word's, own voice.

Maria Maddalena's use of language is not descriptive; she does not speak in order to narrate. For the Florentine, mystic language is the means through which the body of the Word could be evoked; the presence or absence of an audience for her discourses is absolutely irrelevant to her.[5] To perceive the saint's discourse means to become aware of the fact that we are excluded from the text itself. *We do not belong in this text.*[6] We must understand that the corpus of the mystical works by Maria Maddalena de' Pazzi reflects our misunderstanding; no reassuring agreement exists between our comprehension and the written text. To listen to Maria Maddalena's monologues primarily means to know that we are *mis*listening. To read these pages means to perceive that we are excluded from them. Unlike our typical and active way of listening to a text, de' Pazzi's mysticism asks us to be "humble" readers and to let its words *happen within* ourselves.[7] Instead of decoding the meaning of her visionary discourse according to some rational interpretation based, for instance, on our knowledge of other mystical works, the texts by Maria Maddalena de' Pazzi ask us to perform an act of radical humility. As the mystic reiterates that the soul must abandon itself to the Word in order to let the Word speak himself, the reader must understand that his/her presence is unnecessary.

However, although the saint's language comes to us as a sort of echo, we realize that her words somehow concern us. We sense that when we actually let her words occur they are not foreign to us, even though we cannot *appropriate* them. It is only in this way that we can establish a basic communication with the saint's oral discourse in its edited form. Even though Maria Maddalena does not take into account any human listener, in our humble "overhearing" of her monologues, we come to perceive her words as if they were directed to us. If the mystic's major concern revolves around the act of speaking, we must primarily focus on our act of hearing. What Maria Maddalena de' Pazzi teaches us is that the Word may turn to us; that is, he may ask us to pronounce his being when we recognize that we are not listening to him, for in fact we can neither listen to him nor speak (to) him.

Maria Maddalena synthesizes the goal of her mystical experience through the biblical expression *"Eructavit cor meum verbum bonum, dico ego opera mea Regi"* ("My heart belched forth the good Word, I speak my works to the King," cf. *Vulgate*, Ps. 44:2) which is repeated with different connotations in every volume of her writings. In vision 12 from *The Dialogues*, the most compelling section of her raptures, Maria Maddalena clearly states that she aims to "belch forth" the Word:

> Oh my Jesus, now that you are in me I can really say David's words: *Eructavit cor meum verbum bonum, dico ego opera mea Regi.* I expressed, that is, I will articulate the good word that you are, my Jesus, and that I keep deep in my heart. (1:152)

The expression *eructavit verbum bonum* has a totally different meaning in St. Bernard's *On the Song of Songs.* In the sermon 67, Bernard actually interprets the verb *eructare* as "to belch forth." He holds that, when the soul is full with God's grace, she "belches forth" the Word. St. Bernard clearly states that the spouse/soul overcomes language when she is replenished with love. "She does not speak; she belches forth" *(non enuntiat, sed eructat).*[8] The difference between Maria Maddalena's interpretation and Bernard's is apparent: whereas in Bernard the act of belching out the Word signifies the soul's contentment with his grace, in Maria Maddalena *eructare* primarily means "give linguistic expression" to the Word. *Eructare* is synonymous with *to speak.* Maria Maddalena perceives the sacred texts, either read or listened to during the mass, as God's request for being.[9]

We may go as far as to state that Maria Maddalena's wishes to articulate a language similar to that of the angels. As Origen writes, the angels constantly long for the Word; they feed on the bread of heaven, *panem intellegibilem.*[10] Their contemplation is in fact a constant desire.[11] The angels are their request for the Word; their being reflects the absence of the Word and communicates the absence/Word to the humankind. Thomas Aquinas defines the manifestation of the Word in the world as "the word of the Word."[12] Like the angels, Maria Maddalena announces that the Word is going to be spoken, or better yet, that the Word should/might be spoken.[13] As we shall see later, her announcement is a constant attempt to announce/embody the Word. But the crucial similarity between the mystic's language and that of the angels lies in the fact that the actual message does not coincide with its signifiers. The language of the angels announces a forthcoming language, the transparent, perfect dialogue/understanding between the Word and the human subject. The angels *hint* at the fact that the Word needs both to speak and to be spoken. This is also the never fulfilled task of Maria Maddalena's monologues. However, like Maria Maddalena's mystical speeches, the angels pronounce a word that risks to be mispronounced, misuttered, as a result of their misinterpretation of the divine Word or, better yet, of his silent word.

The most frequent term used by Maria Maddalena to address the divinity is *Verbo* (Word). In the first vision from *The Dialogues*, the initial words pronounced by Maria Maddalena are *Verbum caro factum est* and *in principio erat Verbum et Verbum erat apud Deum*, as if the nuns/editors wanted the reader to perceive the Word as the leitmotif of the entire text.[14] As we have already mentioned, *Word* is and is not a first name. We should also remember that the first vision of *The Dialogues* opens with a fundamental religious feast, that of the Holy Name of Jesus (*il Santissimo nome di Gesù*), celebrated on January 1. Still in vision 1, the nuns go back to some of Maria Maddalena's previous raptures, starting with that one she had had at Christmas, thus commemorating the incarnation of the Word into the world. These are the central premises of all of *The Dialogues*: the name of the Word and his birth among and within us:

> On Tuesday, January 1, 1584, the feast of the Holy Name of Jesus, we gathered, in the name of Jesus, with the beloved soul [Maria Maddalena]…we started by asking her what the Lord had wanted to communicate to her on Christmas night [and she] started with the words of Saint John: *Et Verbum caro factum est* and also *In principio erat Verbum et Verbum erat apud Deum*. (1:51, emphasis mine)

In the passage that immediately follows, Maria Maddalena underscores a crucial theme of her mysticism: the difficulty she faces in expressing the Word. Indeed, she tells her sisters that St. John previously scolded her because she had not recited her morning prayer with the necessary intensity (1:52). By resting on the Word's chest, Maria Maddalena allegedly says, John had been able to experience his infinite love and wisdom, and thus to write his Gospel, that is, to utter the Word for all of humanity:

> While Saint John was resting on his chest, Jesus poured into him. This is how he [Saint John] acquired so much wisdom…that *he*

belched forth that divine conceived Word, as he later wrote in his holy Gospel. (1:54, emphasis mine)

John also tells her that three virtues are necessary in order to utter the Word: *"humiltà, purità, e amore"* (humility, purity, and love, 1:52). In particular, humility is crucial for the soul who wants to receive the Word's holy love, and so she totally loses herself in the divinity and becomes like him:

> And he who has this perfect humility also has very easily the third virtue which is his holy love. His love comes to the soul without being requested, because it depends on holy humility. If we have this perfect love we can perfectly unite with God and thus we can become something similar to him. (1:53)

In order to receive the Word, the soul must become completely humble and passive toward the divine will.

The term *Word* is present in every single vision of Maria Maddalena de' Pazzi. *Word* is a reminder of the mystic's unfulfilled task. According to the transcribers, in some passages the mystic discusses the meaning of *Word* as if she aimed to clarify some of its unique aspects. For instance, in vision 38 from *The Dialogues*, Maria Maddalena distinguishes between the word, that is, human linguistic expression, and the Word, divine language. She reminds us that God's glory lies in the Word's voice:

> ...your idea, your might, your goodness, everything is a language *in Verbo Domini. In Verbo Domini* I hoped, rested, and abandoned my soul...The Word, proceeding from the Word, communicates us the Word and unites him to us. She meant that the word of God, which is pronounced by the mouth of the humanate Jesus, communicates to us and unites us to its source, Jesus himself, while he utters it and we listen to it. (1:435)

In another passage from vision 15 the saint goes on to distinguish the human voice, which can only convey an ephemeral word, from God's voice, which is his eternal being:

> The eternal Father has placed...his right to his right, primarily for the three virtues that he practiced throughout his life,

but particularly during his holy passion…Truth is his holy voice, because it lives forever. *The voice of the creatures is nothing but a little sound that one hears and then it disappears, whereas the voice of Jesus stays forever. Truth is God's being, and also his voice…* (1:172–73, emphasis mine)

Finally, in vision 33 of *The Dialogues*, Maria Maddalena is reported as describing the Word's mouth. As she says, "the Word's mouth speaks":

But there is that sweet mouth…are so many the virtues of that mouth…as from there breath comes out, they will draw the Spirit out of you so that they can infuse in the others *[silence]* then *that mouth speaks*. Oh, how necessary this is! (1:335, emphasis mine)

Maria Maddalena perceives her task as unachievable. Whereas the divine word coincides with his being, her language is only a repeated attempt to evoke divine presence.

In the mystic's language the signifier, coinciding with the physicality of the Word, is never fully expressed, or better yet, the speaker, the mystic herself, constantly doubts that the ultimate signified, the Word, can be expressed through her words. In vision 11 of *The Dialogues* (1:145–46) the saint speaks of the "idle word" (*parola otiosa*), which prevents God from meeting with us. Our idle word is a "stain" on our soul; God cannot tolerate it. Although this idle word sometimes could seem a minimum flaw to us, it actually makes our communication with the Word impossible. This is why the believer unsuccessfully repeats the very same act, the articulation of the Savior's language.

Indeed, repetition is one of the most frequent rhetorical devices of the saint's style. In her visions Maria Maddalena makes a statement, repeats it, and varies it by using terms thematically related to each other because her language never succeeds in "saying" what it was asked to say. Moreover, Maria Maddalena repeats and varies the themes of her visions as well. As we shall see later, in vision 48 of *The Dialogues* she is allowed to follow the Word to his tomb. The visionary takes up this very "plot" years later and performs it in a quite different manner. The convent writers point out that her new vision, which took place on March 22, 1591, a Sunday, shows striking similarities with a previous vision the mystic had had seven years before, in 1585, as reported in *The Dialogues*.[15] The nuns themselves point out the fact that their blessed sister had already done "these acts, as one can see in the book of *The Dialogues*" (*Probation*, 2:49). Indeed, as this anthology of the mystic's texts clearly shows, Maria Maddalena had innumerable visions on the Word's passion and death.

The mystic's attempt to utter the Word is constantly jeopardized by the presence of the Enemy. Indeed, as our selection attempts to show, the devil is a recurrent presence in Maria Maddalena's raptures. She sees him, speaks to him, and cannot help but hear his words. For instance, in vision 48 of *The Dialogues* the mystic is assaulted by a throng of demons. Demons are disturbances, sound interferences in the ongoing process/dialogue with the Word. While she is sitting next to the Savior's corpse in the sepulcher, the devil attacks her as an army, an untamed mob:[16]

> [S]he also said about the bad Angels: "So confused before, but now in everything *[silence] Et collocavit eos in infernum [silence]* Who has ever seen such a speed?"
> And raising her head and then lowering it down, she made gestures with her hands and her arms, bending over the window, as if she were sending them down to Hell with her own hands, and saying: "Go *[silence]* howl, scream as much as you want *[silence] Et sublimavit humanitatis nostre* with their confusion *[silence] Non cognoscetur amplius.* (*The Dialogues*, 2:299)

The demons scream; they do not articulate any idiom. They are beasts, as often depicted in medieval iconology. In vision 48 the devils attempt to derange the mystic's performance of the Word's death. They occur as an instant of blurred memory, the Aristotelian *phantasiai* or "after-images" that drift in and out of the mind.[17] Devils can be almost-images, almost-feelings, a disquiet arising from nowhere. Devils are afterthoughts. In vision 48 of *The Dialogues* Maria Maddalena easily dismisses them, grabbing them as ferocious and noisy animals and throwing them out of the window, down in the courtyard/hell. Like St. Anthony tempted in his solitary dwelling in the desert, the mystic does not doubt about their being mere images, nothing but *vociferous* images. Her body performs the imaginary act of dumping images in the abyss of absences, hell itself. Hell is indeed the nonplace where the disturbances of the mind annihilate themselves.

However, in the above vision the dismissal of the demonic presences is simplified through the narrative of the mystic's performance. To be assaulted by devils is both a present occurrence and the reenactment of a remembrance. The Latin sentence *"Et collocavit eos in infernum"* ("And he placed them in Hell") is in the past tense. The divinity, the mystic says, "placed" the devils in hell. And *now* she herself "places," throws them into hell. The mystic's self-confidence lies in her in-between being, in a not-quite-being there.

Paradoxically, in vision 48 the physicality of the devils renders them less threatening to the mystic. In vision 39 of *The Dialogues* Maria Maddalena is tempted by the demons in a quite similar manner. She hears voices. A multitude of "bad angels" swears in her ears:

> [D]uring our conversation we asked her what she had been experiencing when she was shaking so intensively and crying so much that we feared that the Devil himself was hitting her like Saint Anthony, for she kept saying: Oh good Jesus, screaming, crying, shaking as if she were being hit.
>
> She told us that no, she was not being hit, but she was rather hearing voices swearing in her ears, so that she was compelled to shake as she did each time that she heard those swearings, because those swearers' voices terrified her. (2:16)

In this second passage Maria Maddalena is terrified by voices. She is not assaulted physically; curses echo in her mind. She does not see the Enemy; she hears him. His absence is more haunting than his image. The devil articulates his message of disturbance, of doubt, through his speaking absence. If the Word's absent speech is exclusively a request, the devil's language testifies to his, the devil's, presence *somewhere*. The devil troubles the mystic's attempt to realize her being, which equals the Word's Word, as Thomas Aquinas says. The devil exists insofar as he curses the absent Word. The devil's word may annihilate the Word. This is the most terrifying power of the Enemy.

The devil's word also affects the mystic's body. Whereas his image triggers her active response, his saying is both a curse and a subtle whispering. A whisper makes the mystic ill. As the nuns remark, she shakes as if she were being hit. By entering her mind, the devil comes to endanger the entire identity of the subject. The Enemy replaces the subject's thinking with his, the devil's, own thinking. The mind thus becomes divided into two acts of thinking, a thinking denying one's own thinking. As a consequence, the body attacks itself. As the mind questions itself, the body dissects itself.

To clarify the relationship between demonic speech and the mystic's thinking, on the one hand, and demons' physicality and the mystic's physicality, on the other, we must analyze the *Probation*, which recounts the painful temptations Maria Maddalena faced for five years, from 1585 to 1590. If *The Dialogues* focuses on the Word, the *Probation* revolves around the Enemy. The devil visits the mystic daily, affecting both her body and her mind with excruciating sufferings. The modalities of the devil's offenses are diverse. The devil can appear as a beast, as a multitude of roaring beasts, or as himself, although no actual description of his body is present in the text. Unlike the Word, the devil has a body that does not need to be named, for it is *naturally* known to the human being. The Word is a request for being; the devil is a multiplicity of beings.

In the *Probation* the devil attacks the "blessed soul" for the first time on June 16, 1585:

> [S]he heard with her ears the horrible screams and howls that the Devil...pronounced to offend God. And sometimes these screams occupied her hearing to the point that she had difficulty in understanding us when we spoke to her. This blessed soul suffered a constant martyrdom, because of her internal and external sufferings...the devils afflicted her body by pushing her down the stairs, making her fall down; and other times, like vipers, they wrapped around her body biting her in the flesh with great cruelty. (*Probation*, 1:33–34)

In this passage the devils' speech combines the two elements present in visions 39 and 48 of *The Dialogues:* The devil both screams in the mystic's ears and speaks to her. His speech as disturbance conveys a message and deafens the mystic's hearing so that she cannot help but listen to his curses. In another passage (1:124) the transcribers stress that at times the mystic could not hear them because of the devils' loud swearing. Maria Maddalena becomes deaf to the world's speaking, to the Word's creation, and is compelled to focus on the curses of the Enemy of the creation.

But why should someone else's cursing affect the faith of a believer? Why does the mystic feel her identity jeopardized by the demons' offensive words?[18] In fact, the devil articulates a language of negativity that resounds like an echo of the mystic's own saying. As the guardian angels, according to Origen, repeat our prayers to the divinity without being heard by us, so does the devil encourage the subject to recognize the devil's speaking as his, that is, the subject's, speaking.[19] In other words, the subject's language and the devil's always risk overlapping because the signifiers they articulate are the same. Hearing the other's, the devil's, voice *might* become hearing our own voice. Teresa of Avila alludes to a similar experience when, for instance, she writes that "he [Satan] tells us directly, or make us think, that we poor sinners may admire but must not imitate the deeds of the saints."[20]

The devil's speaking is indeed a *crossing*, a traversing of the speaker's subjectivity. The Enemy speaks and by speaking *distracts the mystic from her attempt to acquire the Word's voice.* How should we otherwise interpret the devil's physical offences, his pushing the mystic down the stairs, his biting her stomach, his making her trip? The Enemy aims to distract her from her self with sudden, disruptive actions. In those moments, when the body falls, the soul as well *might* fall. The soul, the heart, *might* forget its sole task, the articulation of the Word.

The Enemy's attacks are in fact never physically fatal. The devil, like the Word, needs an interlocutor. He makes himself heard through the ear and the rest of the body. On September 17, 1587, Maria Maddalena becomes ill. She cannot leave the bed; intense fever gives her painful migraines for more than fifteen days

22

(1:114–15). When she tries to stand up and participate in the morning Mass, the devil makes her fall down the stairs. She falls again on November 1 (1:119) and on February 9 (1:134).

Other female mystics experienced similar demonic *disturbances*. Benvenuta Bojanni[21] sometimes was taken up in the air by the devil and then thrown on the floor with extreme violence. Once she wrestled with him on the ground:

> Sometimes it happened that [the devil] took her and raised her up, and then with great violence he hurled her down... once...she stood up against him, grabbed him and pushed him down under her feet. Then, putting a foot on his neck, she scolded at him with outraged words.[22]

As Maria Maddalena threw the demons out of the window in dialogue 48, Benvenuta responded to the devil's physical assaults by fighting back. In the *Vita beatae Benvenutae Boianae* the devil ends up by begging the strong mystic for mercy. She has humiliated him. Instead of stones, Teresa of Avila used holy water: "I have learned from the experience of several occasions that there is nothing that the devils fly from more promptly, never to return, than from holy water."[23]

In the *Probation* Maria Maddalena has a reaction similar to Benvenuta's and Teresa's. A devil all of a sudden jumps on her, as if he wanted to devour her. She picks up some big stones and throws them at him, screaming: "Leave me alone, you horrible beast, don't come close to me. In the name of Jesus, I tell you, leave me alone" (1:73). Months later, while she is praying with her sisters in the chapel, the mystic detects a crowd of demons trying to enter the room unnoticed. Because one of them has already entered that sacred place, Maria Maddalena grabs a crucifix and, using it as a weapon, she kicks the beasts out of the chapel (1:179).

The relationship between Maria Maddalena and the Enemy, however, only rarely acquires such a distinct theatricality. The devil's *disturbances* are usually less "histrionic" but much more distressful because they tend to refrain from any physicality.

To resume the narration of Maria Maddalena's sudden and intense fever, when she recovers from her disease, a drastic change occurs in the devil's language. The devil succeeds in making Maria

Maddalena think his own words. He starts by instilling doubts about her way of thinking. The mystic has difficulty in drawing the line between his thoughts, his images, and hers:

> [T]he Devil [started] to put doubts and fears in her mind about the holy and austere life she has embraced for God's will. He made her doubt that that was not God's will, like walking barefoot and wearing only a gown, both in winter and in summer, as she had decided to do a few months before. (1:116–17)

Maria Maddalena goes so far as to contemplate the possibility of abandoning the religious life (1:124). "She had the impression," the nuns report, "that whatever she did, either externally or internally, would deepen her damnation" (1:140). Rather than disrupting her daily life with sudden attacks, the Enemy makes the mystic play his own role. The mystic becomes the Enemy of herself. As Michel de Certeau says about the famous possession that took place in the monastery of Loudun, the nuns possessed by the devils affirm "I is another."[24] The possessed nuns perceive the fact that they have become the *site* where the Other resides. The battle between the Inquisition and the devil is a matter of language. Indeed, the devil refuses to speak because he has taken over the identity of the subject. In order to defeat him, the judges of the Inquisition must force him to pronounce his name(s).

Maria Maddalena experiences something similar. The devil speaks by not speaking any longer. The mystic's life/world, which awaits the Word in order to perceive itself, in order to become real, questions its own performativity. Is walking barefoot licit? Is testing one's body resistance legitimate? What does it mean to do something licit and legitimate?

The mystic's daily life and her familiar places, that in *The Dialogues* had turned into settings of the Word's death, that is, the kitchen garden, the staircases, the dormitory, the scriptorium, the chapel, are now *doubtful*. Her life, her sisters write, has become "an exile" (1:156). The language of the devil, his most eloquent speaking, is a sight that doubts its seeing and thus exiles the subject from her self.[25] The nuns themselves ask Maria Maddalena to explain the nature of her demonic oppression. What does she actually see?

Does she see him all the time? Does she always see him with her "corporeal eye"?

> She told us that she does not always see him with her corporeal eye, but she always sees him with the eye of the mind with no respite, as when (similarly) a creature sees something with her corporeal eye, and then that something stays in her mind so clearly that, even if she does not see it concretely, she has the impression that she always sees it. (1:73–74)

The devil has the substance of memory. Remembrances *cross* the subject's mind without any warning. Maria Maddalena knows that, like any memory, the devil has impressed his image in her mind. Not only does he not need to speak, he also does not need to be visible. Indeed, more than merely seeing him, Maria Maddalena states that "she has the impression she always sees him." The devil *is* even before acquiring an image, as any memory lingers in the mind before expressing itself in an image.

Whereas the devil signifies his presence through a lack of presence, because the mystic has absorbed his image, the Word's image causes intolerable pain to the mystic's "internal eyes." On January 28 of the same year, Maria Maddalena faints when she comes across a picture of the Word's crucified on the cross: "She cried for a long time and screamed a lot because of the intrinsic light and knowledge that she had of herself; and often she said: 'I would go to hell if there I could undo my offenses'" (*Probation*, 1:133).[26] Both the devil's absent image and the Word's present image torment the mystic. If in *The Dialogues* the pains primarily derived from the devil's cursing in her ear and from his bestial attacks, in the *Probation* her anguish comes from the vision of the Word. However, through the vision of what the Word is not, or better yet, what he is not for her, the mystic acquires a deeper understanding of the faulty nature of her language, and thus, of her being unable to express the Word. As every treatise on demonology underscores, the Savior often allows the devil to tempt a soul in order to show that soul its sinfulness, and thus compel it to repent.[27] For Maria Maddalena de' Pazzi, the long and distressing probation is nothing but a process toward a more "refined," purified articulation of her voice.

III. MARIA MADDALENA'S ESSENTIAL TERMINOLOGY

De' Pazzi's mystical discourses make use of a few recurrent terms, which have a great relevance to her mystical language. We have already analyzed the obsessive repetition of *Word* in every page of the seven volumes of de' Pazzi's texts. Rather than *Jesus* or *Savior* or *Son*, for Maria Maddalena de' Pazzi the second Person of the Trinity is almost exclusively *Word*.[28] The Florentine mystic consistently repeats a number of other words. The most significant ones are *blood, contemplation (risguardo)*, and *love*.

Let us examine briefly how the mystic uses these three words. First of all, for Maria Maddalena de' Pazzi to speak of the Word's language necessarily means to "analyze" his blood. The connection between language and blood is one of the basic aspects of her mysticism. Indeed, in several passages she compares divine language/voice to the Word's blood. For instance, in vision 35 of *The Dialogues*, Maria Maddalena states:

> [W]hen you, Word, come down to us, you show all your works and communications…and you necessarily communicate to us through blood, sweet blood, delightful blood…Oh, Word, you conceive the soul of blood, you give birth to it in blood, you wash it with blood, you nourish it with blood, you dress it with blood, and you crown it with blood. (1:379)

The Word's blood not only allows God to communicate with the soul, it also gives birth to the soul itself; it nourishes it, and it radically transforms it. However, because the soul exists insofar as it strives to give the Word an idiom, blood also signifies that the Word's blood gives birth to the soul so that the soul might generate the Word's blood. The soul, born in/from the Word's blood, is asked to give blood to the Word's blood. As we will see, *blood* signifies both the humanate Word and his "lack of blood," that is, his request for blood.

In biblical language *blood* has a variety of meanings.[29] However, it is possible to say that blood indicates both a physical and a spiritual element; it refers to humanity and to the human soul. As far as the first facet is concerned, blood plays a fundamental role in the

26

INTRODUCTION

Holy Week and paschal liturgy. Jesus sweats blood in the Gethsemani episode (Lk 22:44) and during the Last Supper he gives his disciples a cup of wine saying: "This cup is the new covenant in my blood which will be poured out for you" (Lk 20:20).[30] According to the New Testament, the blood shed by the Savior for all of humanity is an instrument of salvation and of spiritual transformation. The Old Testament had already tackled the blood–humanity relationship in some crucial passages. In Leviticus 17:11–12, we read: "The life of the flesh is in the blood. This blood I myself have given you to perform the rite of atonement for your lives at the altar; for it is blood that atones for a life." The Old Testament also tends to relate blood to the alliance between God and the his people (Ex 24:3–8; Zec 9:11). Furthermore, blood is synonymous with expiation (Lv 16) and repentance. The consecration of altars and priests, for example, was performed with blood. We might infer that in the Holy Scripture the image of blood has a twofold nature: It indicates both human transient condition with its bodily nature and its very opposite, the sacred relationship between God and his people.

Let us examine now how Maria Maddalena uses Scriptural texts on blood. In Genesis 4:10–11, God says to Cain, who has just killed his brother: "Listen to the sound of your brother's blood, crying out to me from the ground." In some of her visions Maria Maddalena appropriates this passage; for example, in *The Dialogues* she states that: "On Doomsday each drop of the blood that Jesus shed during his passion will cry out for vengeance against the damned" (1:98). In the same book we read: "All the blood drops you shed will be tongues that thank you" (2:27). In the *Revelations and Knowledge*, the mystic goes on to attribute to God's blood a "musical voice":

> [T]he blood, of which each drop is a tongue that cries out: Union, union, union with whom you have redeemed *[silence]* these drops of the Word's blood speak in a sweet musical voice to the Word himself, reminding him that he shed them for love. (146)

According to Maria Maddalena, the Word communicates to his creatures through his blood; his blood is his actual voice. In vision 48 of *The Dialogues* we read that the Virgin "plays" the bleeding corpse of the Word as a ten-stringed psaltery. The Word's blood utters a melodic saying, as a music of signifiers.

According to the mystic, blood plays another fundamental role: It helps both the Word and the soul to come into contact with their own selves. Indeed, at several points the Word and his blood are two distinct entities; by interacting with his own blood the Word becomes aware of his own love and generosity: "Who could narrate your love and kindness better than your blood?" (2:385). In another passage Maria Maddalena goes so far as to ask the Word to answer his own blood; only his blood can fulfill his message:

> Do not answer me, since I am too presumptuous, but answer your blood. You cannot fail yourself: answer, answer then, Word, your blood...Oh, how powerful is your blood! (1:104–105)

Blood is the awareness the Word obtains by contemplating his own being. Blood is a mirror of the Word's being. By gazing at/listening to his own blood, the Word perceives his love, that is, his being for love. The Word's blood thus speaks both to the creature, as the biblical passage from Genesis underscores, and to the second Person of the Trinity. The Word has apprehended the blood's language by becoming incarnate, by acquiring a physicality made of blood.

Moving now to the relationship between blood and the soul, in vision 5 of *The Dialogues*, as she describes the Savior's five wounds, the mystic explains that, drinking from each of Christ's bleeding wounds, the soul progressively acquires a deeper knowledge of itself and finally turns into blood:

> [I]n the left foot [of Christ] the blood annihilated, and the soul acquired knowledge of itself. In the right foot the blood was purified, and the soul fortified itself. In the left hand, the blood was enlightened, and the soul acquired knowledge of God. In the right hand the blood was clarified, and the soul became stronger in charity. The chest was nourished, and the soul was transformed into blood, so that it understood nothing but blood, it saw nothing but blood, it tasted nothing but blood, it perceived nothing but blood, it thought of nothing but blood, it spoke and could think of nothing but blood. (1:97)

In this excerpt Maria Maddalena clearly states that when the soul finally identifies with the Word, it thinks only about blood and utters only blood; blood becomes both its sole thought and its sole language. However, it is important to note that the language articulated through/by blood essentially recounts the Word's death. Blood utters the speaker's act of gazing at the Word's corpse. Indeed, the Virgin plays his corpse as a psaltery, and the mystic herself describes the "phonetics" of this idiom by observing the Word's open wounds closely. Although, as the mystic says, each drop of the Word's blood is a voice that invokes the divinity, each drop summons the image of a corpse and the narration of an execution. The subject (the Word, the Virgin, Maria Maddalena) starts to articulate the language of blood when she/he commemorates a death.

We have seen so far that, according to Maria Maddalena, the Word's blood not only purifies the soul of its sins but also first and foremost articulates a language that leads both the Word himself and the soul to a deeper awareness of themselves. However, in some crucial passages Maria Maddalena associates blood with two other highly significant fluids: water and milk. In fact, according to the mystic, blood "contains" both milk and water; that is, blood has all the properties of milk and water. If we examine how blood interacts with these two liquids for Maria Maddalena, we shall be able to understand better the nature of her divine blood/language.

Let us first see what Maria Maddalena says about the relationship between blood and water.[31] In *The Dialogues* the mystic reminds us that water and blood issued from the Word's wound in his side; the water is connected to his soul, blood to his human body:

> [S]he saw that blood issued from Jesus' humanity, with which washing his creatures he removed their impurity. From his soul there came out a very clear water which was his grace, with which he fortified his creatures (1:262)

In another rapture of the same book, the mystic elucidates the above point. She sees some souls entering the Word's bleeding side. They first turn into blood through an act of love; then they change into water through suffering. However, the mystic adds, water is "inferior" *(inferiore)* to blood; although it is water that purifies the soul from its "dirt," it is blood that "adorns" the soul with the Word's love:

> She saw that those that entered Jesus' side produced two effects: first they turned into blood thanks to love, and then they changed into water through pain…in his side water is inferior, blood is superior; water…purifies and blood adorns. (1:87–88)

The soul entering in the Word's bleeding side is a standard image which goes back to the thirteenth century.[32] In another rapture Maria Maddalena specifies that divine blood adorns the soul as a dress:

> [I]n the morning…during her spiritual Communion, as usual she entered a rapture…and she had the impression that she was dressed with this blood, and she also saw others [her sisters] dressed with the blood of Jesus as well. (1:147)

The image of the soul dressed with the Savior's blood is fairly common in mystical literature. For instance, Gertrude of Helfta, the female mystic contemporary of Mechthild of Magdeburg and Mechthild of Hackeborn, writes: "Christ's voice: I will make you a robe of the noble purple of my precious blood."[33]

However, in some other visions Maria Maddalena seems to ascribe the qualities of blood to water, as if she used the term *water* as a synonym for *blood:*

> [S]he saw Jesus so beautiful with his side open, and it seemed to her that his side was like a source of very crystalline and clear water; she understood that that water was first of all the clarity of his divinity, the sweetness and overflowing of his humanity, and the purity of his soul. (*The Dialogues,* 1:159)

This passage shows that when the mystic stresses the spiritual and regenerative element of Christ's blood over its corporeal one, she may use *water* rather than *blood*, although her concept of blood/water always contains a clear reference to both the Word's human and to his divine nature. We might synthesize the above discussion concerning blood and water by saying that blood is a purifying fluid, and in that it is similar to water. However, because it expresses the Word's love, blood has also a regenerative force; it transforms the image that the soul has of itself, what Maria Maddalena calls the soul's "appearance." Indeed, blood has also an extraordinary purifying power. In many raptures she sees the Word's blood as a fluid that "cleanses" the soul from its sins. In dialogue 42 Maria Maddalena says that Christ's blood cleans his spouse of her dirt (2:86).

Blood relates to a second fluid, milk. When Maria Maddalena mentions milk, she underscores the nourishing aspect of the Word's blood. Indeed, as Caroline Walker Bynum reminds us, medieval medicine considered milk to be a derivative of blood; blood turns into milk:[34]

> You take it with your mouth from the breast of Jesus' humanity...Jesus communicates that sweet feeling of his divinity to the soul through...the mouth of his humanity, and the [your] mouth attracts it to itself with the mouth of his [the creature's] desire. The abovementioned milk originates from within the creature, and it belongs to his [the creature's] substance and being. So, this feeling is Jesus' actual divine being, that is God's substance, that is so delicate and sweet, that it cannot adequately be uttered. (*The Dialogues*, 1:111)

If we add this long and intricate passage to those already discussed, we understand that according to Maria Maddalena divine blood is at least three-faceted: First, it is blood when she emphasizes its relation to Christ's human death and resurrection; second, it becomes water when the mystic refers to its purifying character; finally, it turns into milk when she stresses its nourishing quality. Moreover, this multiform concept of blood modifies its physical features. When Maria Maddalena speaks of blood as milk, she emphasizes its taste: the Word's blood/milk is sweet and delicate. On the other hand, blood/water is first of all remarkable from a visual standpoint: It is extremely clear and luminous.

In the above excerpt, however, the mystic introduces a new element in her concept of blood/milk. Divine milk originates, she says, both in the Word's breast and within the creature. Blood/milk does not belong exclusively to the Son; by sucking from his breast, a human being recreates that very blood/milk within himself.[35] The connection between blood and milk produced in the female breast refers to a crucial belief of medieval anatomy, that is, the basic equivalence among blood, milk, and sperm. These three fluids are in fact nothing but blood. As Maria Maddalena says, "[y]ou take it with your mouth from the breast of Jesus' humanity." Once it has sucked the Savior's milk, the soul is able to generate the same "milk" in itself. The term *milk* is a clear synonym for *blood*. Is not the "blood" created in the soul's womb a divine semen? In his description of the formation of milk in the female breast, Galen directly relates its genesis to the blood present in the mother's genitalia.[36]

We might say that the Word's blood is both a nourishing milk and a generating semen. Moreover, his blood also signifies the end of any generation because it is connected with the subject's death. The Word's blood speaks of generation and of the dissolution of what has been generated.

The relationship of blood with milk is one of the main topics of God's sermon in Maria Maddalena's longest rapture, vision 48 of *The Dialogues*. In the Father's discourse, uttered through the mystic's voice, the distinction between blood and milk and their complex interaction acquire a deeper theological connotation. God tells Maria Maddalena that when the Word entered his (the Father's) breast, their mutual contemplation *(risguardo)* produced two springs: one of milk and one of blood. These two sources flowed over the church and the human soul. As a result, both the church and the soul generated two sources: one of milk and one of blood:

> [T]hat look of my Word into me and mine into him…produced two springs: one of milk and one of blood, which sprinkled the two spouses, the spouse soul and the spouse Church…this sprinkling…generates two more springs in each spouse in the same way: one of milk and one of blood (2:343–44).

Why does God distinguish milk from blood? In the first part of his explanation, the Father says that the spring of milk embodies his purity, whereas the spring of blood corresponds to the Word's humanity. Maria Maddalena interrupts the Father's sermon by asking him how the soul can reach divine purity. In order to attain his purity, God says, the soul must be nothing, understand nothing, know nothing, be attached to nothing, and desire nothing.[37] Moreover, the Father states that the soul must also fulfill four basic requirements: First, the soul must die, as if it were crazy and beside itself; second, it must direct all its thoughts toward him, its Creator; third, it must be a virgin; fourth, it must be totally humble (2:345–47).

When it receives God's purity through his milk, the soul starts feeling such an anxious and "dead" *(morto)* desire that it turns to his second spring, that of blood. At this point, drowning in the Word's blood, the soul sees only blood and desires only blood:

> [T]his purity then generates in the soul that anxious and dead desire that later leads the soul to the source of my humanate Word. In this source the soul drowns and annihilates itself so that it tastes nothing but Blood, sees nothing but Blood, wishes and wants nothing but Blood, lives and feeds on nothing but Blood. (2:348)

According to Maria Maddalena, milk is a divine fluid which leads the soul to a deeper appreciation of divine essence. By drinking God's milk, the soul receives a perfect purity, which allows it to taste the second, more important divine spring, that of blood. To taste God's milk means to come in contact with one's own nothingness. Only after having realized fully its nothingness can the soul encounter the Word's humanity. This encounter, the mystic says, is the sole sense and goal of human life. Becoming nothing, realizing oneself and drinking the Word's blood is a simultaneous and three-faceted event.

Blood is both the language and the "place" where the soul meets the divinity. If we consider how Maria Maddalena de' Pazzi describes her encounter with the Word, we notice that in several passages she defines her meeting the Word as a *risguardo* (contemplation), or that she and the Son *risguardano* (contemplate) each other. The mystic also uses this word to characterize the relationship between the Father and the Son. If we examine what *risguardo* means both in Italian in general and in de' Pazzi's texts, we shall understand better the nature of the mystic's relation to the Savior.

The verb *risguardare* has three basic meanings:[38] (1) *riguardare* ("to look at attentively, to examine");[39] (2) *rispettare, osservare* ("to respect, to observe");[40] (3) *avere relazione con, dipendere da* ("to have a relation to, to depend on").[41] As far as the noun *risguardo* is concerned, first of all it indicates the act of looking attentively *(risguardare)*. It also means "respect" *(rispetto, considerazione)*.[42] *Risguardo* and *risguardare* can have also a specific mystical connotation. For instance, in Loarte's *Istrutione et avertimenti*, a book that Maria Maddalena read when she was still a child, *risguardare* is present fairly often: "I humbly beg you to open the eyes of my soul, so that I can examine *[risguardare]* and understand what you accomplished;" "Consider how tenderly Mary Virgin and Mother received the dead body...carefully looking at *[risguardando]* his wounds and his sores with an immense sorrow."[43]

Maria Maddalena makes use of *risguardare* and *risguardo* in several visions. Although the mystic does not alter the basic meaning of this word, she interprets it in a deeply personal manner. More than simply describing the act of "gazing at" or "meditating upon" something or someone, in Maria Maddalena's raptures this word acquires a crucial theological sense—*risguardo* always entails a double act of seeing, both "to see" and "to be seen."

However, *risguardo* can have an even more complex meaning. In some visions Maria Maddalena connects *risguardare* to the "inner" senses of every human being. To fully understand this central point, it is necessary to bear in mind Origen's distinction between "inner" and "outer" sense. In the *Commentary on the Song of Songs*, interpreting a passage from 2 Corinthians, Origen writes:

> In his letters he [Paul] wrote more openly and clearly that every person is two different men. This is what he said, "Though our outer man is wasting away, our inner man is being renewed every day" (2 Cor 4:16).[44]

Interpreting the above Pauline text, Origen holds that man has two bodies. Both the visible part and the invisible one have their own senses, desires, and sensations. Origen believes that in the scriptures, sentences such as "Break the arm of the sinners and evildoer" (Ps 10:15) or "you have broken the teeth of the sinners" (Ps 3:7) actually refer to the invisible body of each human being and not to the carnal one.

Maria Maddalena de' Pazzi often refers to Origen's concept of "inner senses." In *The Forty Days* she reminds us that God attracts to himself the creatures who look at him with their "interior eyes." By looking at the Creator with their inner eyes, the believer responds to God's *risguardo* toward him. In other words, when we "look at" God, in reality we respond to his previous attentive look toward us:

> I saw that with his look he drew all creatures to himself, I mean those who looked at him with their interior eyes, and who collaborated with the grace of that look. At this point I remembered Saint Peter when he denied Jesus, but then, when he looked at him with his divine, so beautiful, and piercing eyes, he [St. Peter] suddenly recognized his sin and repented. (140)

According to Maria Maddalena, St Peter's *risguardo* toward the Savior is nothing but a recognition that Jesus had previously contemplated him. First the creature directs his interior eyes toward the divinity; then he realizes that God has always been looking at him.

The act of gazing at the Word takes place only if we acknowledge that he is gazing at us. The soul needs the Word's face, we may say, in order to see its own face. The Word *reflects* the soul as the soul is nothing but the Word's *reflection*. Maria Maddalena clarifies this central element in a passage from *The Dialogues:*

> God could never unite with that soul, even though it is perfect, if he did not look at himself. By doing so, he realizes that it is another himself, first because he created it in his own image and likeness, and also because he united it to himself through his redemption. Similarly, we will never be able to abandon ourselves in God, unless we look at that God who is in ourselves. (1:234)

As the above excerpt shows, in Maria Maddalena's discourse the term *risguardare* has a reflexive element. God *risguarda* himself in order to *risguardare* the soul, and vice versa—the soul *risguarda* that

God who dwells in itself in order to rest later in God. The act of looking at either the Father or at the Word or at the soul itself is always double. Whereas in Italian *risguardo* is usually meant to signify a private act of meditation on a specific divine person, for Maria Maddalena *risguardo* is a synonym for communication or exchange. God *risguarda* himself in order to attain a deeper comprehension of the object of his attention, which can be either the Word or the Virgin Mary or the soul. Similarly, the object of his gaze responds to him by contemplating his image.

As far as the above passage is concerned, Maria Maddalena uses another crucial verb in order to explain the soul's total abandonment to God: *rilassare* ("to relax into, to abandon oneself to"). As the mystic says, the soul can rest in God only when it has looked at the divinity present in itself. Maria Maddalena's *rilassare*, or the much more frequent *relassatione*, is similar to Tauler's concept of "abandonment" *(Gelassenheit)*.[45] Maria Maddalena knew Tauler through the *Istitutioni*, an anthology of German mystics that included passages from both Eckhart and Tauler. As I pointed out at the beginning of this introduction, the Florentine mystic refers to this anthology in a letter now edited with the title *Renovation of the Church* (167).

In his sermons Tauler states that in order to accomplish *unio mystica*, the subject must destroy himself *(die Vernichtung des Subjekt)* and totally abandon himself to God.[46] *Gelassenheit* is a typical word in Tauler's sermons. In the sermon for the feast of the Epiphany, he writes that there are two kinds of people according to the way in which they abandon themselves to God: The first kind abandons themselves to God by using reason, trying to understand why they must do it; the second kind does not try to justify their decision rationally; they rather refrain from any thinking because they simply trust the divinity:

> They [the first kind] have to abandon their presumptions and arrogant ways and begin the strenuous work of self-denial, following the steps of our Lord Jesus Christ in humility and love...we encounter noble souls [the second kind of people] so steeped in truth that it shines forth in them. They permit God

to prepare the ground, leaving themselves entirely to him. By this act of self-surrender they refuse to cling to anything of their own.[47]

Tauler rejects the first sort of behavior, believing that instead of attempting to interpret God's intention the soul should simply deny itself and surrender itself *(rilassarsi)* to him. Tauler's *Gelassenheit* requires a complete surrender to God's inscrutable will.

The Italian *relassatione*, a term related to Tauler's *Gelassenheit*, is a crucial word in some of Maria Maddalena's most interesting visions. In vision 45 of *The Dialogues*, the mystic explains that every good action, desire, or thought derives from the soul's abandonment to God: "Oh, how many are the operations of abandonment? Every operation, every feeling, every desire, every thought is before you a great work of abandonment" (2:187–88). In vision 46 that the mystic dedicates a significant part of her rapture to the word *relassatione*. In order to defeat some devils that harass her, instead of fighting against them she abandons her body to God. By so doing, Maria Maddalena succeeds in fortifying her face, her mouth, her chest, her heart, her intellect, and her eyes against any possible attack from Satan:

> *"Propter relassationem istam comunicavit se Pater ad me, ad utilitatem animarum*[48] *[silence] Domine probasti me and cognovisti me*[49] *[silence] in relassatione que feci in te."*[50] Then, she joined her hands, resting her finger tips against her head. Her hands were slightly apart, so that she hid her face in them and said: *"In relaxatione ista abscondit faciem meam."*[51]…She crossed her hands on her heart and said: *"In relaxatione ista custodivit cor meum."*[52] Then she crossed her hands on her temples and said: *"In relaxatione ista elevavit* and *illuminavit intellectum meum* and *voluntatem meam"*[53]…Finally, she crossed her hands on her eyes and said: *"In relaxatione ista illuminavit oculos meos"*[54] (2:196–97).

It is interesting to notice that, for Maria Maddalena, the act of "relaxation" is similar to a ritual that involves her own body. God "cleanses" each part of her body in order to defend herself against Satan and thus to be able to enter a full contemplation of the divinity.[55] If we relate the above passage to the previous one concerning the mystic's and God's mutual contemplation, we understand that in order to observe the divinity and to be observed by him, the soul must have previously destroyed itself and must have abandoned itself totally to God.

We might say that *relassatione* indicates a first step in the process leading the soul toward a perfect reflection of the divinity. To gaze at the divinity actually means to annihilate oneself and thus to become similar to a mirror that simply reflects God's image. As we have seen in a previous passage, God starts interacting with a "perfect" soul after having observed his own image and thus having realized that that soul is nothing but "his second self"; that is, the image of the soul is simply the image God has of himself. The soul is thus a mirror of the divine essence. Maria Maddalena directly refers to this topic in an interesting passage from the *Probation* in which she says that the Word is a mirror, which actually reflects the Word himself dying on the cross. The mystic adds that we must purify our eyes to be able to see clearly:

> The mirror I must contemplate in the humanate Word is nothing but the Word himself nailed to the cross *[silence]* one must have pure eyes in order to be able to contemplate well: *si oculus tuus simplex fuerit.* (2:103).

The mirror is a very frequent metaphor in mystical literature.[56] In 2 Corinthians 3:17–18 Paul compares the graced soul to a mirror which reflects "the brightness of the Lord":

> Now this Lord is the Spirit, and where the Spirit of the Lord is, there is freedom. And we, with unveiled faces reflecting like mirrors the brightness of the Lord, all grow brighter as we are turned into the image that we reflect.[57]

Almost every visionary in the Christian tradition makes use of the metaphor of the mirror.[58] For example, Hadewijch interprets the act of understanding as follows: "in your mirror/ always ready for you.// It is a great thing to see/ In nakedness, without intermediary."[59] Speaking of the effects provoked by the act of contemplating a crucifix, Gertrude of Helfta writes:

> [S]he was given to understand that if anyone were to look with a similar devout attention at an image of Christ crucified, the Lord would look at them with such benign mercy that their soul, like a burnished mirror, would reflect, by an effect of divine love, such a delectable image, that it would gladden the whole court of heaven.[60]

In the *Mirror of Simple Souls* Marguerite Porete associates the concept of divine self-reflection with the final stage of the soul's mystical journey. When the soul annihilates itself and returns to its precreated state, the soul no longer sees or knows God. The actions become reflexive:

> She [the soul] has fallen from grace into the perfection of the work of the virtues, and from the virtues into love, and from love into nothingness, and from nothingness into the clarification of God who sees himself with the eyes of his majesty, who at this point has clarified her through himself.[61]

Porete states that when the soul embraces its own nothingness God comes to contemplate himself through his own eyes and thus he "clarifies" the soul which is the actual means of his self-reflection. This passage from *The Mirror* highlights the main difference between Porete's interpretation of the mirror and Maria Maddalena's. Whereas for Porete God's self-reflection symbolizes the final step in the soul's mystical journey, for Maria Maddalena the act of *risguardare* indicates the very first step in the mystical transformation of the soul.

Because *risguardo* indicates the initial contact between God and the soul, let us now see how Maria Maddalena explains the subsequent steps of their relationship. In many of her monologues the mystic associates the act of "looking at" with that of breathing. In particular, she distinguishes between "breathing in" or "inspiring" *(ispirare)*, also in the sense of "giving inspiration to," and "breathing out upon" *(respirare su)*. Whenever she attempts to describe a progressive interaction between either two divine Persons or a divine Person and the soul, Maria Maddalena uses the images of contemplating *(risguardare)* and "breathing in" or "breathing out upon."

For that matter, the *Revelations and Knowledge* contains some insightful passages concerning the act of contemplating the Word and being contemplated by him. In this book Maria Maddalena interprets the creation of the human race as a result of the Word observing himself. She states that, after having contemplated himself, the Word as Truth "comes out" of himself and creates man. Later, the Word himself decides to take a bodily form in order to save all of humanity, which has gone astray because of its sinful tendencies:

> [T]he incarnate Word contemplated himself, and coming out of himself, he saw himself as Word both as inferior to the Father and as equal to him...then this Truth went in and out in himself and from himself, because, if it had not gone out of itself, it would have not created the creature and would have not given being to it. The Word later took on its [the creature's] being, so that he could save the lost man. (141)

The Word/Truth looks at himself and, by going in and then out of himself, he creates human beings. We might say that, according to the mystic, man is the result of a divine gaze upon himself; man reminds God of himself.

In another passage Maria Maddalena holds that God has established a fundamental peace in the whole creation, including also the three Persons of the Trinity. This divine peace exists between the Father and the Son, between the divinity and the humanity, between the Word and Mary, and between the Word and the creature (*Revelations and Knowledge*, 76). Explaining how this essential peace moves from the divinity toward the created world, Maria Maddalena states that the three Persons, starting from the Father, "breathe into one another" and, by so doing, are united in a perfect peace:

> And it [this peace] was given through a breathing from the Father into the Word, and from the Word into the Father and into the Holy Spirit. And this peace was given among us, the three divine Persons and one in essence and it was a peace of breathing...and it was not given only once, many times it was given among us, the three divine Persons.

The mystic describes divine peace as an act of "breathing into" *(ispirare/inspirare/spirare)* that paradoxically moves from one Person to the other.[62] However, this first act of "inspiring" does not lead divine peace to its full completion. After having breathed in, the Trinity contemplates itself, which deepens its inner peace:

> Much more peace was given when, each Person meditating on the other, we conceived the already conceived man. And this peace was not based on inspiring but rather on contemplating, and in that contemplation we fell in love with our greatness and goodness so deeply, that without desiring we desired with an immense desire to communicate this goodness. (76–77)

By contemplating themselves, the three Persons of the Trinity fully perceive that love is their essence, and thus they feel urged to communicate their love outside of themselves. The creation of the world derives from this act of awareness.

As Maria Maddalena then explains, after having established a perfect peace within himself the Word shares his peace with the Blessed Virgin. The mystic believes that in this case divine peace is based neither on *ispirare* ("breathing in") nor on *risguardo* ("contemplation"), but rather on *compiacimento* ("delight, pleasure"). By looking at *("risguardando")* the Virgin, the Word feels such a deep gladness, that he wishes to become incarnate in her body. The act of "looking at" does not actually found a new form of peace; it is however the means through which peace is founded:

> Then peace was given between the Word and Mary neither through inspiring, nor through contemplation, but rather through delight. Indeed, when the Trinity looked at Mary, it was so pleased with her, that my Word decided to become incarnate in her, and by himself took on his humanity. (78)

Also in this third kind of peace, the Trinity is drawn outside of itself after having performed an act of observation: Earlier the divinity had gazed at himself, now he contemplates Mary and feels drawn toward her. As a result, the divinity, in the second Person, moves out of himself in order to become incarnate. However, the Word takes a bodily form only when the Virgin responds to his *risguardo* by breathing into him *(un respirare)*. In this way she summons a new kind of peace:

> [T]his peace is based neither on inspiring nor on contempla-
> tion, nor on that so little known and loved delight, but rather
> on Mary's breath into the Word...[she] gave the Word his
> peace by recreating the Uncreated. And how? By her breathing
> into your idea, Father, while she pronounced the following
> words: *Ecce Ancilla Domini, fiat mihi secundum Verbum tuum*, in
> which words she performed that breathing. (79–80)

Mary's act of giving life to her Son by breathing on him reminds us of God making man a living being by breathing into him: "The Lord fashioned man of dust from the soil. Then he breathed into his nostrils a breath of life, and thus man became a living being" (Gn 2:7). However, the mystic specifies that Mary breathes life into her Son by pronouncing the sentence *Ecce Ancilla Domini, fiat mihi secundum Verbum tuum* (Lk 1:38). In other words, the Virgin Mary breathes life into the second Person of the Trinity when she aban-dons herself to God's will and performs a speech act. The Virgin gives birth to the Word by articulating language.

In *Revelations and Knowledge* the mystic restates and expands her interpretation of the Word's birth in Mary's bosom. Speaking through Maria Maddalena's voice as he had already done in vision 48 of *The Dialogues*, the Father reminds us that the three Persons have created the human being by contemplating each other and that the Virgin participated in their creation by giving birth to a new man, Christ himself:

> Mary contributed to that peace that was based on contempla-
> tion and that we, the three divine Persons, shared with each
> other, when I looked into the Word and the Word looked into
> me and into the Holy Spirit, whence the new Trinity of man
> was created. And since Mary could not create man whom we
> had already created, she collaborated with us to create him
> again through my Word's incarnation in her. (87)

According to Maria Maddalena, their *risguardo* indicates an act of awareness which subsequently leads to creation. *Risguardo* is also the basis of the relationship between the Word and his creatures. Every soul is constantly "recreated" by the Word, who contemplates both himself and the soul:

> The Word contemplates himself and they [the creatures] contemplate him...and this cannot be done without a participation of grace, through an amorous affection, and the intoxication of Blood *[silence]* the soul contemplates God every time it sees God in every thing. He contemplates the creatures every time out of his amorous affection he aspires to their salvation. His aspiration is so intense, that he does not limit himself either to one, or to two, or to three cities, but he also contemplates those creatures who have still to come...again he generates himself, again he recreates the creature. (122)

The mystic believes that by contemplating himself and his creatures the Word "aspires to" *(aspira)* their salvation. It is important to remember that in Italian the verb *aspirare* is also a synonym for *ispirare* ("to inspire, to breath in"). In her discourse the mystic actually merges the two basic meanings of *aspirare*. As we have seen in some previous passages, Maria Maddalena believes that the three Persons of the Trinity communicate with each other by "breathing in" their love. We may say that, when he contemplates himself, the Word aspires to his creatures' salvation by "inspiring" and "breathing in" his love for them.

Love is another central term in de' Pazzi's mystical spirituality. In her use of this word, however, she oscillates between two opposite approaches. On the one hand, following the medieval mystical tradition, she draws up long lists of different definitions of *love*. On the other, in some raptures she focuses less on what *love* means than on how she may utter love, that is, on how she may perform an act of love. These two approaches do not correspond to two different phases of her mysticism. We must bear in mind that Maria Maddalena's spirituality does not have a progressive character. The mystic does not *move toward* a more profound understanding of the divinity. As Bernard writes in *On the Song of Songs*,[63] Maria Maddalena is visited by the Word from time to time.

Let us examine the first approach, the more theoretical one. In vision 49 of *The Dialogues*, Maria Maddalena presents a complete categorization of divine love(s). While she is praying, the Father "calls her to him" because he wants her to learn all his different forms of love. The mystic feels extremely pleased and responds to God's request by repeating the Father's long list of "loves":

> Oh, how many are the loves through which you love us! And everything is love *[silence]* separate love, unifying love, recreative love, consuming love, love which always exists and at every moment sees its goal; and it is eternal love, glorifying love, beatific love, transforming love, which is a compendium of every love *[silence]* separate love. From what is it separate if it unifies? It is separate from every thing that is separate from God; [it is] separate from every image and figure; [it is] separate from every voice and word; [it is separate] from every seeing and understanding; [it is] separate from every action; [it is] separate from myself, eternal, and [it is] even more separate from the essence of my idea *[silence]* the other loves are neither to be tasted nor to be understood, they rather serve it [this last one]. (2:374–75)

What is striking in the above long list of "loves" is the fact that only the "separate" love is actually performed by the soul. All the other forms of love (unifying love, recreative love, consuming love, eternal love, glorifying love, beatific love, transforming love) are received by the soul from the divinity. Moreover, all the other loves "serve" the soul's separate love. The soul loves the Word if it separates itself from itself, if it separates itself from "every image and figure, from every voice and word." By distancing itself from itself, the soul becomes pure exile. The soul's love for love is exile.

According to Simone Weil, our status of émigrés from ourselves is God's most enduring expression of love: "Through love, he abandons them [the creatures] to affliction and sin."[64] Affliction is the condition proper to exile, and exile is the condition proper to the soul: "The soul," Simone Weil holds, "has to go on loving in the emptiness."[65] Love occurs when the subject perceives her distance from the Word, when she senses that, as Maria Maddalena says, she is "separate" from herself. We might infer that the soul (and "soul") itself is a synonym for love (and "love") because both love and soul result from exile.

In *Revelations and Knowledge*, Maria Maddalena goes back to this topic in a more detailed manner, dedicating an entire rapture to the various manifestations of divine loves. Although in this second text she makes use of the same style—that is, she enumerates a series of adjectives that either precede or follow the term *love*—in this case she explains each type extensively (*Revelations*, pp. 206–12). In this second list of divine "loves," Maria Maddalena changes many of the adjectives used in her previous rapture. In particular, instead of "separate love" *(amore separato)*, she calls the last kind of love "dead love" *(amore morto)*, a definition quite common in the western mystical tradition. Let us read now the final passage of this long vision from *Revelations:*

> A passive love, an anxious love, a satiating love, and a dead love…it is lazy, because it contemplates God and sees his supreme goodness…but this love, or better yet, the creature, I mean, who has this love, passively considers God's infinitely perfect qualities…and lets God do everything…anxious love…the soul that has this kind of love with a constant and passionate desire desires every creature to know God and desires to know God herself, and it desires God to let everyone to know him…the following love is satiating, because it [the soul] enjoys God completely, it takes delight in God…the last love is dead, because it does not desire anything, it does not want anything, it does not long for anything, and it does not look for anything. By deadly abandoning itself to God, the soul that has this love desires neither to know him, nor to understand him, nor to enjoy him…all these loves lead to the Word, but one must dwell only in the last one, I mean, in the dead love, of which the Word lets his spouse taste a bit (*Revelations*, pp. 210–11).

In this passage the mystic seems to reverse the logic of the previous excerpt from vision 49 of *The Dialogues*. Whereas in that vision she recounts the different ways in which God loves the creatures, now she seems to be describing how the soul loves the divinity (passive love, anxious love, satiating love, and dead love). We might see these four loves as four steps toward a closer relation to the divinity. The soul abandons itself to God (passive love); it realizes how distant the other creatures are from God (anxious love); it is filled with a sense of divine satisfaction; and it finally ceases to feel, think, or perceive anything.

In fact, no actual difference exists between vision 49 and the passage from the *Revelations*. What does *love* actually mean? Is not *love* the name of love? Is not *love* a synonym for the Word? The mystic's different "love(s)" are nothing but different names of the Word. Indeed, if we analyze the four loves of the *Revelations*, we notice that more than expressing the soul's love for the divinity, they are different ways in which the divinity manifests itself in the soul. The Word is a passive, anxious, satiating, and dead love. The soul is never capable of conceiving an "active love" for the Word. It is the Word that lets the soul call him with *different names that correspond to his different manifestations. Love*, like *Word*, is first and foremost a name that needs to be qualified. To qualify the Word means to give *love* a meaning, such as "anxious," "satiating," or "dead." By manifesting himself to the soul, the Word/Love lets the soul pronounce his "face." There is a substantial difference between "naming the Word" and "being allowed to name the Word." The Word names himself by letting the soul perceive, but not see, his face. The word *Word* reflects itself in the word *love* through the mirror/soul, which is the "dead" soul. The soul is the "dead" surface in which the Word contemplates *(risguarda)* his love. The soul is not a being but rather eyes that see the Word seeing himself as love. The soul is the act of seeing how the Word loves and contemplates himself.

In the above excerpt from the *Revelations*, Maria Maddalena enumerates a series of different loves, which characterize the Word's different approaches to the soul. However, the Florentine mystic primarily performs the third kind of love, the so-called "anxious love": "anxious love…the soul, which has this kind of love, with a constant and passionate desire desires every creature to know God and desires to know God herself, and it desires God to let everyone know him." "Anxious love" occurs when the soul gazes at the Word and thus perceives the unbridgeable distance between its, the soul's, gaze and the Word's denied response, due to the soul's "incapability"

46

(incapacità). At that point, the soul identifies with every creature "who neither loves nor knows love," as Maria Maddalena says in a powerful passage from *The Forty Days* (136), and asks love to grant her the desire both to see the face of the Word/Love and to be seen by the Word/Love.

For that matter, the long vision 48 of *The Dialogues*, presented in this volume in its complete version, clarifies how the soul gazes at the Word. After having participated in Jesus' burial, Maria Maddalena finds herself in the Savior's tomb and is allowed to contemplate his corpse, and in particular his closed eyes. This narrative moment describes a pivotal aspect of Maria Maddalena's mystical discourse. The Word's face, the object of the soul's desire, shows itself as a flat and inexpressive surface, what Jacques Lacan calls *objet a*, that "mute thing" on which the subject projects her own discourse and desire.[66] The closed eyes of the Word urges the mystic to speak and to attempt to speak the Word's inexpressive face. Lacan's astute pun "I soul" *(j'âme)* for "I love" *(j'aime)* is a direct response to the mystic's conflict between its desire for the Word and the Word's denied gaze. Lacan asks himself whether we should consider the soul as a "love's effect":

> The soul could only be spoken as whatever enables a being—the speaking being to call him by its name—to bear what is intolerable in its world, which presumes this soul to be alien to that world, that is to say, fantasmatic.[67]

Maria Maddalena's soul springs from the vision of the Word's closed eyelids. Her soul in fact "souls for the soul" *(âme l'âme)*. In the act of "souling for" itself, the mystic's soul is compelled to speak. The vision of the Word's dead body leads Maria Maddalena to acknowledge the present absence of her interlocutor and her own (as interlocutor of her interlocutor) absence. "Love" is thus the name pronounced by an absence to an absence. The soul is indeed the gift of the Word in that it is by gazing at the Word's corpse that Maria Maddalena *perceives the absence of her own soul.*[68] In vision 48 of *The Dialogues* both the perception of the Word's corpse and the awareness of her own missing soul compel Maria Maddalena de' Pazzi to articulate an invocation, an exclamation, utterances directed to a noninterlocutor. "Love," "Word," are invocations both to God and to her own soul.

"Love" is always an invocation, is always expression of an "anxious love," as Maria Maddalena says, and it should always be written with an exclamation mark, *love!* Some of the most fascinating visions of Maria Maddalena de' Pazzi are indeed dominated by the repeated exclamation "oh, love!" or simply "love!" See, for instance, a powerful page from *Probation*. As the transcribers report, on May 3, 1592, the mystic entered a very painful rapture. Feeling restless and anguished, Maria Maddalena runs through the convent and the kitchen garden, and asks her sisters to answer her distressed questions: Do they know love? Why does no one love love? Does love know that she, Maria Maddalena, is willing to do everything to be with him? While she screams "Love! love!" she starts ringing the convent bells to remind every nun that they must love Love. Let us read the last lines of this vision:

> [S]he ran all around the kitchen garden several times, and nearly throughout the entire convent. She said that she was looking for some soul who knew and loved love. And she always either called love or spoke with love. Sometimes, when she met a nun, she grabbed her and holding her tight she told her: " Soul, do you love love? How can you live? Don't you feel like you were consuming and dying for love?"...After having walked through the convent for a while, she grasped the bells large and small, and rang them crying out loudly: "Come to love, oh souls, to love Love who loves you so much! Souls, come to love!" (*Probation*, 2:189).

Maria Maddalena "grabs a soul" in order to see/face Love; she asks a "soul" to utter its love for Love/the Word. In this passage the encounter between the subject and her soul is performed as a dramatic confrontation. The mystic "grabs" the image of herself through another nun (a "soul") and questions her/herself about the absence of Love. "How can you live?" Maria Maddalena asks her sister, meaning "How can you live without love?" "Don't you feel like you were consuming and dying for love?" she adds.

48

INTRODUCTION

As I have pointed out, Maria Maddalena primarily focuses on an "anxious" love. In her words, "anxious love" takes place when the subject feels the presence of love as a reminder of its absence in the world. "Come to Love, souls!" the mystic screams ringing the bell of the convent. It is actually by gazing at the other's, her sister's, face that the mystic recognizes that the Word is absent. The other's life itself exists as long as it "cries out" the absent Word. More than "belching forth" the Word, Maria Maddalena invokes him. To cry out the Word is a performative act that is not directed to the "name" invoked, but rather to those who witness the subject's invocation.

A meaningful element of the mystic's "anxious" love is that in her raptures the traditional mystical discourse about the different kinds and stages of divine love acquires a performative connotation; that is, for Maria Maddalena love is not only a topic to explain, but also and more importantly a truth to manifest, an inner feeling to perform through both spoken language and her physicality. When the Word asks her to respond to his request for being, the mystic cannot help but speak and move about the convent. Her voice and her body have the very same task: the expression of the Word. Whereas some of her visions are predominantly discursive, others are dominated by the expressions of her body; words and body are two facets of the same language.

The most eloquent vision concerning Maria Maddalena's "anxious" love is in a long passage from *The Forty Days* (133–80) that opens this anthology. During this four-day rapture the nuns tell that the mystic is ill and "in an rapture of mind." On Monday, June 11, 1584, although she feels restless and anxious, her sisters force Maria Maddalena to stay in bed and constantly ask her to drink some broth. Maria Maddalena keeps repeating, "I can't stay here, please let me get out this bed, I can't." She stares at a small crucifix that she keeps on the altar in her cell. She poses questions to her sisters and to her confessor, who has been asked by the Mother Superior to assist the "blessed soul" in her malaise:

> All of a sudden she saw everything God has worked for the creature that is so base and corrupt, so that she was forced to

49

scream out loudly, externally, so that she was heard by all those who were present: love love, oh God, you love the creature with a pure love, oh God of love, oh God of love.

And since she saw that the creatures were so ungrateful toward such a great love, she burst with sorrow, screaming and saying:

Lord, no more love, no more love, you have too much love for your creatures. No, it's not too much, I mean, for your greatness. But it is too much for the creature, that is so base and corrupt. Lord, why do you give so much love to me? (*The Forty Days*, 133–34)

What is striking in this passage is that Maria Maddalena, like the female speaker of the Song of Songs, is "sick with love" (Sg 2:5c). However, unlike the Song of Songs, *The Forty Days* does not recount the lover's weakness or disease because of an abundance of love but rather because the Word's love for the lover reminds the lover that in fact she does not love Love/the Word. The Word's love shatters the subject's love by making the lover doubt her own identity as lover; in other words, God's love leads the mystic to perceive the void of her alleged love. More than an actual act of caring, divine love questions the creature's perception of love. Love is in fact a reminder of the lack of love. God's love is "too much": It makes the mystic scream and cry. The Word's love is perceived by the mystic as a persecution: "Why do you give so much love to me?"

Love makes Maria Maddalena sick because love, as the Word, manifests itself as missing. The mystic grabs the crucifix she has in her cell and stares at it:

If at least, my Jesus, you were not naked on the cross. Such a dishonor increases their sneer. Yes, love, you wished so. Love love, love drove you crazy, and you went crazy for such an ungrateful creature. Oh, blindness, oh man's malice, toward such a great love. Nobody, nobody loves my love. Oh, my love, when will I have you? When will I be united with you perfectly? When will I love you infinitely?…My Jesus, no more love, 'cause I can't take it anymore; and if you want to give it to me, give it to me as much as you want. But give the strength to tolerate it. Oh holy Virgin, how could you be there? You saw

him; and he was your son, and he was also God. And you knew
that he was doing this because he loves the creatures. (134–35)

The Word, which is love, was "driven crazy" by love. Love
deranges both the creature and the divinity who dies for love. Love
engenders destruction and death, folly and disease. Love, as the
term *blood*, is a negativity in the sense that it works against the world
and the subject. This is why the mystic can only associate love with
death, with the death of love on the cross ("If at least, my Jesus, you
were not naked on the cross…Oh holy Virgin, how could you be
there?"). Love is what does not exist, what does not exist in the
world, and what makes the creature sense her own nonexistence in
the world. Maria Maddalena can only recall the end of love, his
dying on the cross for love. Love is always the end of love because
love itself engenders its end: "My Jesus, no more love."

Maria Maddalena cannot "conjugate love" in the present tense
because love is exclusively its past. There would be no love if love
were not absent here and now: "Nobody loves my love. Oh, my
love, when will I have you?" Love is intrinsically nonlove, for it can
exist only insofar as the subject longs for it, misses it, and recall his
death. The crucifix is a token of love's death, of his presence in the
world as a being—for death. The mystic is unable to love love
because of her "baseness." Speaking to the Virgin, Maria Maddalena says: "You saw him; and he was your son, and he was also
God…But, I mean, how could you be there without bursting with
sorrow? I do not see him and still burst with a great sorrow." Moreover, Maria Maddalena underscores that she loves a love that she
has not seen or met. Her sorrow springs from an act of remembrance that does not belong to her. She loves someone else's love.
Love is not only absence, but it is primarily a remembrance that
"makes us sick" without belonging to us.

In a fundamental passage from book 10 of the *Confessions*,
Augustine asks God how it is possible that the subject has an innate
desire for happiness, even though he/she has no experience of it:

When I seek for you, my God, my quest is for the happy life. I
will seek you that 'my soul may live' (Is 55:3), for my body
derives life from my soul, and my soul derives from you…Is

not the happy life that which all desire, which indeed no one fails to desire?...My question is whether the happy life is in the memory. For we would not love it if we did not know what it is...Even when sad, I remember my times of joy, like a wretched person thinking of the happy life. It is never by bodily sense that I have seen my joy or heard or smelt or tasted or touched it. I experienced it in my mind when I was glad, and the knowledge of it stuck in my memory, so that I could remind myself of it.[69]

Augustine comes to the conclusion that God has instilled the memory of the happy life, that is, of himself, in man's consciousness.[70] The human being in fact remembers what he/she has not experienced. The gift of God's remembrance lies in man's consciousness. This is why, Augustine infers, everybody spontaneously longs for happiness. According to Augustine, God is the remembrance of a perfect joy: "You [God] conferred this honor on my memory that you should dwell in it."[71]

Maria Maddalena de' Pazzi offers a radically different concept of memory and remembrance. Although she shares with Augustine the central idea that to love God means both to remember him and to reenact this very memory of the divinity in one's own life, she does not believe that God is a memory of a "happy life." As she stresses in many passages of her raptures, for her God is the remembrance of his suffering and death for all of humanity. At the beginning was God's suffering for the creation. This is what the creature actually remembers. From the very beginning, from the moment when the Father generated the Word, the divinity descended upon the world as the memory of the Word's forthcoming death. For the Florentine mystic, to love God and to love oneself are the same as recalling the Word's death. Maria Maddalena holds that the human life is a constant commemoration of the Word's passion and death. As she says in many passages from *The Dialogues*, Jesus wishes us "to practice pain more than joy." It is through suffering that the subject "remembers" the Word. Both psychological and physical pain are a sudden insight into the Word's past.

Rephrasing Augustine's concept of memory, we might say that for Maria Maddalena God has granted us the memory of his original absence from the world. Whereas for Augustine the divinity, which coincides with a perfectly "happy life," is a sense of fulfillment similar to Bernard's act of "belching forth the Word," for Maria Maddalena the Word is "history," narration, the tormenting memory of an act of injustice.[72] Injustice, suffering, guilt, affliction are the actual means through which the soul remembers the Word and expresses its longing for him.

A Note on the Translation

In my translation I have attempted to reproduce the oral tone of Maria Maddalena de' Pazzi's discourse. I have neither corrected nor simplified her numerous incomplete, convoluted, and grammatically inexact sentences. When the mystic coins a new term, I have resorted to an English neologism. For example, the verb *squallidare* becomes *to squalid*. I have not translated the mystic's innumerable Latin quotations, even when she uses Latin and Italian in the same sentence. I give a translation of the Latin expressions in the footnotes when the sense of a Latin sentence is not immediately evident. For instance, when Maria Maddalena mentions a well-known passage from the Gospel, I omit its translation but give the reference. Also when she herself translates her Latin, I have not considered necessary to offer any additional translation. Following Giovanni Pozzi's graphic interpretation in *Le parole dell'estasi*, to signify the mystic's frequent pauses I use the term *silence* in brackets *[silence]*.

The result is a text that is often puzzling and syntactically unpleasant. Overall, however, this translation is much clearer than its original. Indeed, in several passages I have been compelled to interpret, and thus to simplify, in order to avoid an excessive obscurity.

The translations were made from *Tutte le Opere* (7 vols., Eds. Bruno Nardini, Bruno Visentin, Carlo Catena, and Giulio Agresti [Florence: Nardini, 1960–66]). Notes in parentheses within the text indicating volume, edition, or page numbers refer to locations in that original source.

The few direct translations from biblical sources are from the Jerusalem Bible.

Selections from

The Forty Days

The Forty Days[1]

June 11 to June 15, 1584 (ed. 1:133–80)

In two occasions during the same day [Monday June 11, 1584] she had a great transport of love and looked as if she were about to burst. Then she had a marvelous vision of pure love. She saw God all pure in himself loving himself and loving the creature with a similar pure and infinite love. All of a sudden she saw everything God had generated for the creature that is so base and corrupt that she was forced to scream out loud, externally, so that she was heard by all those who were present: "Love love, oh God, you love the creature with a pure love, oh God of love, oh God of love."

Because she saw that the creatures were so ungrateful toward such a great love, she burst with sorrow, screaming and saying:

"Lord, no more love, no more love, you have too much love for your creatures. No, it's not too much, I mean, for your greatness. But it is too much for the creature, that is so base and corrupt. Lord, why do you give so much love to me? I'm so base and corrupt. There are still other creatures; I am not the only one. My Lord, please communicate this love to the other creatures. I know, I know, you give it, yes, you give it, but those betrayers do not want it. Oh my Jesus, what took you to the cross but love?"

She kept a crucifix in her hand and spoke to it because with her internal eyes she saw in her hand something different from what she saw with her external eyes. During this day she constantly stared at its holy feet because in them she saw the great malice of the creatures. And she said:

"My love, what pierced your holy feet but the malice of the creatures? My Jesus, last Friday you made me foresee very clearly the martyrdom I am suffering now so intensely; [You showed me] that those who are malicious pierce your holy feet. Oh, my Jesus, why am I not on the cross as I see you now? If at least, my Jesus, you were not naked on the cross. Such a dishonor increases their sneer. Yes, love, you wished so. Love love, love drove you crazy, and you went crazy for such an ungrateful creature. Oh, blindness, oh man's malice, toward such a great love. No one, no one loves my love. Oh, my love, when will I have you? When will I be united with you perfectly? When will I love you infinitely? *Satiabor, satiabor, cum apparuerit gloria tua.*[2] My Jesus, no more love, 'cause I can't take it anymore; and if you want to give it to me, give it to me as much as you want. But give me the strength to tolerate it. Oh holy Virgin, how could you be there? You saw him; and he was your son, and he was also God. And you knew that he was doing this because he loves the creatures. But, I mean, how could you be there without bursting with sorrow? I do not see him, and yet I burst with a great sorrow. Oh my Jesus, last Saturday you showed me very clearly that she was prepared for everything."

And turning to the nuns that were there she offered them the crucifix, and said:

"Love him, love my Jesus, love him, because nobody loves him."

And she repeated this several times, speaking words that were both amorous and full of compassion. I am able neither to express them nor to explain them. And in this day she suffered a very intense pain both internally and externally, crying and moaning a lot because she saw that love was neither loved nor known because of the creatures' malice.

Tuesday, June 12. After receiving communion, I meditated on those words, *"et delitie mee esse cum Filiis hominum."*[3] And I understood that God's "delights" in his staying with the children of man; that is, he takes a great pleasure in staying in the souls that are pure and that love him with a pure love. This is why he calls them his delights. And for a while I meditated and saw the great delight God finds in the souls, but in particular I dwelled on enjoying the great love he has for them. It is impossible for me either to express or to speak about this great love of his.

That day she had such a great transport of love that she looked crazy; and this lasted for three hours until the twenty-first hour. Its vehemence was so overwhelming that she could not stay in bed. She jumped out of her bed, took a small crucifix that she keeps on her altar, and started to run around the room screaming "Love love love." And she smiled in such a sweet and cheerful manner, that it was a consolation for us to hear her, but also a great dismay because of her screaming "Love love"; but we were not afraid. She stared at the crucifix often, looking as if she were in an excess of mind. Then she stood up, hugged it, and pressed it against her breast, and with a great transport she said again:

"Love, love, love, I will never stop calling you love. Love neither loved nor known by anyone. Oh my Love, joy of my heart; you are love."

And turning to those who were present, she said:

"Love, love, you laugh, you cry, you scream and keep silent. Love!"

And turning to those who were present she said:

"Don't you know it? Oh my Jesus, love, crazy for love, crazy for love, I say it, oh my Jesus. Oh love, you are all lovable and joyful love! Old and new truth. Love, love, you are recreative, you are consoling, love! Love, love, you are loving and unifying love! Love, you are pain and relief; Love, you are toil and rest, death and life you are, love! Oh love, what's not in you? What's not in you? Love, love, you are wise and joyful. High and profound love. Love love, you are admirable, inexpugnable, unfathomable, incomprehensible, you are love!"

During this day she always stared at the open side of the crucifix that she held in her hand, but her internal eyes stared at the actual and consoling side of Jesus much more intensely. Like in a mirror, in this crucifix she saw every creature, but in particular she saw the spouses of Jesus, that is, the nuns. And she had the impression that the thalamus had been created only for Jesus' virgin spouses, as she had seen that

Wednesday after the celebration of the Holy Trinity.[4] And she said that at that time she saw all the nuns of the convent staying in Jesus' side; she saw that some other nuns were there, but only a few, and many of them came out of it. She also saw the angels, those who were in that side like in a delightful garden, gathering flowers, as she had seen the previous Wednesday. At that point, she said, the angels were gathering many, many flowers; and she said: "Now now, in that spot they gather so many [flowers] to make wreaths." And first of all she saw that her little angel was making one for her. Later she said that she saw all these nuns under the mantel of the Virgin Mary. And woe betide those who came out of it. She also added:

"Woe betide those nuns that break all the three vows they have made to God, and primarily that of obedience. If they break only the first two, that is, chastity and poverty, love can still take those strings and tie them back to him very easily because he keeps his arms stretched out on the cross and can reach for them. But if they break that of obedience along with the first two, nobody can tie them back, but love moved by himself. Mary, our Mary, Mary our mother can cover us under her mantel, but she cannot tie us back. Love, only love can. Love, love, you are that bond that binds fast the soul to God; but woe betide those creatures that break that bond because there is no love that can tie it back, but you, love. The Father with you, the Holy Spirit with you. Only you, love, can do it; you that suffered the pain, you are the only one who has tied it back. Mary, Mary, our mother, she can show you her breast with which she fed you, and in this way she can force you, love, to tie it back. Oh, pure love. Pure love. Oh unity of the Holy Trinity. Oh wisdom of the Father, oh benevolence of the Holy Spirit. Oh, my love, my Jesus, you are crazy for love, my Jesus. When, my love, will I be united to you? Love, old and new truth; love, love, I know you want the soul to come back to you as pure as it was when it came out of you. Love, and when you see that it soils itself with sin, you cross its path and send it to purge itself with love. Love, love, I see you wounded for love. Please, in the name of love take out of your open wound the lance that has wounded you for love so that it can come and rain down that water that is inside of your grace and of your love. Love, love, rain it over the hearts of your creatures, created for love. Love, love, yesterday these feet of yours gave me such a pain and martyrdom because I saw that the creatures do not love you, but today away from me, away from me that sorrow and pain; and everything be as love is, joyful and delightful, love! Oh love, you make my heart rejoice, love!"

And when a companion of hers, Sister Veronica, asked her how long she would last in this way, she answered:

"Love wishes to keep me in this way until the moment when love ended up on the cross to show his love for his love toward the creatures created for love. And tomorrow my love wants [to keep me in this way] from the fifteenth hour until he, love, was lifted up to the cross for love, I mean, my love wishes me, his creature created for love, to suffer from love all that time. And my love wants me, his creature created for love, to start to suffer from love around the second hour of the night of the following day, which is Thursday, until that hour of Friday when love was lifted to the cross. I believe that this will be a torturous pain and sorrow. And I will have it neither always externally, nor always internally, but I will have it some time in a way, some time in another."

And because we paid a close attention to this, we saw everything that followed as she had said. She also said:

"Because he finished his external passion, my love wants me to finish this vehemence of love that now I have externally. But my love does not want me to finish the internal pain because he always always wants to be in it, and my love will never leave me."

And at the twenty-first hour, when she had said that she would finish, before that hour rang, she placed her mouth on the side of Jesus, I mean, of that crucifix that she had always kept in her hand, and said:

"Yes, now it comes into my soul, and the body will have it no more."[5]

And she stopped in a way that she looked engrossed and totally outside of her corporeal feelings. She stayed like this for quite a while; then she recovered from it as she had had nothing. It seemed a marvel to us.

Wednesday, June 13. After receiving communion, while I was considering those words of the psalmist, *"Cor meum, et caro mea exultaverunt in Deum vivum, in porticum Salomonis,"*[6] first I had the impression that I was seeing Jesus amorously sitting to the right side of his Father; and that his eyes were so beautiful that I would never be able to explain or to tell you their beauty. And I saw that with his look he drew every creature to him, I mean, those who looked at him with their internal eyes and partook of the grace of his look. At this point St. Peter came up to me, and it was when he denied Jesus, but later, when Jesus gazed at him with his beautiful and piercing eyes, he recognized his sin and repented. And on the contrary, those who crucified Jesus during his passion and sneered at him and laughed at him, their eyes only gazed at him aslant because of their great hatred for him. However, if their eyes had looked at him directly, they would have not been able to feel attracted to his beauty and to the gentle look of those divine eyes. Then, going back to that verse that I have mentioned before, the one that the soul recites, *"Cor meum et caro mea exultaverunt in Porticum Salomonis,"* I had the impression I was seeing that our flesh and our heart rejoiced and celebrated Jesus' humanity, that I saw similar to a loggia or to a porch; and I call it in this way so that you can understand me because in fact it was neither a loggia nor a porch but rather a place of enjoyment and of recreation; and I saw that our flesh rejoiced and exulted in Jesus' humanity for two reasons: first, because it was exalted, sublimated, and magnified through Jesus' humanity—indeed, when the Word had become incarnate, he had exalted and magnified it, placing it at the right side of his eternal Father—and, second, it exulted for the incorruptibility that it would attain in heaven because at that time it will be immortal, incorruptible, eternal, and equal to Jesus' humanity. It seemed to me that our heart also exulted and rejoiced for two reasons. The first reason is the peace it gave Jesus inside itself; the second were the influences that God exerted on it through his grace. Then, on the contrary, it seemed to me that Jesus recited that verse to our souls, *"Cor meum, et caro mea exultaverunt in te."* In other words, it seemed to me that Jesus' humanity exulted within ourselves in one way, thanks to the fact that our soul is made to his image and likeness, and his heart exulted in a different way in order to rest in ourselves. Then, as usual, I recommended to Jesus every creature, in particular our father and you, Sister Veronica."

That day, around the fifteenth hour, while she was speaking to her companion, Sister Veronica, she told her:

"I am going crazy, and I can't stay in this bed any longer. Please, let me get up."

And because Sister Veronica suggested that she stay in bed because the nurse was not there, she turned and tossed, unable to stop because of love's great transport. And when the nurse arrived, she begged her to let her get up. And as soon as they let her get up because of her insistence, she jumped out of her bed, run to her small altar, took her crucifix, unnailed it from the cross, pressed it to her breast, and started to run up and down the room, saying:

"Love, love. Love, no one loves you or knows you."

And taking that companion of hers by the hand, she said:

"Come, come, run with me; help me call love." And she added: "Scream loud, loud, louder; you speak so low; he doesn't hear you."

And screaming very loudly, she said:

"Love, love, love. I will never tire of calling you love. Oh, love. *Cor meum et caro mea exultaverunt in te*, my love."

And running around the room again, she pressed her Jesus against her breast and kept screaming "love love," and sometimes she burst into a wonderful laughter with such a joy that it was a pleasure to hear her. And then, stopping for a while, she repeated once again:

"Love, love. Oh love, give me a strong voice, so that when I call you I can be heard from the East to the West, and in every part of the world, even in hell, so that everyone will hear and love you, love. You are strong and powerful, love. Love, love, only you can penetrate and pierce; you break and overcome everything. Love, love. You are heaven and earth, fire and air, blood and water. Oh love, you are God and man, love and hatred, joy of a divine nobility, old and new truth. Oh love, neither loved nor known. But at least I see one person that has had this love."

And when we asked her who this person was, she said:

"Mother Sister Maria knew my love.[7] Oh love, make every creature love you, love. But I mean, sooner, because the way they love you now is less than nothing. And that nothing [is even] mixed up with that pestilential poison of self-love because your love and self-love cannot stay together. They are opposed; they are opposed. No, no, only you love. And no other love, oh love, love, and who on earth, who on earth, and who on earth could even think or tell your greatness? You are infinite and eternal, immutable, incomprehensible; love, you are inscrutable. What does *inscrutable* mean? Who knows, who knows, who knows, please, who knows it please tell me, because I know nothing about it."

And given that the father confessor was present, she turned to him and said:

"Perhaps you, perhaps you are able to tell me."

And he answered that it was such a great thing that no one could understand it. Then she smiled and said:

"It's so great, I believe, so great, love."

And staring at that crucifix that she held in her hand, she kept quiet for a little while. Then she continued:

"Oh, love, you are so strong, and then I see you so weak. So strong that nobody can resist you, but you are also so weak that a creature so base as I am defeats you, overcomes you, just by calling you love. Oh love, love. What you said was right: *Desiderio desideravi.*"[8]

And the father confessor continued saying "*hoc pasca manducare vobiscum, ante quam patiar.*" She said:

"Love let you finish it for me. Oh love, why did you long to have the last supper? Ah, love, because you wanted to show your love for the creatures. Oh love, love, what a privilege do the priests enjoy when they handle you, love, and administer you to the others. But, oh love, there are so few priests who are as they should be! Oh, love, I wished, I wished that what I said were a lie because, you see, love, I would be proud of telling such lies. But, love, unfortunately what I said is true."

We asked her if one of those priests was present in the room. She answered:

"Because there is only one here I cannot say who they are, because now love does not allow me to do so. Love, love, I say love, who could ever penetrate the great privilege of the priests. But alas! Love, love, Catherine knew how to speak about it. And if, my love, they could fathom and understand how appropriate is that worthy offer that they make of you to the eternal Father in that great act. Oh love, not once, but thousand times, if they could, they would make this offer so dear to you, love. But, love, I want to pray to that who has made this offer to you many many times, that he may offer you, love, for me."

And when a nun asked her: "But, Sister Maria Maddalena, can't we make this offer ourselves? Can't we offer Jesus to the eternal Father?" she smiled and said:

"Ah, love, listen to what she says. Of course you can. But not in that way. For there is a big gap between the offer the priests make at the altar and that that you can make. Oh, love, love old and new truth; you are love, love love. Who will I say that has written more profoundly about you? John, who said: *In principio erat Verbum* or Augustine, who expounded those words? Love, who will I say that has gone deeper? Augustine, love! Oh, love, love, is it possible that you have no other name than love? You are so poor of names, love! Of course you have names, of course, and so many, love, but you prefer to be called by this one, oh love, because with this one you have revealed yourself to the creatures. Even the saints in heaven call you with this name of love; they always say love, love; every other name is in this love. Always repeating *Sanctus Sanctus*, they in fact say love, which is all the same. But that Sanctus contains everything in itself; they say *Sanctus, Sanctus*. You are God, you are Father, you are Spirit, and you are also love. Never, never will I tire of calling you with this name of love."

During that day she constantly stared at the right hand of Jesus crucified that she held in her hand. Sometimes turning to the nuns, she showed the open wound of its right hand and said:

"Do you see, do you see how much love?!"

A nun said: "I don't see anything but this bruised hand." Smiling she answered:

"Ah, love, they don't see anything else, but if I didn't see anything else I would not stare at you so intensely; and if, taking away this image of wood, I would see nothing else, I would take it away at once because love would show himself to me anyway, but I hold this in my hand to satisfy my corporeal eyes. Oh love, love, so few love you and know you. Oh love, love, happy and blessed is the soul that has you, love, love, love. Woe betide, oh love, woe betide those religious that break that one that nowadays only a few observe."

And when someone asked her if she meant the vow of obedience, she said:

"No, no, I mean observance."

And we asked her if she had doubts about this convent, she said:

"I do not doubt those who are there now, but watch out those who are going to come. Be careful that no one will mar it, because, since we lack any support now, it [observance] might lack in the future. Oh love, woe betide, woe betide those who mar it. I don't mean that it will happen necessarily, but it could if love's support lacked. Oh love, love, woe betide, woe betide those who mar it and break the ties that unite [us] to you, I mean, the three vows, along with the bond of charity. These three vows, oh love, are like a chain that if one breaks the first ring all the others break up. Love, love, these rings are already broken, you know where, you know where, in that place where I stayed for an entire year. That of obedience is already broken, and that of poverty as well. And, love, and that other also, it's broken."

And when a nun asked her if she meant that of chastity, she answered:

"No, no, I don't mean this one. I mean that of chastity; you know what has happened to you because of your lack of chastity."

At this point she wept a little bit out of sorrow. Thus, she did not speak for quite a while, as she usually does. In this case we leave a space, when she says "love, love," because almost every time she keeps quiet for a while she starts again with these words "love, love."[9] Then she continued as follows:

"But love, how better it would be, I mean, love, as you said to the traitor, how better it would be for the bad religious if they were never never born because they do not observe what they have promised. Oh, love love, who do they think they have made a promise to? To someone who is deaf or blind, maybe? Ah, love, later they find themselves blind and deaf, love. Love, love and justice are the same in you, love, although it seems to me that justice, oh love, is not as great as love is because love, more than justice, has manifested love to the creatures. But, oh love, time will come, yes love, when you manifest justice as well. Old love and new truth, wisdom of the Father, supreme goodness, infinite love, love neither known nor loved. But love, these two, these two knew you, and loved you."

We asked her: "Who, perhaps Mother Sister Maria?" And she answered:

"Yes, Mother Sister Maria has loved my love; love, love; and then they fear that she is going to be recognized; oh love, their lukewarm and apathetic faith makes their beloved remain unknown. But, oh love, you'll make her known, yes, when time comes. Oh love, love, if the creatures knew how much they offend you, they would choose not one but thousand hells, with thousand devils more than they are in hell. Love, love, you are incomprehensible, you are immense and worthy of every praise; but, oh love, no one would ever be able to praise you, love, as you deserve. If all human languages, along with the angels and all the stars of the sky, the sand of the sea, the plants of the earth, the drops of water, the birds of the air, became languages to praise you, they would not suffice to praise you, love."

And when someone told her: "Sister Maria Maddalena, don't you remember your father confessor?" Then she said:

"You ask me if I remember him. If I were obliged to a creature, that creature would be him, but I cannot, I cannot be obliged to any creature, but to love. Love, love, oh love, see, see how they struggle, love, and by the way they struggle it really seems that they only have one soul. Love, love, oh, they are so many. Oh, see how they strive for it. As you, love, love the souls so vehemently that it seems like you have only one, so they strive for it so much that all of them seem to have only one; love, love, send them away, send them away, love. Well, let them stay as long as you wish. Love, but don't let them win."

And turning to the nuns who were there, she said:

"Yes, yes, I speak to you! I want you to take hammers and break the walls, I mean, the obstacles that the devils, the enemies, try to raise to prevent you from receiving my love's grace. Oh, how they are striving for it, love! Oh love, I was right when I said that you only needed to stretch your powerful arm in order to put them to flight and rout them. You see, love, how soon you have run away. Oh love, only you have power over everyone."

Someone asked her if the waker had already arrived. She answered:

"Oh, if he has arrived? I am surprised that you haven't heard him ring because he made a big noise. Didn't you hear my love? When he, the 'waker' as you call him with a very material name, gave out that great and echoing sound after being lifted on the cross, didn't you hear him? When he said '*Sitio*,' didn't you hear him?[10] That sound was so great that all, all of you could have heard it. Oh, love, who doesn't hear the waker is deaf, deaf, oh love. Oh love, if I could and if it were possible, I would take all your love away from you and would give it to the creatures so that they would be able to love you, love. Oh love, you are a loving love. Love, love, you do everything for love. You also give everything for love. You give heaven for love, purgatory for love, everything you give for love. Even hell you give for love, because, oh love, the love you have for the creature is so much that you cannot see any offense in her. But for love you give hell to her. But, oh love, how many descend in this sea and abyss of darkness. You see, love, as water rains from the sky down to us, so they descend down there. Ah love, what am I saying? I see many many more raining down there than the rain does and I hear them falling down in that chasm and infernal abyss. And that one, that woman, I mean, yes that virulent and malignant woman that is persecuting you so much; I see her falling and sinking like an arrow into the most horrible and obscure place. Oh love, love."

We understood that she meant Queen Elizabeth of England, the heretic. At this point she stopped because we wanted to give her a little bit of broth. She looked to be suffering a lot for having spoken for so long and with such a vehemence. And we said to her: "Sister Maria Maddalena, we have the feeling that you are suffering. We would like you to drink a bit." Then she said:

"Why do you think I am suffering since I am with my love? Don't you know that love cannot feel pain? So, how could I possibly suffer?"

And when the nuns said to her: "Sister Maria Maddalena, you see, the father wants you to drink," then she said:

"I do believe that the Father wants me to drink, my Father of Light wants to give me something to drink."

And placing her mouth on the right hand of the crucifix she was holding in her hand, she said:

"I drink, I drink, and they do not believe it."

And even though we insisted that she take that broth, she said:

"Please, love, you are still so benign. And how could I act differently since I am with you, love. But, love, in order to satisfy the creatures and recreate this body of mine, I'll take what they want to give me."

And so she drank that little bit of broth. And resuming her discourse, she recommended all the heretics, the Jews, and all the infidels:

"Oh love, love, love. You are full of love. Love love, give it to every creature and, love, make all all of them love you, love, desire you, love, long for you, love; and those who are still waiting for you, love, don't make them wait any longer because once you have come, love. But, oh love, make them recognize this and stop waiting for you, because, love, their waiting is useless; love, love, and also those who have left you, love, I mean the heretics, love, make them come back to you like a lost flock, I mean, come back to you, love, their good shepherd; make them revere and love you, love. Love, love, make all those who don't believe in you come back to you, love, because they are your creatures too, love. Oh love love, if a soul were able to see, I mean a soul that is without you, love, it would die not once, but thousand thousand times, love. And if it could penetrate what is in you, love, love you are the only one to know it. Oh love, you do not allow me to say everything; the only thing that really matters, love, what really matters is that you know it, what it is, love."

And because it was almost vespers and the father confessor wanted to leave in order to confess the other nuns, he asked her if she wanted anything from him. She answered:

71

"I wouldn't ask you for anything else but love, and I don't know what to ask for besides love because if I have love I have everything, and if I don't have him, I miss every good."

And when he said: "Sister Maria Maddalena, God be with you," she answered:

"God with God, and you with God."

And when the nuns said that he was going to confess, she said:

"Yes, he must make you vases more suitable to receive love. Love, love, incorruptible purity, incomprehensible love. Oh love, love. Love, I will never stop calling you love, wisdom of the Father, goodness of the Holy Spirit, Unity, Unity of the holy Trinity, love, love; love neither loved nor known; oh love, love, old and new truth, love, love."

After these words, because the other nuns had gone to recite Vespers, one of them told her: "Sister Maria Maddalena, the nuns go to Vespers." She answered:

"Let them go give birth to love. Each time they speak a word, they will give birth to love. Love, love, who tastes you, is always satisfied by you, love."

And saying "Come, come in me, love, because the body could not tolerate more love," she placed her mouth on the right hand of the crucifix that she was holding. And suddenly she stopped, without speaking anymore. And she kept quiet for quite a long time. And it was indeed the eighteenth hour, as she said she would conclude at that time.

In those three hours that she was in that way, during that day and the previous two, she said many things that we could not remember precisely, and even those words that we did write down we could not report them as correctly as she spoke them. She pronounced them in such a wondrous manner that no one would ever be able to explain or communicate them unless one had listened to them. And we saw that everything she had told Sister Veronica the previous Tuesday came true. Indeed, she started to speak exactly when she said she would, which amazed us greatly. As her confessor has ordered her to do, she describes to Sister Veronica all her raptures and everything that happens to her internally or externally.

72

She also told her that during those three days the Lord let her taste and feel also externally those things he had shown her the previous Friday, that is, that man's malice pierces Jesus' feet. And she perceived it this Monday with a great pain. But because the body is unable to tolerate all this, she said:

"Jesus does not want me to suffer too much during these two days, Tuesday and Wednesday. However, he wants me to stay at his side and at his right hand. Then, Friday, he wants me to stay at his left hand, while I am considering his passion, as you will see from the second hour at night until the eighteenth of that day. And he wants and wishes me to long for love in a cheerful and happy way in order to animate me."

As we said, on Tuesday she was at his left side, and today [she is] at the right side of the crucifix she holds in her hand.

Thursday June 14, 1584. When I received Communion I meditated on those words written by St. John, *"In principio erat Verbum, et Verbum erat apud Deum, et Deus erat Verbum,"* and I had the impression that I understood that at the beginning, without any beginning, and also without end.[11] That beginning and that end was the eternal Word generated by the Father. But it says *"erat Verbum,"* and the Word was God himself. And *"Verbum erat apud Deum"*; it seemed to me that the Word, that is God, was next to God; I mean, he was next to himself. *"Et Deus erat Verbum"*: If before I said that the Word was God, now I say that God is the Word, that he is the same thing, but, on the other hand, because the Son is the Word because he has been generated by the Father, and he is God because he is one thing with the Father.

Then I had the impression that I was seeing the great union between the holy Trinity and that pure and infinite love that is constantly breathing out, and it breathes from the Father into the Son and from the Son into the Father. And from the Father and the Son, [it breathes] into the Holy Spirit, and from the Holy Spirit into the Father and the Son. And then from the whole Trinity it is breathed first into the Virgin, and after [being breathed] into heaven and the Virgin, [it is breathed] into the whole Trinity. But one thing is to taste something, and another thing is to speak about what has been tasted because, although I know what I have tasted, I am unable to tell you anything about it, nor would I be able to find words with which I might or could explain it to you. After contemplating the issue that I have mentioned to you, I made a big jump I don't know how, because some words from the Pater Noster suddenly crossed my mind, that is, *"Fiat voluntas tua, sicut in Cielo, et in terra. Panem nostrum cotidianum."* And it seemed to me that God's will was done in heaven in two ways, first of all through a conformity of will; that is, every saint conforms to God's will, and because he conforms to it, he realizes it. They also do God's will in a second way; that is, they see God's will even before God carries it out, although God's will and God's working are the same act. And because they see that God's will is to breathe his love and his grace into his creatures, they are so willing to do it, given their conformity to his will, that if God needed their help to achieve this, they would offer it to him immediately. But this is impossible because God's might does not need any help, and he can do everything by himself.

Then I also saw that God's will was done on earth in two ways: First, because the creatures receive God's influences, I mean, his love and his grace, and they let God rest in themselves, they come to do his will. Second, the creatures do God's will in another way—because they know that it deserves to be done, they do it. Then it seemed to me that Jesus was the bread we call "our daily bread," and I saw that Jesus had all the qualities of bread.[12] First of all, bread, that is, corn, comes out of the earth. In a similar way, Jesus came out of the earth, I mean, out of the Virgin's womb. Moreover, corn is ground, and during the time he was on earth Jesus was ground by numerous persecutions, offenses, and abuses. Then flour is worked into dough, and this is, it seems to me, what happened to Jesus when he was hit at the column because that was the first act through which Jesus began to erase sin, removing what was between God and the creatures; and he began to unite them with God and to make us his coheirs. Then bread is cooked, and in a similar manner Jesus was cooked on the wood of the holy cross with the fire of his love. When bread is cooked, it is then tasted and eaten, and in a like way I perceived that Jesus gave himself to us to be tasted when later he rose from the dead, ascended to heaven, and sent us the Holy Spirit. And in heaven he will give himself to us forever.

74

Thursday night, while she was physically in bed, between the first and the second hour she felt drawn by love to follow him in his passion. Thus, she said to the nurse:

"I would like to get out of this bed. Please, let me get up because I feel my love and I have already, at least it seems to me, run around this room several times, and now I see myself in bed. Let me get up."

And, jumping out of her bed with a great vehemence and transport of love, she spoke those words of the psalmist *"Supra dorsum meum fabricaverunt peccatores."*[13] Then, as usual, she grabbed her crucifix holding it tight against her breast. She started to run around the room screaming out loud:

"Love, love love."

And then, after resting a little, she said:

"Now now he communicates it."

And she sat down for a while; then she jumped up and run around again, screaming out loud:

"Love, love love."

And then she added:

"Betrayer, betrayer, oh betrayer; he gives himself to you and you betray him, betrayer."

She repeated these words many times. And after stopping for a moment, she said again:

"Love, love, how little they know you; this one is one of yours and, nonetheless, he betrays you, love. Betrayer, betrayer, how little you knew him. You pretend to be a friend of his, and then you betray him, my love. Betrayer. Love, love, oh love. Here he comes, here he is."

And she said to the nurse:

"You see, you see, do you see him?"

And when the nurse said: "Who? Jesus?" She said:

"No, no, I mean the betrayer that goes to betray my love, oh iniquity; thousand thousand hells I would give you if it were up to me. Love, love, love."

While she kept running, she screamed so loudly that she was heard from far away; and it seemed like the whole room was shaking, what unsettled the present beyond any imagination; but it was not fear. And after behaving in this room in this way for quite a while, she obeyed the nurse who told her: "Sister Maria Maddalena, I want you to go to bed. You see, Jesus wants you to." And sitting in bed holding her crucifix, she leaned back her arms and hands on a pillow. In the meantime, she stared at the left hand of that crucifix, seeing in it the whole course of Jesus' passion. And she said with a controlled and compassionate voice:

"Now now he betrays him, my love. They deliberate about him, don't you see it? Twice, two different deliberations. In heaven the eternal Father deliberates in order to save the creatures, and on earth the betrayers deliberate in order to execute my love. Love, love, you were right when you said, '*Desiderio desideravi,*'[14] for you desired to save the creatures."

Then she kept quiet for a moment. Then, when she resumed speaking, she said:

"*Hec mando vobis, ut diligatis invicem sicut dilexi vos.*"[15]

At this point she stopped again for a long time, looking very sorrowful. Then, being visibly upset, she spoke the following words:

"*Tristis es.* Oh love you are not powerful any longer, but rather afflicted and melancholy. Your face makes the angels happy and gives glory to heaven, but now you look so upset. Oh love, you are not the truth anymore. You said through the prophet: "*Ego Deus et non mutor.*"[16] And now, why are you so upset?"

And keeping silent for a while, then she said:

"Now he leaves him. Oh love, you would have never left me."

Then, after a short while, she said:

"Oh, what a beautiful face; how distressed and upset you are. I cannot say, my love, what the prophet says: "*Speciosus forma pre Filiis hominum,*"[17] because I see your face full of blood. Oh love, who will come and console you? Maybe the eternal Father? Who, love? The Father, I don't think so. So, who will come? Oh, a servant?"

And giving a big sigh, she said:

"One of those that you created so that they would praise you, I mean, an angel is now coming to console you. Only one, and there are so many. Daniel did say: "*Millia millium ministrabant ei, et decies centena millia assistebant ei.*"[18] But I see that only one is coming."

At this point she stopped speaking for a long time, being pre-occupied and sorrowful in a great excess of mind. Then she said these words:

"You withdraw. If you didn't withdraw, you couldn't suffer."

We understood that at that point she saw Jesus for the first time praying to his eternal Father in the garden. And she said other things full of compassion and admiration, but we have not kept them in mind. Around the third hour she indicated that Jesus was going to wake his disciples up. Thus, she said:

"Oh love, they are asleep. You, Peter, Peter, you that seemed so zealous, you can't be on the alert not even for an hour. You don't show that love you seemed to have for Jesus. Oh Peter, you are asleep, yes, you are. And John sleeps. Oh John, and you, you that were the chosen one, you too, you sleep. I am not surprised that Peter does, but that you, you that had tasted the celestial secrets by resting on his chest, now your love fails. I can't believe that. And also that one is asleep. Oh love, everybody is asleep; I am surprised that they are not moved by that bloody face. There is nothing that makes a face uglier than blood. Oh, oh, it's ominous, it's ominous."

When the third hour rang, she indicated that she was seeing Jesus praying for the second time. Her gaze moved from the left hand of the crucifix toward the face. Staring at that face intensely, she seemed to be seeing drops of blood dripping from it to the floor because her eyes, totally absorbed in this contemplation, first looked at the head of the crucifix and slowly, little by little, moved down to the feet. And she said:

"And he is sweating blood."

Then, after a short while, she said:

"Oh love, not only your entire body sweats blood, also your eyes shed drops of blood instead of tears."

After keeping silent for a while, she added:

"Oh love, I wish I were that earth that received this blood. Love, please, let the creatures' heart receive it. Yes, it was a garden of love, because it was going to fructify in the hearts of your chosen."

Then, around the fourth hour, she said:

"The more you show them your love, the more they increase their hatred against you. Oh love, no, for them it won't be enough that you shed your blood."

And after a short pause, she said:

"My love, your heart and everything that was in you foresaw everything that it was going to happen during your passion."

Later she said:

"Love, the Prophet was right when he said *'Ipse fecit nos, e[t] non ipsi nos.'*[19] And he repeated it many times. I can say that myself. Oh love."

When the fourth hour rang, we understood that Jesus had gone back to the apostles. And she said:

"Love, love, they are still asleep. And you, Peter, you said *'Relinquimus omnia;'*[20] you said that you had left everything. It doesn't seem that you have left yourselves. And you, John, you had been with him for so long. When two people converse, they usually understand each other's speech, but now I see that you do not understand him because you do not do what you say. My love, please, put up with their fragility because you know that Peter will be the founder of your Church. My love, forgive them, because you know that when Peter asked you how many times he was supposed to forgive who hurt him, you know what you said to him, you said that he should forgive not seven times, but seventy times seven. And John will praise you so highly. You, eternal wisdom, foresaw and saw everything before time. My senses may deceive me, or someone may deceive me, but you would never do it. Love, *omnia in sapientia tu fecisti.*"[21]

She kept silent for quite a while. During this time she looked totally removed from her physical senses. As long as we could understand, she saw Jesus going to pray for the third time. And she also saw Judas, and the Jews preparing themselves to come take him. Thus, she said:

"The time is coming, and they try to reach you. They speak, question, try, and try again. The betrayer tries and tries to hail you in that insincere way. My love, I burst with sorrow."

At this point she stopped again and then said:

"Love. *Non mea sed tua voluntas fiat;* my love, yours [your will] be done. My love, make every creature speak these words."

And after a long silence, she said:

"If Gabriel was so content when he brought that message to Mary, that is, that you would become incarnate in her, a much greater sorrow would the angels have now if they could because now they bring you the chalice. It's not that he actually brings it to you; it's only to make us understand."

Almost right after, she said:

"*Inclina aurem tua et exaudi me,*[22] oh my God. Oh my God love, let us be always united with you, so that we will be able to pronounce that verse: '*Ecce quam bonum, et quam iocundum habitare fratres in unum.*'[23] My love, I don't mean *in unum*, but in you, first of all in you and then *in unum*. No one can say that he loves God, if he does not love the one who derives from that God."[24]

After a little while, she said:

"*Exinanivit semetipsum formam servi accipiens.*[25] Oh my love, much more than that of a servant."

Right before the fifth hour, after gazing at that crucifix for a long time, she recovered all of a sudden and said these words in a voice louder than usual:

"Oh, what can I do now? I can't do anything, if love wants to suffer! Oh love. Here he is, the betrayer, I see him."

And after a short pause, she said:

"He greets him with the kiss of peace. A greeting of peace, but not for peace and affection, but to betray you, my love."

At that point, the fifth hour rang. She continued as follows:

"Oh love, you said 'friend,' but if he had been a friend, he wouldn't have betrayed you, love. For you he was a friend, but he has made himself an enemy."

And, turning to Judas, she said:

"Satisfied, now, satisfied.[26] Love, if you let him kiss you, don't let your spouse be inferior to him, and not only your spouse, oh love, but also the others, not because we want to betray you, no, my love, but to love you and be united with you. Although the betrayer seemed to be united with you he was not united with you but with that who was disunited from you. You passed along, passed along, my love, but you didn't stop!"

After a while we understood that Jesus was asking the crowd who they were looking for. And when they answered: "Jesus the Nazarene," she said:

"Oh, they mention that holy name, that is venerated by those in heaven, on earth, even by those in hell."

Then she indicated that Jesus was saying *"Ego sum,"* because she said:

"Ego sum. Oh love, it is true indeed that only you are; the other creatures are nothing without you, but with you they are something."

At this point we understood that she saw the soldiers falling on the ground and staying there for a while. In the meantime she said:

"Love, you show more power now in making them fall than when you were going to come because, at that time, being invisible, you protected yourself, but now, because you don't protect yourself, you make visible what your power really is."

Then we understood that when the soldiers stood up, Jesus asked them again who they were looking for. When they answered "Jesus the Nazarene," she said the following words:

"Again, they mention that holy name again with their infectious and malignant tongues. Oh love, tell them again: *'Ego sum.'* They won't be able to say that they didn't know you because you, you, love, you spoke to them with your own voice."

Then she saw the soldiers falling for the second time, and when they stood up, Jesus asked them again who they were looking for. And when they said "Jesus the Nazarene," he said *"Ego sum,"* and they fell for the third time. This is what we believe she saw because she showed this more with gestures and movements than with words. Indeed, she was engrossed and quiet for a long while. Then she said:

"Love, weaken those who intend to do harm."

Around the sixth hour, she showed that she was seeing Jesus being taken and his disciples running away because she said:

"Oh love, they leave you; if I had the power that you have, they wouldn't have taken you. A short while ago I said that you were powerful, but, love, now I correct myself. Now I say that you are extremely weak. But, oh love, you have made yourself powerless in order to be powerful within us so that we would be able to win with your weakness. Oh love, I know well that, if you had wanted to, but you didn't, not twelve legions of angels but the entire heaven would have come down to defend you."

She also said: "Let them go," meaning the apostles. Then she said:

"Oh love, you wanted to be taken alone because you don't want the soul to take anyone else but you, and you want to be taken alone by the soul. You don't want the soul to love anyone but you."

After a while she said:

"Oh love, they tie you up with the chain of iron. Oh love, how many lovers tie you up in different ways with the chain of love. Oh, those hands tie that who did everything for them and even created them. Love, tie me to you and these others as well. Love, make us tie you within ourselves, and you, love, tie us within yourself. They tied you up out of hatred and to torture you, dishonor you, and give you death. But we want to tie you up in order to praise you, honor you, and so that you give us life; and you want to tie us within yourself out of love. And, love, tie them back, I mean, those that revolted against you and came untied from you, and unite them with yourself. Those, my love, those that don't have faith, please enlighten them so that they know you, their love and creator. And those, love, those that are waiting for you! Make them all, make them love you."

After these words, she kept quiet for a while, showing that she was feeling a great pain and compassion. Her face changed expressions, making gestures and movements with her whole body. It seemed like her body were falling apart inside. She sighed, cried, and sweated and shook also externally to such a degree that her hair stood on end. And we understood that Jesus was taken by the Jews; and the tortures they inflicted on him while they took him to Annas, and those of the other chief priests.[27] And she spoke these words:

"Oh, my love, how many tortures! Oh Mary, oh Magdalen, if you saw him now you would act like two fierce lionesses when someone takes their young away from them; they run infuriated and tear to pieces whoever they come across."

She said this when it was almost the seventh hour. From that moment until the eighth hour she only said:

"Oh love, how much you suffer, oh love; and it's nothing. It's just the beginning. Oh love, will I be strong enough to see so much pain? Love, love, I can't say: *'Rex Regum, Deus Deorum, et dominus Dominantium.'*"[28]

At the eighth hour we realized that he had arrived at Annas because she said:

"He questions you."

Then she became silent for a little while. When she resumed speaking, she said to St. Peter:

"Oh Peter, Peter, you haven't been strong; you haven't kept your promises. Love was right when he said that your deeds were not as ready as your words."

And turning to Jesus, she said:

"Love, and then he repented. Love, it was necessary that that who would be the head of the church felt his own frailty, so that he would be able to feel compassion for the others."

At this point she stopped for a short while. We understood that Jesus was taken to Caiaphas because she said:

"Love, love, they pull you; one pulls you this way, another pulls you that way. They also show very clearly that you offered yourself for everybody and that you wanted to save everybody."

Then at Caiaphas's, she said to Peter:

"Oh Peter, you, you warm up. You show very well that the cold you had inside was much more intense than that you felt outside."

Again, after a pause, she resumed speaking as follows:

"So many things are done here. Love, you speak, keep quiet, question, answer, and generate. Me, I don't understand this."

From this moment until he got to Pilate's, she spoke very few words, and with such a low voice that we could not understand what she was saying. And she stared at the crucifix, in which, as far as we could understand, she saw like in a mirror all the things that were happening during Jesus' passion, exactly when they really took place. She said later to Sister Veronica that was the way it had being shown to her. Then, according to what she said, we understood that Jesus was before Pilate.

"My love does not deserve to be accused of anything."

Then, after a while, she said:

"You are *Rex Judeorum*."[29]

She stopped for a moment. Then she said:

"*Regnum meum non est de hoc mundo*.[30] Oh love, you were right when you said that your kingdom is not of this world. Our souls are your kingdom. Love, let my soul be your kingdom, and also the others."

Then she said:

"*Deus iudicium tuum Regi da*."[31]

After a while, she said to Pilate:

"You did the right thing when you left because you were not worthy of understanding what truth is, because truth is God himself, and you were unable to understand and know God because you made yourself unworthy of it."

At this point she stopped speaking, and for quite a while she stared at the crucifix that she was holding in her hand. Then she indicated that Jesus was before Herod by uttering these words:

"Oh Herod, because of your curiosity you didn't deserve any answer at all."

Then, after a short while, she said:

"Oh love, and they put the white gown on you, and they do so in order to deride and dishonor you. But they are mistaken because they didn't understand what they were doing, and against their will they showed your innocence and purity and also that you were a Virgin and that you had taken flesh from the pure blood of the Virgin Mary. Love, make us similar to you; dress us up with the gown of innocence and purity."

Then she said:

"*Homo cum in honore esset, non intellixit. Comparatus est iumentis insipientibus, et similis factus est illis*.[32] It is true that man is comparable to a mule, which is such a dull and base animal. When man loses his mind, he lets himself be guided like a foolish beast. Oh love, because they considered you crazy, they put the white gown on you to make the others deride and dishonor you, but in fact they honored you much more."

We understood that she meant Herod and his army. At this point she became silent, showing with these words that Jesus was coming back to Pilate:

"Love, take me with you; love, take me with you because if the groom is considered crazy, it is unbecoming that his spouse be not similar to him."

Right after she said:

"Love, for you, for you, Herod and Pilate become friends. Love, hatred and pain oppress you, and they become friends."

She became silent for more than an hour, showing with gestures and movements that she was suffering intensely because she felt pity for Jesus whose suffering was beyond description. Sometimes she gave deep sighs, and almost at the end of the hour we noticed that her face had become transfigured and looked now deeply different.

"Love, oh love, I can't see you suffer so much, and so much must still happen."

And showing that Jesus was scourged at the column, she said:

"Love, I really can't say now what the prophet said, '*Non accedet ad te malum, et flagellum non appropinquabit tabernaculo tuo.*'[33] Love, why do they hit you so much? What have you done? Love, what do you lack? Do you lack wisdom? goodness? mercy? pity? Could you lack love?"

After a short pause, she said:

"Oh, they're hitting his head."

Then she said:

"Love, your love does not let me penetrate your great pain fully because I would not be able to tolerate it. Oh love, the arrows you send to your creatures' hearts are much more numerous than the blows that they are giving you now."

Then we understood that she was seeing Jesus crowned with thorns, because she said:

"Love, you wanted to be crowned with thorns in order to crown your spouses in heaven. Love, who deserves this piercing crown more, love or his lover? Love, I, I deserve it; love, give it to me; give it to me."

After a long pause, she added:

"Love, now no one can say about you what was said about me, *'Induit me dominus ciclade auro texta.'*[34] No, love, yours was not out of gold but of thorns. And, oh love, what could we ever do to alleviate this pain? A great purity of mind and a profound humility."

As usual, she stopped for quite a while. Then she said:

"Oh, they are not satisfied with hitting that holy face, that the angels wish to look at. Now they inflict many more torments on it. Oh love, you cannot say that your joys are with the sons of man but only torments and insults. Oh love, the soul, your spouse, call you the glory of heaven and the delight of the angels; and now I hear you saying: *'Opprobrium hominum et abiectio plebis.'*"[35]

At this point she indicated that Pilate was showing Jesus to the crowd, because she said:

"*Ecce homo.* Here is the man God. Pilate said showing him to the Jews, 'Here is the man.' And with a great love he shows the creature to the Father and tells him, 'Here is the man, the sinner.' Here is the man, saved. Here is the man, redeemed. Oh love, do not allow this creature, redeemed at such a high price, to lose herself again."

As usual, she had a short pause. Then, turning to Pilate, she started to say:

"You appropriated power by taking away that that belonged to God, and pursuing honor, you lost it."

After this she said:

"I don't know how to call it, but I'll say it anyway. A curse on human respect! Where does it lead man to! Oh Pilate, what did it make you do? Because of human respect, you sentenced the innocent to death. But let's stop speaking about him because he's lost anyway; let's remember those who are among us now. Because of this pestilent vice, they offend God immensely. Oh God, how many, how many do worse than Pilate, and first of all among the superiors, who should be examples for the others. Oh my love, take this human respect away from the creatures so that they won't offend you so much any more. Many believe that you, Pilate, are rather excusable, but I don't think so because love showed more benevolence to you than to the others. He spoke with you for a longer time, giving you a great chance to get to know him, but you missed it."

Afterward, she said:

"*Tolle, tolle, crucifige eum.*[36] Love, love, they say, '*Tolo, tolo, crucifige eum.*' Oh love, they say '*Tolo,*' but they should have said 'Give him to us,' and not '*Tolo,*' but they didn't know what they were saying.[37] Since they weren't worthy to have you, my love, they also said, '*Crucifige eum.*' Oh, why don't they say, 'Crucify that man whose name is Jesus,' and instead they say '*eum*'? Because they shouldn't have crucified the divinity, but our sin that is this '*eum*' that he had taken over himself becoming incarnate.[38] This should have been crucified."

After this she kept quiet for a long while, then she said:

"Only a few moments before these very tongues had said '*Benedictus qui venit in nomine domini.*'[39] It is really true that you received those expressions of honor in the same way you receive now these expressions of blasphemy and dishonor. My love, don't let me rejoice in the happy things, and don't let me grieve in the doleful ones. And the same for all the others."

She became silent for quite a long time. Then she said:

"And that beautiful hair that with their beauty drew the heart of creatures to itself; and that beautiful beard that adorned that mouth so beautifully, it was the trumpet of the Holy Spirit; and those ears? They used to listen to the beautiful melody of the angels in heaven and Mary's sweet words; now they hear curses."

After a bit she said:

"If I had thousand hells, I would throw them all into it."

And then this verse:

"*Non est qui faciat bonum, non est usque ad unum.*[40] Oh love, no one does it, no one."

At the fifteenth hour, she said:

"They want Barabbas."

Here she looked as if she had a wound in her heart because she showed that she was feeling a great pain through gestures and the expression of her face. Shaking greatly, she burst into these words:

"Oh, oh, I can't stand that my spouse is placed after such a base person and that they want the servant instead of the lord."

She kept quiet for more or less fifteen minutes, and then she said:

"I know that you have always disliked pride, but in this case I want to be proud, because I can't stand their comparing you to such a base person. I'll say what Caiaphas said: '*Expedit ut unus homo moriatur pro populo.*'"[41]

Then she indicated that she was seeing Pilate washing his hands, because she said:

"He is washing his hands."

And pausing for a moment, she said:

"Oh, will I be able to tolerate that last word? I wish I never had to get to that point. I would like to do like a deaf evildoer in order not to hear. I would like that moment never to come."

She paused a little. Then she gave a very moving and disturbing cry and said:

"Oh, I've got there. He passed that unjust sentence. The one who is going to sentence him and all the other creatures now tolerates to be sentenced."

And turning to the Jews, she told them:

"Be happy now. Feel satisfied, feel satisfied because you won't be satisfied anymore."

At the sixteenth hour she said:

"Oh, where is my love? I don't see him."

After a short while, she said:

"Love, love, I had never thought that I would find you up here. I would have looked for you forever."

We think that this was in that room where they put the cross on his shoulders. After keeping quiet for quite a while, she resumed saying:

"They put you between the two thieves; you were a thief yourself, my love, because you stole our souls from the devil. One can really say that you left the ninety-nine lambs to look for the hundredth. And you placed it over your shoulders, leaving those that always praised you in order to take this one out of the wolf's mouth. I am not surprised that they rejoice for a sinner because my love has descended from heaven and has suffered so much, and he would suffer again for one single soul."

Then she said:

"*Dominus regit me.*[42] Because, my love, you have led me to this pasture, lead me also to that other one, that of the eternal life; and the other souls as well."

After a long pause, she said:

"This is that stake that Moses erected in the desert, on top of which there was the snake that would heal and reconcile the people. My love, they had to be in the desert."

Waiting a moment, she said:

"Now I can actually say: '*Sicut passer solitarius in tecto*'[43] because everybody has left you. Love, they do not know you, that's why they leave you. Love, allow me to be with you alone, and never to leave you."

After this, she said:

"The time of your satisfaction is approaching."

And turning to the prophets she said:

"Now I see that my Spouse has gone on a journey; who wants to follow him must set out. You shouldn't worry about every obstacle."

She paused a moment. Then she said:

"Love, love, love."

After quite a while, she said:

"Oh Mary, when you see him. Even though you knew about it, time had not come yet. You won't be able to hug him as you wish because you'll fall down on the ground."

Then she said:

"If we could find at least one person who would be willing to tell him a good word, I would be satisfied."

Later she said:

"Love, if I could help you to carry this cross a little bit, I would be more than willing to do it—not like Simon from Cyrene, but to share your pain, my love. They don't help you for love, but only to take you to death sooner."

She paused a moment. And she said:

"Yes, then you'll be satisfied. Against your will, hatred and love go together."

After a short while, she said:

"*Christus factus est obediens usque ad mortem: mortem autem crucis.*[44] Love, let me be crucified with you."

She paused, and then she said:

"Life dies. I will die with you. Love, love, we have got there, my love."

At this point she started to cry desperately, screaming out loudly:

"Oh God, oh God, my love undresses. Alas, the suffering! The cross is laid on the ground, and he, he, my love, undresses by himself. It is the same when a soul divests itself of its innocence."

At this point she intensified her crying, raising her voice more than usual and making gestures that showed such a great suffering and compassion that moved and made all the present cry. She shook intensely, quivering in such a way that we could hear it. It seemed like she was falling apart inside; and she said:

"Alas, if at least they didn't hit so strongly. I see the innocent being killed. Alas, alas. Alas, I can no more. No more, love. No more, I can no more. If at least they hadn't made those holes so deep.[45] Alas, my love, alas. Don't stretch my love so much. Oh, my love. *Expandit alas suas.*[46] Alas, love, I can no more. Love, we still have three hours. Please, communicate them to some other soul because I can no more, love. However, if you want to, I'll be happy, but give me the strength to tolerate it. Love, hammer me into you. I will never leave you, love. If you do not hammer me into you, well, hammer yourself into me. Please, love, I want to hammer you into myself with those three nails, of faith, hope, and charity. And when the moment comes, when you are put down from the cross, choose my heart as your sepulcher, and also that of my sisters."

Here she finished, staring at the whole figure of the crucifix. She kissed its hands, its side, and its feet with a great expression of love. Then she offered it to the Mother Superior. All of a sudden she came out of this rapture. And it was indeed the eighteenth hour, as she has said the previous Tuesday, as one can read above. When she came back, she looked like a dead person; she looked so disheartened, weakened, and transfigured because of her great suffering during this excess of mind and also because of her long ailment. This time her pain was so intense that nobody would ever be able to imagine it unless he had seen it. She had sweated so much, that it had passed through the feather mattress. We had to change and dry everything. It lasted six hours thirty minutes in a row, without her moving her eyes away from that crucifix she was holding in her hand. She stared at it so firmly that we believe she saw there everything that happened to Jesus during his passion and death. At that time it was as if he were present to her because she was seeing everything as it had actually happened, although she knew that Jesus was not going through his passion at the present time because now he was at the right of the Father in heaven. He deigned to show himself to her in that way for her great desire of accompanying him through his passion and suffering with him. Sometimes she looked at the face of her crucifix totally engrossed for many hours; some other times she turned her eyes to his left hand and to the right; and then, again, she looked at the whole body in a way that it showed that she was seeing what the Jews were doing to Jesus and also what he was suffering; and sometimes she looked as if she saw them going, staring at the crucifix with a great wonder. She made gestures with her mouth; she ground her teeth, and she shook her body as if she were being dismembered. Other times she gave very deep sighs, and she felt inside as if her bones and her entrails were being dismembered. Sometimes she kept quiet for more than an hour, and sometimes less, and it seemed as if everything she saw she considered with a great wonder and awe. And then, because of her transportation of love, she burst into words full of compassion and admiration. Although we have transcribed many of them here, nonetheless they are not all what she said. We could not transcribe everything she said because sometimes she spoke so softly that we could not understand her; and sometimes she started to say something, and then she either became silent, or she pronounced them very softly. Sometimes she showed signs of compassion more than other times. And first of all we saw this during those fundamental mysteries of Jesus' passion, such as when he was in the garden; when he was arrested, hit at the column, crown with thorns, shown to the crowd; and when Pilate sentenced him to death. It seemed as if this pierced her heart. But the most intense and fierce sorrow she showed was when she saw Jesus being crucified at the cross because at that point she started to cry and scream very out loudly, shaking much more than the previous times. She held the crucifix tightly and made other gestures with her body, through which she manifested the great pain she was suffering and tolerating inside her soul and also outside her body. No language could ever express her movements, her gestures, her words, the sighs of compassion she gave during that act, and during that time that, as we said, went from the first hour thirty minutes of Thursday night until the eighteenth of Friday. And although we have attempted to gather her words and gestures as much as possible, nonetheless we missed quite a bit of what we saw and heard. But if we will succeed in showing and fructifying what we have written, it will be enough. Our compassionate Lord grant us this with his infinite goodness and mercy.

Amen.

MARIA MADDALENA DE' PAZZI

July 22, 1584 (ed. 1:248–52)

Sunday July 22, 1584. While I was at the Mass, I considered the words pronounced in the Epistle that morning. *"Pone me ut signaculum super cor tuum."*[47] And I heard Love saying: "The holy Trinity wants to mark your heart with his sign so that your enemies will see you marked with his seal and will not dare to come close to you." And first I saw the eternal Father writing on my heart with Jesus' Blood, and the Father said, "My dear daughter and spouse of my Son, crucified Love." And he wrote these words in Latin. Then Jesus wrote on me with the milk of the Virgin Mary: "I am forced to stay in you because of the Love I have for you in my heart." And the Holy Spirit wrote on my heart with the tears of Saint Mary Magdalen, and it said: "Love, that it is myself, forces me to generate marvelous things in you, things that you would not be able to do by yourself because they are above nature." And it concluded recommending the archbishop, the father, the nuns, and every creature to Jesus.

The same day she had a marvelous insight into herself and into her baseness, along with a knowledge of God and of his greatness. And considering this, she started to cry copiously, saying these words:

"Oh God, please do not show me anything more of myself, 'cause I can't see myself anymore."

And she saw that God's purity was so great, that the slightest imperfection the soul generated was an offense to that purity. And she saw that her self was a nothingness, and even less than that. And she saw that she was not the only one to be like that because in a similar way every creature was less than a nothingness in comparison with God's greatness. At the same time she saw all the offenses given to God, first of all by her and then by every other creature. To see that such a great and finite baseness had offended God in his infinite greatness was unbearable to her. She would have fallen apart if the Lord himself had not supported her. And at that point, in the act of passing away she would have thrown herself into thousand hells if it

92

had been granted her to have them before her. And her internal pain was so intense that she did not care about the exterior one, although it was so great that she seemed to be going to die. And she felt all her bones shaking and that great pain that she had and felt. And then she had the feeling that she was similar to the devil because of her offenses to him, God. Moreover, she had the feeling that she was similar to the damned souls in hell because they would rather never be born than have those pains and torments. And she as well, I say, would rather never be born than offend God, even though she loved her having come to the world so that she could praise and honor him. For this reason she did not regret to have come to the world. But she also wished every creature, included the irrational and insensitive ones, to be like her so that God would be honored and praised more by everyone. However, as I have said, because she had offended him she wished she were never born, and similarly [she wished] every creature that had offended him never to be born.[48] Indeed, at that point she felt how great were the offenses given to God; and she said:

"Oh God, why don't you grant me thousand hells so that I could throw myself into them, and thus my pains could make up for it, though I know that I will never be able to make up for it because I have given offense to you, who are infinite, whereas I am finite and very base. Oh God, why don't you send me a creature here, someone who would kill me many many times, and coming back to life I would die the cruelest death and would be cut into tiny pieces and burned. And thousand times every day, being born again and again, I would die the cruelest deaths ever and ever again, until Doomsday, so that I will not see myself so dissimilar to you, God." And she said: "I know it, I know that I have offended you, but please do not show me myself anymore because I cannot look at myself anymore; otherwise I will die." And there was nothing we could say to console her because everything caused her a stronger pain. And she told Sister Veronica that she suffered more today than that night when she saw Jesus' passion, even though that time we saw that she suffered a horrible pain. But now she says that this is twice as much. And the more she saw God's greatness, the more she understood her baseness and the offenses given to God. And thus she felt devastated even more. And she stayed like that for an hour and a half, more or less. And then she stopped and joined her hands in prayer. She kept quiet as if she were not there. And it was clear that the Lord had relieved her of the vision of herself and left her only the vision of his greatness and of his Love. And she was in this vision for a long time. When she recovered from it, she was in a sweat and exhausted.

Selections from

The Dialogues

The Dialogues

Dialogue 36
Participation in Jesus' Passion

On Good Friday we did not have a chance to converse with our blessed soul because she remained in her vision of the passion until the twenty-first hour. And she was like dead when she came out of that rapture. This is why we decided that it was better not to disturb her and to let her rest on Saturday as well. And this time we will write down what we saw with our eyes and what we heard with our ears, rather than what she herself told us, which will be almost nothing.

That rapture started on Maundy Thursday when it had just struck the eighteenth hour, and it lasted until the aforementioned hour on Good Friday. She never came out of it. No one could ever describe how marvelous she was during that vision of the passion. She physically accompanied her dear love to each place and each mystery where he suffered. She showed that she was seeing him suffer all the pains he had suffered in his passion and that he granted his passion to her insofar as her frail and sweet being could tolerate it. But for those who saw her, it was an extremely moving and edifying scene, almost impossible to be described and to be believed by those who have not eyewitnessed it.

She walked through the convent going from one room to another, according to the mysteries Jesus suffered, and she did this or that gesture.[1] She showed his mother's departure in the scriptorium, where we usually hold our conversations with her. Indeed, she entered her rapture while she was there with us. After being quiet and absorbed for some time and keeping her eyes downcast, she spoke these words:

"What a sweet dialogue between Mary and the Word *[silence]* and this work is the work of piety." And she referred to the work Mary Magdalen did for Jesus when she poured her ointment for him. She saw her doing it with the eyes of her mind as if it were a present thing. "No more deeds of admiration but of compassion," [she said] when she saw and heard Jesus talking with his sweet Mother, telling Mary about the rest of his passion, whose sorrow she would experience later along with all the sorrows and pain Jesus suffered. Indeed, as she told us, she would see and experience all of this, as she learned at that moment. Then she continued to say:

"*Sic Deus dilexit mundum ut filium suum unigenitum daret*[2] *[silence] et dilexit Mariam et non fecit cognita de omnia.*" She meant that because of his tender affection toward his holy mother, Jesus had not revealed her everything he had to work in order to achieve our redemption, I mean, how much he had to suffer, because he did not want to give pain to her, not only while he spoke with her but also in the end when he revealed to her many things of his passion but not all of them. She continued as follows:

"Oh, could you share with her a working more important than our redemption?"

This blessed soul spoke sometimes with Jesus and sometimes with the Virgin and sometimes with herself. And between one speech and the next, she kept silent for a while, as she usually does.

"In her the greatly exercised charity exercises in the conformity of her will." She meant that the Virgin exercised her charity for us by conforming her will to that of her Son, who was about to suffer his passion and a very painful and shameful death.

Now she speaks with Jesus. "Oh, if you asked Mary to exercise so much, I mean, suffering, no wonder you want us to exercise this suffering as well because we are sinners and deserve every pain *[silence]* What a pain with infinite joy! Oh, Mary Magdalen also had to share his sorrows a little bit, *[silence]* but I'm sure you didn't tell her about your passion and about your resurrection along with all the glorious workings you were about to do *[silence]* and what do you teach us with this? *[silence]* other than an amorous compassion with a different union *[silence]* and who was more chosen than her? *[silence]* chosen among thousands *[silence] et cum essem parvula placui tibi.*[3] Before you established the heavens and settled the abysses, she was already with you. Surely, the waters had not been limited yet, and Mary had already conceived you; nobody had been confirmed either in grace or in glory; and nobody down here with our humanity had risen to heaven to perceive and understand *[silence]* but this knife would pierce your heart *[silence]* Mary was that wine store where you ordered charity, where you and Mary dispensed that charity," she meant that he was going to suffer for us. "In the meantime John was getting ready for those high and profound secrets he would see, hear, and taste later *[silence]* but Mary shared his pain more than the others, because she loved more than the others *[silence]* and in this way you, Word, conceive us with pain and sorrow, and suffer so much when we abandon you *[silence]* you went to the winepress by yourself, and this vineyard was Mary *[silence]* a winepress that squeezed her soul so well."

Now it is clear that this soul is answering and speaking about what she sees and hears. She does not utter questions, but only answers, but she could easily perceive what Jesus was telling her, what she was seeing and hearing, and who was with her in that room while she was speaking.

"This narration of your workings tormented Mary so deeply *[silence] elegi eam apud te [silence] et confirmasti eam de manu tua*[4] because she was about to give birth to you, I believe so *[silence]* down here you granted her that [working] of sorrow, because you would grant her that of joy and dignity, as no human being had ever been able to receive *[silence]* but in this dialogue she surrounded you with the grievous flowers of her words, I mean, with the words of the Word, your Only Begotten, the same words that later you granted us down here with joy *[silence]* he nourished you, and you nourished him; and he took away and sucked his nourishment, for if he hadn't taken it away you would have died of tenderness *[silence]* in this dialogue your head was adorned with those gentle bees that suck honey out of every thing *[silence]* in this dialogue you were not adorned with sun and stars, but [you were] surrounded by *varietate*

Passionis Verbi [silence] desire inspired, love inflamed, will comforted, intellect glared and died *[silence]* and those breasts that had nourished the incarnate Word were ready to nourish those who had been created anew *[silence]* with the right breast she sprinkled and nourished heaven and with the left one [she sprinkled and nourished] earth; one makes sprout and the other makes fructify. You could really say that you were mother of every beautiful charity *[silence]* your charity had every beauty, even though it could only be a superior beauty because it joined the Word and adjusted to It; and [even though] it could be measured only with the Word's measurement *[silence]* her face had those beautiful eyes; with one she looked with compassion and with the other [she looked] in order to grant fruition of it *[silence]* that sweet mouth that tasted his indescribable glory, and our infinite nothingness *[silence]* I'd like to help someone else understand and taste this profound, amorous, and impatient dialogue—this is how I want to call it—because by myself I'm unable to understand it *[silence]* if one penetrated love and pain, greatness and baseness, suffering and compassion, one would dissolve and annihilate oneself in you *[silence]* you chose Mary, because you wanted to crown her as the Virgin, and now you crown her with pain *[silence]* you make her die and live with love and pain so that it would come true what Moses saw about her, that burning and never burned-up bush *[silence]* things are infinite *[silence]* but in particular you made her perceive the love you wanted to share with us; the faith with which you wanted to confirm us; and the vision you wanted to give us *[silence]* how great is the vision you wanted to give us, and the glory you wanted us not to share with you, I wouldn't dare to say that, but rather to taste and appreciate. If your glory weren't superior to your suffering, I would stop here *[silence]* vision *[silence]* vision; vision of the truth and of the Word *[silence]* but today is a day of passion and not of vision, yes, but still."

She kept the rest in herself, penetrating and tasting.

"If they hadn't been uttered by that which can do everything, they would have pierced Mary's heart. But his tender gaze mitigated what he showed her with his words *[silence]* but what can I take out of this dialogue? A right will, a sweet compassion. But how often we taint this compassion. Patience in every suffering; a firm, immense,

and ardent love toward you; a burning wish to act out all your workings; a working toward a nonworking; annihilation of every being and
of every possible being; caution in every deliberation; wisdom in
every dispensation both of working, words, desires, and feelings;
strength in every temptation *[silence]* oh, I wish those betrayers had
heard these words! But they heard and will hear so many. But Mary
omnia conferens in corde tuo[5] *[silence]* oh Mary, if the angels and all the
elect constantly infuse into us every working they undergo, much
much more you'll do it! Indeed, you underwent many more workings
than any other created creature! *[silence]* you infuse and instill a cognition both of God's greatness and of the humanate Word.[6] But where,
where do you lead us? *[silence]* oh Mary, with the sweet breath of your
breathing you lead us to the side of the humanate Word, where we
taste God as a man, and man as God. [He has] confused the devils;
fulfilled the angels' wishes; accomplished our redemption; and
achieved the holy Spirit's working *[silence]* great is to satisfy the
Father's wish *[silence]* oh Mary, you take us to a gentle place *[silence]*
non dormitavit neque dormiet qui custodit Israel[7] *[silence] cum accepero
tempus ego iustitias iudicabo*[8] *[silence]* with your passion you showed that
the time had come, and now you communicate it to Mary *[silence]* I
want to consider what you achieved with that painful and glorious
dialogue *[silence]* they certainly could *[silence] et procidentes adoraverunt
eam dicentes: ista est digna accipere dexteram virtutis Dei."*[9]

At this point she understood that the Virgin, because of this
excruciating dialogue with Jesus before his final departure, would
receive the above worship. And because her intellect fathomed this
greatly, she answered with those words: "They certainly could,"
meaning that it was a suitable thing because she would be placed at
the right side of her humanate Word.

Afterward she kept silent for a long time. And when Jesus
spoke to her, she said to him: "When you told Mary that you would
suffer very much, oh, I wish I could have taken you away from the
Jews' hands, as she did from Herod's. Oh, I would have loved to do
it! *[silence]* We can take the creatures away from ignorance, but not
from malice *[silence]* yes, yes, because those who sin out of ignorance offend your person, humanate Word; and you can have pity
on them. But malicious people offend the person of the Holy Spirit;

and it can't have pity on them because it has not become human, although you are one in your divine essence *[silence]* but, oh, when we get to that departure, oh, oh! *[silence]* the Word is that cornerstone, but you too, Mary! He has united the creature with the Creature; and you [have united] divinity with humanity *[silence]* *dixit Dominus Domino meo*,[10] the Word said: *cogito cogitationes*[11] *[silence]* he gives [us] strength so that we be able to suffer."

She saw that Jesus was about to leave and go to Jerusalem where he would suffer his passion. Thus, she added: "You sent three apostles because they were united with the Trinity *[silence]* when you, Word, came out of the Father's bosom, you were still there; but it was not so for Mary *[silence]* it was not so for Mary *[silence]* for the creature you are both present and absent everywhere *[silence]* oh Word, it seems like you failed the creature, your mother, but you did it so that she would have more where one rejoices. You do the same to those you love the most; since you want them to be more glorious, you make them more sorrowful down here, like Mary *[silence]* oh, oh, *intellexit* and *videbit anima mea*, and *participavit in opera ista*."[12]

At this point she knelt down because she saw Jesus kneeling down before his mother and asking her for her last benediction. Mary too knelt down and asked him for his [benediction]. "Oh, what a painful departure! Oh Mary, you wanted it, I know *[silence]* but you'll do like the turtle dove when she loses her companion *[silence]* disunion in order to unite *[silence]* oh, you'll let Judas give it to you; let her too give it to you! *[silence]* Give her the benediction that Isaac gave to his beloved son Jacob *[silence]* you are not only a father for her, but also a son and a spouse; and although this benediction seems to be suitable for the angelic nature, like for a first-born brother, nonetheless because she guarded your humanity, oh Word, she has become superior to the angels, and thanks to that benediction not only the angels and the hierarchies, but the Trinity as well will be pleased with Mary, extolled above the hierarchies *[silence]* not the abundance of the earth, but the fruits of the Word's divinity *[silence]* please, no more, because the more, more pain."

She rushed upstairs to a large room, to the highest place in the monastery, that for her was the mountain Zion, where Jesus had his supper with his apostles, because she showed that she was seeing

Jesus have this supper, wash the apostles' feet, communicate his body and blood to them. And, as we shall write later, in this room she recited the whole *Mandato* until Jesus went to the kitchen garden to pray. She was on her knees with her hands on a chest that was there, with her eyes open and such a wonderful expression on her face that she seemed to be in heaven; and sometimes she looked sad, and sometimes [she looked] happier, according to what she was seeing and perceiving. Her gestures indicated that she wished Jesus to give her Holy Communion and to all of us. During this time she never came out of her rapture and, although she went from the scriptorium to this room—it was indeed a big distance, and she also had to climb up three stairs—, nonetheless she never came out of it, and she did not seem to walk but rather to be carried because she walked with such a liveliness and celerity, with clasped hands and her eyes up to the sky.

She left the scriptorium when the twenty-second hour had just struck, exactly when it is commonly believed that Jesus left his mother and went to Jerusalem to the Zion mountain, where he had his supper. And she remained in that room until the second hour in the morning. During that time, after having kept silent for quite a while as she usually does, she said all the following things. After her long silence these were her first words:

"*Desiderio desideravi*[13] *[silence] adimpleantur scripturae*[14] *[silence] mirabilis Deus in operatione humanitatis sue [silence] eructavit cor meum humilitatis*[15] *[silence] fundavit eam in humilitate abiectionis*[16] *[silence]* oh humility, we cannot imitate you; we can only admire you! *[silence]* Why didn't the heavens descend and the earth rise before such a profound humility? You took off your clothes because, if you hadn't cast off that immense greatness that made you consubstantial with the Father, you couldn't have worked so much humility *[silence]* you left your being and took on the human being, who is no being *[silence]* humility, you extoll the thing which is not, and debase that which is, for you extoll man who is nothing, and debase God who is everything *[silence]* humility, you are triumphant, and dancing you get to the throne of the Trinity *[silence]* oh you, the truth, you said: '*qui se humiliat exaltabitur*, and *qui se esaltat humiliatibur*'[17] *[silence]* with your workings you appease and show that you are the truth *[silence]* you, humility, as a nanny you produce purity from your breasts; purity with sincerity; sincerity with purity. As a mother you cherish the poor in spirit and lead them under the Word's shadow *[silence]* you welcome the uneducated and take them to the womb of your spouse, the church *[silence]* you sustain the uneducated, nourish the poor, crown the virgins, and elevate the martyrs; up there in heaven you adorn your christs down here on earth *[silence]* you grant a satisfying vision of yourself to the hermits; in a word you, humility, satisfy every saint. You make us patient in our pilgrimage."

She said that after having seen Jesus leaving the dinner table the first time and getting ready to wash his apostles' feet. And now she saw that he was pouring water in the basin to wash their feet, and thus she said: "Then you take and pour water to wash their feet *[silence]* oh, I shall dare to say that now that you are in heaven you do the same, because it seems to me that it's a greater humility to impose our soiled feelings into your heart, than to wash your apostles' feet with your holy hands *[silence] non lavabis mihi pedes in aeternum.*[18] Oh Peter, you didn't penetrate *[silence]* how often we want to teach to the wisdom and compare our judgments with yours! *[silence] si non lavero te non habebis partem mecum in regno dei.*[19] I tell you most solemnly, if we don't place our feelings in your blood, we won't enter God's reign. And if we penetrated it, we would drown with Peter in his blood *[silence]* but John keeps silent. Who penetrates everything, silences everything and loses himself into your benignity's abyss *[silence]* oh Word! *[silence]* to him too! *[silence]* oh traitor! *[silence]* traitor *[silence]* worse than the devil *[silence]* all your knowledge and *[silence] et accepi vestimenta sua*[20] *[silence]* oh Word, you didn't need to show such a humility, but it was suitable that you take your being back *[silence]* and when I come to receive you, I should take my being back, I mean, that being you gave me when you created me, that pure being; for if I did it, I would come to you with a greater participation in you.[21] Moreover, my body, which is a nothingness, should come with a greater annihilation *[silence] mirabilis deus in operatione comunicatione corporis* and *sanguinis sui* *[silence] sola fides sufficit*[22] *[silence] tantum ergo sacramentum*[23] *[silence]* and like the sun is in heaven and on earth, in a similar way you, Word, are in heaven to the right side of the Father and on earth in the form of the sacrament *[silence]* and what compelled [you] to such a love? Your being, which is all mercy *[silence] misericordia tua super omnia opera tua*[24] *[silence] misericors and miserator Dominus escam dedit timentibus se.*[25] What an immense communication! We are greater than the seraphim; they are close to the throne of the Holy Trinity, but we unite both with your humanity and your divinity at the same time *[silence]* we have such a greatness, and still we make ourselves so base that we fear a nothingness *[silence]* oh oh *[silence] hoc facite in meam commemorationem.*"[26]

Here she showed that Jesus was administering Holy Communion to her, opening her mouth and holding her hands on her breast; she showed that she was enjoying it. And she said:

"*Dilectus meus candidus* and *rubicundus*[27] *[silence] speciosus forma pre filiis hominum.*[28] *Electus ex millibus.*[29] *Diffusa est gratia in labiis tuis*[30] *[silence] collocavit se in anime nostre [silence] dilata cor meum ut inducat omnem creaturam ad communionem corporis* and *sanguinis suis*[31] *[silence] quam bonus Israel Deus*[32] *[silence]* oh John, it is right, because you had to protect the woman whose womb cradled the Word *[silence]* and you also had to shed the Word's word in order to nourish your spouse, the church *[silence]* this Word, I shall dare to say, produces in us the effects he produces in heaven, by giving us the four gifts; and while we are in this mortal body you give us a liveliness that only who experiences it and tastes it actually knows it."

She enters the *Mandato:* "*Ego sum via, veritas,* and *vita*[33] *[silence]* oh livable life, you are sweet and lovable, and always enjoyable! *[silence]* oh sweet truth! *[silence]* truth, you must verify all your truths and all our lies; truth, you penetrate the hearts. Whose hearts? The hearts of those who have humility and enter the secrecy of the soul *[silence]* [you are a] life that vivifies; truth that manifests the Word *[silence]* path that leads the blind; path in whose path there are many seeds; seeds to nourish the soul, to cherish the body; to enlighten the mind; to satisfy the will; to let memory die *[silence]* but in order to nourish the soul you must become a turtle dove; to nourish the body you become a dove *[silence]* to satisfy the will you become an eagle; to enlighten the mind one must become a pure man; to satisfy memory one must be a fleet deer. The turtle dove leads us to moan and cry; the dove leads us to the cave and here it makes its nest; the eagle leads to the essence of God; man reaches divinity; the deer leads us to eternity *[silence]* oh, what a delightful seed; oh, what a precious seed! If you know me, oh, we will love each other. In this way we shall understand if we are your sons, if we love each other *[silence]* oh, if I could instill some love among so many animosities, hell would seem heaven to me *[silence]* oh love for your neighbor, unknown to so many! For our neighbor we must leave not only the conveniences of the soul and of the body, but also God himself; and this can be fathomed only by those who receive your enlighten-ment, because otherwise."

She did not say anything more.

"But you, who are the investigator of the hearts, who knows love and hatred, hatred and love *[silence]* and we say that we love our neighbor when we actually offend him *[silence]* oh, oh, how different are our judgments from yours! *[silence]* you are the vine and we are the palm trees *[silence]* and the vine shouldn't be different from the palm tree, and the palm tree from the vine. But these creatures are different from you. But those who are different from you, you'll do what one usually does with the vine, you'll cut its branches and throw them away. Where? In the eternal fire *[silence]* if we don't want them to be different from you, we must tie them up to you so that they fructify *[silence]* with a strong and powerful bond so that it can't break. And this is your blood; and this is common to every sta-tus because you do not yield to people.[34] And there is another one which is threefold, and these are the theological virtues. There is also another one, and many hold it in their hands, but then they break it; and these are the three vows. The first transforms us, the second unites us, and the third leads us to the prize, that we [nuns] have, of the holy virginity. But not everyone can have it. Everyone can have the blood and the theological virtues.

"*Ubi sum ego ibi* and *minister meus erit*[35] *[silence]* who are these ministers of yours? And who glorifies your Father not the way he glo-rifies you? Where you are, there they are, oh good Jesus *[silence]* you are everywhere, and they are everywhere because they are in you who are everything, and they are everything. You are in them who are a nothingness by themselves, but since they are in you and you [are] in them, they are something. Your Christs are your ministers, and they acquire (but only if they exercise their ministry with sincerity), I mean, they acquire a name that is above any other name, like yours, of which we say: *'in nomine Jesu omne genu flectatur, celestium, terrestrium,* and *infernorum.'*[36] In a similar way, you have made the name of your priests known to the creatures in heaven, on earth, and even the devils fear their name, I'm sure *[silence]* because when these priests offer you, Word, to the Father, every angel and every blessed soul, I mean, every blessed soul prostrates itself before the Father with a new prostration, and thus the creatures are taken away from the devil's hands, and through them the devil is deprived of every power he had over these creatures *[silence]* and we could never stop praising them. If every star in the sky became a tongue, and every grain of sand could speak, we could never praise your Christs as they deserve; and unlike those who carry this name unworthily. *Et procidentes adoraverunt eos dicentes: isti sunt digni accipere capacitatem Sanguinis Verbi. Et procidentes* etc. three times. *Et Pater meus clarificet eos in semetipsum [silence] Pater clarifica filium tuum; et ego clarificavi te super terram*[37] *[silence]* but Word, if you proceed from the Father, how can you say that you clarify the Father? And if you are the truth, why do you say it? *[silence]* but you clarify the Father every time you work; and because your workings are infinite, you clarify him infinitely. But this is only fathomed by yourself, through yourself, and in yourself *[silence]* from *Deum venit,* and *ad Deum vadit*[38] *[silence]* you go there where you came from, and you have always been a bridge, but everything is said for our teaching *[silence]* but you go because, as like with every other creature, I come from your idea, everyone must go back there *[silence]* we must go back there where we came from. What will happen the last day of our life? And also at Doomsday, when we really go back there where we came from, and everyone will enjoy you either in a vision, or in love, or in a working, or in wisdom, in power, or in goodness, or in justice, or in truth, in eternity, or in participation? But you passed through this world in love and vision *[silence]* you are the Spouse; it would be good if your brides too could pass [through the world] in love and vision *[silence]* glorious things are said about the city of God, but even more glorious are the things said about your workings! *[silence]* oh words of an infinite consideration! *[silence] os justi meditabitur sapientiam*[39] *[silence] et collocavit anima mea* in the words *Verbis mei.*[40] *[silence]* With a profound reverence, sincerity, devotion, humility your words should be listened to! They came out of you, infallible Word; at this time your word has been spread everywhere, in every place! But how many, how many go to it only because they are curious and have other goals in mind. You know how many have been converted to it *[silence]* poor apostles, they got upset. Oh poor John, he had tasted so much *[silence]* where I go you can't come *[silence]* but this does not occur to us who can go anywhere; if we can't be anywhere any moment since we are mortal and passing creatures, let us enter God, and we will be everywhere *[silence]* oh Peter, you cheer up and then? *[silence]* so many people do the same; I wish they continued this way later as well *[silence]* how many say that they love and fear him, that they have charity and compassion; and if one considered them closely, [one would see that] they have nothing, and their words are hypocrisy *[silence]* oh Word, of Word! *[silence]* *modicum,* and *non videbitis me.*[41] But let us always always see you in every creature in your being; but not as some people see you because they have your image, yes, but they scourge and mistreat it to the point that it becomes unrecognizable *[silence]* but even though we don't see you during this short and long time, we'll see you forever up there *[silence]* oh, down here, among so many obstacles, there are so many, how difficult it is! *[silence]* who can possibly understand the glory and the reward you give to your elect? *[silence]* but the heart of every creature must take courage, because then you send your Spirit *[silence]* but oh, eternal Father *[silence]* *et quem misisti Jesum Christum.*"[42]

She showed that Jesus had finished the *Mandatum* and that he wanted to go and pray, leaving the apostles by themselves. Thus, she said:

"Affection of equality." She saw Jesus grieving and becoming sad. Therefore she said: "You were right when you said '*tristis est anima mea usque ad mortem*'[43] *[silence]* '*vigilate* and *orate ut non intretis in tentatione.*'"[44]

And as soon as she uttered these words, she left that room where she was at the moment in a rush, and, walking down the stairs still rapt, then with clasped hands she walked upstairs to the dormitory in front of the room for the novices. Here she knelt down, close to a small altar, keeping her arms up and her hands open, her eyes engrossed as if she were suffering an intrinsic pain. Her face was grave, disconsolate, and very pale. And after being silent and absorbed in that position for quite a while, when it was the second hour in the morning, she said:

"If it is possible *transeat ad me calix iste*[45] *[silence] non mea voluntas, sed tua fiat.*[46] Oh, oh, oh."

After a short pause, she clasped her hands, still absorbed and motionless, looking toward the sky. And after staying in this way for a third of an hour, she spoke these words:

"God prays to God himself *[silence]* and equality seems to contradict itself *[silence]*, but in order not to withdraw from his creature, he lets his own divinity withdraw from himself *[silence]* but who will ever dare to have a will?

She showed that she was feeling an intense pain:

"Oh what a penetrating pain!"

And it was apparent that she was participating in it because her face became transfigured more and more and showed a great sadness. Then she said:

"*Cor meum dereliquit me*[47] *et dolor passionis mee assunsit me [silence] et peccatum omni creaturae [silence]* oh, oh, it seems like now you don't remember what you said: '*Filius meus est tu*'[48] *[silence] et non audisti eum.* Oh, oh, and everything for the creature *[silence]* oh Word, I wonder if I should say: '*transeat ad me penis ista,*' even though it is glorious."

She was feeling Jesus' pain insofar as she was able to tolerate it.

"*Non mea voluntas, sed tua fiat.*"

Then she gave a big shriek that came from inside herself; then she said:

"In her womb you wished to suffer, and now? *[silence]* but your sadness sends all our sadness away *[silence]* but, oh Word!"

And after these words she fell on the floor, half sitting, with clasped hands and arms dropped down like an exhausted person who can't take it anymore, and her eyes were downcast and her face stiff. And after a long time, she shook and gave a deep sigh. Then she said:

"And you suffered this for all your elect."

And keeping quiet again for a long while, after an hour she stood up on her knees, holding her hands and arms wide open with her eyes toward the sky, as she had done the other time. She showed that she was praying for the second time; and after staying like this for a while, she said:

"*Transeat, transeat. Non mea sed tua voluntas fiat.*"

And after a while, she shook and said:

"Oh, oh, oh." And she threw herself on the floor, lowering her eyes, and clasping hands like the other time. And after staying like this for a half-hour, she gave a deep sigh saying:

"Oh, oh, oh."

And when the hour was over, she said:

"Oh Word, and you suffered this for every sinner."

And after a short pause, she stood up again on her knees, with her hands and arms open, eyes to the sky in the same way she had done before. And after quite a long time, she said:

"*Transeat, transeat a me calix iste.*"

And after a short while, she fell down on her face, exhausted, staying like that for more than forty minutes. Then, kneeling up straight on her knees, after a brief pause she said:

"The Consoler of the angels is being consoled by the angel *[silence]* and you suffered this for the damned souls *[silence]* here he lets all his will go *[silence]* and he wishes it to happen soon, and it will be soon."

She saw Jesus preparing with immense fortitude to go up to Judas, and [she saw] Judas urge the mob to take Jesus.

"Oh, if the flesh was sick, he couldn't do anything about it *[silence]* you sweated a sweat of blood *[silence]* oh, why? Because these people became disunited from you, and when one cuts a member from a body, that body oozes blood *[silence]* oh, why can't I take up every man's will and give to you? *[silence]* oh, if I could give them to you, it seems to me that I would be able to relieve you somehow *[silence]* you also suffered that agony for that anguish and fear that we are going to suffer at the moment of our death."

She saw Judas coming with the mob to take Jesus.

"But the traitor is arriving *[silence]* oh, here he comes, the traitor!"

And all of a sudden she stood up and left that room with such a liveliness and celerity as she had done the previous two times, without coming out of her raptures, still with clasped hands. She went to another room close to the previous one, and when she stopped there, she stood motionless with clasped hands and eyes open, leaning over a small altar, having such a joyful and grave expression on her face that she looked royal. And here she spoke the following words:

"Oh Word, I'll see them taking you away *[silence] ad quid venisti?*[49] *[silence]* oh, how can you possibly call him your friend? *[silence]* but you have taught your spouses that they must love even those who offend you, because for those who love it is imperative to love who offends the lover *[silence]* oh, with the kiss of peace you showed how much you loved peace; and you have taught us to love it and to look for it, because, when you were still in heaven, before coming down here, you made justice and peace kiss *[silence]* you took and were taken *[silence] beati pacifici quoniam filii Dei vocabuntur*[50] *[silence]* oh, even the son of perdition can teach us *[silence] quem queritis?*[51] *[silence] ego sum.*[52] Yes, of course, because you are who you are *[silence]* in this you show the Trinity with the humanity, because you are four, yes *[silence]* and in this you also manifest your eternity, *ego sum*, and eternal. And similarly, your power *[silence]* they said it three times, so that they cursed the whole Trinity."

She meant that the Jews said three times, "Jesus the Nazarene." And Jesus perhaps said four times "*Quem queritis?*" before they answered him twice; and then each time that they fell on the ground. Indeed, this soul said: "In this you show the trinity with the humanity, because you are four, yes."

Then, she said: "*Venisti ad me sicut ad latronem*[53] *[silence]* oh Peter, you'd like to impede our salvation, and yours as well *[silence]* they do the same, those who try to remove their inner hearing *[silence]* how many, how many take out the knife of hatred, and who tries to impede your passion;[54] they don't renew it, they rather impede its fruit *[silence]* who ties is tied, and with his arms he holds us tight to himself and himself to us *[silence]* and how do we tie you? By offering you this tie again and again *[silence]* you tie yourself in us and us in yourself; and like precious stones adorning a robe, our souls adorn your humanity *[silence]* where the holy Trinity is pleased, the angels rejoice, and the creatures rest *[silence]* here he is, the strong Samson *[silence]* oh, holy feet! *[silence]* oh, it draws so much! But you drew and draws even more *[silence]* they jeered at the wisdom; they insulted goodness *[silence]* a great patience in tolerating those people around you, who were so different from you. But it is not inferior at all to the patience you now have in tolerating us. But we show a greater power in receiving so many influences of your grace without being converted to you *[silence]* those hands tie so that we tie your working *[silence]* but as they were able to multiply their bread through your power, so now your workings multiply in us through your pain and your passion *[silence] erraverunt ab utero, locuti sunt falsa;*[55] *erraverunt in via,* and *non cognoverunt eam*[56] *[silence]* oh, these hands would deserve such a great admiration. *Et procidentes adoraverunt manus Verbi dicentes: iste sunt digne accipere potentiam in omni loco dominationis Patris eius*[57] *[silence]* and they even wanted to take you away and accuse you. Oh, Word, how many, how many offend you! And with this you teach a humble pride. No greater humility than enduring, and no righter pride than refusing to yield to the malignant people *[silence]* and with your numerous mockeries you taught me to be clothed and rejoice in my affliction *[silence] non enim mihi conscius sum, sed non in hoc iustificatus sum*[58] (and she said this three times). But you, Word, you couldn't sin; and everything they said about you was a lie *[silence] adversum me malignaverunt iniqui."*

At this point she left that room, and after going down through the room of the novices she walked down the stairs of the infirmary; then she went to the refectory next to a low closet; and she had the impression that she was led to Annas's house. The eighth hour had just struck, and after being quiet for a while in this place, she said:

"Are you afraid of not having enough time? Is this why you are doing it so fast? *[silence]* oh that face that the angels wish to contemplate!"

She saw Jesus being slapped on the face when he was before Annas, the chief priest. And she said: *"Faciem tuam illumina super servas tuas.*[59] But your soul, oh Word, was dark and adorned. *Plorans ploravit in noctae* and *lacrimae eius in maxillis eius.*[60] But not only the tears, but also the slaps of the iniquitous servants; *in maxillis eius,* because it didn't pierce the body, but the interior of the soul *[silence]* yes, because they offended that fortitude which holds every working,

112

like the jaw holds the teeth *[silence]* oh, that ruddy and pale face *[silence] et obscurata est facies virginis*[61] *[silence] et obscurata est facies sponsi [silence] faciem meam non averti ad increpantibus* and *conspuentibus in me*[62] *[silence]* and teeth lead to the bosom of the eternal Father, because hell is full of good intentions *[silence] non abscondas ad me faciem tuam [silence] et procidentes adoraverunt faciem eius dicentes: ista est digna accipere splendorem Divinitatis sue.*"

She said all the above things while she was with her soul in Annas's house. Then she left the refectory with her usual lightness, with clasped hands, and went to the chapter house, where she knelt down before the grating over the church. And after being silent and engrossed for a long time, she spoke the following words:

"There is no reason for death *[silence]* oh Peter, don't you remember the promises and suggestions? *[silence]* and not once, but three times you deny it *[silence]* and we deny it too *[silence]* indeed, don't we deny his power when we apologize for not doing good and repent justifying ourselves with our frailty? And don't we deny his wisdom when we oppose his workings? And, moreover, we deny his greatness and abundance when we stick to the transitory things of this world *[silence]* and when the Word raises his divine eyes, he penetrates the interior part and gives any knowledge *[silence]* but how many times, infinite goodness, you allow your servants to fall into some minor fault, only because in this way they'll be able to feel compassion for others! *[silence] et cum perversio perverteris*[63] *[silence]* oh, oh oh! *[silence] et oculi mei languerunt pre inopia*[64] *[silence]* oh those eyes; with their sight they make heaven glorious and make the earth shake! *[silence]* oh, oh, oh!" And at this point she cried heartily; after two deep sighs, she said: "Oh Peter, you could admire the eyes of my Word! *[silence] et procidentes adoraverunt oculi sponsi mei dicentes; isti sunt digni accipere visionem Divinitatis eternitatis par-ticipationis sue.*"[65]

And she repeated this prayer three times.

"Oh, oh, oh, they demand him like crazy[66] *[silence]* you were right when you said: *oculi mei semper ad Dominum quoniam ipse evellet de laqueo pedes meos;*[67] *et evellet me de laqueo venantium.*"[68]

She left the chapter house in a rush. Walking through the court room she went to the guest rooms, which are pretty far away, always in a rush, as we just said, and with clasped hands. She walked so fast that we could not reach her. She was drawn by her spirit and went to those places where she saw Jesus stay. And here she turned the guest rooms into Pilate's palace, the most appropriate place she could choose in our monastery because there are several rooms in the basement, in the mezzanine, and upstairs; and at first she knelt down next to the sink where, after a long silence, she said:

"Oh iniquitous! *[silence]* you say that he is an evildoer and in this you confess to your iniquity, and that you are the iniquitous, for if he is that who makes everyone, he also makes you; thus, if he were, as you say, an evildoer, you too would be evil, because if the doer is evil, that who is done is evil too *[silence]* but he is a doer of infinite goodness, but later the creature becomes a doer of infinite malice and iniquity *[silence]* and disparagers give this same offence *[silence] pone Domine custodiam ori meo, et hostium circunstantie labiis meis, et non declines cor meum in verba malitie ad excusandas excusationes in peccatis.*"[69]

After keeping quiet for a short time, she left this guest room and, going through the Choir, she stopped at the stairs in front of the Choir. Here she showed that Jesus was before Herod. After being here for a short while, she said:

"Oh you rejoice, against your will *[silence]* you wanted to see him jeer at him, it seems to me *[silence]* they do the same thing those who rejoice at goodness, and then they condemn it with their workings[70] *[silence] bonitatem* and *disciplinam* and *scientiam doce me*[71] *[silence]* wisdom and knowledge, *oh altitudo divitiarum sapientie* and *scientie Dei, quam incomprehensibilia sunt omni caro*[72] *[silence]* oh what a vestment! *[silence]* you want to jeer at him, and at the same time you manifest his greatness and his innocence *[silence]* he dresses us with the vestment of innocence in the holy baptism and constantly dresses us with his grace, granting us his body and his blood in the holy sacrament. And then in heaven he wants to dress us with his glory and immortality *[silence] in odorem vestimentorum tuorum curremus.*"[73]

All of a sudden she stood up and left this place, going down the stairs that take to the first floor, and went back to the guest room in the same way she did the first time. Kneeling down in the same place, after a long silence she said:

"Oh, but if he is innocence itself?"

She showed that she was with Jesus before Pilate again and that she heard him questioning him and Jesus' love answering him; and she said:

"*Regnum meum non est de hoc mundo*[74] *[silence]* and you are our kingdom itself *[silence]* and if yours were a kingdom of this world, you would have it." And, as she often does, she said nothing more and does not finish what she has begun, keeping it in herself.

"But your kingdom, oh, oh, oh!"

And then, after keeping quiet for a long time, she became much more sad and grieved and spoke the following words:

"*Et persecutus est hominem inopem* and *mendicum*[75] *[silence]* that Joseph [was] persecuted *[silence] Dominis regis terre.*"[76]

And at this point she understood that, as Joseph had been put in a cell by his brothers, so was Jesus put in an old cell at Pilate's. And she saw him being put in it; and she followed him inside. And she signified that when she threw herself on the floor and curled up, she became like a clew. She repeated the following words three times:

"Here he is, here he is in the cell."

A bit later, while she was with a sister, she saw a small lamb that was resting in a broken vase, rolled up as they usually do. She told her: "You see, Jesus was like that in that cell at Pilate's house." She remained in that cell for an hour and a half, looking dead and speaking no word. Then she stood up; and it was the eleventh hour. And after a little while, she said:

"*Magni consilii Angelus [silence]* oh, oh, and then they will feel content *[silence]* you let them pull your holy beard away, in order to adorn us later with the magnificence of your divinity *[silence] veritatem meam [silence]* who comes from truth knows what truth is *[silence]* why can't we make the truth known? Because those who don't have the truth cannot enjoy that glory *[silence] veritas a Patre venit per me*[77] *[silence]* you let them spit on your face in order to adorn your spouse and make her effulgent in your blood."

During this time of the passion, I mean, when Jesus went to the kitchen garden to pray, until the end, she spoke very little and so low because she had difficulty in articulating the words, given the intense suffering she felt inside and the great pain she showed externally.

Indeed, she told us that she could hardly cry, but once in a while she gave those deep screams of hers. She did so because she felt so tightened inside that she could not breath. Thus, most of the time she kept quiet and engrossed, showing that she was suffering a lot and speaking those rare and brief words. She had long pauses between one thing and the other, and one can see that from the fact that in this long vision, although she was rapt for many hours, she spoke only a few words. And she signified the rest of the passion more through her walking and her external acts than through her actual words; in particular those major mysteries, like being hit at the column, receiving the crown of thorns, carrying the cross, and being crucified—all these events she showed to be seeing them and be suffering [because of them] in a very clear way.

At this point she saw the torments that were inflicting on Jesus at Pilate's house, when he came back from Herod. Indeed, she said:

"*Multiplicati sunt qui tribulant me*[78] *[silence]* a lie can never know the truth."

Here she meant that Pilate first asked for it [truth], but then he refused to listen to it because he was a mendacious and deceitful man and did not deserve to learn from Jesus what truth is. And there are many people like Pilate. This is why she spoke the following words in the person of Pilate:[79]

"You let them pull your beard away, and your hair too, in order to reward us for every minimal thing, as he had promised *[silence]* *vestri capilli capitis omnes numerati sunt*[80] *[silence]* *non invenio in eo causam*[81] *[silence]* he is impeccable.[82] I agree!"

And all of a sudden she stood up and went to the room next to that where she was, that is, to the small grocery room. Going around the room still with clasped hands, she stopped and leaned against the sink that was there, crossing her hands on her breast. She stayed there with such a great humbleness, that she could have made the stones weep. And after being quiet for a little bit, she said:

"You let them compare you to Barrabas, though you are that *qui mortificat* and *vivificat*[83] *[silence]* you let them choose that who is full of malice and ignorance. And still, you are *Deus Deorum et Dominus Dominatium*[84] *[silence]* oh, can you believe it. And you want

116

to satisfy that people, but in any case they won't be satisfied, and you won't satisfy them."

And after a short pause in this room, she left again and, walking through the previous guest room, went downstairs, where she put her hands behind her back leaning against a column that was right next to the door. Bending her head and looking down, sometimes she writhed and showed a great pain. And the twelfth hour had just struck, but she remained there more than an hour. During this time she spoke the following words, with long silences between one word and the other. Her first words were these:

"Against the column with your hands behind your back, oh, oh, oh *[silence] supra dorsum meum fabricaverunt peccatores iniquitates*[85] *[silence]* oh, if the Almighty's virtue didn't hold you, you would have died at once *[silence]* you did it to fulfill what you had promised: *"in domo Patris mei mansiones multae sunt"*[86] *[silence] flagellatus sum tota die, et castigatio mea in matutinis*[87] *[silence] congregaverunt in unum*, and *fragellaverunt te*[88] *[silence]* you are the house where the divinity rests, and your wounds are its rooms *[silence] considerabam ad dexteram* and *videbam*, and not *erat qui adiuvabat me*[89] *[silence]* they are more than willing to take turns to hit you, but we can't take turns in loving, no *[silence] fragellaverunt corpus tuum, ut confortentur membra tua*[90] *[silence] quoniam angeli[s] suis mandavit de te, ut custodiant te in omnibus viis tuis*[91] *[silence] mandavit itaque in operae redentionis nostrae*[92] *[silence]* you could rightly say: *"unam petii a Domino, hanc requiram,*[93] *ut liberem de fragellis corporis Ecclesiae meae"*[94] *[silence] ponam consilio in anima mea adversum me.*[95] Your acts of mercy are innumerable; their blows are also innumerable. Please, make our workings innumerable, and also our desires, like those of our ancient holy Fathers *[silence]* oh Mary, if you saw that whom you suckled with so much affection you would die before him *[silence]* but if the souls penetrated it, they would burst for love *[silence]* oh traitors, you don't want to look, because you don't to feel any love and compassion *[silence]* you tied the Word up and untied yourself from him."

After a rather long pause, she fell on the floor as if she had been untied from that column. And after lying there for quite a while, she stood up and, walking very slowly, went up those same stairs she had come down from before. She went back to that same guest room, exactly where she had been the first time. And kneeling down there for a little while, she spoke the following words:

"They put together the harsh thorns to make a crown for my beloved *[silence]* to find thorns for him, who gives us his body as food *[silence]* oh, oh, oh!"

She showed that she was receiving the crown of thorns by sitting up straight with clasped hands in her lap and her head bent over. And almost right after she said:

"*Et incoronaverunt Sponsi mei* with piercing thorns. That who crowns the soul with joyfulness and glory *[silence]* they penetrated through his brain and made, made that infinite wisdom exude *[silence]* alas, they put a reed in the Word's hand as a scepter."

And she moved her hand as if she were receiving the reed; and she kept it in that way until she had to put the cross on her shoulders. As we shall say later, at that point she put it down.

"*Et percusserunt caput eius arundine*[96] *[silence]* the head of divine essence. But, time will come when they are trampled on; the Word's feet will trample on these traitors *[silence]* they want to hide the light of light *[silence]* oh, oh, he sees where you'll never be able to see *[silence]* they do the same those who don't trust you and say that God doesn't watch over his creatures *[silence]* but you hold in your hand the sceptre of your virtue, so that with it we are able to strike the head of the old serpent *[silence]* and, and, you recognize him as the king of the Jews; but he is the king not only of the Jews, but also of heaven and earth, of the abyss, of hell, and of every existing thing *[silence]* and who do you prophesy about? it's him who has been prophesied; it's him who saw everything before you had been created; and he shows us the forthcoming things, of which you'll be deprived much to your vexation! *[silence] filiae Sion*, come out and see your king crowned with a diadem. His mother synagogue crowned him the day of his wedding."

And after a short while, she slowly went to the same grocery room. Walking around as she had done the other time, she stopped and leaned over the same spot. Here she showed that Pilate was showing Jesus crowned with thorns to the people; and she said:

"*Ecce homo;* here is the man who is the real God *[silence]* ecco homo *[silence]* here is the man who has made man God *[silence]* yes, man, but the man who does everything that the divinity himself does *[silence]* you say that Caesar is your God, but in fact you do not deserve to have my Spouse as your king, but rather as your judge *[silence] ecce rex vester*[97] *[silence]* what are you doing, you ungrateful? Before you said: *"Benedictus qui venit in nomine Domini"*;[98] and now you say: *"Crucifige, crucifige eum"*[99] *[silence]* you fulfill what this truth said with his mouth, that is, that you praised him with your mouth, but with your heart you were far from him."

She left from here walking around very slowly, and walking up a stair she went to a room upstairs. Kneeling down on the landing, she prayed to the Father, speaking the following words and showing that she was rapt in contemplation:

"Father, do not regard the thoughts of these impious people, but regard the salvation of the humankind *[silence]* Father, accept the anguish and suffering of your Word for the comfort and consolation of your elect."

Afterward, she kept silent for a very long time; then, all of a sudden she stood up and leaned with her left arm against a corner of this landing, which was like a small balcony, and looking down she spoke these words:

"Although you think so, you can't free the Word *[silence]* and if you wanted to free him, you wouldn't look to Caesar *[silence]* and he even says that he finds no reason to condemn him, and nevertheless you sentence him to death."

She was covered with tears and gave a deep sigh. It was the sixteenth hour when Pilate had just sentenced Jesus to death. And when she knelt down again, she prayed to the Father one more time saying:

"Oh eternal Father, if at least this was not shed in vain!"

And after being on her knees for quite a while, she turned a little, speaking these words:

"Damnable human respect, cause of every evil *[silence] dixi tibi in principio.*"[100]

And after a while, she stood up, turning toward the stairs, her hands crossed on her breast. She said:

"Now, now the sentence against my Word. And in a hurry they prepare the cross for that who wants to prepare his glory for us."

119

And after a little while, she made the gesture of putting down the reed that she had been holding in her hand. Laying it down, she turned and made the gesture of putting the cross on her shoulders. She turned an arm on her back, placing a hand on her shoulder to set the cross straight.

And starting to go down this stair very slowly, she walked downstairs. And when she was halfway down, she fell on her back on one of those big steps; after a short time she stood up and got to the end of the stairs. And when she reached the ground she walked through the loggia to the main room. Here, she walked around and around, still in her rapture, with clasped hands on her breast and her eyes looking down; her face was melancholy and so pale and livid that she looked like dead. And once in a while she screamed so desperately that she could make a stone weep.

Leaving the main room in the same way, she went back to the kitchen garden, where she walked through every path. Leaving the kitchen garden from that side, she walked through the loggia of the infirmary heading for the chapter room. And when she was close to its door, she gave a deep sigh and fell on the ground. She remained there for a long time. Later, we helped her stand up because she had a difficulty in doing it by herself. She headed for the chapter room, where she walked around, and then left through the door opening on the courtyard. She walked up the stairs leading to the refectory; then, passing through the refectory, she crossed the Chorus and went upstairs to the room where the nuns work in wintertime. After walking around the room as she had done downstairs, she went to the room of the novices. Walking up the stairs, she went to the big dormitory, and going downstairs she headed for the dormitory of the novices. When she entered their oratory, she knelt down next to the altar with clasped hands. Here she prayed for a half hour, always in silence. And it was the eighteenth hour.

Then she resumed walking, carrying the cross in that way for more than an hour. During this time she only spoke the following words three times. The first time was when she was in the main room downstairs. She said:

"*Tanquam oves ad occisionem ductus est,* and *non aperuit os suum.*"[101] And her voice was so low, that we could hardly hear it. In the kitchen garden she said: *"Filiae Hierusalem, nolite flere super me sed super vos ipsas flete."*[102] And another time she said: *"Non aperiet os suum."* And after having prayed to the Father for that half hour, she spoke these words: *"Pater, offero ad te istam operationem redentioni omni creature."*

At the end of these words she stood up. Taking off her slippers, she left them there at a corner of the altar, and going to the other side of the oratory, she lay on the floor. Opening her arms she showed that she was lying on the cross like Jesus. Staying still for a short time, she signified that they were piercing her feet because she shook and gave a deep sigh. Then she signified that they were piercing her left hand, again by shaking and wrenching her hand, and by stretching her arm with a deep groan. Later she signified that they were piercing her right hand by shaking greatly and wrenching this hand and also by stretching her arm in a way that only those who saw her could understand it.

And I, the writer, testify that, when I put my hand under hers so that it would not touch the floor, as soon as they put the nail in it she shook and wrenched this hand; it became like a piece of wood, yellow as if it were filled with saffron. And we were greatly amazed and surprised when we saw the nerves of her arm twisting and moving.

And she lay on the floor in that position for, say, fifteen minutes. In other words, more or less thirty minutes passed between the crucifixion and her lying on the floor. And then she stood up and, leaning against the wall with her arms open, remained in that position until the twenty-first hour, when she spoke the following words. She had long pauses between one sentence and the next.

After quite a bit, she pronounced the first sentence: *"Pater ignosce illis quia nesciunt quid faciunt*[103] *ad Verbum tuum, qui dignatus est partecipare pena ista mecum."* Second sentence: *"Hodie mecum eris in Paradiso*[104] *[silence] mulier, ecce Filius tuus [silence] ecce Mater tua*[105] *[silence]* oh my Word, recommend me too to John *[silence]* give me what Mary had, her holy humility *[silence]* oh Word, express the other word: *Heli, Heli, la mazzabatani."*[106]

After a new long silence, she pronounced the fifth sentence as follows: "Express the other word: *sitio."*[107] And before the sixth sentence, she paused for more than a half hour. Then, when the twentieth hour had just struck, she said: "My Spouse, please say it: *in manus tuas commendo spiritum meum.*"[108]

And again, she waited so long before she spoke these words that it was very painful for us to see her lying there like dead. It did not seem to us that she would be able to come around. As far as I am concerned, I must confess that I thought she might be dead; and it was really painful for me. Her arms and her neck were so stiff that her entire body seemed to be like dry wood. And around the twentieth hour and a half, she said: "*Consummatum est*[109] *[silence]* and finished [is] the working of our redemption; finished [is] the working of communication; and finished [is] the working of reunion." And then she said: "*Et inclinato capite emisit spiritum.*"[110] And at once she slackened her arms and her head that she had been holding rather stiff, and she fell in our arms. Then, relaxing slowly, she woke up and came back to her corporeal feelings.

And she recovered so well both in her strength and her complexion that she did not seem to be herself, although she felt very tired. We took her to bed despite her strong protests. However, thanks to her holy obedience, she did everything we asked her to do and rested as she deserved.

She recovered from this rapture a little bit before the twenty-first hour, exactly when the Friday before the holy passion she had entered a vision. That day the Lord shared with her the pain he suffered when he breathed out his Spirit on the cross, as it is written. Later, during our conversation, she told us that Jesus wanted to give her that pain before. The pain had been very intense because of her frailty; she would not have been able to tolerate it on Good Friday because she was so tired after all the other pains he had shared with her during his passion. This rapture of the passion lasted from Thursday at the sixth hour and a half of the night until the same hour on Friday. They were twenty-six hours altogether, during which she never came out of her rapture, as we have already said, although she moved and made all those gestures we have described and also many others. We were unable to write down every single detail.

Among others, when she went to the column to be struck, she made the gestures of undressing and leaving her clothes on the floor. And when she said *"Filie Hierusalem"* while she was carrying the cross, she turned toward those women; and many other things that we neither understood or comprehended. We were able to keep in mind only those things that we saw, understood, and comprehended. We asked her if, when she went to those places, she followed Jesus and saw him. She said that yes, she saw him and suffered with him to the point that sometimes she felt as if she were Jesus himself, as we could infer by the way she recounted this to us.

Let us always praise, bless, and thank the Lord. And here we end our holy conversation.

Dialogue 39
Marriage to Jesus

On April 28, the Sunday *in albis*, 1585 we sang Mass because a girl was taking the veil of our sacred religion. During the ceremony our beloved soul was rapt in spirit. As she told us later during our conversation, although she was separate from her corporeal perceptions she heard the nuns singing, understood what they were saying, and sang in the Mass herself. She also saw that the Lord was sending down many gifts and graces to those nuns, and while they were singing *Kyrie eleison* she saw the nine angelic choirs descend from heaven, a choir for every *Kyrie eleison*. Then, when they were singing the Epistle, she saw that the Lord confirmed the gifts he had given the nuns at the beginning of the Mass and even added some more.

While they were singing the Gospel, she saw that the Lord was giving some beautiful adornments to the girl who was taking the veil. As our order states, that girl had to enter the church right after the Gospel. And while, according to the rules, the priests were getting ready with the cross and the vine to go up to her at the door of the monastery, in the church our blessed soul saw a cherub who held a book in his hand. And as soon as that girl started to sing *"Ancilla Christi sum,"*[1] the angel—a cherub, as our blessed soul perceived—immediately started to write and kept writing as the girl went on speaking. And he completed his writing when the girl finally took the veil. Then our blessed soul was told that every time a girl takes the veil, an angel comes and writes in a book everything that girl says to present it later at Doomsday in her favor or disfavor, according to our accomplishments. And our blessed soul understood that that book describes how every nun in our monastery took the veil. And when that girl received the sacred cloth and thus was totally dressed, our blessed soul saw another angel arriving immediately, who, as she understood, was from the chorus of the seraphim. This second angel had also a book, which concerned, as she realized, the lives of the religious. And first this angel recounted all the good deeds that girl had ever done until then: her desire to enter the religious life and to become Jesus' spouse, and all her good thoughts, ideas, feelings, desires, and every other good deed. And then he enumerated all the good things that girl would have to do in the future and all their good effects in our holy religion. Finally, he wrote her name in that book.

And about this morning our blessed soul did not tell us anything more.

That same day, around the seventeenth hour, feeling very melancholy and sorrowful, our blessed soul went alone to the dormitory for the novices, where, as we realized later, she entered a rapture at once. However, we did not know that she was there until we went to the choir to sing Vespers. Because she was not with the other novices, our Mother teacher sent some of us to look for her. And they found her on her knees in the dormitory, rapt in spirit. And our blessed soul was speaking, both her words and her face showing that she was in great pain and distress. She repeated the following words several times: *"Circundederunt me dolores inferni;*[2] *dolores inferni circundedit me."* And other times she said: *"Comedit me dolores inferni pro multitudine iniquitatum nostrarum."* And we understood that that day the Lord repeatedly showed her the offenses creatures give to him and the numerous iniquities and sins that are committed all over the world. And so once she said: "Oh Word, I can't anymore, iniquities, oh no, no more, no more, and if they don't want to remove their sins and their iniquities, please remove these iniquities from my sight, because I can't anymore." Then, after a short while: *"Respiciunt vanitatem,* and *cadunt in iniquitate; respiciunt elevationem,* and *cadunt in profundum abissi*[3] *[silence] Non habitabit in domum tuam qui blasfemant nominis tui [silence] Comedi ego iniquitates eorum, dolores inferni circundedit me. Discedit ad me anima eius,* and *accedit to you."*[4] Sometimes she seemed to be seeing particular sins that had been committed by particular persons, but in particular it seemed that that day the Lord showed her how serious the sin of cursing was, and that was why she was in a great pain and distress. She remained in this rapture until the twenty-first hour, often speaking about different things but always going back to those iniquities. And she seemed to be suffering a lot, sighing deeply, crying, throwing herself on the floor, and making gestures that expressed affliction and internal pain.

When the twentieth hour rang, after a deep sigh she cried out: "Oh good Jesus, as much as you want." Then, after a short silence, she said: "Oh, I don't know *[silence] Et relaxabo me in liberalitate tua*[5] *[silence]* oh good Jesus, oh, oh, oh *[silence]* oh Word, oh good Jesus! *[silence]* oh *bonitas immensa [silence] Vir linguosus non dirigetur in terra*[6] *[silence]* oh, aren't they like curses! *[silence]* oh good veritas, you give strength, even though the soul and the body don't think it's possible. Oh Word, let me die a living death, so that I can carry out your project. *Omnes declinaverunt, non est qui faciat bonum, non est usque ad unum*[7] *[silence]* oh, let blindness see, whose seeing gives it pain, whose pain gives it glory; this glory is its beatitude, and its eternity is incomprehensible, inscrutable, and can be understood only by you, for you, and in you *[silence]* but no novelty is a novelty to me! *[silence] omnes declinaverunt a te*, and *non cognoverunt te, et nolunt intelligere ut bene agerent*[8] *[silence]* they don't know you, and don't want to know you. But in any case they will know you. *Et mors depascet eos*[9] *[silence]* Oh Word, even though always, you always show them to us in the same way *[silence]* you showed us your open wounds, your hands, your chest, so that we are not incredulous anymore, but faithful *[silence]* how immense is the ingratitude of your creatures!"

At this point she burst into tears and said: "Oh, oh, oh *bonitas.*" After crying and sighing many times, she threw herself on the floor again as if she were dying, and said: "Oh death, you give life *[silence]* I die alive *[silence]* oh, oh, oh *[silence] appone iniquitatem super iniquitatem*[10] *[silence]* oh, it is so little understood. Wisdom seems folly and folly seems wisdom *[silence]* oh iniquity! *[silence]* oh offenses, they can't penetrate them, even if they try to, yes *[silence]* oh, oh, oh good Jesus."

She was in such a great distress that it was painful to see her; and she gave sighs and shook, as if someone were hitting her. And she said: "Oh glorious sorrow, you are glorious and sorrowful." She meant that for her that suffering was glorious because she desired to suffer for God's love and for the creatures' salvation; but it was also sorrowful because she was feeling such an internal and external sorrow. Thus she said: "Sorrow that gives me delight, and delight that gives me sorrow."

After keeping quiet for a long while, she came out of the rapture when it was already the twenty-fourth hour. So we did not dare to ask her what she was seeing. Still very grieved, first she went to the Choir for Compline with the nuns and then to the refectory with the whole convent. Having expressed her thanks to God, on her way to the kitchen garden she became deeply grieved and started to cry. So, we walked her out of the kitchen garden and took her to the oratory for the novices, where she burst into intense and scalding tears as if she were about to die. She moaned and shook so vehemently that we could neither look at her nor listen to her. And this lasted from the twenty-fourth hour to the first hour sharp, when all of a sudden she calmed down and was rapt in spirit again. We understood this by the fact that she quieted down and became very stiff, as she usually does when she is in a rapture.

Later, during our conversation we asked her what she had been experiencing when she was shaking so intensely and crying so much that we feared that the devil himself was hitting her like St. Anthony, for she kept saying: "Oh good Jesus," screaming, crying, shaking as if someone were hitting her.

She told us that no, she was not being hit; she was rather hearing voices swearing in her ears so that she was compelled to shake as she did each time that she heard those swears because those swearers' voices terrified her. And she also saw a big profusion of offenses against God; that was why that day, until night, she had suffered a hellish pain. And we think that the Lord let her experience this to purge her because that night he wanted to give her the great present of his wedding ring in order to marry her, as he had done to St. Catherine of Siena. Indeed, that night was the eve of that anniversary when Jesus, Catherine's Spouse, had taken her to her heavenly *noces*. And he wanted to marry this dear soul as well, who was so devout to St. Catherine; and [she told us] that Jesus Love had told her that he wanted to make her similar to her. As we have written above, we have already seen several signs of this, and we believe that we are going to see many others.

Her loving Spouse Jesus always treats her in this way when he wants to give her some new gifts. He always tests her with some great distress, that is, either a temptation or something else. As a consequence, every time we see her behave in certain ways, we believe that later she will receive some grace and a particular present. That night, after being silent and enthralled for around fifteen minutes, she said:

"Oh immense generosity." When she saw the present Jesus wanted to give her, she rejoiced greatly and said: *"Non coronabitur nisi qui legittime certaverit*[11] *[silence]* oh Word, You too." She meant: "you married St. Catherine too *[silence]* oh Word *[silence]* oh, your holy hands are so beautifully adorned and full of so many wedding rings for your spouses."

She saw that Jesus was very beautiful, with his hands full of rings; and he showed that he wanted to marry both her and the others. However, she said: "Oh, I wished as many as our offenses to you were able to receive your ring! *[silence]* good for us was the day when you married that one." *[silence]* She meant St. Catherine of Siena because it was her day *[silence]* "I will have her as a priest, even though she is a bride *[silence]* and I will have Augustine *[silence]* oh, both of them!"

Then Jesus kindly asked her whether she wanted their wedding to be revealed or not because he knew how much she wished these things to remain secret to the other creatures. Responding to him, she said: "Oh my Jesus, your will *[silence]* but you promised me that, as you hid, I would hide as well *[silence]* who will understand the value and the beauty of this ring? I don't care about its importance and its beauty, just about who gives it *[silence]* when they receive their groom, the spouses make requests. I too, I will make requests. However, since your creatures give me pain, I will make requests for your spouses, although I won't forget all the other creatures. But now I'll pray for your spouses, so that you help them become better and keep the promises they made to you. I'll also ask that you give them a Christ according to your heart *[silence]* I will also ask for those you force me to ask for *[silence]* *cantabo Domino canticum novum*[12] *[silence]* *omnes gentes plaudite manibus,*[13] in honor of the marriage of pure souls *[silence]* on the enamel of the ring you will write what is already written in the heart, *Verbum caro factum est,*[14] and *Sanguis unionis* *[silence]* to the first and to the second you add the third *[silence]* and what will it be? *[silence]* but my Jesus, I don't want to give you orders *[silence]* oh, purity! *[silence] et puritas coniunsit Verbum ad Maria.*"

She meant that, as purity had united the Word with Mary, it now united him with her because he had had that purity written in her heart. But then she said: "The Word, blood, purity. And you, Mary, must give your milk to nourish the bride. If the groom is generous, my Word says, you must be generous too, Mary *[silence]* oh, Augustine, put aside and guard everything he will deign to offer."

She said that because St. Augustine—her spiritual father, to whom she is so devout—has always written in her heart the presents Jesus gave him. And before: *"Verbum caro factum est"* because of the his incarnation; and *"Sanguis unionis,"* holy Monday; and tonight: *"Puritas coniunsit Verbum ad Maria."*

Afterward she kept silent for a long while, seemed to be feeling an immense joy, and was very glad, with a face like a paradise. She kept her eyes open, sparkling like two stars, and her face was so beautifully rose colored that it looked like milk and blood. She remained in this way throughout the night. Then she started to speak again as follows: *"Ecce quam bonum* and *quam jocundum habitare,*[15] yes, in unitate, yes, but much more in the essence of his divinity and his humanity. And the Word, who lives in his Father's gentle and eternal bosom, draws the souls there; he weighs them with his just and merciful scale, and uses his blood, that the creatures and his elect offered to him, to counterbalance God's just justice." At this point it seemed as if she were digressing from her wedding. But, as she has explained to us many times, in her raptures she sees and perceives more than one thing at the same time. She utters, however, what the Lord wants her to because by herself she neither knows how to speak nor what to say. Then she said: "The greater is divinity than humanity, the greater is consolation."

Going back to her wedding she said:

"Oh good Jesus, you have some of them in your hands and in your side; give those in your side *[silence]* the enamel will be *"Verbum caro factum est et Sanguis unionis"; "Puritas coniunsit Verbum ad Maria, et Sponsum ad sponsam"* *[silence]* only one thing is absent, and strength is missing; well, your blood will compensate for that." *[silence]* She was speaking about her indignity because she doubted whether she was adequate for such a wedding or not. But, trusting the blood shed by Jesus her Spouse, she said: "I offer you the blood of your incarnate Word, I mean, I offer it to you Father, I offer it to you, Word, and I offer it to you, Holy Spirit. And, how could I ever forget you, I offer it to you, Mary, so that you be able to offer it to the eternal Trinity, in order to make up for all the possible flaws of my soul, and also to discharge all the possible flaws of my body."

Then, after staying in this position for a while, she moved her arm away from her body just a little bit and, offering her hand, she graciously raised her ring finger. Keeping her hand still, she said: "Catherine and Augustine will hold my hand. But let the Word put it *[silence] desponsavit me in dulcedine suavitatis* and *liberalitatis Amoris sui; in unione S.me Trinitatis.*"[16]

And she suddenly lowered her finger and drew back her hand, placing it over the other and forming a cross on her knees because now she was sitting; and in silence, with that same cheerfulness, she pleasingly showed that she was enjoying the present she had received. And after quite a while:

"Oh Catherine, you preserved this wedding so well! How will I preserve it? *[silence]* I will use it as a bright mirror, in which, by constantly contemplating it, I will see how in this wedding the generosity, goodness, and gentleness of my Word have united with Holy Trinity, to Whom he has married my soul. I will see the Word in myself, and myself in him. And he will be crucified in myself, and I will be crucified in him, as his beloved apostle St. Paul said: '*Vivo ego iam non ego vivit vero in me Christus Crucifixus.*"[17] In that ring I will also see the Word my Spouse stay in his Father's bosom in a motionless motion that can never cease because of his vehement desire to come down to earth to redeem the creatures; it is moved by his vehement transport of love to be pleased by the creature who has already been conceived in his inner heart. Whence I will derive a vehement desire to glorify God and a constant fervor to lead the creatures to him, seeing how much he has loved them, and that he can be fully glorified only by them; and that I must force myself to help the creatures not only with my prayers, but also with my words and deeds and, if it were necessary, even with my blood and life, as he himself did.

"Later, in this mirror I will see my Word rest in Mary's womb like in a valley of purity; and then, coming out of it, I will see him do so many marvelous and wonderful workings that the angels in heaven are still filled with wonder and surprise; he has done so to show the creature what she is supposed to achieve. And, although she won't be able to imitate him fully because of her littleness, at least she must make profession of gratitude to him and thank him for everything he has done for her. And from this I will draw a rule on how to proceed and do all my workings. Then from his profound humbleness I will learn that I must always humiliate myself and humble myself in every thing; and with this humbleness I will be able to acquire a knowledge of my baseness. From his obedience I will draw a willingness to do nothing in my way, but I will always respond to the others' will. From his generosity I will learn how I must love my neighbor.

"In this mirror I will also see that ardent and infinite love he has wanted to show us by giving himself to us in his Holy Sacrament, so that we can constantly be with him. And he gives it to me, wretched and miserable creature, with such an abundance; but from it I will draw a constant thankfulness for his lovingness toward me and toward every creature, and also thankfulness for all his presents and blessings, since this sacred Sacrament summarizes all the love he has had for us and everything he has done for us in all his life, passion, and death. I will also see the blood he has shed to bathe us, in which we can continuously wash our souls of our constant faults; and with that blood we can adorn ourselves, so that we can appear beautiful in his presence. Whence I will draw a continuous memory of what my Word was willing to suffer for me. And I will dress myself and cover myself with this blood, uniting with it all my thoughts, words, and deeds, so that they will be more welcome and accepted *[silence]*.

"Moreover, I will always be able to see in the ring like in a mirror the love with which the Word has prepared his glory for us; he has decided to go ahead and prepare this glory for us, so that the glory we will enjoy be greater and more copious, because he himself, who is so great and supreme, Lord of this very glory, has prepared it for us. And in this way, so to speak, our souls will be more suitable to adorn the Word with this glory because, as the stars, in the way they are in the sky adorn it with a very intense splendor, so do the souls of the blessed ones in the skies, being placed and united with the Word, adorn him with the greatest splendor; they let his glory shine with much more intensity by showing how generous he was toward them when he exalted them so high and united them to himself. These blessed souls are placed in the Word; each of them [is placed] in one of his organs, higher or lower according to her merits. Some of them are placed in his chest, others in his head, others in his mouth, others in his hands, others in his feet, and some others in his divine heart. Oh, in your side are the virgins, your spouses, because this place has been made for them! And they adorn the Word in a manner more specific than the other saints, because each of these blessed souls adorn and embellish the Word more or less, according to their merits. And not only do they shine and adorn [him] by being in the Word in that way, similar to the stars and the planets in the sky that with their movement provoke several effects in the sky, and whence the creatures down here draw great utility and great pleasure; united to and placed in the Word these blessed souls do so much, that through their delectable movement the beauty, the splendor, the adornment that they have given to him echo in the skies and in the souls themselves. Therefore, a joy, a satisfaction, an unspeakable delight, and a greater glory arise in them; and thanks to this glory the Word is constantly moved to enjoy them, and to be merciful with the creatures here on earth.

"And what will I draw from this? I will draw a total abandonment of myself to my Word, so that the Word himself will actually work in me and do all the workings that I will do. I will also see how he led his souls toward him, I mean, to the vision and fruition of him; and as various are the deeds and the merits of everyone, so are the paths and ways the Word uses to lead them to himself, although the path is in fact only one: love. He drew the prophets through a secret love, since they walked the path of the Word's faith who had promised them that he would come and save the creatures; although they knew this through a revelation and held it for sure thanks to a prophecy, it was nonetheless still unknown to the others;

[he drew] the apostles by means of a strong love, having fortified them with his example and his words; [he drew] the martyrs by means of an ardent love, because through the blood that he had shed he gave them so much ardor, that they neither feared nor minded giving their own blood and life for his love; and [he drew] the confessors with a quiet love, because in all their temptations, afflictions, and pains they always quieted down in God; [he drew] the virgins with a pure love, having purified them with his blood and having always drawn them in his intrinsic path.

"And from this I will also draw an ardent desire to walk toward him, and to go and enjoy the vision and the fruition of him as soon as possible. And in that mirror I will also see Mary's purity, that united her with the Word and united the Word with her. And I will recall the present he gave me, and also that thanks to that purity the Spouse joined the spouse: *Puritas coniunsit Verbum ad Maria*, and *Sponsum ad sponsam*.

"I will see in it [the mirror] Catherine's loving kindness and Augustine's sanctity; and as love is a compendium of all things, so will this ring be for me a compendium of all the presents, graces, and benefits that I have received from my Spouse, the Word; and like in a mirror I will always see in it what I must do. And if it ever happens to tarnish, the Word's blood will make up for it because, as the sun sends the clouds away, so will the Word's blood do what is in the enamel of this ring; and *Sanguis unionis* will send away any tarnish that I might cause to this mirror."

After she spoke all the above words at length, in a rush, even though she had uttered them very slowly and with long pauses, she eventually stopped and kept silent for quite a while, with a cheerful face and shining eyes, as if they reflected the paradise. Then she repeated three times:

"*Eructavit cor meum verbum bonum*,[18] I mean, *ego desponsationem Verbis ad anime meae. [silence] non cor meum*, but *costatum tuum*; no *verbum*, no word, but the bond of a ring, of union, of love, of preciousness *[silence] ortus conclusus*[19] *[silence] conserva me Domine*,[20] *quoniam innocentia mea regeneravit me Sanguinis sui*.[21] *[silence] multi videbunt*, and *timebunt, et exaltavit cornum*, and *confregit iniquitas peccatorum. Sanctus Deus, Sanctus*, yes, but in what? In your mercy. And in what is your mercy greater? I shall dare to say, and I shall say it, and I shall always profess it: It is greater the mercy one shows in tolerating constant iniquities than that [one has] in giving one's own blood one time *[silence] vidi Deum sedere super thronum magnum et elevatum*[22] *[silence]* seven and ten *[silence]* variety, yes, yes, *[silence]* varied of an equal variety *[silence]* 33 *[silence]* 40. First and all in unity. *Et procidentes adoraverunt Deum dicentes: Magnus Deus, magnus Deus, magnus Deus, in participatione gloriae suae, ad anime cum ipso, unite in desponsatione Verbis suis.*"

And after she spoke these words she was silent and dazed for a long while, and then she said: "But where do I leave Mary?"

And musing in this way a little, she showed that she was seeing the nuns under Mary's robe, as she had seen it other times; and they were not only under this robe, some of them were at her breast; and so she said: "All of them yes, and all do not fit under your robe, so some come out of it. But you keep your robe so large and open, that if they do not force themselves to be out of it, it will be hard for them to stay out of it. Oh, great benevolence, oh sweet mother. *[silence]* oh, oh, what a difference. Many of them are at the breast, others out of it. What mind will be ever able to do it? Mine no, unless you force me, so to speak, to understand."

Later we understood that she was praying for the nuns, both in general and in particular; and so she said: "You have actually said that you do not despise desires, and that you want to be prayed to. Now, listen to me, a wretched and miserable creature *[silence]* and what shelter is there? *[Silence]* a memory, a mind, a will, a desire, a passion, an intention, everything abandons itself to you, Word. And this abandonment is necessary *[silence]* oh Word, who will be able to thank you for the present you gave me? *[Silence]* only your blood will be able to to do this; and all the drops you shed will be voices thanking you. But I want to offer you all the drops of your blood, that you shed for me with such a burning love, in order to thank you for having married me."

And after these words, she remained quiet and dazed for a while. She came out of this rapture at about the third hour and thirty minutes, and then she went to rest quietly.

Let us always praise and thank the Lord.

Dialogue 43
The Regeneration of the Church

On Monday May 6, 1585, during her exercise, our blessed soul was suddenly called by the Lord with this address: "Come, my spouse, come, for now I want you to regenerate and renew the entire body of the holy church with my blood by offering me every state of my creatures. You must remain in this exercise the whole night until my minister comes to give you my holy Sacrament."

Immediately after this address she rushed to the room for the novices. When we found her, she was on her knees speaking the words: *"Ego sum."* And we heard her saying these words three times. Later, after keeping silent and engrossed for a while, she said: *"Vivo ego iam non ego,*[1] *sed vivit in Verbum caro, et sanguis Unionis Sponsi mei."*

And she repeated these words three times as well. She uttered the above words *(ego sum)* in the person of Jesus, and these others as herself: *"Et eduxit me de umbra mortis, et induxit anima mea in latitudine regenerationis humanae."*[2]

Then she shows that she has been called through the above invocation: "Oh Word, although this night will be short because I am with you, here on earth it is long. Please, give strength to my weak body, for my soul is ready *[silence]* tonight this brief exercise of mine, in which I shall offer you all the creatures again and again, will last until your minister, yes my Word, comes to bestow your body and your blood upon me; and although this offering is always the same, albeit in a different way, it will result in a perfect union with your blood."

Having spoken these words, after a short pause she became very upset, her face showing a great grief and sadness. And we understood that she was seeing the devil by the fact that she crossed herself and said many things against the devil and in defense of herself. For instance, she must have repeated *"Verbum caro factum est"* more than thirty times, pausing between one sentence and the other. She also said: *"Jesus Nazarenus Rex Judeorum"*;[3] and *"Sursum corda."*[4] Other times she crossed herself hastily, turning to every side. Other times she spoke to the devil with a great readiness to intimidate him: "Oh, you are strong aren't you? *[silence]* I myself am weak, but the Word is in me and the Word is stronger than you *[silence]* oh, I shall take the weapons of my Spouse's cross to defend myself." And she crossed herself all over her person. First, raising her hand she crossed herself on the forehead three times, then on the right side of her head three times, and on the left one three times as well. Then putting her hand on her eyes she crossed herself on each eye three times. She did the same thing on her ears, her mouth, her hands, and all her senses and members three times. She did the same on her breast; she crossed herself on her heart, not just three times but infinite times, if we consider that this first struggle lasted more than one hour. During this time she suffered every sort of temptation, but she defended herself bravely and despised and derided the devil by repeating *"Verbum caro factum est"* and other words. And now she spoke and now she kept silent.

And after the above words, crossing herself again she said: "And as a shield I will take those words: *In principio erat Verbum*, and *Verbum erat apud Deum*, and *Deus erat Verbum [silence]* oh what a multitude! Oh what horrible beasts! *[silence]* oh, oh, you ignorant, don't you see that I am with my Word? Don't you understand that you can't hurt me? *[silence]* oh why are you spying on me? If I come, I'll be there, I'll be with my Word. So, what do you have to say? *[silence]* don't you see that the more you try to hurt me the more I win? *[silence]* they try to stop my offering. Well, despite you I shall begin right now *[silence]* angels, archangels, thrones *et* dominations, *principatus et potestates* please come and help me."

At this point she became very happy, showing that all those tempting devils had left. The devils perceived that that night the offering of our blessed soul to the Lord would defeat them, and thus they attacked her vehemently because they did not want her to do it. And they did not attack her only at the beginning, but also every time she made a new offering. Once they attacked her in her faith, once in something else, as we shall see in the rest of this rapture.

Sometimes they tempted her with vanity, sometimes with pride. And the more she acquired new souls for the Lord, the more they assaulted her; she always fought against them with a great fortitude, beating them and sending them away from her. As soon as she had defeated them, she resumed her offering. She dispelled the devils twice with her discipline.[5] The first time she was on her knees for a long time, hitting with her discipline here and there vehemently, with such a swiftness and vigor that it was amazing to look at her; the other time she walked through the whole oratory hitting with her discipline everywhere and on the benches with a zeal, I believe, similar to Jesus', when he overturned the temple. And then, hiding in the same place, she quietly resumed her offering, and as soon as she was done with one offering she had one of those fights, and after a fight and conflict with the devil she started to make a new offer. And she continued the whole night in this way. The devils interrupted her first offering three times: at the beginning, in the middle, and at the end, but she always defeated them.

And continuing her first offering, she said: "*Offeram a teipsum omnem creaturam in unionem Sanguinis tui [silence]* I want to offer you every creature, according to their personal condition; but I want to begin with your virgin spouses, who please you so much and are closer to me."

She meant us, the nuns of this convent. "*In principio erat Verbum*, and *Verbum erat apud Deum*, and *Deus erat Verbum [silence]* in the beginning and before time you elected them and pre-elected them *[silence]* you have elected and pre-elected them so that they lead the elect to you, I mean the creatures, for every creature was elected when you shed your blood. You have elected every nun, but not every nun has been pre-elected, because not all of them do what you requested at the moment of their election *[silence]* others, like these ones next to me, are where your Christ is. You have pre-elected these ones so that they take you the souls redeemed by your blood."

She meant our Capuchin sisters in Rome. She has seen many times how devoted they are to God and give a great help to the holy church. This blessed soul knows them in general and in particular, even though she has never met them. Nevertheless she sees and knows what they lack and what they abound with, I mean, as far as their spiritual and not worldly life is concerned. She is very fond of them, and often remembers them in her prayers, as she clearly shows in this rapture. Continuing her offer she said:

"I offer you those who fight under Mary's protection and also those who belong to your seraphic Francis. I dare to say that both of us are unique. And I say this even though I shouldn't say it. They overcome us with their poverty, and we overcome them with our union; they have poverty in affection and in effect, but we [have it] more in desire than in effect *[silence]* thus I offer you, Word, one of these and one of those. I shall accompany one from the order of Mary and one with the hood of St. Francis. And I shall place this couple, coming from each order, at the beginning of this solemn procession. And all the others will follow, your youngest ones finally closing the procession. I recommend them to you. Please, help them persevere in the purity and integrity of your observance. Oh Word, I recommend to you in particular those who are under Mary's mantle, I mean, both those who are there now and those who are about to come; and I also pray to you for those you committed to my custody. Please, give them light. And for all of them I ask you for a perfect patience. Give them a spark of your light necessary to them, so that they can see and understand that not only have you elected them, you have also pre-elected them to lead the souls to you."

She looked very upset, showing that the devils were coming to tempt her again. Thus she said:

"Oh Word, please help me, they're coming back *[silence]* *Verbum caro factum est* *[silence]* oh Word, send them away please *[silence]* *sursum corda* *[silence]* what do you gain by doing that? *[silence]* oh stupid and ignorant, what do you think you're doing? You're hurting yourself! *[silence]* don't you see that the others are gone? And you are so defiant to come up to me. Don't you see that my Word is defending me? *[silence]* go, go! *[silence]* oh Word, make them understand how fertile is the spark of your light *[silence]* and now I put all your pre-elected spouses into your divine side, next to your heart, because this is where they must settle their nest and their safe and comforting cell."

At this point she spoke up with a sweet and marvelous contentment, because she saw the pre-elected spouses entering Jesus' side in pairs. She said: "Oh what a wonderful procession! Who ever saw more beautiful couples of doves? One with the vestment of Mary, the other with the hood. Oh, they enter so beautifully!"

And keeping quiet for a while, with a happy smile on her face as if she were feeling an immense joy, at once she became upset again, looking very sad. With an angry voice she said: "Well, yes, yes, we started! And? Yes, I am coming too, I'll be there. The Word will be with me *[silence]* don't you see I'm in heaven? Why do you want to pull me down? *[silence]* well, yes. If they want me to, I'll be there. Oh *[silence]* don't you see I'm dressed with blood? And you still want to take me down? *Verbum caro factum est [silence]* well, this time you were not opposed. *In nomine Jesu omne genuflectatur, coelestium, terrestrium,* and *infernorum*[6] despite you."

Then she crossed over the devils. And crossing herself, she said: "Now I have crossed over you, do you want to cross over me?" And she crossed herself on her forehead, her heart, and her whole body three times, repeating *"Verbum caro factum est."* And after having fought against the devils for a while, she left the place where she was on her knees, I mean, the left side of the oratory next to the altar, and went to the right side in front of the altar where she usually stays when she enters a rapture.

And it seemed to us that she was acting like St. Catherine of Siena, when she wanted to escape the devils that tormented her in that place. Sitting down on a bench of the oratory, she said with a very tranquil voice:

"Oh amorous Word and sweet and pure Spouse, they were so envious that they couldn't stand the fact that you were infusing that spark of light. Although they are ignorant, nonetheless they knew that a great fruit would come out of that *[silence]* but, oh Word, please infuse, infuse it, for even if they don't receive it all they'll receive part of it *[silence]* the soul rejoice, the heart be happy, the mind sing *[silence] offero sponsi mei electae suae*[7] *[silence]* my Word, now I want to offer you your elect, who are also your spouses. However, even though they have been elected, they neither know nor understand their election, let alone their pre-election, because they don't keep the promises they have made to you, Word *[silence]* for this reason I want to pray to you so that you enlighten them about their

139

duties; and for them I offer you the blood you shed in the kitchen garden with such a deep agony, that you were compelled to speak those troubled and anguished words: *'Tristis est anima mea usque ad mortem' [silence]* but, oh Word, those little ones who have been placed there, I wish I could take them out of there with my own hands! *[silence]* oh Word, I want to speak to you the way you spoke to us: oh Word, I tell you, thousand times I would give my life if I could get thousand of them, and I would go among them and, if I only could, help them know how evil they are; and I wouldn't care if they considered me insane and stupid. And if they considered me a devil, I would scream until they hear me. And I wish justice preceded me, so that they couldn't say that they did it out of ignorance and because they didn't understand it. Oh, how many go to hell, and if some of them are saved it's only thanks to your generosity! Oh, I wish I could show one of them who she really is and take her there among those ones to show her how horrible she is. I wish I could, so that if they don't want to do it for love at least they'll do it out of fear and awe.

"Oh Word, what shall I say of your Christs? They degrade their greatness so much, that you make me see many of them commit so many abominable sins and thus debase their bodies. And dishonoring you, others become slaves of creatures who are much more corrupt and inferior than them. And may I say more? They follow the most ignorant and rebellious creatures, and become slaves of the most abominable and ignominious things, like those who starve longing for a bit of mud *[silence]* those eyes that see you, Word, coming down and descending from the bosom of the eternal Father, those eyes also commit so many deadly sins and even go to the altar with those deadly sins. Oh God, oh Word, how can you tolerate them? *[silence]* how many are they, how many! I can't even count them all. How many in the past, how many in the present time! I wish they wouldn't come in the future *[silence]* they hear innumerable curses, but they don't reprove them at all. And what does it mean to give one's own life for the sake of truth? Didn't the holy John do this? And when they don't reprove these curses they show that they don't find them evil *[silence]* oh Word, I won't leave from this place where I'm with you and with them until I see at least one of them being enlightened. I don't ask you, Word, to enlighten all of them, because I don't deserve to be responded to. Don't respond to me, since I am too proud, but to your blood. You cannot fail to respond to yourself. Word, respond, respond to your blood *[silence]* oh eternal Father, move, move that love that moved you to show us your communication in creating the angelic spirits; and if this doesn't move you, move for that love that moved you to create the entire human kind, among those I am myself, ungrateful and unthankful. Oh Father, move also for that love that moved you to send your Word to recreate the creature by shedding his precious blood; and he shed it for me too, ungrateful and unthankful creature *[silence]* Word, I offer you the profound act of humility you performed in descending from heaven to earth into the womb of the Virgin Mary; and [I offer you] also the meekness you showed in letting the Virgin nourish you. In this way you showed that you needed help like us, poor creatures. Oh Mary, if they are not willing to receive the light, please open them to the Word, so that he can infuse it into them *[silence]* oh Word, I shall never leave you, and won't offer you the other creatures unless you grant me your grace and enlighten some of your Christs *[silence]* oh Word, punish me for their faults; and since my weakness cannot sustain their great ignorance, make me die as many times as your justice requires it *[silence]* oh my Spouse, I want it for some of them; please show me what I am supposed to do. Whatever it is, I'll do it *[silence]* I offer you all the blood that you shed in your circumcision, in your agonizing prayer in the kitchen garden, and that [blood] you shed at the column, and in your passion *[silence]* all your deeds during your thirty-three years among us, and all you did and suffered in all your life, passion, and death *[silence]* oh Word, I offer you the sweet and tender love you had for your holy Mother, and I also offer you the love she had for you, along with your holy merit and privileges *[silence]* oh Father, I offer you the blood of every martyr in union with the Word's blood *[silence]* I also offer the wisdom, constancy, the words, and the toil of every holy doctor in union with the Word's blood. I offer you every fasting, penitence, and fortitude of the hermits against every temptation, in union with the Word's blood *[silence]* I offer you every desire, tear, prayer, and devotion of the holy confessors, in union with the Word's blood *[silence]* I offer you the purity, beauty, and union of the virgins in union with the Word's blood; in a word I offer you every merit and deed of every creature, the humility, obedience, charity, patience, mercy, and virtue of all your elect, in union with the Word's blood.

"Oh, oh, oh, I've called for so long, I've invoked for so long, and I've offered so much, that I see some of your Christs, oh Word, being enlightened, although only a few *[silence]* oh Word, how powerful is this blood! *[silence]* and who could ever thank you? I offer you this blood of yours to thank you for your blood. This blood thanks itself, is pleased with itself, and glories in itself. But I won't be content until I see myself burning with a perfect desire for your creatures, I mean, a perfect desire to lead them to you, Word. *Desiderium animarum tuarum comedit me.*"[8]

At once she became upset. Then she said: "Yell, scream as much as you want, come on, you only increase your own affliction *[silence]* and you won't be able to catch me here; I know that I have been made out of earth and shall nourish worms; I would be worse if I weren't united with my Word." Here she showed that she was being tempted with vainglory. And after keeping silent for a moment, at once she revived with a great impetus and said: "*Verbum caro factum est [silence] ego sum vermis* and *non homo.*"[9]

And taking out her discipline from her side, like a zealous judge she stood up and started hitting here and there, showing that she was hitting the devils whom she saw tempting her. And they tempted her, but she continued to hit with her discipline for the duration of three Misereri. Then, she went back to her seat looking very tired. After a short while she said: "I acknowledge that my being is a nothingness, and that if I were not united with my Word, I would be worse than the devil *[silence]* yes, either in heaven or on earth, or in hell, wherever I am thanks to my Word's generosity *[silence]* please, my soul, resume your offer. That who has given the strength to make the first and the second, will give it to make the third too *[silence] offeram Verbo meo animas omnium credentium, quae requiescunt in tabernaculo Sponsae tuae ecclesiae [silence]* oh, how much malice, how much arrogance, how much ingratitude, how much pride, and how much ignorance lie in this estimable tabernacle! *[silence]* and like Noah's ark which contained so many different sorts of animals, pure and impure ones, bad and mediocre ones, your church as well, Word, has pure and impure animals, good, bad, and mediocre ones *[silence]* and for these ones, given that they are infinite, I offer you the infinite drops of the blood you shed so copiously when you were hit at the column; and as you shed it from every member of your body, I offer it to you for every member of the holy church, governed by you and whose members are your creatures. But Word, my love, I wish I had some from each [member] *[silence] in patientia vestra possidebitis animas vestras*[10] *[silence] beati qui esuriunt* and *sitiunt iustitiam quoniam ipsi saturabuntur*[11] *[silence] conserva me Domine quoniam in desiderio animarum consumavit anima mea*[12] *[silence] collocavi me in desiderio, Verbo meo, quem ipse habuit in humanitatis suae*[13] *[silence] custodivit desiderium quem dedit mihi Verbo meo, quia si non invenerit in me possibilitate, inveniat tamen desiderium*[14] *[silence] beatus qui tenebit* and *allidet parvulos suos ad petram*[15] *[silence]* oh when shall I be able to say with all my desires and feelings: *In exitu Israel de Egypt!*[16] But I believe that sooner I'll be able to say in the name of the multitude: '*Super flumina Babylonis illic sedimus* and *flevimus dum recordaremur tui Sion*'[17] *[silence] considerabam ad dexteram* and *videbam,*[18] and *non erat qui impleret desiderium animae meae*[19] *[silence] supra dorsum meum fabricaverunt*[20] *desiderium salute omnium credentium Verbi mei*[21] *[silence]* oh Word, your blood will compel you. And what will it compel you to do? What else but to achieve the salvation of every creature believing in you, Word? *[silence]* your useless and unusable servant would like to compel the Almighty, but she should be able to say: '*cum essem parvula placui Altissimo,*'[22] as they say about your Mother *[silence]* I see the Word bend and kiss his spouse as the bridegroom does, but they step back as blind people do when they sense that someone is coming up to them. Since they're blind, they can't tell whether the person approaching them will bring them good or evil *[silence]* my Word's blood is nothing but a magnet drawing the souls toward himself *[silence]* my Word's blood bends the tree of life, as a tree does when heavy fruits bend its branches down *[silence]* oh Word, your blood is also a snare that deceives your power and your wisdom, and [it deceives] also our ignorant knowledge, for as soon as it wishes to ascend it encounters your blood and recognizes its ignorance *[silence]* but even though I see and recognize before your goodness that every creature in your church steps back when you bend before her, nonetheless I see that your blood is so powerful that it is a press squeezing grapes and sending out sweet wine. Similarly, oh Word, your blood presses your power to send out your love, which is your mercy. You make such a great use of your mercy for all your creatures, that many times they misuse it. Oh, how devastating can your mercy be! You may rightly say: *"Conversa es in amaritudinem vitis aliena"*[23] *[silence]* when the thirsty soul is willing to offer this blood it may rightly say: *'Crastina die delebitur iniquitas,'*[24] because as soon as it has made its offer every iniquity is removed from every creature and from every heart."

At this point she was shown that by having offered and continuing to offer the Word's blood, some creatures had converted to the Lord and iniquities had been removed from some hearts. And in particular, as we shall clarify later, at that point she sensed that the mind of some priests had been enlightened. Thus she continued as follows: "Oh Word, what don't you answer, why don't you work, why don't you consume, why don't you make us taste hell and lose our life, so that we could appease your Father's wrath at least in part? *[silence]* to have no pain gives me a great pain *[silence] vidi videre assumere ab inimicis animam sponsae suae*[25] *[silence] et collustrare* some of your Christs."[26]

And at this point she looked vexed, showing that she was seeing the devils coming to fight with her. She went up to them very bravely, saying:

"Were there more in hell? Yes, of course. But see, I shall defend myself with the weapon I fought with, and shall fight against you with the weapon I defended myself with *[silence] Verbum caro factum est* (three times). Oh, don't you know that when a stronger one arrives he takes the weapons and disrobes him who had all the strength, and overcomes him and defeats him? *[silence]* I proclaim, I have proclaimed, and I shall always proclaim that what the holy church shows us is the true and Catholic faith. And if I became eternal in this world without any vision, I shall always proclaim that I believe in the holy Trinity, and that there is one sole God who created heaven and earth *[silence]* and if you want me to say it I shall, but you're going to suffer even more *[silence] credo in unum Deum."* And she said this with a great austerity; and after that she kept quiet for a long time. Indicating that Jesus was pleased with her immensely and that he was showing her his goodness, she said with a great happiness and relief: "Oh Word, how great is your contentment! *[silence]* it overcomes [your] goodness and also the malice of your enemies, who'd like to hinder your working!"

And turning to the devils, she spoke to them with a great vehemence:

"Oh, do you believe that his blood is useless? You are wrong. You are really mistaken."

Although on one side she saw Jesus being pleased with her greatly, on the opposite side she saw the devils. Thus she said: "And what do you want? If I had thousand tongues, I would proclaim it with all of them. And since I am weak by myself, I ask you all, blessed spirits, to proclaim it for me *[silence]* oh think about it, if my soul were about to abandon my body, what would you do? *[silence]* oh, if your strength increased, my Spouse's power and fortitude would increase as well. Don't you know it? Everything is present in my Spouse, and I myself am present to him. Do you have something to say about it? *[silence]* well, if you suffer, you see your loss yourself. I believe, I believe in everything my mother church believes in. Go, go, ask her [the church] *[silence]* and keep in mind that my Spouse is always with me, and he is powerful *et dextera illius amplexabitur me*[27] *[silence]* oh, he created heaven and earth, and hell too, besides heaven and earth, and [he created] you too, with all your followers, although you made yourself unworthy *[silence]* oh, oh, and he created everything that is, was, and could ever be, yes, yes *[silence]* no, no, leave the others and come to me because, although you don't let me spend my time as I'd like to, I'm sure that I won't give in since my Word is with me. But I am not sure about the others. Leave, leave the others alone *[silence]* and if she was a Virgin, she was what she was, God knows, and I myself know that too. Go now, I don't want to waste my time with you *[silence]* you think you can confound me. Go ahead, but my Word will confound you in me *[silence]* oh, here we go, three Persons but one essence: God the Father, God the Son, and God the Holy Spirit. Yes, yes, what could you possibly say now?"

145

She looked very tired. Her face was swollen and sweaty, and she was gasping as if she could not breathe any more. And turning to her sweet Spouse the Word she told him: "Oh my Spouse Word, you are in me and I am in you. Oh good Jesus, why don't you help me?" And very sorrowful and anguished she said many times: "Oh good Jesus, oh good Jesus, Jesus *Nazarenus Rex Iudeorum [silence] sursum corda! Habemus ad desiderium salutem animarum omnium credentium.*"[28]

And after speaking these words three times, with a great vehemence she stood up and grasped the discipline that she had used the other time, and going around the oratory she struck everywhere with that, more scrupulously than the previous time. And she did this for quite a while. Then, going back to her place, she sat down anxious and exhausted. And after a short pause she said:

"Oh Word, oh my soul, oh my anxious mind, please, let us resume our offering *[silence]* Word, now I shall focus on your believers. My enemy tried to prevent me from doing this, I mean, he tried to take your holy faith out of my heart so that I wouldn't be among your believers. I also see the blood of my Spouse and my soul's life being questioned *[silence]* oh Word, I see so many, so many rejecting your blood, but I also see that many accept it, and this makes me feel blessed and dejected. After this, oh Word, I offer you the multitude of the miserable and wretched ones who don't know you and worship their enemy as their god, leaving you, their Father and Lord, friend, brother, and advocate. *Advocatus habemus apud Patrem.*[29] However, your goodness is so great, that you deign to give them as their defenders those noble spirits that serve you and that, if they could suffer, would have a great pain, seeing their constant losses. I make this offer both with happiness and sorrow. With happiness for those who receive it, and with sorrow for the multitude of those who don't want to receive it. But what blood shall I offer for these ones to the undivided Trinity, so that It will be merciful toward them? For, since they deride and ridicule you, I offer you what you, despised and ridiculed, were forced to shed (albeit willingly), I mean what you shed from your venerable head, when they made you wear that piercing crown of thorns *[silence]* the love that moved you to create them, this same love moves you to infuse your light in them. I know that you never miss to infuse it, but they don't receive it. And what is the reason? My ingratitude. I acknowledge that, because of my misery and ingratitude, all my offerings of your blood are not offerings, but rather withdrawals *[silence]* yes, Word, I know my ingratitude, but I am unable to penetrate it fully *[silence]* *quod vidi, quod audivi, univit me in unione Sanguinis tui [silence] omnia per omnia*, and *in ipso omnia*[30] *[silence]* oh, I am so unhappy and too happy. Unhappy for my ingratitude *[silence]* oh, my ingratitude causes every evil! *[silence]* punish me for every offence. Oh, I am a miserable wretch, for I am the cause of every evil and ingratitude *[silence]* as a result of their ingratitude they deny themselves the milk of your divinity, the fruits of your humanity, the wine of your eternity, the vestment of your essence *[silence]* I wish I were not, and now I wish I had an infinite being; I wish I were powerless, and now I wish I could have everything. I wish I were despised, and now I wish I were extolled; for if I could I'd take them all and lead them to the womb of your holy church. And I'd like the church to purge them of their sinfulness with its pure breath, like a mother with her children. And then [I'd like the church] to offer them its sweet and pure breast to nourish them with the sweet milk of its sacraments. Oh how wonderfully the church would nourish and nurse them with its breast! Oh, if I could, I would do it myself, but I can only be sorrowful about myself, for my ingratitude and ignorance are the sole causes of my being incapable *[silence]* *montes exultaverunt ut arietes* and *colles sicut agni ovium.*"[31]

And she spoke these words because she saw that some infidels had been enlightened and were coming to our faith, rejoicing like rams and lambs. And although, as she said above, she was unable to lead them because of her ingratitude and ignorance, nonetheless the Lord had relieved her frailty and had responded to her. Thus she said: "Your goodness is so great that you never fail to respond to your creatures' wishes, ignoring their nothingness and baseness. As a discreet Father [you follow] them and adjust to their steps, as a father adjusts to the small steps of his little ones. *Adesit pavimento anima mea, vivifica me secundum verbum tuum.*"[32]

She meant that the Lord revives, that is, he responds to those who humble themselves.

"Oh amorous Word, how great is your generosity *[silence]* you let your blood, which descends from your head crowned with thorns, descend over these dark beings, so that it can enlighten their darkness."

At this point she kept silent for a while, considering that, even though we have the gift of faith, we still have sin and thus must work hard if we want his grace and obtain a victory for ourselves and the others. And she said: "And as your holy apostle John says: Who says that he has never sinned is a liar and no truth is in him;[33] and Saint Paul: *Non coronabitur nisi qui legitime certaverit.*"[34]

She showed that she had finished her offering for the infidels and that now she was looking at every sinner in order to offer them to the Lord, along with all the other members of the holy church. And she said: "*Respice de coelo et vide*[35] *omnes errantes in via sua, non est quid faciat bonum, non est usque ad unum*[36] *[silence]* but, oh Father, what must we do to move you to pity for them? *[silence]* oh, what must we do? We must do as those who want to catch a beast or a bird. They bend a strong bow with a big ball or arrow inside, according to what they aim to catch. Then they take aim, bending the bow with all their strength. In this way they catch it. We must do the same; we must take the strong bow that the Word has bent toward us, I mean, the holy cross *[silence]* and what shall I use as a ball or arrow? Oh, I shall keep your word and your promises, and shall remind you of them; and I shall aim at your bosom, Father, where my prey lies, I mean, my Word; and from your bosom I shall also take your mercy, because outside your bosom everything is justice *[silence]* my aim will be my pure and right intention, for we must bend this bow with the wound of faith and the hand of charity and [we must] aim at you only, so that you, as if dead, can be captured and be merciful toward those poor sinners *[silence]* yes, if we need something strong, my Word's cross is very strong *[silence]* but what do you think I shall do once I capture you in this way? I shall feed on you, Word. But why do I say that I'll feed on you? I won't be the only one to feed on you, because otherwise I would become hungrier and sadder. I intend to nourish my neighbors more than myself, depriving myself of you for the sake of them if it is necessary."

148

And after a pause, she showed that Jesus was telling her that it was good to deprive oneself of his consolation for the sake of others. She responded to him as follows: "Yes, of course in your house it is better to be poor for the sake of you and of our neighbors, than to abound *[silence] elegi abiectus esse in domo tua*[37] *[silence] magis quam abundare propter te, Verbo meo.*"

And after these words she became sad again, indicating that she was seeing the devils tempting her. Keeping silent and somber for a while, she said:

"Oh Word *[silence]* you do things with a great wisdom, although since I'm ignorant I can't understand them. I don't think that my being exposed to this horde is senseless. You know its meaning *[silence]* and if I'm alone and you are legions, you'll be able to do only what my Spouse will allow you to; be sure of that *[silence] Verbum caro factum est [silence]* but I tell you that from now on I shall answer you with these words only: '*Verbum caro factum est.*'"

And this is what she did, crossing herself repeatedly and whispering many times: "*Verbum caro factum est.*" And after doing this for a while, all of a sudden she stood up straight and spoke these words with fervor: "*Et signavit me signaculum vitae.*" And she crossed herself on her forehead three times, and on her mouth, her heart, and then on both eyes. And when she crossed herself on her ears she said: "Oh, I'm the spouse of generosity. *Verbum caro factum est.*" Then she crossed herself on both hands, with the right hand she made the sign of the cross on the left hand, and with the left hand she did it on the right one, always repeating "*Verbum caro factum est.*" And in a similar way she crossed herself on her breast three times, repeating the same words. Then she crossed herself three more times as everyone usually does, still saying "*Verbum caro factum est.*"

Then she stopped, keeping quiet for a long while. During this time she felt very melancholy and exhausted. However, it looked like Jesus was with her and consoled her by showing her how triumphant were her battles against the devils for the sake of the soul of every believer and of every member of the holy church; and he showed her how deeply she pleased him and satisfied him. Thus she spoke these words: "*Quemadmodum desiderat cervus ad fontes aquarum, ita desiderat anima mea*[38] *liberalitate tua in comunicatione sponse tua* and *omnium credentium [silence]* I confess this to you, Word, but please don't reveal it."

She meant that she wished that the devils did not realize how generous he was toward her by communicating himself to her for her sake and for the sake of every believer. I mean his blood, that she offered for the creatures so that the devils would not be able to attack her any more. But when she realized that she had to hide from the devils, she said: "Oh amorous Word, one can hide in your side also. I know that I shall go in there, and they will go back to their dwellings confused. In this way I shall be able to bring my offer to an indisputable conclusion *[silence]* oh, how beautifully you build your dwelling. Oh, both the right side and the left one."

And raising her eyes all of a sudden, this blessed soul showed such a happy and beautiful face, that we could not get tired of staring at her. And she said:

"Oh amorous Word and glorious Spouse, now that your enemies have left I'll be able to resume my offer. And what shall I offer you, Word? *[silence]* oh, oh, I shall offer you those who are, so to speak, so horrible and numerous that I am not sure I'll be able to count them all. You are the one who knows them all. I mean those incarnate devils, the heretics; and for them I shall offer you the blood you shed when you were on the mount Calvary to be crucified. For they try their best to ruin and destroy your vestment, tearing it into pieces and damaging it with their poisonous words and deeds *[silence]* they constantly try to usurp your glory and your honor. And for that cursed woman, [who is] worse than Jezebel,[39] I do not intend to pray, because I have neither hope nor interest in her convertion. I rather hope that she will be annihilated, for she seems to be rejected by you. But I do want to pray to you for the others; that you may show them their faults and thus lead them back to you *[silence]* I pray you in the name of your love, that regenerated them through your blood. Only your blood can reunite them with you *[silence]* but in making this offer, I should be totally free of what is inside of me, I mean, my ingratitude, arrogance, and pride. Oh, how much purity, humility, and self-negation this offer requires! *[silence]* those who try to take away the fine gold of your divinity by denying this or that thing. And others with their infected tongues claim that thanks to your sacrifice they have no duties. You did sacrifice yourself for everybody, but we must respond to you with our workings. Some others deny your power, by failing to obey to your Christs on earth, to whom you gave the power of opening and closing heaven. Others deny your generosity, by repudiating your holy sacraments and the gift of your flesh and blood. And others are immersed in thousands of errors, to that point that our souls should be like turtle doves, constantly mourning and lamenting their blindness. And although we can't succeed by ourselves, through our incessant persistency they would be able to give birth to themselves again and again; once they would give birth to themselves in their own being, I mean, in the being you, God, gave to them *[silence] exurgat Deus* and *dissipentur inimici eius et fugiant qui oderunt cum a facie eius*[40] *[silence] non dormitavit neque dormiet qui custodit Israel*[41] *[silence] congratulamini mihi omnes qui diligitis eum.*"[42]

And at this point through the above and the following words she indicated that she was seeing some heretics being enlightened: "When you, Word, divested yourself on the mount Calvary you shed you blood and the virtue of your divinity. But now, when we divest ourselves of ourselves, you shed the ointment of your mercy: *Unguentum effusum nomen tuum.*[43] Oh, we should divest ourselves of our pride and of ourselves, because in so doing we acquire so much both for ourselves and for others."

Later, after a pause, she showed that she was seeing a multitude of heretics rejecting the blood that had been offered to them and refusing to convert. Thus she said: "*Dilexerunt maleditionem et veniet eis, noluerunt benedictionem et elongabitur ab eis*[44] *[silence]* oh Word, yes, it's true that when you let us meet you in our childhood and youth you give us a great gift, because those who have offended you have a great difficulty in going back to you *[silence]* yes, yes, there are two chains. One is out of the purest gold, the other is out of the heaviest lead *[silence]* oh, how important is to listen to your inspiration and follow your inner arrow."

And she said the above things considering the harshness of those heretics who did not want to repent, even though God himself tried to move them with the offer of his blood. Then she continued:

"Why do they fail to penetrate the glory and the punishment expecting them and [why do] their heart become so hard and blind? *[silence]* oh, those who stop seeking you and themselves pass from one error to another, from error to sin, from sin to malice, from malice to iniquity, and then fall into the chasm of hell; and down there *in inferno nulla est redentio*,[45] and in heaven [is] eternal glory. God always makes them perceive what glory and punishment are in there. And as he makes the sun rise over the just and the wicked, he always sends his light over everyone and shows his mercy to everyone, but they don't want to receive it *[silence]* you pick roses among thorns."

Showing a great happiness because she saw some heretics coming back to their true light: *"Vidi Deum sedere super thronum magnum* and *elevatum*[46] *[silence]* but what act does my Word carry out from that throne? No one can understand it *[silence]* now I see that his sole act is to constantly offer himself to the eternal Father, giving him this present along with his other infinite members *[silence]* the sun penetrates the heart making it blossom less than the Word's offering penetrates the idea of the Father's essence and makes him generate deeds of compassion, mercy, and love *[silence]* but the time will come when the Spouse will take the power for a short while, I mean even if he is still there, and will condemn and elect *[silence]* then he will come for the sweetest time for those who long for him and have chosen him in their pilgrimage, which will manifest your act; and they will have glory and eternity. And those who are thirsty will be satisfied with a satisfaction that will make them thirsty forever; and these ones will glorify and praise my Spouse the Word forever *[silence]* but the miserable and wretched ones deprive themselves of this good because they waver in their faith for you *[silence]* oh Word, how can I possibly stand seeing a creature, created and molded by you, separate from you, supreme good, and from your blood?"

And after these words, all of a sudden she lowered her eyes, looking very upset and anguished. For she saw the devils again. Thus, as usual, she said:

"*Verbum caro factum est [silence] non nobis Domine, non nobis [silence]* he thinks that I'll pride myself on my nonbeing and weakness *[silence]* yes, you'd like to hide me in hell. *Verbum caro factum est [silence] Verbum caro factum est [silence]* don't you know that my Word is aware of everything? You can't judge me. *Verbum caro factum est [silence] per aspersionem Sanguinis Domini nostri Jesu Christi [silence] Jesus Nazarenus Rex Iudeorum [silence] non nobis Domine non nobis, sed nomini tuo da gloria*[47] *[silence]* no, you'd like to gag me and then put me to death *[silence]* you think I wish to take the glory away from my Word. Don't you know that, if I were like him, I would abandon my being to give it to him? I would like thousands of thousands of thousands, and a thousand millions of thousands to repeat these same words: '*Non nobis, Domine, non nobis, sed nomini tuo da gloria.*'"

And after these words she crossed herself three times and stood up with a great enthusiasm. Stretching her arm, she said:

"In virtue of the Word's blood and in virtue of the Father's essence, I demand that you leave from here."

And sitting down, she became very happy indicating that all the devils had left; and I am convinced that they left very confused because they could not achieve any form of victory. Thus that night they did not disturb her. And until the morning she continued this rapture with a great liveliness, gentleness, and contentment. And speaking to her amorous Spouse the Word, she spoke these sweet words:

"Oh my amorous and sweet Spouse Word, you rule over heaven and earth; you confound everyone and send your enemies away. I myself am weak, extremely weak; and if one had their same power one would be able to defeat them. But you, Word, with a brief glance you send them away like a tiny grain in the wind. But before doing that you let them fight with your servants. The more you want to enlighten them, and thus to make them able to understand you, the more you make furnaces and fires, where they get purged and more precious and pure stones are produced. For the time being, they'll be staying in their dwellings *[silence] in columna nubis loquebatur ad eos*[48] *[silence]* in your fortress you grant us the power to fight; and those who want to battle for your glory in a forceful way, must go down still being in heaven in order not to be confounded *[silence]* now, amorous Word, although a lot should be done to regenerate and renew the body of your holy church—and this is why you called me at the beginning—, nonetheless, since I do want to understand something about you, now I am not going to examine all the others but I shall focus on those blessed souls of purgatory who are shut up, so to speak, in a prison. But blessed be those who go down there, and blessed me if I eventually go down there. But since I have offered all the other members of the holy Church to the Father, and to you too, Word, now I want to offer this only to you, immensely pure and simple Word. I shall imagine that you are a janitor, for when a janitor of some grand palace lets someone in, the Lord, I mean the lord of the palace does not prevent those who have been let in by the janitor from living in his palace, primarily when they share the same will. And what shall I offer you for these people? Oh, I shall offer you Mary's white and red, red and white milk. And her breasts will be like two springs from which milk will flow down to these blessed souls, cooling down the flames and nourishing them with milk, which will soothe their constant thirst for your vision. And you, Word, sending also your blood to them, will adorn them with it and attract them to you. Thus we'll be able to say *[silence]* and what? *[silence]* and *procidentes adoraverunt eas dicentes: Iste sunt dignae accipere aspersionem Sanguinis Verbi [silence]* this blood adorns these blessed souls as spring adorns flowers and boughs."

And at this point Jesus showed her that he was sprinkling his blood over these souls, as she had asked him to. Thus she showed a great happiness and contentment, saying: *"Laetabitur iustus cum viderit iustitia*[49] *[silence] laetabitur sponsa cum viderit aspersionem Sanguinis Verbi sui [silence]* oh, oh, oh! *[silence]* oh generous you are!" Being engrossed and motionless, she indicated that she saw these souls ascending to heaven. Then, becoming very happy with her eyes shining like two stars, she said:

"Oh my beloved and precious Spouse, [who is] known and perceived only by you and understood (I mean the whole of it) only by you, oh, you generate in the body of the holy church (forgive my poor saying) as Mary generated you, Word. For when we offer you all the members of your church, with your blood you form a well-organized and well-disposed body of which you are the head and whose beauty the angels enjoy, the archangels admire, the seraphim love, all the angelic spirits cherish, and all the blessed souls of the celestial land feed on! *[silence]* oh, oh, and what does the holy Trinity do? What does it do? It is pleased by it in a way that we can't fathom. And although this body has rotten and stale members, what does the wise Spouse do? He sends them there to a corner, and makes it sure that they do not sully this well-organized body. But the time will come when, if they want to, he will call them all back to him, but if they don't want to *mittet eos in caminum ignis.*[50]

"The eyes of this well-organized body are your Christs because, as the eyes see everything and are so noble that a minimum thing can offend them and are able to distinguish what is good from what is evil *[silence]* so are your Christs so noble that a minimum flaw offends their greatness and purity, even a venial and minimum sin, because their brilliance is as tender as the eye's. They must see everything, I mean, the creatures' deepest needs, and must be able to distinguish good from evil, and to know the difference between sin and nonsin, and before absolving someone must be sure of what they are doing.

"They must take care of their cattle, which is the eye's cover, and lead it toward the right path. And moreover, as the eyebrow over the pupil defends [it] from evil, so must they watch over their love, and protect them against their enemies the devils, and against every evil and danger that they may face. For they are entitled to know the soul's dangers and protect it from them.

"The ears of this body are the contemplatives. While they are contemplating you, they listen to your sweet and persuasive voice, and fathom your secrets insofar as you are willing to disclose them. Then they communicate them to the others. And these people are those who come to you with a total honesty and sincerity, leaving aside any deception. And you manifest yourself to them according to their capability of receiving you; and you let them perceive the essence of your Divinity according to their capability. Yes, yes, Word!

"And what are the hands of this body? They are your holy virgins: *per manum sponsae tuae venerunt signa* and *prodigia magna in unione Divinitatis tuae*[51] *[silence] vidi Mariam sedere super naviculam*[52] *[silence]* but doesn't this mean that you govern and crown virginity? *[silence]* this ship doesn't fear any wave *[silence]* its sail is truth, its sailor is intelligence, its rudder is mercy. Will it fear the winds? Certainly not. They can be as strong as they wish; the temptations as powerful and great as they wish, they will be able neither to over-whelm it nor to sink it *[silence]* Mary is surrounded by sixty-three unicorns, and under her feet are seven little lions *[silence]* she is dressed with ermine. She doesn't keep it for herself, no, she gives it to her maids, every time they want it *[silence]* precious stones, of a similar purple, are woven into her mantle. The horns of six deer hold this mantle *[silence]* three little eagles carry and guard Mary's ring *[silence]* twenty-four Seraphim hold her crown *[silence]* thirty-three little bears carry and give her the chain to tie and to embrace her maids spouses *[silence]* oh, and these little bears look like evil! *[silence]* and sixteen doves give her and hold her bracelets to sanctify her maids' deeds *[silence]* hundred turtle-doves carry her belt to for-tify and embellish the spouses, her maids *[silence] millia milium* are approaching, I mean, an infinite number of lambs; some of them are very strong, some others less strong, and some very weak *[silence]* a great multitude of wild wolves is approaching. They start fighting and opposing the lambs, and devour the weak ones. They oppose the less strong ones. However, although they have bites and open wounds, nevertheless they defeat the wolves. They fight against the strongest ones. Not only are the wolves defeated, they are subju-gated and crushed *[silence]* the wolves thus turn to the spouses, try-ing to take away from them the benediction and fortitude they have received from Mary *[silence]* but what does she do to defend her maids? *[silence]* she does what the strong David did. She holds three shiny slings and simply shows them to the wolves, sending them away from the spouses. The first sling is the divinity and the humanity of her Only Begotten; the second is her humility, I mean the humility of his Mother, Mary, who let the Word descend from heaven to earth; the third is her conformity to God's will *[silence] ab initio* and *ante secula creata sum, et usque ad futurum seculum non desinam, et in habitationem sancta coram ipso ministravi*[53] *[silence]* con-*formavi voluntati meae eterno Patri*, and *Verbo quem nutrivi* and *gener-avi visceribus meis*[54] *[silence] tres pueri adoraverunt eam*[55] *[silence] duodecim adolescentulae adoraverunt eam, triginta tres seniores ante eam procidentes*[56] *[silence]* and what do they do? Oh, what do they do?

They extoll her, bless her, and praise her. Then they narrate to the whole heaven her power, glory, and eminence, inviting every blessed soul to congratulate her and to rejoice in her infinite greatness with these words: *Congratulamini cum eam.* Congratulate himself, I mean, the eternal Father, the Word, Son and Spouse, and the holy Spirit, who are one essence, one divinity equal in glory, greatness, and power, in wisdom and goodness; and they give her every glory, greatness, and power *[silence] sed Patris* and *Filii*, and *Spiritus Sancti una est divinitas, equalis gloria, coeterna maiestas.* And the Trinity infuses this into Mary, since she is the mirror of the Holy Trinity Himself *[silence]* fifty Cherubim follow her closely, and the entire Celestial Court as well with a constant gait and a steady firmness, saying: *Ista es digna accipere capacitatem incomprehensibilis Dei."*

She saw that the Virgin was armed, not to defend herself, but to protect her maids, her Son's spouses. And she started from the Virgin's hands saying:

"Mary holds a polished sword. As soon as she sees her well-armed enemy coming toward her, she crushes him. And when his soldiers realize that their head is on the ground, they yell, scream, and rush to hide him so that no one sees him. But in her great benevolence Mary does not offend them and send them back to their place *[silence]* she also has some arrows at her side. She grabs them and throws them at every wild beast, I mean some noxious and hurtful bird such as the crow and others, and kills them. And then without touching them she burns them to ashes that she scatters around to confound and condemn every adversary *[silence]* and in her left hand she holds a shiny and, so to speak, blazing lamp, to enlighten the spouses, her maids, and thus to support them through sown lands, but also through deserts *[silence]* she also keeps a round shield in front of her face and uses it when she needs it, I mean, when she was a pilgrim herself, because now she doesn't need it anymore. So, how does she use it? She gives it to her maids so that they can use it when it's necessary *[silence]* she also has gloves to protect her hands, but they don't bother her *[silence]* then spreading her beautiful and golden hair she sends it down to us, like beautiful ropes and chains, with which she ties us to herself so that later she will be able to tie us to the Spouse, her Only Begotten *[silence]* and she also uses her hair to hide somewhat her beauty and greatness from us, for we wouldn't be able to tolerate it; and she hides it with a great wisdom *[silence]* she also keeps a sallet on her head, but since iron is heavy, hers is out of gold *[silence]* the eternal Father, in agreement with his Word, has given her more than she desired. And she enjoys her greatness and vision so much, that she lets others have it.[57] And, oh eternal Father, what did you give her? And you, Word, what did you give her? You gave her a balance, that she holds with her right hand, so that if she wants to she can dispense justice; and in her left hand she holds a precious vase, with which she can dispense her mercy every time she wants to *[silence]* and her feet wear silver ankle boots, not to be offended *[silence]* oh Mary, oh Mary, oh Mary, is there anything else? *[silence]* and all these things are not for you because you don't really need an armor, but for the sake of your maids, the spouses."

She kept silent for some time, and when she resumed her speech we understood that she had gone back to her previous resolution, that is, to generate and renew the body of the holy church. Thus she said:

"Oh, now that this body is arranged and embellished so well, we must organize it and embellish it again. For I myself and others need it immensely. Let's say that, since the body of the Spouse has been embellished, we must embellish the body of his spouse the church as well, since her Spouse is her head. But what is the head of the spouse? Oh Word, oh Spouse, what is the head of your spouse but her faith and participation in you? *[silence]* her eyes: mercy and justice *[silence]* her ears: truth and pity *[silence]* her smell is humility *[silence]* taste is contemplation *[silence]* her hands: wisdom and science *[silence]* her feet: awe and prudence *[silence]* and once your Christ has been renewed, we shall renew your holy footsteps."

She meant that the new pope had just been elected. Indeed, Pope Sixtus V had succeeded Gregory XIII. Thus she meant that because the head had been renewed, the other members would be renewed as well. Let us hope that our Love and Spouse Jesus grant us this grace. Then she said:

"From the Spouse's breast I see springs and streams infusing and bathing. But for many people these waters taste too bitter. And what could we possibly do to make them sweet? *[silence]* oh, let's take the Spouse's scepter and throw it into them. It'll make them sweet! *[silence] vidi spo[n]sam recumbere super pectum sponsi sui* and *gustavit* and *confortata est*[58] *[silence] non manufactum [silence] rex meus* and *Deus meus [silence] omnes de Saba venient aurum* and *tuis deferentes* and *laudem Domino annunciantes*[59] *[silence]* yes, let's start from the bottom to reach the top *[silence] accedet homo ad cor altum* and *exaltabitur Deus*[60] *[silence] abissus abissus invocat in voce catarattarum tuarum*[61] *[silence]* who will be able to discern the unordered order of this worthy spouse's body? Wisdom looking like foolishness, power being frailty, fortitude being a weakness. The angels admire, the archangels cherish *[silence]* be the Word pleased in himself. And me, if I am not allowed to help him, I shall take pain and pleasure, confusion and profound calm, fortitude along with frailty, and fear with a confinding love *[silence] gustavit te in me*, and *me in te.*"

And all of a sudden she became silent for quite a while, showing that she was enjoying the sweetness and tenderness of his Spouse, the Word. And after a long time, she became upset and said: "Oh, I wish your offenses were over once and for all!" She meant that she keeps seeing God being offended. Then she continued:

"It would be too much! I would taste the air of heaven. You want this sweet honey to be mixed up with absinthe. If I forget them all, at once, all of a sudden, in a trice they come back."

And after a short pause, she indicated that she was praying for a certain sinner. Thus she said: "Oh my Jesus, convert him, convert him! *[silence]* oh Word, your blood shouts. Oh, oh! *[silence]* oh Love, respond to your blood! *[silence]* yes, double it, it doesn't matter." She meant that she was asking him to double her punishment for that person as she had already prayed in the past. Then she continued: "Double it, as long as such a great ignorance leaves. Please, infuse your light, send a spark, a drop of your blood, which is able to penetrate thousand hearts, not just one *[silence]* oh, Word, I would suffer every form of torture, if I could see him converted; and it wouldn't be a torture for me, no, rather a paradise *[silence]* oh Word, please, give him your blood, even if he doesn't want it; respond to the prayers of your maids *[silence]* oh, this blood is so refreshing! *[silence] cor mundum crea in me Deus*[62] *[silence]* oh, it is coming soon, but we don't know the moment! *[silence]* oh Word, if you want him to be open to you, force him *[silence]* cursed be our habit to sin! Oh, we need to be more solicitous in doing good than in sinning, or better yet, we must double our solicitude more and more *[silence]* *voluntatem timentium se faciet.*[63] Oh, who doesn't love you or fear you! I am not worthy to be listened to; listen to your blood, which is united with you and loves you *[silence]* oh Word, I shall pay attention to everything you say, and shall love what you love, and shall do whatever you want me to do. But, please, give your light to those who must work, and don't care about what I want *[silence]* but Word, let's go back to the intrinsic part."

And at that point she stopped speaking.

And after keeping silent for a while, she came out of this rapture at the seventh hour sharp, when the father confessor had just arrived to administer Holy Communion.

Dialogue 44
On the Humanity of the Word

On Tuesday May 7, 1585, the day before St. Michael Archangel, about the twenty-fourth hour at night, our blessed soul went to the oratory of the novices and, kneeling down close to the altar, she entered a vision at once. According to what she told us later during our conversation, she had been drawn by a call, as the first words of this rapture clearly show. She said: "Ascend! What do you want from me?" She recited a prayer and asked that question as an answer to that call. The prayer was that he would allow her to ascend to him; the question was what he wanted from her. Since he was calling her, she said *"Ego sum"* in the person of God.

After keeping quiet for a bit, she showed that God was speaking to her and telling her what he wanted her to do that night—and not only that night, but also all the two following ones because she was called to perceive and to see the three divine Persons: Father, Son, and Holy Spirit; and each of them wanted to subject her to his own probation. And the first probation would be with the Holy Spirit. Because it is a spirit of generosity and purity, it would expose her to the spirit of malice which is the devil. And she had to go through this probation that first night, as the words that she uttered, sometimes more and sometimes less, will clarify later. As usual, we shall mark her pauses and signs so that one can understand when she was silent and when she spoke in a rush. And then she said: "When our eyes are in the dark, you give me light."

She meant that, while night was coming down on us, light was coming down on her. Then she said: "Not magna now, but vision." [She meant that] this vision would not be *magna* because it would not be about the divinity but rather about the Word's humanity. It would be an actual vision but not *magna* as her previous ones.

Then she said: "Oh Father, oh Word, oh Holy Spirit *[silence]* I don't comprehend anything more. That is, you show me these things about you, but then I don't comprehend them *[silence]* you know my strength better than me *[silence]* yes, last night passed rapidly *[silence]* three more nights, right? *[silence]* the one that just passed doesn't count, right? *[silence] in te Domine speravi non confundar in aeternum."*[1]

She understood that she would be tested by devils. "Oh amorous Word, you do not test us with your elect, but with your enemies *[silence]* one test will be conducted by the Father, one by the Word, and one by the Holy Spirit. And the one that just passed came from the whole Trinity *[silence]* oh holy archangel, please be close to me *[silence]* oh, the angelic spirit, when he became a devil, did he turn his purity into malice? *[silence] magnificate Dominum mecum, et exaltamus nomen eius in idipsum."*[2]

And after these words, all of a sudden she became very upset, showing that she was seeing the devil. Thus, raising her voice she said: "Oh, oh, here he is *[silence] et probavit me cum inimicum suum*[3] *[silence] fortitudo mea,* and *laus mea Dominus."*[4]

And stretching her hands on the altar, she said in a very anguished way:

"Oh Word, oh Word! *[silence] in te Domine speravi, non confundar in aeternum."*

And giving a deep sigh, she turned to the devil and said:

"And what do you want from me anyway? *[silence]* oh good Jesus! *[silence]* showing me your offenses and your enemies I wonder if you want me to taste Hell *[silence]* please, and if it swallowed me you would be forced to take me out."

And then she smiled showing that she laughed at what the devil was telling her, and after a while she showed that she felt a strong pain and that she was suffering a lot. Indeed, she shook and grinded her teeth. And her face became ashen and sweated like when one is in agony. And all of a sudden she was thrown on the floor with a great thrust. And staying like this for some time, she started to flounder here and there, hitting her head, her face, and her entire body on the floor. If we had not held her, she would have hurt herself seriously. Nonetheless, she did hurt herself a little bit; her face and her nose were swollen, and it became so livid, that it remained like that for several days. Other times that malign spirit tortured her so much that her body bent backwards. When we asked her why she moved in that way, she told us that the malign spirit threw her on the floor and fought with her in that manner because God had granted him that power over her, as he had done with Job. However, he could not hurt her the way we might have thought because he could only go so far as God allowed him to and no more. This is why, when at the beginning she was thrown to the floor, she said: "If the Word gives you this power, I myself give it to you; and even though I'm suffering, I feel content more with the external one than with that you make me feel inside. Do as you like."

And as soon as she spoke these words, he began to torture her as we said before. And after being tortured for quite a bit, she became still and said to this devil: "And when you have enough shaking me here and there, what are you going to do? *[silence] Verbum caro factum est [silence] benedicam Dominum in omni tempore*[5] (three times)."

Then she stood up straight, lightly laying her hands on the altar, and after a long pause, at once she was pulled back and thrown on the floor again. She said: *"Exurgat Deus, et dissipentur inimici eius."*[6]

She showed that Jesus was consoling her; she said: "Yes, Word, I know it." And turning to the devil, she told him: "And you may do only what my Spouse wants you to *[silence] adesit pavimento anima mea, vivifica me secundum verbum tuum*[7] *[silence]* oh, think about what those poor damned souls do *[silence] benedicam Dominum in omni tempore, semper laus eius in ore meo*[8] *[silence]* oh good Jesus."

And after being shaken for more than a half hour, at once she stood up and, leaning against the altar with clasped hands and looking upward, stared at the painting over the altar, still and firm for quite a while; and then, all of a sudden, her face became very happy, with a radiant expression and her eyes like in Heaven. She said: "Oh amorous Word!" And she showed that he was telling her that he did not want the devil to have power over her any longer; thus, turning to the devil she told him: "Go away, away with your other devils, because for the moment my Word doesn't give you any power over me."

And being quiet and engrossed for a while, with the same cheerful expression and her happy face she said:

"*Vidi Spiritum moventem a Patrem*, and *assistentem ad humanitatem Verbi. Et ipse conferet eum nobis*[9] *[silence] Redde mihi letitiam salutaris tui*, and *spiritu principali confirma me*[10] *[silence] in unione Sanguinis tui, ut liberentur dilecti tui*[11] *[silence]* I see that Spirit of purity moving from the idea of the Father, and descending with an immobile motion, and with ardor infusing itself into Mary. And he does so that she can grant humanity to the Word. Who then infuses into us this same Spirit of purity assisting him *[silence]* and what? We can discuss it as long as we want to, but we always go back to the same purity, generosity, goodness. But as light is different from darkness and darkness from light, so to taste you is different every time *[silence]* oh you are given so much, but you are tasted so little! *[silence]* oh indescribable purity, how important it is to prepare to receive you inside! *[silence] omnia diiudicat, omnia diiudicat, omnia diiudicat*[12] *[silence]* oh Word, how deeply you examine our desires, affections, and resolutions before you unite us with that Spirit of purity! *[silence]* oh, and then they believe—those mundane and sensual people with their filth, sensuality, and malice—they believe that they can reach this divine and immaculate Spirit, and that he will descend into them. Oh, they are more mistaken than the devil, when he wanted to become equal to God."

After these words she kept quiet for a bit. Then, turning toward the nuns and leaning against the altar with her back, with clasped hands and looking upwards, she spoke the following words with a smiling expression and a happy face:

"*Vidi thronum in coelo, Spiritum moventem descentem in terra*, and *circundantem eam*.[13] And what does he do? He penetrates the hearts and draws them to him; then he goes back to Heaven, and with the humanate Word he penetrates those skies and rests with him in the Father's bosom. Then he goes down to hell, and condemns and confuses his enemies *[silence]* oh throne of joy, of contemplation, and of consolation for us! *[silence]* fifty flaming mouths surround this throne *[silence]* it is surrounded by millions of millions of stars; it can't be seen, but only tasted *[silence]* this throne is without form and is a being in form; it draws from every form and every being of ours *[silence]* drawing arrows that penetrate and divide the creatures' hearts and prepare them to receive his grace. And he does this because he is generous. And then when these hearts are ready and have received these arrows, they send them back to the Spirit and move it to send new gifts and graces. Thus, receiving more and more gifts and graces, these creatures become able to prepare other creatures to receive these arrows that are sent by the generosity of this divine Spirit. Oh, why don't we make our hearts big enough to embrace every creature? And not only the creatures, but also all the angelic choirs and all the blessed souls who are in Heaven? And even the throne of the holy Trinity, and if this is not enough there are the elements, earth and hell itself *[silence]* oh the creature's great dignity! You, oh Word, have extolled and glorified it! We can glory in it and, so to speak, pride ourselves on it with a holy pride *[silence]* oh misery of ours! We make ourselves so miserable with our sins! *[silence]* and nobody has a more sinful humbleness than a proud man; nobody has a wiser pride than a humble and just man."

And after these words she left the altar and went to her usual place, sitting on her bench. Being silent for a while, she said: "The Spirit comes out and is there in those clouds, I mean, in the hearts of those creatures. But they must be waters because the clouds bend toward the waters; and when they bend the Spirit will take them *[silence]* oh, yes, yes, we must lead ourselves beyond ourselves."

And all of a sudden she stood up, raising both hands and having such a devout expression in her eyes that she would inspire a stone with devotion, apart from every creature. Asking the Holy Spirit to come down to her, she said: "Descend, Spirit, for yourself." And lowering her hands, she said: "Oh, now." And after a little while, and raising her hands again, she said: "Descend, Spirit, for the Word *[silence]* descend, Spirit, for the Father's essence *[silence]* descend, Spirit, for Mary's purity *[silence]* descend, Spirit, for the angelic choirs *[silence]* descend, Spirit, *per Aposotolorum chorus.*"[14]

The seventh time, she stood up with a grave swiftness, faster than the other times; the other times, when she received the Spirit, she sat down crossing her hands on her knees, and every time she said: "Descend, Spirit," she stood up first raising her hands. But this last time she raised them much higher, showing a burning desire to

165

receive it. And she said: *"Descendat Spiritus per martires* and *virgines* that you love so dearly."

And then, sitting down again, she kept quiet for a while. Afterward, she stood up again as she had done before. She opened her mouth seven times as when one draws breath in, waiting a little in between. In this way she showed that she was receiving the seven gifts of the Holy Spirit. And she made these gestures and movements with an incredible grace. And after the last one, waiting a little, she said: *"Confirma hoc quod operatus est*[15] *liberalitate Sanguinis tui [silence] veni Spiritus amoris [silence] veni Spiritus puritatis [silence] veni Spiritus unitatis [silence] veni Spiritus eternitatis [silence] veni Spiritus equalitatis [silence] veni Spiritus sapientiae."*

She sat down; and then she said: "No, I am not happy to be the only one to have it, because what is the use of having it for oneself? What can I do by myself? I can only communicate you to the creatures. Thus, oh Spirit, communicate yourself *[silence]* but what is this, oh Spirit? They don't want to raise their hands *[silence]* and do they open their mouths? Yes, they open them, but to curse and to condemn *[silence] confringam omnia cornua peccatorum, et exaltabuntur cornua iusti."*[16]

And then she kept quiet for a while. Later, becoming very happy, we understood that she had gone back to her first statement, that is, that the Spirit always sustained the Word's humanity from the beginning of his incarnation to the moment when he went back to Heaven. Indeed, during his humanity the Holy Spirit assisted the humanate Word in all his workings and deeds. And after having explained how the Spirit assisted the Word in his incarnation, now she moves to his childhood saying:

"Then the inspiring Spirit rests in the humanity of that sweet and ruddy child, I mean, in the cute little body of my Word while he was sucking milk from Mary's breasts, his dear mother *[silence]* later, when thanks to your goodness and generosity you run away from Herod's hands and went to Egypt, oh how inspiring was that Spirit; he overthrew all the idols and broke them to pieces, and [he overthrew] Herod's evil resolution as well. During that time he always accompanied you, since this Spirit was always united with you, Word *[silence]* when you came back from Egypt, this Spirit inspired you so deeply, that he helped you speak with so much wisdom, when you questioned and responded to those doctors, I mean, when at the age of twelve Mary and Joseph found you discussing with them in the temple *[silence]* but, oh Word, what shall I say when I see you jumping so high with that Spirit? where does he take you to? [He takes you] to the river Jordan to ask John to baptize you. And, Word, why do you do this? To transform us and to unite us with that Spirit in you and with you. In that baptism you gave your grace to our baptism; this was a necessary, useful, and fruitful gift. And what could we be without this gift, this real gift of the Holy Spirit, or better yet of the whole holy Trinity, since we are baptized in the name of the Father, of the Son, and of the Holy Spirit? You were also moved by the Spirit to sanctify the waters and to give us back that innocence in which you had created us. And the water descends on our head less quickly than the Spirit and your grace come down upon us; indeed they saw the Spirit in the form of a dove coming upon you *[silence]* you also heard your Father's sweet words: *"Hic est Filius meus dilectus in quo mihi bene complacui."*[17] I would dare to say that, if we weren't blind and ignorant, the eternal Father would pronounce these same words when we receive the holy baptism ourselves. I don't want this to become an arrogant and vain act, but through the holy baptism we become sons of God and, when he descends upon us in the third Person since the three Persons are one unity, the holy Trinity itself descends upon us and rejoices in us *[silence]* then I see you in the Spirit, and the Spirit leads you to the desert, where he inspires so strongly that he overcomes the Spirit that is against you; but more than inspiring and giving strength to you, he gives vigor, strength, and virtue to every human being, so that he can overcome the devilish spirit who is so contrary to the Spirit and to you. Then through the Spirit you start spreading your wisdom; and with this Spirit you draw the creatures' spirit to you. Indeed, since we are made of such a noble spirit, we can't help but be drawn by the inspiring and divine Spirit through you, my humanate Word *[silence]* but, Word, I must jump. For later, when you began to show not only your wisdom but also your power, which at the present moment you let every creature admire, and we still gaze at it in admiration, I mean, when you did that great miracle turning water into wine, where who had and has now a bit of light was and is aware of this mutation, and through this mutation you let the Spirit spread in us.

"Oh Word, with the Spirit moving you and being moved by you you do wonderful miracles; he gives life back to the dead, sight to the blind, hearing to the deaf; he heals the lepers and, in a word, cures every infirmity *[silence]* you convert the souls, but before you diverts them from evil, from vices and sins; and when they are totally diverted from their evil path and are moved by this moving Spirit they convert to you, their sole goal, and totally and completely rest in you *[silence]* oh greatness of my Word, if they knew you I am sure everyone would admire and adore you.

"Then I see you giving life back to the dead supported by this inspiring and moving Spirit *[silence]* yes, you were right when you vivified the dead, since you are life itself. It seems difficult to cure and remove those infirmities that eventually make the bodies lie dead, but much more difficult is to remove sins and bring back to life those souls dead in those sins. But I see the Spirit, similar to a flying eagle, taking them [the souls] upon himself and raising them, and with his inspiration making them live again.

"Word, you gave hearing back to the deaf who like dead can't hear anything, understand anything, and since they don't hear they can't speak. And doesn't their being deaf and mute result from their being possessed by the malign spirit and the filthy spirit? They can be freed only through this Spirit of purity, if the finger of God's right hand, which is you, demands it. Thus you say: '*Si in digito Dei eijcio Demonia.*'[18] The deaf are the souls possessed by sin. And is there anything filthier than sin? Sin makes the soul unable to listen to your voice, and if it can't listen to it it can't be worthy of you *[silence]* for by listening [to you] we become worthy of you, who can be fathomed only by yourself. Oh, you make us worthy of it [yourself] through the Spirit of purity that purges and purifies the souls with your beneficial water. By drawing this water the Spirit purifies the souls. And from where does it draw this water? Oh, it draws it from the Father, from his bosom, that living spring that lies in his bosom *[silence]* oh Word, how beautifully that water flows from your Father's bosom! It flows down, and the Spirit infuses it into those poor souls, whence they become totally purified *[silence]* then

you order, yes, that filthy spirit to depart from them; and you say:
'Oh deaf and mute *spiritus, exii ab eis*'; oh filthy spirit, depart from
them. Thus, being freed from the dirt of sin, not only do they hear
your words, they also perceive what you want them to do; and so,
when the Spirit moving from you accomplishes that purification,
they get their hearing back *[silence]* this purification is so necessary
that without it they can't hear.

"Then you give speech back to the mute. And, Word, how are
they mute? Yes, they are mute for your confession, for your praise,
but because of their curses, slanders, and betrayals they don't have
one tongue, but thousands and thousands of tongues. They are
mute and have no tongue when they should bless, glorify, thank
you. And what do we need in this situation? As you, Word, did
yourself, the Spirit must blow in order to give them speech. But at
the same time they must open their mouths in order to receive this
insufflation. *Os meum aperui* and *attraxi spiritum;*[19] and also: *Domine
labia mea aperies et os meum annunciabit laudem tuam*[20] *[silence]* oh how
beautiful it is to hear your elect's mouths praising you! On the contrary, it's neither beautiful nor precious the way the sinners' mouths
praise you *[silence]* the language of your praise penetrates the idea of
the holy Trinity and sends down to us whatever we want, to the
point that, if we want to become God through participation and
union, it [the language of praise] attains it.

"Word, you also give strong legs to the lame. Oh, how many,
how many people are lame! Those who questions their faith; those
who are uncertain about [divine] power; those who are weak in generosity. Oh, what an ignorance! But your Spirit must bow down and
do not consider his own being, which is perfect goodness, infinite
power, and unfathomable truth *[silence]* oh Word, Word! *[silence]* the
Spirit leads his Word who transforms in his name *[silence]* and where
does he lead him? he leads him where he abandons himself to the
creature, I mean, your body and your blood as food and drink. And
for how long? Truth itself says it: '*Usque ad consumationem seculi,*'[21] so
that the soul can have it not only once, no, not only every year, no,
not only every month, no, not only every week, no, but every day,
every morning; the soul can have it every time it wants to, and it can
rest with it as it likes *[silence]* oh my Word's great generosity! Oh, I

am such a miserable wretch; I have plenty of it and bring forth nothing! *[silence]* but about the soul receiving this Sacrament we can say what we say about Mary: *"Quia quem coeli capere non poterant tuo gremio contulisti,"*[22] since this soul has become very similar to Mary *[silence]* thus, as I believe John saw her adorned with the sun's rays, so is this soul receiving you in itself adorned with the sun's rays, which is yourself: *"Sol iustitiae Christus Deus noster"*[23] *[silence]* and I shall also dare to mention the sun of your vision, for this soul wants you to allow it to penetrate your vision, but only per *gratia gratis data [silence]* and in the way Mary was crowned with stars, the Seraphim, who form the crown of your spouses, shine in the empyrean much more than the stars in our sky; and instead of shooting stars they have wings *[silence]* but with an incredible ignorance we go to the Sacrament; we do not wear that sun! *[silence]* Mary had also the moon under her feet; and what more could this spouse desire, than to put the moon under her feet? Those who taste it now know it, those who put every gift and grace under their feet, because they don't consider the gifts but the giver *[silence]* pride makes us despise this crown; vainglory does not keep the moon under its feet because it merely considers the gifts and graces it has received and not their giver *[silence]* but when you showed your profound love Judas the traitor was there; it would have been better for him not to be how he is now, for many become almost like him. I wish there were no Judas now! *[silence]* Oh, *cum perverso pervertiris,*[24] we can really say this today *[silence]* no creature, nobody will be ever able to fully understand how pleased the Holy Trinity is when someone goes to this holy Sacrament prepared and eager; and on the other hand, how nauseated it feels when someone goes [to it] without any preparation and eagerness *[silence]* any pain would be glory for me if many of those who come to you would eliminate their inconsiderateness and ignorance.

"The Spirit also leads my Word to such a valley of humility, that he goes so far as to wash his disciples' feet. And won't the Spouse take his Spouse with him? *Exemplum enim dedi vobis, ut quemadmodum ego feci, ita et vos faciatis.*[25]

"The Spirit keeps leading his Word. And where does he lead him? And to do what? Oh, he leads him where he can have a pure meditation and conversation with his beloved apostles, where he granted us so many treasures that even one word leaves every mind, even a divine one, astonished. *Ego sum vitis* and *vos palmites: qui manet in me et ego in eo, hic fert fructum multum*[26] *[silence]* well, those who remain[27] in you fructify a lot, and as a consequence those who do not remain in you do not fructify at all *[silence]* but since the vine shoot remains and persists in the vine, it turns into the vine itself, and first of all when it is underground *[silence]* and the spouse, by annihilating herself and going underground with her Spouse, turns into a fruitful vine *[silence]* the press, which is the desire for your honor and salvation of our neighbors, squeezes and sends out a wine that intoxicates the Spouse and rejoices the spouse, warms the creatures' hearts and pleases the angels. *Et vinum laetificet cor hominis.*[28] And the abundance of this squeezed wine is so copious that the spouse has not enough vases for it. In fact, the more she tastes it the more she keeps it inside herself, but when she is filled up with that she is forced to send it out with words and external gestures, belching forth for the others what she has inside *[silence]* and what does the Spouse do? He asks his spouse to preserve it. And what does he give her? He gives her a precious and large vase, which is his heart, because he knows that this wine is so powerful that it would break any other vase. And when the soul has reached this point it must abandon every desire for God's honor and the others' salvation, and must abandon itself to God totally and completely, because the desire for God's honor and the others' salvation would make the spouse both sorrowful and glorious, given that good and bad creatures will always be among us.

"Then the Spirit leads the Word to pray *[silence]* I am so ignorant that I'm unable to believe, understand, penetrate, taste what my Word did at this point. Oh my Word, you took the holy Trinity with you when you chose those three apostles and told them: *'Tristis est anima mea usque ad mortem.'*[29] You showed them your humanity and also how troubled your soul felt, with fear and awe *[silence]* but, oh Word, you did let your soul be troubled, but you, my love, primarily did it to comfort us, so that our soul would not feel troubled with your same trouble, when we sometimes think that we have lost your Spirit *[silence]* then, when you prayed to the Father, you spoke those words: *'Non mea sed tua voluntas fiat'*;[30] and everything [was] for the creature. Was equality unequal? Was this the reason why you had to say: 'Let your will be done, not mine'? And was it in a way that your sanctified and deified humanity could feel pain? No, but you wanted to leave your deification and sanctification and embrace your contradiction, so that we could embrace his sanctification and deification, and through it [we could] find comfort to our contradictions and troubles. Your sanctification and deification is given to us through the combat we fight when we must abandon ourselves to your will *[silence]* and you renewed this three times, yes, because we constantly fall back into doing our own will. For you, Word, you would have needed to say it only once: 'Let your will be done,' because it would have immediately conformed to the Father's [will]. However, even though in our prayer we leave our will to you and promise never to do ours, still because of our frailty we often do [our will] again and again and take it [our will] away from you. Thus, we must constantly abandon our will to you. And you wanted to set an example for us by leaving your will into the Father's hands repeatedly; you have also given us the strength we need to accomplish this. Indeed, every time we drown, deny, and restrain our will, we acquire one of the three Persons of the holy Trinity; and by multiplying our denial we receive the infinite workings of the Trinity, since it is three Persons but one divinity in its essence.

"You, oh Word, the consoler of every creature and the glory of the angels, wanted to be consoled by the Angel. And Word, my love, why did you do it? So that in our afflictions and worries we would accept to be consoled and a bit relieved. Many of us wouldn't accept any consolation in their afflictions if they hadn't found an example in you, Word. And I would've been someone who accepts consolation only from you, neither from a creature, nor from the angels and saints, nor from any thing whatsoever. But since we have seen that you, Word, wanted to accept this consolation for our sake, we also accept to be consoled both by the angels and by the creatures, for our own consolation *[silence]* for surely no creature would accept any consolation if you, Word, had not accepted to be consoled yourself *[silence]* moreover, in order to help us send out some word in our afflictions (although it would be better for us not to send it out), you

172

decided to speak those words: *'Transeat a me calix iste.'*[31] And you uttered them to console your humanity, but even more to console and sustain us.

"But, oh eternal Word, you also wanted to sweat blood. You sweated because of your agony, yes, but even more to teach us not to dwell in our desires and good will, but to proceed in our workings. For, if we hadn't seen how your desire was followed by your working, we could have thought that good desires were enough, and needed no working. But they are not enough, they are not, because hell is full of desires, whereas Heaven is full of workers *[silence]* three are the things that should compel us to work: God's honor, our salvation, and the condemnation and abhorrence of every lie *[silence]* you went back to the apostles three times, so that we—woe to those who don't do it— so that we always go back to consider our origin and that [God] who compels us to do this or that thing. And again, once we have considered it, we must go back to consider it one more time; and, as I said, woe to those who don't do this. And we must always contemplate the goal of this working, which is God *[silence]* and you yourself wanted to go up to your traitor in order to show us that we must be willing to suffer for your honor and [be willing] to give our life for our neighbor, leaving you for you, and abandoning us to you; but only a few, only a few reach this perfection.

"The Spirit keeps leading *[silence]* oh, where does it lead to? It leads the Spouse there where he is arrested and tied up. That who ties everything and gives the authority to tie and untie us from our sins, and makes us both free from our enemies and enslaved by them, wanted to be arrested and tied up by his enemies *[silence]* oh Word, although it would have been suitable, you didn't want to be defended and to enforce the law against those iniquitous men, because you wanted to tell your spouse that she must give up every revenge. And you reprimanded Peter to show that, even though our mind may consider revenge as a reasonable response since sometimes it is necessary to defend ourselves, nevertheless we must refrain from pursuing it.

"You wanted your enemies to tie your hands up so that we brace ourselves to tie up your hands, and also the eternal Father's hands, so that he does not enforce his law against the sinners. But woe betide if nobody tied these hands! You also let Judas the traitor

173

kiss you so that we could hope to reach a perfect union with you. How many people, disguising their pride and ignorance as humility, could ever be able to attain such a union! But seeing that you let your traitor and beloved apostle kiss you, they discarded their blindness and ignorance that they disguised as a virtuous humility *[silence]* you also wanted to show your power when you made the soldiers, who were coming to take you, fall on the ground. In this way you taught your spouse that sometimes she must manifest your gifts and graces, I mean, [she must] show the ignorant people the virtue she has received from you; and in so doing she'll be able to show them their own ignorance and the offensive nature of their certainties.

"And then you made them stand up because you wanted to be merciful to them, yes, but also because you wanted to tell us that when we see a soul lapsing into sin we must help it stand up again; and [you wanted to tell us] that we must forgive this fallen soul if it throws itself to the ground totally humiliated and it recognizes its fault; in the same way God forgives us every time we humiliate ourselves and recognize and confess our faults. Indeed, he said that as soon as the sinner repents: *'omnium iniquitatum suarum non recordabor.'*[32]

"And the moving Spirit still moves you and makes [you] fly. It takes you to Annas. And, oh Word, why did you let him lead you? Because you wanted to lead the working of our redemption, yes, yes, yes, and also [because you wanted] to lead us to you in a way that pleases you, either by means of our desires, or our deeds, or our afflictions, hunger or poverty, or by means of some creature, so that we don't do what many do, those who decide to serve only in a way that pleases them. Even if a devil led us to you, we should let him do it, without looking at the path we are led through, provided that we are actually led and move toward you *[silence]* and [when you were] taken to Caiaphas, here you are beaten and keep silent in order to show your spouse that when she is offended she must pride herself on the offenses she has received in the name of your love, as Paul the apostle says: *'Nam et gloriamur in tribulationibus'*[33] *[silence]* and you also did it because, as the Scripture says, it's no good holding a sermon where nobody hears. Oh, how many, how many make themselves unworthy of your word! And the support of the Holy Spirit is a crucial gift for us, so that we become able to consider and weigh when it is appropriate to speak and [when it is appropriate] to be silent, to speak the word and to keep it for ourselves. Oh, if your spouses were more considerate when they speak, how more useful they would be to their neighbors! *[silence]* then, oh moving Spirit, you led my Word to that other judge. And why did you, my Word, go to him? So that we could learn that we shouldn't dwell in our good deeds, we should rather move from virtue to virtue. And here, what did they do to you, my Word?"

All of a sudden she became silent, being engrossed for quite a long time. She did not speak a word and kept for herself everything Jesus did before Pilate the first time he was taken to him. Later, after a long silence, she uttered these words:

"The Word goes and is led to Pilate. And he is pleased and dresses him up with a white gown. Tell me, oh Word, why did you want to be dressed with that white gown? In order to make your innocence known, yes, but even more because you wanted to dress your spouse with that gown of purity, which brings about a great joy in the spouse's heart. Indeed, rushing to serve you she moves toward you. And as a result of your mutual satisfaction, you dress her up in white. And, oh Word, where do you take this gown that you want to give to your spouse? *[silence]* when he had that gown put on you, Herod didn't take it from a honorable place, but at random; and he put it on you to laugh and sneer at you. But the gown you wish to give your spouse you take it from a very virtuous and honorable place, I mean, you take it out of your side and put it on her in order to honor her and make her more pleasing to you. And in exchange for the rope you were girt with, you give her a marvelous stole; and this is the pleasure coming from a participation in and fruition of your divinity; and this stole is adorned with the most precious gems, which are those secrets and wisdom about the soul's greatness and dignity you communicate to whoever you like *[silence]* yes, the spouse too wants to give a vestment to her Spouse, and wants to dress him in white as well, since she knows that he delights in lilies. And what kind of vestment will she give to her Spouse? Oh, it [the vestment] will be the offering of himself to himself, a magnificent vestment indeed. But since it is appropriate for the spouse to give something hers, she offers her heart and her soul; and the more it

175

[her soul] is pure the more it is appreciated; and the more her heart is chaste the more his vestment is beautiful, and he rejoices in it.

"Then you went back to Pilate to give us an example, so that we are not confused when first we are raised and later are lowered *[silence]* and here, Word, you were questioned so many times, but you rarely answered *[silence]* What do you say, Word? What I and your other spouses, and every creature, should profess: '*Regnum meum non est de hoc mundo.*'[34] But woe to those believing that theirs is a kingdom of this world, for they only think about accumulating gold and silver, and pursue stuff that is nothing but a handful of earth; they condemn their souls for that bit of earth. And they will be buried in that earth of theirs. But your spouse does not want hers to be a kingdom of this earth, she rather wants her kingdom to be yours, Word *[silence]* you said that you had come to bear witness to the truth. Oh, how much this truth should be manifested! I dare to say that those who do not manifest this truth do not believe that you are the truth itself *[silence]* then the Spirit leads the Word to the prison; and you, Word, lead your spouse to the prison. And to what prison? And to what prison? To a prison that is so secret that only a few know it, in which the Spouse keeps her tied up so strongly that she can't leave. And this is the plenitude of a grace that, even if the devils and all the creatures tried to take her out of it, they would be able neither to take her out of it nor to make her fail. For she is completely tied up and imprisoned *[silence]* then the Spirit leads you, Word, there where you are shown to the people, so that your spouse can be shown to you before the Holy Trinity. There you will say: '*Ista est in qua dolus non est,*'[35] as Pilate stated before the people that you were innocent, and that he could find no case against you.

"Then he leads you to the column so that later you can lead your spouse to your sweet conversation: '*In columna nubis loquebatur sapientia*'[36] *[silence]* then Pilate shows you to the people and says: '*Ecce homo.*' And you say to your spouse: '*Ista est speciosa inter filias Hierusalem*'[37] *[silence]* the Spirit also leads the Spouse where he hears that cruel sentence, which is very merciful for us because by means of it he calls the spouse while she is still in her pilgrimage. He says: '*Surge, propera amica mea, columba mea, formosa mea* and *veni in foraminibus petrae in caverna maceriae.*'[38] And also because you wanted to hear those other

176

words: *'Venite benedicti Patris mei'*[39] *[silence]* but those who say that God doesn't care about these things sentence you to death; they think that God is dead and obtuse, and don't know that God is everywhere and sees and hears everything. *Si ascendero in coelum tu illic es, si descendero in infernum ades. Si sunsero pennas meas diluculo* and *abitavero in extremis maris etenim illuc manus tua deducet me* and *tenebit me dextera tua.*[40] Oh, how many, how many are in this way!

"Then the Spirit leads him where he must carry his cross. Oh amorous Word, why do you let him lead you there? To give a bunch of myrrh to your spouse. *Fasciculus mirrae dilectus meus inter ubera mea commorabitur;*[41] and also so that his cross be light to him *[silence]* he meets his mother so that later he can have sweet meetings with his spouse, while she is in this world, I mean, in her pilgrimage; and so that the creature can meet you and you can meet the creature, and neighbors can meet as well, and angels can meet men and men can meet angels, and the Old Testament can meet your pure Gospel.

"Now the Spirit has led the Word to the mount Calvary; and [he has led] every creature, especially his spouses, to the Word, in order to lead them to the mount Zion of the city of Jerusalem, called vision of peace; instead of stench he lets them perceive the fragrance of the slaughtered lamb's blood *[silence]* now the Word, moving from the Spirit, prays to the Father in order to teach his spouse how to adore the Holy Trinity when she enters her fatherland *[silence]* he undresses to show that, if we want to be led up there, we must divest ourselves of everything, both of our body and ourselves completely; and then he will dress us with himself, giving us his vision and glory *[silence]* yes, as if he divests the Cherubim and Seraphim of their glory, since we shall appear much more glorious with the vestment of the Word's humanity. His humanity is indeed superior and much more glorious than any angelic virtue. And at that point the Bridegroom and the spouse will consider themselves equal; and he will give to every spouse a radiant vestment, which will be every virtue and splendor containing the Word.

"He stretches on the cross, moving from the Spirit remaining in him. Then he opens his arms to embrace and hold tight the spouse and every creature, with every being of ours *[silence]* he lets them nail his holy hands in order to unite our workings with his perfectly, so that they will please him *[silence]* and he lets them nail his feet, so that our affections and effects unite with his *[silence]* and to give more caves to the spouse he lets them wound him five times in his holy body *[silence] sicut passer solitarius in tecto*[42] *[silence] et eduxit me in caverna eius*[43] *[silence] sicut passer erecta est de laqueo venantium*[44] *[silence]* yes, and to offer them to the Father in case his spouse wavers; and these caves are also the seals of the human kind itself *[silence]* the Spirit grants the Word those seven arrows of love corresponding to his seven gifts." She stood up and said: "Let us count them one by one." And she became silent because she started to count them by herself. Then she sat down again and said: "He makes him taste gall so that later his spouse can taste his sweetness. Yes, yes *[silence]* Oh moving Spirit, you are always with the Word; you inspire him so that he sends out his own Spirit. How can you inspire without expiring? And if you are with him, how can you withdraw from him? How will you be able to be with him in the Father's bosom, I mean, with the Word's soul, and with his body on the cross? With his soul in limbo, and with his body in the sepulcher? Oh, Spirit, how will you be able to inspire your inspirations? *[silence]* of course, Word. You will withdraw your Spirit into the Spirit expiring into you, and with him inside of you you will inspire, aspire, and expire, so that your spouse will be able to aspire, inspire, and expire into you *[silence]* this moving, inspiring Spirit moves into you, Word. [We must] inspire this Spirit in order to inspire it in ourselves with all his gifts *[silence]* [you] inspire with the Spirit in the Father's bosom; [you] inspire [with him] in limbo; [you] inspire [with him] in the sepulcher; [you] inspire in the soul so that it can expire in him *[silence]* [you] inspire in the sepulcher so that your spouse can bury you in herself and you [can bury] her in yourself *[silence]* you inspires in limbo so that your spouse can transcend everything, not only limbo but hell as well *[silence]* you inspire in the Father's bosom so that your spouse, after her toils, can rest in an eternal calm enjoying and contemplating the holy Trinity's essence.

"Oh inspiring Spirit, you inspire with the Word's soul into the Father's bosom, into the Word's humanity itself, into his spouse's soul which, expiring into her Bridegroom, is dead and vivifying! *[silence]* you inspire into the Father's essence, from the Father into the Word's soul, from his soul into the Word's body, from his body into his spouse. When his spouse inspires into the humanity of her Spouse the Word, his humanity expires into you, moving Spirit; and then you inspire into the unity of the Holy Trinity *[silence]* oh, then the moving Spirit takes his Spirit again, and in so doing he takes inspiration for life; uniting his holy humanity with the Word's soul, he glorifies it and makes it resurrect to justify us. Consequently his spouse, already dead in herself, can be vivified by you, moving and inspiring Spirit *[silence]* then the Spirit moves the Word so that he goes to Mary, and together they have a divine conversation, not through words, no, but through aspirations, inspirations, expirations *[silence]* still moving, the Spirit leads the Word to his apostles, but before to Peter and then, in his final glory, to his conversation with us for forty days *[silence]* no more, now no more *[silence]* he is already."

She meant that she had sensed that her confessor had already arrived to give her communion. We asked her about it, and she confirmed that that was what she meant with those words: "He is already"; he has arrived. And it was the seventh hour sharp.

Let us always praise and bless the Lord.

Dialogue 45
An Inner Test

On Wednesday night, May 8, 1585, while our beloved soul was at the statue of the Virgin Mary in the room for the novices, all of a sudden she entered a rapture. She was called by her Spouse to continue the working of the three Persons of the holy Trinity. Indeed, that night he himself was going to test his spouse. His test would be a test of annihilation because he had annihilated himself when he, God, had become a man.

And after a pause, she *"procidit in faciem suam."*[1] She threw herself on the floor exhausted, crossing her arms and hands under her head. And she said:

"Verbum probabit me in annihilation [silence] will I be able to have your body and your blood?"

At this point the Word told her how long she would have to remain in this rapture. She then asked him if she was allowed to take communion, that is to say if she would have to go beyond the time of her usual communion. But she recovered from her rapture when she had to take communion, and then she went back to it [the rapture], as we shall explain later. This is what she said:

"Cor meum dereliquit me,[2] *et postea Sanguinis Verbi assumsit me*[3] *[silence] Verbum dereliquit me*[4] (three times). *Probavit me in aqua contradictionis*[5] and of annihilation *[silence]* you hid in Mary's womb and then revealed yourself."

She always had long pauses between one sentence and the other; and she remained more than an hour in that probation of annihilation. Then, after a long and exhausting silence, she said: "I can't anymore."

And removing her hands from under her head, she placed them on the floor. With a low, mournful, and hardly audible voice she said: "I am sorry for the others, and the others should be sorry for

180

me, since my offenses are so numerous *[silence]* woe betide you, my soul, if you don't remove every possible thing from yourself, even hell will hate you *[silence]* and if you don't get rid of your pride, the devil will abhor you, let alone the Word *[silence]* you are the almighty God; nonetheless I will dare to say that neither does hell have enough punishments for me, nor do enough hells exist to punish me, miserable wretch *[silence]* woe, woe betide me, receptacle of wickedness and innumerable iniquities. However, although I mistrust myself, I will not mistrust you *[silence]* I wish I were punished for the others' offenses; I can't find a punishment appropriate to mine *[silence] complacuit* the Word *in annihilatione sponsae suae*[6] *[silence]* I don't dare to ask the devils for help, let alone the angels *[silence]* how can the earth sustain me? Why doesn't hell swallow me? *[silence]* every miserable thing, I believe, is aware of its being slave of its own misery *[silence] recogitabo tibi omnes annos meos in amaritudine animae meae*[7] *[silence] et in prufundum maris immersit me."*[8]

After these words she stood up slowly, slowly, and while she was still on her knees with clasped hands she said: *"Exurge Domine in requiem tuam, et sanctifica arca sanctificationis tuae."*[9]

And after these words, she stood up leaning a little bit. With clasped hands she said: *"Propter Sanguinem tuum, non avertas faciem tuam a me."*[10]

And then she sat down, keeping quiet for a long while and looking very engrossed, as if she were comprehending great things. And then, at once, she became very cheerful and stood up straight. She said: *"Vidi thronum Verbi altum et elevatum,* held by hundred chameleons *[silence]* oh, surrounded by twelve roaring lions, which invite everyone to admire such an admirable, marvelous, and incomprehensible throne *[silence]* its stable movement amazes the angels and astonishes the archangels *[silence]* fifty-five unicorns constantly contemplate its gaze *[silence]* oh, please multiply them for us down here."

She was speechless and stupefied between one thing and the other; her face was so beautiful; her flesh looked like milk and blood; and her eyes shone like two bright stars. And continuing she said: "Thirty roebucks, yes, but ten by each side *[silence]* twenty-four lambs hide in the shade of this throne and surrounded by its splendor *[silence]* an innumerable multitude of doves feed on and eat the crumbs of the Word sitting on that throne *[silence] relaxa facinora plebi tuae.*"[11]

And then she sat down, crossing her hands on her knees. She looked as if she had been raised above herself, looking upward. Looking extremely happy, she said: *"Narrabo proprietatem Verbi mei que sunt pulchritudo, mirabilia, sapientia, scientia, potentia,* eternity, imperturbability, union, and communication[12] *[silence] postula a me,* and *dabo tibi gentes hereditatem tuam*[13] *[silence] inclinabo in parabola aurem meam.*"[14]

First quality: Beauty.

"Invisible beauty *[silence] speciosus forma pre filiis Hominum*[15] *[silence]* your beauty is like that sweet fruit called pomegranate, whose fruits hold so many small red seeds *[silence]* and look, they bend downward so much to invite everyone, and especially children, to pick them. You were right when you said that only those who are like children can appreciate that beauty. And when the pomegranates are open children put themselves under them with their mouths open to receive the falling seeds. But we must shake [the plant] a lot before they actually fall *[silence]* similarly, if we want the fruit of your blood fall on us, we must take our cross and shake; it lets us taste an absolutely unique sweetness. But those ones we pick with our hands without shaking them, we can preserve them for a long time. In the same way, those who accomplish their workings with a pure desire and without any inappropriate mingling, they are able to preserve their good desires for a long time, but if we preserve nothing of ourselves we fail soon *[silence]* but, even though the rind of this fruit tastes rather bitter and harsh, as soon as we take the knife of your word and remove it [the rind], we savor the sweetness of that fruit. Oh, in your passion you looked bitter; *omnes videntes me deriserunt me factus sum tanquam mortus a corde*[16] *[silence]* that tree, yes, it has several different flavors, because you are beautiful in your divinity, totally incomprehensible and unfathomable. You are also beautiful in your humanity in an impenetrable way. Yes, you communicate your beauty to the soul, I mean, to the soul but also to the body, since many times the beauty of the soul adorns the

182

body; and in some cases you embellish our intentions, along with our desires and feelings, and finally our words and workings *[silence]* the soul's and the body's beauty is indescribable; and the beauty of words and of workings is delightful *[silence]* many creatures' malice despises the beauty of your divinity. Lies and rumors despise the beauty of your humanity *[silence]* the malevolent and hypocritical people despise the beauty of the soul *[silence]* your elect's goodness extols and enjoys the beauty of your divinity *[silence]* those who long for your truth extol the beauty of your humanity *[silence]* those who are pure and simple in their hearts extol the beauty of the soul *[silence]* justice attracts the beauty of this beauty *[silence]* virginity enjoys this beauty *[silence]* wisdom wishes to join this beauty. In this beauty charity gives birth to a desire for a union with you and makes us manifest your advice. *Cupio dissolvi, et esse cum Christo.*"[17]

Second quality: Miracles.

"*Mirabilis Deus in Sanctis suis*[18] *[silence]* admirable in the Father, admirable in the holy Spirit, admirable in yourself, Word, admirable in all your workings; the more [your working is] humble and base the more [it is] admirable *[silence]* you are admirable in the Father when you appease his wrath (if he can have wrath in himself) against us; and isn't blood a marvelous means to appease him, since it is what incites us to wrath the most? And he becomes admirable to us if we consider that he, who is infinite, immensely great, and powerful, and containing everything in himself, lets himself be offended and is offended by such a base and a contemptible thing, the creature; and then he calms down when the creature humiliates herself just a little bit. This is an admirable miracle that you, Word, do before your eternal Father by means of your Blood. And who can understand it? Only those who experience it can understand it; and only those who you allow to experience it can understand it *[silence]* oh Word, you are admirable in the holy Spirit because you ask him to infuse himself into the soul, and through this infusion the soul unites with God; it [the holy Spirit] makes her give birth to God, taste God, and delight only in God. And if the soul missed the infusion of the holy Spirit it would become like a devil, would feed on what the devil feeds on, and would enjoy what he [the devil] enjoys *[silence]* oh, we have so many, so many incarnate devils nowadays, danger on the sea, danger on earth, danger *in falsis fratribus*[19] *[silence]* admirable, you are also admirable, oh Word, in yourself. I mean, you are admirable because you discern yourself in us; [you are] admirable because you understand yourself, possess yourself, and leave yourself to us *[silence]* those who don't recognize your greatness and don't fear your judgment deny your admirable being; they spend their time sinning, with no respect or awe whatsoever *[silence]* on the contrary, your elect do recognize your admirable being, because they acknowledge that nothing could move without your providence and your divine will; and [they acknowledge] that you give us all our goods, without looking at our sins which deserve infinite punishments *[silence]* oh, infinite glory of your elect! But we feel an intolerable pain because we are unable to share this glory with everybody. Oh admirable being of my Word, so few know you; so few recognize you! *[silence]* whose admirable being is like the sea that, taking all the rivers' water, leads them to their end and confounds their name; thus we don't call them rivers any longer, but sea. The sea produces precious stones and fish having in their stomach gems and inestimable stones *[silence]* in the sea of your admirable being we constantly navigate and risk to drown because of the incessant waves; and when we deny to follow your flow, because we don't know your admirable being that only wants to save us, we make ourselves unable to receive the salvation you want to grant us."

And after these words she stood up because she had finished to analyze the admirable being of her beloved Word and wanted to move to his next quality. And she always did this, every time she finished with one quality and wanted to examine the following one. As David is reported to have done, that is, after having composed the psalms totally rapt in God, when he was done with everything he had received in himself, he stood up and walked toward east to understand all the divine and profound secrets God had revealed to him during his composition of the psalms.

And after standing for a while, then she sat down again in silence. Later, after a long pause, she explained everything she had perceived.

184

Third quality: Wisdom.

"*Et sapientia eius non est numerus*[20] *[silence]* et sapientia illius implevit me*[21] *[silence]* wisdom is the propriety of your Trinity, life for your spouse, thalamus of her Spouse, the Word, comfort for those who are tired, shade for the pilgrims, kingdom and haven of the virgins. Word, wisdom that only those who become totally unwise can understand; *nos stulti propter Christum, vos autem prudentes in Christo.*[22] Only those who don't know what wisdom is can taste this wisdom, because human wisdom is like a flower that, when it is cut from its fruit, soon withers and does not flourish any longer; this foolishness, that the world considers wisdom, ensnares so many, so many! But if we tried to join it with your divine wisdom, we would obtain a preservative coating beneficial both to ourselves and to the others; we shall feed on it, and the others will find comfort in its word. And, although everyone has either one or the other [word], everyone should seek yours *[silence]* oh Word, your wisdom is like that bush you deigned to show to Moses; it burns but it doesn't burn out. Yes, oh Word, it burns; *ignem veni mittere in terram*[23] *[silence]* it doesn't burn out, as you said: '*Qui manducat me vivet propter me; et qui manducat hunc panem vivet in aeternum*'[24] *[silence]* those who seek and follow human wisdom, which is nothing but foolishness to God, abhor your wisdom. They are so many now! You, Word, you know those who can say: '*Nihil inveni manu mea*'[25] *[silence]* also those who deny their union with you abhor your wisdom. They offend you and deny you and themselves *[silence]* wisdom of [the Word], you dilate the soul! *[silence]* wisdom of my Word, what do you do? You raise the soul up and plunge it into the abyss *[silence]* wisdom, you erect and tear down every building *[silence]* wisdom that always mourns and sings, watches and sleeps, walks and never moves *[silence]* wisdom, you hold every treasure and are held by every foolishness *[silence]* and do we acquire this wisdom? Perhaps with intelligence? Nothing, we would be really foolish if we thought so. Do we acquire it in time? At the right time. Not with wealth, since everything is vanity. With words, maybe? No, because *vir linguosus non dirigetur in terra*[26] *[silence]* so, how do we acquire this wisdom? We acquire it with the enlightened intelligence of God's being, with a constant affection and desire for God in God. And those who have reached this have acquired the pleasure of wisdom. Those who taste it experience it, and those who know nothing understand it. Oh, why don't we constantly move with a constant movement to acquire this wisdom? *[silence]* wisdom, you establish the skies perpetually in motion; you glorify the angelic and human spirits; wisdom that nourishes its spouses; wisdom, you make your christs powerful; wisdom, you confound every wisdom and extol every ignorance; wisdom, you verify every truth and confound every lie; wisdom, you are the crown of your spouse, the church, and fertility of your spouse, the soul."

At once, she stopped speaking. After a short pause, she stood up and understood, as we said above. Then, sitting down, after quite a while she started to speak about the fourth quality.

Fourth quality: Science.

"*Scientia Dei abissus multa [silence]* science, you are like that sweet fruit of the palm tree that makes very sweet fruits; and [it makes fruits] not in every corner, but only where the soil is suitable for it. And the palm tree also casts the most pleasing shade *[silence]* in this way your wisdom, Word, fructifies in those who are receptive *[silence]* but those who are not receptive can acquire as much wisdom as they want, they will neither attain it, nor will they have a minimum of your science *[silence]* oh science of my Word, who will ever be able to recount it? For everything we say is a lie and foolishness *[silence]* oh science of my Word, like the palm tree you are evergreen *[silence]* your science, Word, is nothing but possessing you; with it you created the human being *[silence]* you infuse your science with the internal—shall I dare to say this? I can say it but I can't understand it—with the internal gift of your soul to us. And as your soul is the medium between your divinity and your humanity, so is your science the medium through which we move to you *[silence]* and, Word, how does your science influence our soul? Oh, it does this: it turns our soul into that animal called ox, which keeps chewing the food it has taken. In the same way those who have this science constantly chew, chew, to the point that they almost reach an equality with the idea of your Trinity; and so they have a glimpse of the highest good *[silence]* this divine science has four legs, which it

186

uses to go to you. I mean, it wishes four things. First, it wishes to join you; second, [it wishes] to come to enjoy you; third, [it wishes] to honor you; fourth, [it wishes] to consume for you, and with its consummation it wishes to nourish its neighbor *[silence]* with our pride we stifle this science that you always infuse, and you would infuse it even more if we detached our pride from ourselves *[silence]* you make our life longer so that everyone receives what he deserves with justice; indeed justice means to give everyone what he merits. God deserves honor and our neighbor [deserves] our care, charity, and love. But this justice is not done properly. Oh how many of us are in fact full of injustice; and we are so foolish to believe that we do justice to our neighbors and to ourselves! We are unjust toward ourselves because so often our pride takes us away from ourselves! And every time we take ourselves away from ourselves we deprive ourselves of ourselves, because every being comes from you. We don't give our neighbor what he deserves. You ordered us to love him unconditionally: *'Diliges proximum tuum sicut te ipsum.'*[27] We take away from God what belongs to God every time we take ourselves away from him, because we are his and he is ours: *'Empti enim estis,'*[28] and the apostle doesn't say: *'estis vestris'* *[silence]* oh good Jesus, how many, how many wish they had their neighbor's life. I wish I had thousands lives to satisfy this desire of theirs. Oh, I see so many, so many coveting gold and silver, but everything is vanity! If I could, I turned into vanity itself to satisfy their desire *[silence]* mercy toward each other is totally dismissed; and you are full of mercy and are always merciful toward everyone, although most of the time we make ourselves unworthy of it *[silence]* oh, you are so merciful in putting up with me, full of misery and cause of every evil because I don't know how to make myself a wall and a partition wall; and my offenses cause every evil *[silence]* woe, woe my soul, cause of every evil. Its [my soul's] offenses are so many that it can't defend and be in defense. I shall dare to say that I would like to be your Spirit in order to infuse myself in everybody. Indeed, although everybody is a sinner and I am a miserable wretch, I would infuse myself in everybody *[silence]* oh John, your voice has been forgotten: *'Diligite alterutrum.'*[29] And then everyone is offended because bad people and good people are mingled; and the bad ones always try to disturb and offend everyone *[silence]* oh, I'm so miserable, I, I cause every evil; because of my ingratitude and my pride we don't respect this principle. I wish I could turn into water to sprinkle every heart *[silence]* great wonder is when we starve, see some bread, and can't take it. I'm sorry for my impotence; I am unable to satisfy the need you show me. Oh Word, I wish I could be in every place, get to every place, and be in no place, but only get to you, and be with you and in you."

We can really say about this blessed soul: *"Beati qui esuriunt e[t] sitiunt iustitiam."*[30] She longs so intensely for the soul's salvation that she consumes like burning wax. It is clear that the Lord has created her for this, and has drawn and draws her to this vocation, so that she lead some souls to him. And she never fails to respond to this vocation. Oh, if you had seen her that night—she spoke those words with such a fervor and a burning devotion—you would have been amazed and astonished. We are unable to describe her movements, her words, and her gestures in detail, because we, who saw and heard her, have the feeling that we would spoil everything, which is true. In any case, we shall continue to narrate her vision as accurately as we can, because we do not want to fail to manifest God's working in his spouse.

Later she said: "Today I see that the world is reduced to its worst condition. And why? Because it has totally lost charity, love, and dedication *[silence]* I envy the birds in the sky that can fly everywhere and let everybody hear their voices; one can hear them everywhere. They never, never stay anywhere in order to avoid to be offended. They fear that, if they stayed somewhere, they could be caught and offended *[silence]* oh Word, I wish I could do the same; [I wish I could] fly everywhere, let everybody hear my words. In this way I would be able to place love and dedication in the creatures' hearts. And I know that I couldn't be caught, because I would only stop in you."

And as soon as she had spoken these words, she stood up looking amazed, showing that she was seeing something. And after remaining engrossed for a bit, all of a sudden her face became very cheerful. Laughing, she said: "Oh Word, come, come, you are little, you'll hide. Come, come, the little ones don't have any fear *[silence]* oh, oh, I see something in one of your christs. Come, come, he has just abandoned the right path. Come, Word, please come; come into him, so that his deeds, displeasing to you before, will please you now. Come, you are little; although his heart is stained and sinful, you'll go into it. It must have one good side, a little bit of good will. Oh Word, come *[silence]* don't you want to come? *[silence]* oh, is the Father holding him? *[silence]* please, Father, let he come. Remember the blood he has shed. Oh, Father, Father, let him come *[silence]* Word, come, come, you are little, you'll hide and the Father won't see you. You'll go into that heart and it will convert to you. Remember that, when you wanted to free the creature from her sin, you hid your greatness by making yourself little. With your greatness you wouldn't have been able to look at our human misery, and thus we would have never been freed. Oh, come, Word *[silence]* oh, he's coming, he's coming. Come, come."

Using one or both hands and raising her arms, she made the gesture of inviting him, as we do when we call someone. And later, following what she said, we recorded these words: "Oh Word, if I could take you I would hide you in him so well! But in any case, don't leave your spouse."

And sitting down she showed that he had gone into that priest and he was thus totally converted. For this reason she said: "See, I made it; after praying and praying I finally got it. But, Word, see, I'm not happy, because I'd like to have many other christs. And, although only a few really serve you, there are so many that one only doesn't satisfy me. Oh, Word, give me others. If you give them to me, they'll help many more creatures come to you. Being like candles on a chandelier, they illuminate the other creatures. Word, send, send your light to them; and let them come back to you. You see how much we need it. Oh, if they who are the light of the world are in fact its darkness, imagine how dark the other creatures are. And if they who are the salt of the world are in fact conceited, how could they possibly season the other creatures and show them the path leading to you, if they themselves are walking on a path contrary to you? Oh Word, and nevertheless they are those who touch you and are close to you all the time more than any other creature. The fact that in reality they are the most distant from you, I can't stand it. Please, Word, give them light, and make everyone convert to you *[silence]* oh Word, you know, I do what the children do; when they taste a fruit, they immediately want a second one. I'd like you to give me some other souls. However, even though they are infinite—and this is due to my ingratitude and my pride—, I shall turn to this one only *[silence]* oh Word, do not permit such a base and vulgar thing to thwart a christ that serves you with sincerity and purity. It is possible that a creature, created in God's image and likeness, becomes more base than a beast. Indeed, beasts serve the creatures and do so because God has created them. But the creature not only refuses to do what she was created for, she also prevents its possible fruits from sprouting. I offer you the milk with which Mary nourished you *[silence]* and to you, Father, I offer my Word's blood. Respond, respond to this blood, because I am not worthy of being responded to and my ingratitude causes every evil. Infuse your blood into them; make them long for it; punish, punish me, and give me either an external or internal punishment, as you like. You forgave the Magdalen. Please, forgive her too and let her hear you internally. Mercy is always good, but you tell me that it is not good when it feeds on iniquity. But I don't want to judge that who ministers you *[silence]* infuse, infuse your blood into them. Even if I had to suffer all the pains of purgatory to save them, I would feel content *[silence]* oh angels, please pray to him. But of course, you want to pray to him but not to force him. Although I could force him, I am such a miserable wretch that I don't dare to do it. Respond, respond to your blood, and infuse it into them. Word, respond to your servant, or better yet, to your servants, and show them what they must do *[silence] beati misericordes.*[31] Unfortunately, here mercy has nourished iniquity. It is a great wonder that, where is immense ignorance, there it is also an immense abundance of light *[silence]* oh, why can't I end, and begin a new life for those who are close to death? Oh, I am a miserable wretch, why can't I consume and be consumed by the other creatures, so that every pain would fall upon me? Oh Word, punish, punish my infinite ingratitude, blindness, and ignorance *[silence]* and, oh Word, what must we do externally? Must we use justice or mercy? I know well that, as far as the interior part is concerned, we need your motion; and [I know that] mercy, an infinite mercy results from goodness, but I can't believe that goodness is everything, because it nourishes so much iniquity. Word, I don't want to listen to you, but to those who minister you *[silence]* oh Word, but you called Matthew to your apostolate, the one who had offended you and who *[silence]* please, call her too, not to the apostolate but to a knowledge of you *[silence] iustus Dominus et iustitiam dilexit, aequitatem vidit vultus eius.*[32]

"Although I live in a time when they offend you the most, you still feel offended the most by those who receive your light and your disposition to love the most *[silence]* science, compendium of yourself."

She stopped speaking for quite a while. As usual, she stood up and walked east to fathom the following quality of the Word. Later, going back to her seat, after a long silence she examined the fifth quality.

Fifth quality: Power.

"Oh power *[silence]* powerful is the Word in all his workings: *Domini est terra* and *plenitudo eius, orbis terrarum et universi qui habitant in eo.*[33] *Ipse dixit* and *facta sunt, ipse mandavit* and *creata sunt*[34] *[silence]* I see the Word having a great power when he takes our souls upon himself; [I see the Word having] a great power when he tolerates them; a great power when he glorifies them *[silence]* you have a great power in everything you do, because your power is so great that whatever you do you do it without power. *Ego occidam* and *ego vivere faciam, percutiam et ego sanabo.*[35] I see that the creatures deny your power in all their activities. In their wrong intentions they deny your power; in their false words they deny your power; in their feeble workings they deny your power, because if they believed that you are so powerful, they would feel fearful and timorous, would constantly watch themselves in order not to offend you, and would be on the alert waiting for your advent, as you said: '*Vigilate* and *orate, quia nescitis qua hora Dominus vester venturus sit*'[36] *[silence]* the foolish virgins didn't understand your power, because otherwise they would have prepared better. Your power is so great that words cannot overcome it. *Domine, Domine.* No, it's not enough, no *[silence]* your power is similar to the tree called pine, whose fruit is so hard and contains many many [seeds]; and if you want the pith of

191

that fruit you must put it on fire. In the same way, if we want to understand and reach the pith of your power, and thus become powerful ourselves, we must put ourselves on the fire of your divine love, and strike ourselves with the knife of your word. In so doing, we shall take that sweet and nourishing fruit out of your power *[silence]* oh, the soul that has and tastes the fruit of your power feels such a marvelous sweetness, since it [the soul] knows that it has such a great power now that neither the devil nor any other creature can overcome or defeat it if it doesn't want to *[silence]* great power is to lead a creature to you *[silence]* great power is to covert a sinner because, as the fruit of the pine contains many [seeds], so does the working of converting a sinner contain many future operators *[silence]* the Father works *[silence]* you, Word, work; the holy Spirit works; the blessed souls work; the creatures work through their prayers *[silence]* this fruit also sends out the sweetest smell. Oh, what a sweet smell was the fragrance of your blood! And what a great power you had when you shed it."

Sixth quality: Eternity.

"Eternity, eternity! *[silence]* eternal, eternal, eternal in giving birth to yourself; eternal in glorifying the angels; eternal in conceiving the creatures; eternal in your workings. And what more? [You are] eternal in generating yourself, through yourself, in yourself, and from yourself. With no beginning and no end; alpha and omega; you have no beginning and are the beginning of everything; you are with no end and will never end, because eternity can never end. And please, grant this to yourself; understand it by yourself; enjoy it through yourself and in yourself, because we are unable to do it *[silence]* eternal eternity, oh my eternity! Eternal in glorifying the angels, who you prepared before creating them, or better yet you created them to enjoy yourself in an eternal eternity. Every past time, every future time—but why do I say time?—every present eternity and every future eternity is disclosed only to you *[silence]* which heart doesn't rejoice and exult just by hearing: 'Your God, our God, your Spouse and your Father, he is eternal'? Oh, oh, oh! *[silence]* eternal also in giving birth to your creature *[silence] ab eterno* you gave birth to her in your idea, when all of them [creatures] were present to you. You prepared them yourself, so that she could enjoy you; and then you took up their being to enjoy them and glorify them: *Et delitiae meae esse cum filiis hominum*[37] *[silence]* and this is similar to the cypress which never rots and sends out a marvelous smell; and it does not fructify because its fruit is not visible. In the same way, your eternity does not generate and does not fructify, since you are your own fruit and send out a powerful smell *[silence]* it ascends; and who ascends more than your eternity, which is so sublime that it is not comprehensible to us down here. Indeed, if I asked what eternity is everyone, unless he knew you, would admit that he doesn't know what it is. Those who confide in the creatures deny your eternity. Cursed be those men who confide in other men and find support in flesh! Your eternity contains your power, since they are like a chain."

Seventh quality: Imperturbability.

"But [to go to] your imperturbability we must go to your humanity, which makes you seem passible even though you are imperturbable. And given that we cannot attain your imperturbability, you had to become passible in order to make us imperturbable later. And you had to become little to let our baseness understand you. But what am I saying? 'To let us understand you'? But if we can't understand the smallest nothing! We can't enjoy even a spark of your imperturbability."

And after these words she stood up in a great surprise, showing with her hands that she was seeing Jesus when he was little, like the other time. He was coming down from the Father's bosom to the floor. And she started to call him with a great joy, clapping her hands and calling with one hand or with both she invited him to come closer to her. She said: "Come, come, please come. Oh, Word, come, come." And after a short while she did the same, saying: "Oh Word, come, come *[silence]* oh, you stop. Come, come. You are little, and the little ones often hide; hide under that throne. The Father won't see you. Come, please come, yes *[silence]* Word, now I shall ask him to come to my heart. I. Come, come *[silence]* but if you don't want to, I don't want to force you because I don't want to enjoy anything without your consent *[silence]* Word, come, come, come."

She signified with her hands that she was inviting Jesus to come to her, and at once she crossed them tight on her breast showing an immense joy. And rejoicing, she went and sat down showing that she had received the baby Jesus. She said: *"Verbum caro factum est,* and *habitavit in me."*

Crossing her hands and arms on her knees, palms up, and in a way that showed that they were holding love Jesus, she stared at her hands. Laughing and speaking to him, she looked so delighted and content that we were amazed and astounded. She told him so many little things. First, she laughed and said: "You, little one! *[silence]* Jesus, those little eyes of yours *[silence]* oh, oh, that beautiful, blond, and cute hair! *[silence]* Jesus, your little hands do good!"

She showed that he wanted to hug her. She said: "Hug me." Bending her neck and pulling it back at once, she said: "And no, no, keep them this way, my poor baby *[silence]* oh my little baby, your cute little feet, oh, oh *[silence]* oh, my poor little one *[silence]* my Spouse, I'd like to kiss you a little bit." And she looked as if she were consuming. She said: "Jesus, I'll kiss you *[silence]* Jesus. Come and look his cute little mouth."

And after being quiet for a short while, she showed that Jesus wanted to leave: "Oh please, a bit more *[silence]* oh, oh, oh, he has given himself these little ears to listen to us *[silence]* then that little nose to smell pure hearts. You are so great that you wouldn't be able to perceive such a base thing."

Then, all of a sudden she stood up, showing that Jesus was going back to the Father's bosom. Slowly raising her hands just a bit, she said: "Now I give him back." And going back to sit, raising her head, and looking up, she said: "Oh, he is better off in the Father's bosom."

And being quiet for a bit, she resumed her discourse about the Word's imperturbability. She said: "You became perturbable so that we could comprehend our imperturbability *[silence]* you suffered too much, but it looks like you didn't suffer at all, since we love you so little *[silence]* it's incredible that men, who are perturbable, turn into earth and food for worms, become dust and ashes, they don't want to suffer *[silence]* I know very well that, if the Word did to me what I deserve, I would suffer so much that I would probably pass away and would lose any hope to be saved. But I hope that the Word's blood will hide my faults and my iniquity. And, and I wish that everyone set his hopes on this blood, and [I wish] that thanks to this hope everyone abandoned every form of sin and pride. In this way, we could hope to receive mercy through this blood *[silence]* oh, those poor damned souls won't receive it! And why did they deprive themselves of the blood's worth? For a nothing, a nothingness, a nullity *[silence]* oh, I wish I could take away and destroy every memory of ingratitude, malice, and pride so that nobody would hear of them anymore."

She turned to the damned souls and said: "You yourselves deprived yourselves of it and will enjoy these pains by yourselves *[silence]* the fruit of this imperturbability is the sweet fig that grows leaves and fruits at the same time. In the same way, oh Word, as soon as it was united to you, your humanity had its imperturbability at once. *Aperiam os meum in parabolis*[38] *[silence]* oh Word, your goodness is so infinitely good that we may compare you with such a base thing, a fig. But you make us more and more certain of it by constantly manifesting your goodness. And, even though I already had it in myself, it keeps growing. Indeed, the more our familiarity with it grows, the more our certainty grows *[silence]* the pith of this fruit is pure and white. Oh, how pure is the soul that retires in your humanity! We take so many of these fruits and dry them so that they can last for a long time. They dry in the heat of the sun and with fire. Oh Word, you took us, your creatures, and generated some of us, like our ancient Fathers, and regenerated some others, those who were present at that time, and [regenerated] also us, who would come later. For first you generated all of us and then regenerated us with your blood; and you constantly put us in your side and dry us, keep us, and preserve us, so that we can last forever and be chewed by you. We are your pure and snow-white gifts to yourself, Word. Oh imperturbability, humanity, and divinity! Oh Word, what a marvel is to be chewed and tasted by your imperturbability, humanity, and divinity! But those who wish to be tasted by you, they need to be burned in the fire of your divine love, and be dried and purified of any form of pride."

Eighth quality: Union.

"Oh union, union, generated when you, Word, descended upon us. You united your divinity with our humanity so well; oh yes, yes, you unite us to you *[silence] Verbum caro factum est, et unitus est Sponsum ad sponsam [silence]* oh, oh, oh, union, who can taste you? But, but, one must unite with your body and your blood!"

At this point she sensed that the father confessor had arrived to give us communion. Indeed, we were told so when he had just got to his usual place. And after keeping a bit quiet, she recovered from this rapture at the eighth hour. And when the father confessor came to give us communion, she took it with the others. Immediately after she went back to her vision and, after being engrossed and silent for quite a while, resumed her discourse about union.

After Communion.

"Oh union, union, union! *[silence]* who will be able to understand it? It's enough to say 'union,' that is, what is equal unites with what is unequal in order to make it equal, and all the angelic spheres are amazed. But in how many ways does this union take place? In many ways. Through faith and admiration, through abandonment, through love, through the sacrament, and through that virtue deriving from certain little animals that proceed from your wounds. They take us up and lead us into your wounds, and there the union takes place *[silence] omnia per omnia facta sunt*[39] *in ipso [silence]* this union takes place through faith by means of that noble bird called eagle, proceeding from the wound in your left foot; and proceeding from the faith which is like our food, we allure it [the eagle] to us, and then it takes us and leads us to the pure bed chamber of your left foot. Here by means of faith it unites us with you. *Sola fides sufficit.*[40] And in order to lead a bigger quantity, what does the eagle do in this bed chamber? When it goes in there, it slowly becomes younger and younger, recovering its strength and renewing itself completely. In this way it can draw more faithful souls to this bed chamber where, tasting their union with your divinity, they hold a pure and faithful conversation *[silence]* oh, what a sweet union there, where the soul becomes a second you! *[silence]* yes, if union turns two things into one, no difference exists any longer because one thing becomes the other, although each of them still maintains its being *[silence]* what does union do? It makes both the soul and the body engrossed in you, Word, and totally in you, as if it [the body] were dead.

"From your right foot the turtle dove proceeds, and there it comes back to stay in the same way and through the same act. Our soul, in a complete admiration, feeds on it and mourns. Indeed, if with the eagle we believe that faith is enough, with the turtle dove we mourn and admire. But we do not admire external things, no, but rather the internal workings God does with the soul. So few of us perceive and understand it [this working], even though we can easily admire it in the corporeal things. And when the soul resides in the wound of your right foot, it keeps mourning because it can't fully understand the working you do with the soul, and also [it does not understand] your honor and your glory *[silence]* oh, how little we can contemplate this union of admiration! Oh Word, how little we can perceive and understand your internal working in the soul!

"Then through abandonment. From your left hand a simple and pure dove proceeds and there it places us in the same way and through the same act, taking us up and drawing us to itself. There, we give birth with the dove and take up the dove's being, which is an intimate meekness. Thus, being there we hold a conversation of meekness and abandonment *[silence]* oh, how many are the workings of abandonment? Every working, every feeling, every desire, every thought is a great working of abandonment before you.

"The other union is a union of love. From your right hand a very loving pelican comes forth. Taking up our soul in the same way and through the same act, it leads it and places it in the enclosure of your right hand, where a perfect union of love takes place. This union thrills it [the pelican] so much that it comes to consider its enemies as its children. And it leads us to this love, which brings about an absent conversation of love. *Sic Deus dilexit mundum, ut Filium suum Unigenitum daret,*[41] *ut universum mundum salvet.*[42] This conversation will be a desiring love, a communicative love, and a unifying love.

"This union also takes place through the sacrament in your holy side, whence the ardent Seraphim with six wings proceeds. Its wings take us up. With two it takes up the soul; with two it takes up the body; and with the other two [it takes up] the powers of our soul, which it then places in the ardent cave of your holy side. There we acquire six wings as well; with two wings we contemplate the earth; with one [we contemplate] the right side and with the other [we contemplate] the left side; and with the other two we contemplate the sky *[silence]* and what do we contemplate with the two wings toward the sky? What do we contemplate? With one wing we contemplate your divinity and with the other [we contemplate] your equality. With the right wing we contemplate God, that is, his mercy and purity: his mercy, *quia misericors et miserator Dominus;*[43] his purity, *quia puritas est Deus* and *purita[tem] dilexit.*[44] With the left wing we contemplate our neighbor with justice and truth; and with the other two we contemplate the earth, because if we only delighted in heaven we would deserve hell, and if we clung to earth too much we would never be able to ascend to heaven. In a similar way, oh Word, as your soul is the medium between your divinity and your humanity, thus it must be between heaven and earth, remaining neither in heaven nor on earth. In the cave of your side we hold an angelic conversation, where each word hides thousands of sacraments. But what does this angelic conversation do? It takes away every will, every knowledge, every power because, since it contains nothing of us, it takes away from our soul every image and every thing that could separate us from God. And here every intellect ends, although one still perceives something like its presence. And this quality of your union is similar to a vine, which at once grafts and unites *[silence]* when a vine is planted it has no rootlets; so in this union we must have no, no root and no foundation at all, being neither in heaven nor on earth *[silence]* when at the beginning one prunes a vine-shoot deeply, it lasts longer and bears much sweeter fruits *[silence]* prune, prune, take away every image if you want to bear sweet and lasting fruits *[silence]* this vine must have a pole, which is the holy cross. What is a soul living on earth without its cross? One must get a cross either from the devil or from the other creatures, because there is no greater cross than being without any cross *[silence]* but one must also have something to tie it with, not something hard but rather something lovesome, so that the vine doesn't break. And this is a correct disposition in every situation, both internally and externally, both in the soul and in the body, in every prayer and every contemplation, in every thought, in every word and working, because this is a sweet and pure that ties everything *[silence]* the fruit of this vine is nothing but giving birth to souls for God, whose desire produces a pressed wine which intoxicates God himself. An image of this was the patriarch Noah who planted the vine *[silence]* this fecundating fruit is hated by those who can't face any minimal temptation and can't have any form of conversation with their neighbors. Alas, for them every little thing is a big cross. *Ecce quam bonum* and *quam iocundum habitare fratres in unum*[45] *[silence]* oh Word, how much more you appreciate a work done in union than one done in disunion; how much more you appreciate an eye twinkling in union than a martyrdom suffered in disunion. Where is union there is God, and where is disunion there is the devil. How strongly we should seek this union, and how passionately we should love it! *[Silence]* in a word, where is union there is every good, copiousness of every thing, of every celestial and earthly wealth; and where is disunion every good is absent, every God's grace, every creatures' benevolence, and only a radical famine is present. *Non vidit iustum derelictum, ne[c] semen eius querens panem.*"[46]

Ninth quality: Communication.

"Then comes communication, which is God's being. Oh communication! And what do you communicate, Word? To whom do you communicate? Why do you communicate? Oh, you communicate in order to make death into life, light into darkness, prison into freedom, a servant into a lord, and a slave into a son. And what do you communicate? You communicate yourself. Could you possibly communicate something more than that? To whom do you communicate? You communicate yourself to those who contemplate, because you communicate to a temple *non manufactum.*[47] And what is the goal of your communication? So that communication can be communicated; and as you said, you communicate yourself so much, that everything the Father had disclosed to you you disclosed it to us: "*Omnia quaecumque audivi a Patre meo nota feci vobis,*"[48] and you did this in such an intrinsic and hidden way that, you see, only you and those who taste it understand it *[silence]* but, oh Word, why don't they become able to understand it? Oh, oh, I am the cause of everything, I am the cause of every evil. Oh, I am the rampart obstructing everything! But with your strong hand, oh Word, you break and demolish everything, because with your communication you nourish the soul, help it grow, and fortify it. One feeds on your communication as a baby feeds on his mother's milk. Then you give us bread, which is your communication as well. But me, perhaps I am too proud, I'd like to ask for bread first and then for milk because, you see, Word, I'll be able to break it with your teeth, not with mine. You know, Word, every milk is aloe unless you communicate it to every creature. But as all things proceed from you, all your graces, all your gifts, and all your things go back to you who are like the sea, or better yet the sea of every good. But could be the soul in love with you deprived of a greater good and a greater thing, than being able to see a soul convert to you? *[silence]* oh my Spouse Word, if you are communicating, why don't you communicate yourself to every creature? And if communication is in transient things, please communicate yourself also in those things, and deprive me of every pleasure and consolation, as long as they come to you. Yes, since in your house less is better than too much, and it is better to suffer than to abound. *Melius est modicum iusto super divitias peccatorum multas;*[49] and it is better to live in your house than somewhere else with wealth.

"But let us go back to your communication. I say that it is similar to the tree called fir, that spreads its branches so that everyone'd like to be in its shade. In the same way you, Word, spread the branches of your communication, but not everyone comes and rests in your shade. *Sub umbra illius consolabit me.*[50] Oh Word, please spread your branches so that at least some of them come back to you."

And all of a sudden she stood up, showing that she was seeing something marvelous. After remaining engrossed for quite a while, she said: *"Vidi Deum sedere super thronum magnum et elevatum*[51] *comunicationis suae, et procidentes Angeli adoraverunt eum dicentes: admiramini omnes qui diligitis eum in comunicatione suae maiestatis* and *bonitatis*[52] *[silence]* oh, what a great communication of my Word to his creatures; he communicates himself, that is not known, not sought, not loved, and not owned. *Redime me a calumniatoris, ut custodiam mandata tua*[53] *[silence] consolamini, consolamini,*[54] *quem non repudiavit desiderium sponsae suae, in comunicatione electorum suorum.*"[55]

She showed that the Lord had responded to her request that he communicate himself to the creatures *[silence]* then, becoming silent again, she looked upset. Lowering her eyes, she said:

"*Dixi tibi ecce non movebor in aeternum.*[56] *Portio mea tu es, dixi custodire legem tuam.*"[57]

And, [looking] exhausted, she threw herself on the floor, as she had done at the beginning of this rapture; and again she entered the annihilation of herself. After being in that way for a bit, she said: "*Domine non est exaltatum cor meum, neque elati sunt oculi mei.*"[58]

And sitting on her knees, she came out of this rapture when the thirteenth hour struck. When she comes out of her raptures, she usually goes back to the beginning of her vision. Thus, we always understand when she is close to recover. At that point, if someone besides the usual people witnessed her rapture, we ask this person to leave. This is what we did this morning.

Let us always praise the Lord, beginning and end of our conversation.

Dialogue 48
Jesus' Forty Hours in the Tomb

On Friday May 17, 1585, from the morning and throughout the day our blessed soul was so engrossed, that she did not seem to be herself. Later, during our conversation, she told us that she heard the eternal Father say that he intended to finish what he had started showing her Sunday morning. So, before the twenty-first hour, she was rapt in spirit, and after a long silence she started to speak and said the following things: *[silence]* "Oh eternal Word, for so long, ah? *[silence]* you stayed underground for so long, forty hours, I mean in the sepulcher, and during that time you were in the Father's bosom in Limbo, and underground? And admiring I will follow you."

Then she kept quiet for a long while and wept. Afterward, we understood that she would have to be in that rapture for forty hours, accompanying her beloved Spouse, the Word, everywhere he went for those forty hours when he was in the sepulcher.[1] And since she had entered this rapture more than three hours before Jesus was buried—he was buried at the twenty-fourth hour and she had entered it before at the twenty-first hour—she realized that during that time she would come out of her rapture from time to time somehow in respect of her physical needs. And these additional hours would be granted to her for her needs so that it would be fulfilled the time of forty hours.

Then she said: "*Anticipationem pro infirmitate [silence]* and the time of forty hours will be fulfilled *[silence]* so that at the dawn of your happy Sunday I will serve. Yes, *[silence]* one can rightly call it the day of the Lord."

At the beginning she spoke in this broken manner, keeping silent from time to time, for she was conversing intimately with her Spouse the Word, who was telling her how long she would have to remain in that same rapture and everything she would have to do during that time. She limited herself to uttering the essence of her dialogue with Jesus. Then she continued:

"Oh yes, at this time you were not in the sepulcher. Ah, I'll go in there myself later, yes, of course! *[silence]* oh yes, at that time the mystery of the Trinity will be fulfilled, because it will be two nights and one day. The day for the eternal Father, the first night for the Word, and the second night for the Holy Spirit *[silence]* two of our nights is one of your days, because it is always light and day to you *[silence]* and during that time I'll be able to have you in the Holy Sacrament, because, even though I am with you, I want to make sure that I have you, ah."

She conversed with Jesus in such an amiable way until the twenty-second hour struck. Then, she sat down with her hands crossed on her knees. And after staying like that a little while, she knelt down on the floor with clasped hands and looking down to the floor. She showed that there she was seeing Jesus put down from the cross, and crying she spoke as the Virgin Mary:

VIRGIN MARY

"*Adoro Filium meum* and *Unigenitum tuum [silence] offero tibi Pater, per omnem creaturam sanguinem quem effudit ipsum Unigenitum Filium tuum pro redentione humana*[2] *[silence]* hurry up, oh Father, your Only Begotten and his Mother who nourished and nursed him."

Afterward, still on the floor, slightly leaning on her heels, she opened her arms and bent them down, showing that she was receiving Jesus in her arms: "*Date mihi Filium meum* and *sponsum meum qui fuit consolatio mea, et hac hora est afflitio mea. Consolavit* and *contristabit me.*"[3]

She lowered her eyes even more. After a short silence she looked upset and gave a deep sigh. Shaking all her body, she showed that she was gazing at every part of Jesus' body and at all the bruises he had received from the beating. In so doing, she penetrated the pain he had suffered in his passion. And she made gestures of pity and of great compassion as, we can imagine, the Virgin did when she had Jesus dead before her eyes and in her arms. She looked up and down, here and there, touching lightly with her hand as if she were cleaning him of his clotted blood and spit. Sometimes she showed great surprise, as if she were seeing something very piteous, crying, sighing, and shaking all her body; some other times she kissed the wounds he had on his hands, his feet, and his side. She looked as if she had in front of her one of those images of Jesus taken down from the cross, as one can see in some *Pietà*. Nor could one ever describe her pitiful manners and gestures. Everyone can imagine it by oneself, although no one would believe every thing she did at this time if one had not seen her.

When she looked at his feet she said: "Oh, Magdalen!" *[silence]* And then she sat up, whereas before she was bent, and pulled back her hands on her knees. Then, looking back to Jesus' side, she said: "Oh, why don't all of us get into your side, which is so open and is such a big cave, oh Love?"

Then shivering and grieving, she showed that they wanted to take Jesus away from her to bury him. Thus she said: "Leave him here a bit more."

And she contemplated his head again, showing that she was taking the crown of thorns from his head; and she stretched her hand toward a nun who was close to her. And she said: "Take it *[silence]* oh Magdalen, oh Magdalen! *[silence]* you were at those feet, but I am at his mouth that has narrated his Father's eternal will so well *[silence]* why can't I turn my heart into a sepulcher?"

Then, sitting up on her knees with clasped hands, she said:

"Once again, oh eternal Father, I offer you his blood for the humankind *[silence]* oh Father, confirm his apostles and his disciples, and let them participate in your vision, because I see them doubt *[silence]* oh my Son, when I had you in my womb, I knew that I would see you in this way, but oh, oh! *[silence]* oh, I nourished you with all my love, but now I do not contemplate you with less love *[silence]* oh, if I could only put my mouth on yours, as you put your mouth on my breast! Oh how willingly I would do so! *[silence]* I gave you my milk, and you want to nourish all of humanity with your blood. Oh how willing would I have given mine in union with yours *[silence]* oh Truth of the eternal Father, my Only begotten and my

Firstborn! *[silence]* oh Word of the Father, My Spouse and my Son! *[silence]* wisdom of the Father, my foolishness and my folly! *[silence]* they will say of me: look at her there, the mother of that crucified *[silence]* you who are eternal, I see you dead and mortal *[silence]* oh John, you rested on his chest, but now he rests on yours *[silence]* oh Magdalen, by kissing his feet now you pay, you pay him the same homage you paid before when you kissed them. But I can't pay mine, I can't nourish him, nurse him, swaddle him, and kiss him alive, and I can't hear him speak, my Love."

And after a short while, all of a sudden she stood up with clasped hands, and slowly she walked toward the door of the room as if she went in procession to bury Jesus. And leaving the room in that way, she walked down the staircase that goes to the infirmary, and through that [she walked] to the staircase which goes down to the parlor. Then, still going downstairs, she passed through the courtyard toward the loggia. Looking down with clasped hands, she was so engrossed and carried herself as if she were really the Virgin. She walked with such a gravity, such a modesty and lightness, that she seemed to be carried more than she actually walked, as if her feet, so to speak, did not touch the ground. And after walking for a while in this way, she spoke the following words: "See how he is carried, that who carries everything! *[silence]* You carry him who carries you."

And continuing her journey she went up the staircase that goes to the living room in front of the Choir, and from there walking in the Oratory of the chapel of the Virgin she went to the Choir above the church. Once she got there she took a lectern that was in the middle of the Choir. She did so with such a dexterity and rapidity, as if it were a pen. Then she placed it in a corner of the Choir. Moving then to the middle she knelt down. With her hand she pointed to the right, and said: "His head will be here."

Afterward, opening her arms as she had done in the room for the novices which for her was the Mount Calvary, she asked to receive Jesus in her arms one more time before they buried him. She said: "Give him to me a bit more." And showing that she had had him, she said: "You are One in essence, and you are the only One who pierces my heart."

And after a short rest: "Go ahead, take him *[silence]* the place of disgrace becomes a heaven. Go ahead, take him *[silence]* why can't I invite all the creatures to chant the funeral for their Creator? I shall invite the angels. Come, oh angels, and bury my Son and your Creator *[silence]* bow, elements you all; praise and chant, birds you all, with jubilation, and also with scalding tears, because this incomprehensible working of Redemption has been offered, your working, Word and my Son *[silence]* incomprehensible today, but later it will be despised by many *[silence]* go ahead, take him away."

Offering her hands and then withdrawing her arms, she joined her hands and was very grieved without speaking any word, bending down in a way that she seemed to be looking down in the sepulcher. And after quite a while she gave a deep sigh, saying: "Why can't I enter with you? *[silence]* but since I can't enter with you you will enter into me *[silence]* they won't be able to say anymore *'Quia quem celi capere non poterant tuo gremio contulisti.'*[4] I won't be able to say anymore *'Exultate filie Sion,'* but rather *'plorate.'* One can now really say that the virgins have gone pale, and their face has grown wan. And your ministers cry, because you, the highest minister, not only do you cry but you are dead and buried. And I, a virgin, have gone pale, since you don't gaze at my face any longer *[silence]* I was boastful and I believed that the virgins would follow me and could boast of having an immortal Groom, but now I see you buried. I believed that they would able to go around daring and bold, and would pride themselves on having a Groom who was the most beautiful and the most distinguished among all the sons of men, and now I saw that you have neither beauty nor dignity *[silence]* you are the crown of the virgins, and now you have been crowned with thorns, and if you give it to them they will despise it *[silence]* now I can truly say that there is more than one heaven, since where your essence is, there is heaven. So, heaven in the sepulcher, heaven in limbo, heaven in purgatory, and what more, heaven in hell *[silence]* oh Groom, oh my Son, the greater you become the more humble you make yourself, since you wanted to be shut first in my womb, and then in the sepulcher! *[silence]* go ahead, go ahead, shut the Word, my Only begotten *[silence]* oh, and they'll keep you in this way, but your might will raise you."

THE DIALOGUES

SOUL

"Oh Mary, oh Word, oh Groom, so many, many want to keep you closed in the sepulcher, because they don't want you, they even fear to announce your name before the creatures! And others, regretting that they don't receive any gift from you, keep you shut up; and others, for their own indolence, lose you."

THE VIRGIN

"Oh, how will I ever be able to leave from here?" And standing up she said: "But will my faith fail me? Will I ever doubt that you are in the sepulcher and still with me? I mean, that you are in the sepulcher with me? Never."

And giving the impression that she was leaving, she moved a little bit from here, and then she went back there to that sepulcher. And she did this two or three times, going up and coming back. And then she set out for the procession, speaking these words: "Yes, you go announcing his name. And I go with John and Magdalen."

And coming back in the same way through the oratory of the chapel of the Virgin, along the way she spoke these other words: "I leave my Son and take my Word with me *[silence]* I leave whom I gave birth to and nourished with my milk, and I take with me the essence of the Trinity."

Walking a bit more, she spoke these other words: "Oh, Magdalen, what shall we do without our Love? *[silence] Confide filia.*"[5]

And she walked a bit more, and then she stopped, saying: "Oh, didn't he prophesy it many times? *[silence]* didn't he say that the temple would be destroyed and then in three [days] would be rebuilt? *[silence]* will you fail to believe the truth?"

And she stopped and then headed for the scriptorium, from where last Thursday she departed when she had the rapture of the whole Passion, as we have already written.[6] And since than time he did not offer [her] that mystery, the Lord has wanted to make up for what lacked the Good Friday, because [that time] he had had pity on her frailty. For that time she couldn't have endured such a discomfort, having suffered with Jesus for so long in her speech about his

Passion. Because for her this scriptorium is the Virgin Mary's house, she stopped here, proceeding with her rapture of the forty hours, which lasted until the dawn of Sunday morning.

When she entered this scriptorium, she sat down in her usual place. After keeping quiet for quite a long time, then she spoke as the Virgin Mary and Saint Mary Magdalen:

"Ah, Magdalen, offer your Master to the eternal Father, so that his Blood will fructify for all of us. Don't fail in your faith."

And refraining from speaking, being silent for a short while, all of a sudden she stood up and with a swift gravity she walked to the door of this scriptorium. She started to beckon and said: "Come in, come in Peter, come, come, come here. Come, come in, come in, because, even though you offended my Word, he is kind, and since he has forgiven you I forgive you too. You know, he has forgiven Magdalen, and he will forgive you too. But, come in, come here."

And moving as if she were taking him by hand and were walking him in, rather quietly she stood at the door without going down the stairs, and then she went back to sit at her place. And later, showing that she was speaking to St. Peter who was here with her, she said: "Besides, Peter, you know that David has written about him: *'Misericors e[t] miserator Dominus,*[7] *et miserationes eius super omnia opera eius'*[8] *[silence]* you know that he said that you are the stone on which he wants to erect his Church: *'Tu es Petrus* and *super hanc petram edificabo ecclesiam meam'*[9] *[silence]* yes, you denied the truth, but he died to pull down the lie and to fulfill his truth *[silence]* you know, you wouldn't have moved him to pity *[silence]* and Peter, strengthen your faith, if you cry now over the past try not to have to cry over the future."

And after keeping silent a bit more, she turned toward the door of the scriptorium, which was open, and said: "Oh John!"

She seemed to be seeing him out there, and this is why all of a sudden she stood up and went to that door once again, and said: "Come, come, oh John, if my Word recommended you to me, why don't you want to be where I [am]? Come in, please, and come here."

And turning over there while she was going back to sit at her place, she stopped a moment and said: "If you didn't feel like coming in because you are suffering, consider that I am suffering more than you."

And back to her seat she said: "If he is your Master, he is also my Son, you know that. If he is your Creator, he is my Spouse. If you rested on his chest, well, I had him in my bosom *[silence]* oh John, you will be so strengthened, that you'll be able to tell what he has done in my bosom. You will tell the union; you will tell the love and the affection, and you will ask them to love each other, and you will write that in the beginning he was by his Father, and you will speak of his divinity, even though you are now so afraid."

And after a short while she stood up one more time and went to that door, and waved at someone to invite him in. According to what we understood later, this was St. James the Great. And when she asked him to come in she said: "Come, come, you too, keep company to these others and to me. Come in, please, you poor things. I love him more than you. Please, come in."

And back to her seat, she said: "Well, here I am in the company of those who followed my Word. And, if you were with him at the time of his transfiguration and his pain in the kitchen garden, you are rightly now with whom has given birth to him."

Turning to St. James, she said: "Even though you are not so sure as others are, you must know that I am the Mother of Pity who has given birth to Pity *[silence]* preserve the words of the eternal Word, you know that you must be his trumpet *[silence]* oh, I shall say to you what the truth did: 'men of poor faith' *[silence]* yes, you don't doubt, and still *[silence]* but the word of my truth must come true: *Percutiam Pastorem e[t] dispergentur oves gregis*[10] *[silence]* in your talk don't lose your Master's talk *[silence]* my pain is bigger than yours, but with more conformity and more light *[silence]* your pain is more for you than for him *[silence]* you don't know what to do with yourselves. Time will come when the entire world will be yours and everyone will fear you."

Then she stood up and went to the door one more time, and said: "Come in, you too, come in."

And she graciously waved at them to let them in. And later we understood that they were St. Joseph and Nicodemus, those who had buried Jesus. And she added: "Come in, come in, although you two, you lack faith, even if you have buried the Word with devotion and love *[silence]* you fear the Jews, but still, come in please."

And she went back to her seat. After a short while, speaking to Joseph and Nicodemus she said: "Although you can't have a seat here, nevertheless I welcome you in this company *[silence]* though you haven't been elected like these ones, still you have been loved, so rest here you too *[silence]* you have asked for his body, you still have to proclaim his divinity and believe in his resurrection *[silence]* here you'll have together a dialogue on my Word, and in my mind I shall accompany him wherever my Only Begotten goes each time. If [he is] in the Father's bosom, I ['ll be] in the Father's bosom; if in limbo, I ['ll be] in limbo; if in the sepulcher, I'll be with him also in the sepulcher."

And interrupting her speech, she withdrew into herself as if she were contemplating and no more speaking. And after being so rapt for a long while, at once she manifested a great happiness; by raising her hands and making gestures she showed that she was seeing a very pleasant and marvelous thing. And it was that she saw the Word's soul come to rest in the bosom of the eternal Father; and she said: "Who will ever be able to fathom what that sacred soul was doing with the divinity in the Father's bosom?"

And raising her hands again she manifested happiness; with great delight she said: "Oh, oh, oh! *[silence]* placed."

And being quiet and engrossed for a long while, then she stood up and went to the window where the desk was; and she put her open hands on this desk, keeping her eyes and her face up toward that window with a great awe and surprise. And after a while she said: "*Vidi Animam Verbi collocare Spiritum suum in essentia divinitatis, potentie idee sue, in complacimento animarum nostrarum*"[11] *[silence]* yes, placing himself and enjoying himself, giving every treasure and gift of wisdom to our souls by means of his enjoyment *[silence]* embraced by that incomprehensible divinity and idea of the Father, this Father wreathing him with his omnipotence. Oh, how admirable is this diadem!"

She paused one more time and showed a cheerful but also engrossed and wonderful face, and then spoke these Latin words that we hardly heard: "*Reservabo in me omnia*, and *dabo Spiritum meum*[12] *[silence] Non respondebo*, and *continuo loquor vobis in ipsum.*"[13]

The eternal Father spoke to her in his Word, making her understand how much he had worked for our redemption, revealing her many things we did not perceive. And she herself was not able to tell us, as she explained us later during our conversation. For she was neither capable of understanding everything she saw and was shown to her during this rapture, nor could she ever express it. In particular, the eternal Father showed her that he glorified and exalted the humanate Word because he had been humiliated and had suffered for the human salvation. And he told her that he had placed our iniquities over him, which were as many as his divinity. We thus asked her how this could ever be, as his divinity is infinite and our iniquities, albeit numerous, are finite. She answered: "They are actually infinite, because they are directed against God who is infinite and offend that who has neither beginning nor end. Therefore, it is correct to say that our iniquities are as many as his divinity; yet I cannot give you any other reason but that I heard it uttered in this way, and then I expressed those words outwardly *[silence]* the iniquities I placed on him were as many as my divinity *[silence]* oh how much the Word's soul rejoices with his divinity in his Father's bosom! *[silence] admirabo* this admiration."

And looking greatly astonished, leaning her hands on the desk, staring over the window, making many gestures with her face, her eyes, and her hands, which she raised up in a marvelous manner.[14] And then all of a sudden she climbed on that desk, which was pretty high, and she looked as if she were flying up there like a dove. And she leaned out of the window lending an ear to something, and when she stared up she seemed to be seeing, hearing, and perceiving great things. And according to what she told us during our conversation, this was the same thing the eternal Father had begun to show her last Sunday morning, that at the time she could not understand completely, even though the following night she had been in a rapture again. And the eternal Father told her so many things, yet she did not understand everything.

So, before she entered this rapture, the Father first wanted her to see what we have just mentioned and she indicated at that point.[15] Indeed, after being absorbed for a long while, making so many wonderful gestures and movements, she spoke these words with a great gravity: *"Et conduxit me in locum magnum* and *altum,*[16] surrounded both from the right and the left side by sounds of trumpets, guitars, psaltery, and other musical instruments, whose gentle sound is indescribable, its sweetness incomprehensible, and its melody unfathomable *[silence] vidi Anima Verbi quiescere, collocare* and expand *in sinu Patris*[17] *[silence]* oh, say something, come on *[silence]* book of life, yes *[silence] et collocavit animas eorum in infernum, et perdent* glory that *preparavit eis Verbum*[18] *[silence] et* their stubbornness *[silence] et occidit eos unus ad unum, et collocavit in tenebris* and *umbre mortis*[19] *[silence] pro superbia Angelo confundit nature Angelice,* and *pro humilitate Verbi exaltavit humanitatis nostre."*[20]

While she was saying the above things, our blessed soul was greatly astonished and astounded, and she made many gestures with her hands, with her face, and with all her body. As one can understand from these few words that she spoke, it seemed that she was seeing and understanding many great things. She spoke rarely, pausing for a long while from one thing to the next, briefly and obscurely. One thus could understand what she was seeing and perceiving better from her gestures and dances, than from the words she was pronouncing, even though from those words one understands that she was perceiving the effects that the human nature, but also the angelic one, received from the Word's passion and death, and [that she was perceiving] the Word's working, when he accepted his humanity, both for the apostate Angels and the bad men, and for the Angels and the good men.

Then she also said about the bad Angels: "So confused before, but now in everything *[silence] et collocavit eos in infernum*[21] *[silence]* Who has ever seen such a speed?"

And raising her head and then lowering it down, she made gestures with her hands and her arms, bending over the window, as if she were sending them down to hell with her own hands, and saying: "Go *[silence]* howl, scream as much as you want *[silence] et sublimavit humanitatis nostre* through their confusion[22] *[silence] Non cognoscetur amplius."*[23]

Being astonished for a long while and looking toward the sky, then she came down from that desk and went to sit down at her place.

After being engrossed for a long while, she said: "*Et sublimavit human-itatis nostre [silence] vidi glorificationis mee* and *omni creatura in ipsum*[24] *[silence] surge, quievit,* and *ambulavit.*"[25]

She was seeing the Word's effects in the Father's bosom. So, she stood up, and then she sat back; and she did this up to three times, standing up and sitting down, to show how that Soul ascended and rested in the Father's bosom. And then, standing up again, she went to the center of the scriptorium toward the right side and then came back, doing this five times, going up and coming back. And she did so on the left side [of the scriptorium] five more times, going and coming back, speaking these words: "In a constant movement, without any movement you are expanding on the right, and on the left, and always coming back to this place *[silence]* on the right glorifying a glorification known by you *[silence]* on the left you do so to give the compendium of this glorification."

And later, going back to her seat, she kept quiet for a little while, and then she said: "Oh, how admirable, wonderful, and intrinsic are your workings! Who knows them? *[silence]* oh, of course, yes who experiences them. Yes, oh, oh, oh *[silence] et non cognoscebam.*"[26]

And later she stood up again, going back and forth, and then she said: "Please," taking one step back and one forth.

And she did this to show how the the Word's Soul moved in the Father's bosom. And [she did] everything very mysteriously. For we did not understand it, but she did, as she had said: "Who experiences it knows it." And after going back to her seat, after sitting for a long while she said: "You are so infinite and so great that you can't be understood. To me it means that more than anybody else I am full of ignorance and blindness, and also in general. Yes. Yes *[silence]* they will understand, yes, later, oh, when! When it will be divided what now for conformity, yes, but not for delight[27] *[silence]* oh, how death is life, and life is death, yes for conformity to him who knows you more, since who knows you more suffers more because he does not have you *[silence]* conformity comes from knowledge, and non-conformity comes from a very intimate nonknowledge *[silence]* oh, how could it be that who is in conformity with you were also able to be in a nonconformity, since who is not with you is against you, as you said *[silence]* oh, there are so many different kinds of conformities, but many are disguised *[silence]* the first conformity is of ignorance, the second of nature, the third of grace, the fourth is of admiration, and the fifth [is] of love *[silence]* the first conformity is of ignorance, since being deprived of God's splendor [the creature] can't know her greatness and also that of her soul, which is God's image. Therefore, she commits that sin that makes her so blind and ignorant, that she believes that she's in conformity with God, but in most cases she fast becomes in conformity with the love for herself. It is from this love for herself that this conformity of ignorance comes forth, since the creature enjoys this ignorant conformity, being unaware of the ignorance that it gives her. And given that she is deprived of God's splendor, of the knowledge of herself, and of the gravity of her sin, she cannot be in conformity with God, but [she is] rather in a nonconformity with God, even though she thinks she is [in conformity] and disguises herself with a false and worthless humility; and since she is not humble she has erected her building on sand *[silence]* the other conformity is of nature, so that she has a conformity with God more naturally than that [conformity] of grace and will, and she is not in a complete conformity, since she disguises herself and soon she leaves, because in its own nature this conformity does not last at all; it cannot persist because our nature is extremely unstable, and it is useful neither to the creature herself nor to the others.

"Another conformity is of grace, and this one brings the veil and is humble, since it proceeds from God, who is the source of humility. And this creature is useful to herself and to the others, but more externally than internally *[silence]* the other conformity originates from admiration, whose conformity of admiration is persisting, humble, and full of every grace; and the creature is a constant movement of vigilance and a conservative consolation for the others *[silence]* the conformity of love is a sublime conformity, originating from that intimate knowledge I've already mentioned, which proceeds from a pure will. And the creature is not disguised, but rather pure, simple, and sincere, and pleases the holy Trinity, and is extremely useful for herself and the others. Being a soul in conformity of love, for her heaven is the same as hell, hell the same as heaven, heaven the same as earth, God the same as the devil, the creature the same as the angel, the rational creature the same as the beast, light the same as darkness, since with that intimate knowledge of God she knows nothing, and abandons herself into God's hands; and this proceeds from her ardent and pure love for God. Oh, sublime conformity, which blends together things so contrary to each other; and it is the nuptial veil of charity! *[silence]* whose soul in love, like a vine, generates the grape, that sweet fruit that makes the wine; she nourishes and squeezes herself. With her wine she intoxicates God; she nourishes herself, and what she squeezes [she gives it] for the salvation of the others. Oh anxious desire, like a sweet press you squeeze that soul's fruits for the salvation of the others, in honor of God, and for your own benefit!"

At this point she came out of the rapture; she took an egg and rested for a short while; and then she went back to her rapture, following the same theme of that conformity for love, in particular about the benefit that it gives to itself. "Oh, how useful to itself! *[silence]* yes, it nourishes itself, giving a comforting and edifying nourishment."

And all of a sudden she stood up and, as she had done before, she went close to the desk of the scriptorium, with her face toward the window, remaining astounded for a long time. She seemed to be seeing and perceiving some great things. And then she started to turn around, around, slowly, slowly, doing this three times, pausing a little bit each time. Then with her hands and her face she made gestures of great admiration, and said: "Oh, great is our God, great is our God!"

And for a long time she could not help but remain so engrossed in that way, that she really seemed to be wasting away. And we saw that she was shown God's greatness, and also the creatures' malice and iniquity, as it will become apparent in what follows. And that night she saw and understood great things, both in general and in particular; and later she said: "Alas, I die alive *[silence]* if at least I could lead the creatures to you!"

And after saying this, pausing a moment, she sat down on the floor and said: "Here I am, on the ground *[silence]* I can't go more down *[silence]* and yes *[silence]* oh, wise madness!"

Then, opening her arms, in that way, sitting on the floor she relaxed completely, staying a bit still. And she began shaking, and making gestures and movements as if she were wasting away. And doing this for a while, she said: "I do not understand *[silence]* yours is better, yes, yes *[silence]* alas *[silence]* you are endless, but I would like to see some end in you."

The things she was seeing about his faculty were so many and great that she could not understand them; and she said so. And after being calm a bit more, she said: "One hundred twenty warriors, divided in six parts. And what is this to me?"

She told us that these warriors were some particular elect by God, who were fighting for God. And by speaking those words, "and what is this to me?," she meant that for her the good ones were too few in comparison to the great multitude of the bad ones that she was seeing. And then, continuing what she was saying, always a bit quiet between one thing and the other: "One hundred twenty-four, bringing beautiful vases, full of the sweetest balm; and they pour it on the Word's head. These are the desires of the pure virgins."

And the Lord was showing her some specific virgins that were performing that act as a response to the many offenses that, as the blessed soul saw, were directed against God. Then she added: "One hundred twenty carry cities in their hands."

She told us that they were specific doctors. "In those cities a huge number of peoples is included. The wisdom of your elect is in a huge number of your workings *[silence]* one hundred thirty-six carry candlesticks of the purest gold, and two of them light them on *[silence]* the price of the confessors, yes."

She told us that those who carried and lit those candlesticks were some saints and that some of the good candlesticks are still down here. "One hundred twenty-eight carry shining columns, and it seems like they are generating a great work. The charity of your lovers down here *[silence]* those who are carrying [these columns] are saints from heaven, and the columns [are] creatures from down here. From the East two ferocious lions are coming, from the West two rapacious wolves, from the North two rabid bears, from the South two lethal asps."

She said that these were men of high status with vices similar to those beasts, which are in the four parts of the world. "But, see, you see a gentle Lamb, and with its shadow it throws them all to the ground *[silence]* but see, you see an immense multitude approaching; this people live with those who place themselves between the sweet Lamb and those animals; and they [the multitude] want to be important before the animals *[silence]* they live in the courts of those aristocrats, and to defend them [the aristocrats] they don't care to offend God and to hurt their own souls seriously *[silence]* but the sweet Lamb strives to send these beasts away, but when he sees that they don't want to be sent away, gently he goes back to his sheepfold *[silence]* then an armed woman comes *[silence]* the Virgin Mary, who wants to throw them all to the ground. But not at all, they—I mean those people—they don't want her, and scoffing at her they send her away *[silence]* oh, oh, why don't you take her? And why don't you want her help? You see that she is strong, and that she can help you *[silence]* then some young girls, sixteen, four from each part; in the East four, in the West four, in the North four, and also four more in the South."

These are the sixteen Virgins elected by the Lord to help those regions, and today they are on earth, four in each side of the world. And, as she told us later, that was what had been shown and explained to our blessed soul that night, although she neither knew them, nor did she know who they were. What matters is that they support us, and they do it, so that the Lord shall not bring his wrath over us as we deserve; and woe betide the world when they [the virgins] won't be there any longer.

And maybe she is one of those who are in our regions.

"These young girls have a particular grace that draws the Lamb and ties him up, when it seems that he doesn't want to come back, since they hold certain ropes, which are the gifts they have from God *[silence]* with that rope they tie the Lamb and pull it, and they bring him back; and also the strong army, in case it had left. And they take it [the army] to the Lamb to force him to come back, because they cannot force him as much as it [the army] can do, since it has a much stronger cordage and can certainly force this Lamb to come back. But if they actually want him, you know it. And when time comes that they want him, you will bring him back and will throw these beasts to the ground *[silence]* but for the moment, seeing that these girls cannot be useful, what do they do? They will eat the Lamb's working, which comes from him, and they will enjoy themselves with him *[silence]* but there are also certain gardens *[silence]* (which are monasteries)[28] *[silence]* they too are in great danger, but the Lamb will defend them from those beasts that would ruin them *[silence]* and the fruits of these gardens are awaited in glory, because they will be placed on those sublime and majestic thrones, to adorn the city of Jerusalem, to please the Trinity, and to glorify those fruits. And woe betide, woe betide, thousand times woe betide those who make themselves unable to give these fruits which live in these gardens. And woe betide, even more woe betide those who will not betake themselves to this city of Jerusalem. And woe betide myself, if I do not betake myself there and do not do my best to take others *[silence]* [it is] written in the book of life, manifest to you, so that you write it in the book of your heart."

She meant that all these things are written in the book of life, I mean, those things he showed her during that night, along with the help she gives to his creatures. And this is exactly what the Lord started to show her last Sunday, which at the time she did not understand completely. The Lord thus told her that she would understand it at the right time, and yesterday morning he called her in order to finish what he had started to show her.

And because it was the time when Jesus died, he showed her everything he [the Word] did, from the moment he passed away until he rose from the dead, which, as she told us later during our conversation, fulfills the mystery of the passion and death of Jesus Love, which she experienced during Good Friday. That rapture actually ended at the moment when he passed away on the cross, but she also experienced a bit of what had happened before, as we wrote at that time. But in that rapture his deposition from the cross and his burial had not been followed by what Jesus did until he rose from the dead. This rapture of forty hours thus completed that other one, I mean that about his Passion, also because he [the Lord] showed her God's greatness and the creatures' malice and iniquities. She completed these two raptures last Sunday, in the morning and at night.

218

Then she added: "Someone is coming to erase what has been written *[silence]* this is the devil's task, who would like to take away the good the creatures do to their minds and, if he could, he would erase everything is written in the book of life, so that nobody will be able to save oneself *[silence]* and two thousand million *adornaverunt faciem Sponse Agni, et milia millium collocavit in thronum suum*[29] *[silence]* and one hundred thousand million *adoraverunt Agnum cum sponse sue dicentes: 'Illumina faciem super servas tuas.'*"[30]

And she spoke these words five times, and then she repeated these others several times: "*Magnus Dominus e[t] laudabilis nimis*[31] *in mansuetudine eius* *[silence]* two hundred thousand thanked him saying: 'great and admirable is our God, and generous and great he is in his power' *[silence]* and an infinite crowd *venerunt contra Deum suum*, and *nolerunt intelligere verba eius, et ipse collocavit in profundum animas eorum*[32] *[silence]* *Ecce quomodo computati sunt inter filios Dei,*[33] they said later *[silence]* My soul will not fail to manifest what it has understood, and I don't refuse to do it *[silence]* more, eternal Word *[silence]* hell and heaven together *[silence]* the bush of Moses burned without wasting away, but I am wasting away without burning *[silence]* oh Word, no more greatness, no more goodness *[silence]* if I died I would taste death once without ever dying *[silence]* but alive, I am dying a thousand deaths *[silence]* since you died, you didn't suffer. *Vivo ego iam non ego*[34] *vivit in me pena inferni* *[silence]* evil hatred, cause of any division."

There was shown to her the great hatred that creatures have against each other, along with many other infinite offenses. Thus we saw her suffer from a pain like someone in agony. Her face was sweaty, and all her body writhed, showing that she was suffering the pain of death. Thus she said: "Oh, in how many ways you test your creatures! *[silence]* oh, if I gave my life and many offenses were canceled, even if [to accomplish this] I had to suffer and to share [the pains of] hell as I am sharing it now, nevertheless it would look like heaven to me, provided that those offenses were canceled."

After that, she kept silent for a bit, and she threw herself to the floor. She hit herself here and there, sometimes arching her back as if she were experiencing the pangs of death, and certainly she showed that she was suffering the pains of hell. It looked impossible that she would not die of that pain; and often she said: "Oh, good Jesus, oh good Jesus, oh good Jesus!"

And then, standing up on her knees, she twisted and quivered intensely; and after a long while she said: "Oh Word, no more offenses *[silence]* no more offenses *[silence]* Where are you, good Jesus? *[silence]* oh Word, so much pain! *[silence]* oh good Jesus."

After this, she came out of the rapture; it was the seventh hour. And she was out of this rapture for, say, one-eighth of an hour. And then, going back to her rapture, she kept very quiet; and later she said: "Oh good Jesus *[silence]* you are merciful when you give pains. Yes, mercy *[silence]* oh good Jesus, yes, yes *[silence]* my Jesus, I'm pleased, but if you want me to feel [it], I shall say what your beloved Francis said: 'So great is the good I expect, that any pain is a delight to me' *[silence]* my Jesus, let the other spouses share it, not the pain, no."

She referred to us, her sisters. Here she meant that Jesus wanted to give her his heart and promised it to her, and she wished each of us could share that gift. And Jesus told her that we had to purify our hearts, before he could engrave his gifts in us. She thus answered him as follows: "Yes, first it is necessary to purify it."

And because she had already received the heart of the Virgin Mary, she said: "Oh, what is going to happen to that of Mary?"

And she kept her hand away from her heart, but she placed it back there when she entered the rapture again; and she held it tight, showing that she was feeling a great pain there. And after a brief silence, she said again: "Give it to one of your spouses."

She meant the heart of the Virgin. And turning to herself she said: "I need to contemplate this heart well, because I will keep it for a short while."

And then, because Jesus told her when he wanted to give his heart to her, she answered him saying: "Yes, later when your soul joins the body *[silence]* and I will have it *[silence] ad vesperum demorabitur fletus*, and *ad mattutinum letitiam*[35] *[silence]* the heart participates in every thing, thus the body must feel the pain *[silence]* oh my Jesus, you need to come and keep it, later, when you give it to me *[silence]* but before having it, I need to comprehend something of your holy soul, what it was doing in his Father's bosom at that time."

And then she kept quiet for a long time, going back to that previous pain; and she understood what she had to suffer and also saw again the offenses that were given to God; thus she said: "Oh good Jesus! *[silence]* my Jesus, then when you want."

After these words, she abandoned herself to God, opening her arms like a *Pietà*, showing that she was feeling a great pain and sorrow, and she said: "Oh, it will happen to me what happened to Job; first he was tested in his things, and then in himself *[silence]* first in my neighbors, and then in me. First in the body, and then in the soul. *Omnia possum in eo qui me confortat.*[36] Oh, eternal wisdom, I understand neither you nor myself *[silence]* oh, eternal Word, assist me, since I am wretched and miserable. *In profundum summersisti me, in profundum summersisti me, et confortata sum e[t] non potero ad eam*[37] *[silence]* oh good Jesus, are you pleased with me now that I do not know you, do not understand you, and do not love you?"

She writhed and twisted, and seemed to be falling apart inside, speaking these words: "My Jesus, I am not sure you want my body to finish in this way *[silence]* I am not sure whether I am on earth or in heaven, in hell or in the abyss *[silence]* oh good Jesus! *[silence] omnes vos qui transitis per viam, attendite* and *videte si est dolor sicut dolor meus*[38] *[silence]* oh good Jesus! *[silence]* oh good Jesus! *[silence]* oh my Jesus, it is clear to me, yes *[silence] si ascendero in celum tu illic es, si descendero in infernum ades*[39] *[silence]* oh good Jesus! *[silence]* oh good Jesus, you are all love, but you are all pure *[silence]* oh Word, when are you coming? *[silence]* oh good Jesus! *[silence]* my Jesus, you want it, yes, yes *[silence]* good Jesus, good Jesus *[silence]* I understand neither you nor myself. If I am in you, you know it; you come out of yourself *[silence]* if I am on earth, I do not know; if I am in heaven, you know it; if I am in purgatory, no, in hell, I'll dare to ask to participate in it. If [I am] at your mother's, no, for I know neither where I am nor what I am *[silence]* I am a nothingness, and an infinite thing coming from you who are infinite. Every creature is infinite, because she comes from you, but in themselves they are a nothingness *[silence]* and since they are infinite, they perceive infinite things, they understand your infinite love, they love you who are infinite, they have you who are infinite *[silence]* if I am, if I am not, you know it. If I perceive, if I understand, if I have, I shall say what your apostle said: *Sive in corpore, sive extra corpore nescio,*

221

Deus scit[40] *[silence]* no, I don't care about knowing it. You are all mercy, you are all justice, good Jesus, good Jesus *[silence] benedicam Dominum in omni tempore*[41] *[silence]* when, when I come out of myself completely, you do not want me to know it, you know it. Oh good Jesus, oh good Jesus, *desiderium anime eius tribuisti ei, e[t] voluntate labiorum eius non fraudasti eum*[42] *[silence]* Word, come, come *[silence] venies autem, venies ad me cum exultatione."*[43]

It was around the tenth hour when she spoke these words, and after a brief rest she came out of the rapture. She seemed to be invoking Jesus so that he would come to her in the Holy Sacrament. And she was out of the rapture enough time to say: *First, Third,* and *Sixth* of the Lord; and when she started *Ninth,* she was rapt, still holding her book. And staying like this for a while, she started to invoke Jesus, so that he would come to her in the Holy Sacrament; and she said: "Oh my Spouse, Lover above all lovers, you are sweeter than any honeycomb; how long, how long will you wait to come to me, I mean, into me in essence, or better yet in presence, since in essence I have you? *[silence]* turn the eyes of your might, look at the creature so crippled by her sin. Only if you make her perceive it can the creature understand her sin and suffer from what she sees. I feel more surprised at those who offend your might, your wisdom, and your goodness, than at those who love you *[silence]* my Spouse, my Lover, my Beloved! Tell me, please, why are you waiting so long to come? What kind of preparation would you like me to make, though nobody can ever prepare oneself properly for you? *[silence]* yes, in your Body and in your Blood, given to us by the priest; yes, I understand that they contain the Soul, the Body, and the Blood, and also that who administers it is made of body, blood, and soul; likewise, who receives it in himself is made of the same matter. It is thus necessary that in this preparation three conditions be present, in the soul, in the body, and in the blood."

ETERNAL FATHER

"Yes, my dear daughter, the soul must try not to lose its nature, which is without origin in my eternal, divine, and pure mind. Therefore, you must go to this sacrament with your noble nature which, as I tell you, is without origin in my mind. And this means that you must never consider the origin of any of your workings as something that has proceeded from you. For you may come to think that your working is something substantial and that you have done or are able to do some good deed by yourself. As a consequence, if you thought that its origin were in you and from you, a great arrogance would arise in your soul, and you would lose your working. But if you know that nothing comes from you, and that the only thing you can do is to sin which is nothing, and that this nothing is your actual origin, you will humiliate yourself. Moreover, if you have the feeling that you are doing no good, you will constantly aspire to a greater perfection. And if no working must be done without an origin, the act of going to the Holy Sacrament must be one of these. Since you know that you have no good adequate to receive in yourself that which is everything, you must abandon yourself completely to that which is your origin, praying to him that he, in himself and for himself, prepare you to his Majesty in a proper manner [silence] being without origin, let your desires, feelings, and intentions be without origin, ignoring where their origin lies [silence] and be aware of the fact that those who come to the Holy Sacrament with an origin, in fact rest in their own tepidness. Having done something by force of habit, they believe that they have, so to speak, paid their duties and have done all the necessary. And, you know, as I said through my beloved John, those are the people on whom I start vomiting, when they are still down here. For I am infinitely displeased by their deeds, since they do not have their origin in me but in themselves. Therefore, you must make the greatest effort to come to me and to my truth without any origin, and not with an origin like those people.

"You must also keep your other being, which is eternity, if you want to be prepared for this Sacrament whose eternity never concerns the present time, but it is always eternal and does not know any corruption [silence] numerous are the corruptions present in the soul, but now I want to mention this one, since it makes the soul condemnable, even though it does not lose its eternity. And this is when the soul commits a sin. There is also another corruption; and this is of those who tarry in these worldly, transitory, and ephemeral things. Although I have given myself to them in order to sustain their nature, so that they can know me and can find recreation in those things, they end up tarrying in those things and finding their goal in them. Thus, what I have given them as a means and for their benefit, becomes their goal. In this way these souls offend me immensely with the benefit I have granted them. From this corruption every soul must distance itself, if it wishes to receive the Holy sacrament without origin, which is indeed the eternity, since I am eternal without origin. And be aware that those who go to this sacrament with this eternity are very grateful to me, because I am the eternity of the soul. Without me the soul is a nothing, a nothingness.

"Oh, I also request that you go to this sacrament with the soul's third attribute, which is its being pure. In this purity you must keep yourself as close to your frailty as possible, since this purity is my actual being, which I have given to you out of sheer goodness. And given that you cannot have it while you are wayfarers, as when you came out of my idea, you must regain it by offering me my Word's blood. Every time you offer it to me I infuse it back into you by means of my Word; and through this infusion of Blood you become purified of any taint of sin and regain that innocence I gave you from the beginning. And the soul which goes to this Sacrament must be so pure and simple, that not only must it feel content with what it has in itself, it must also aspire to the angels' purity and to that of every creature. This purity must adorn the soul, so that it can go to this Sacrament with a pure mind, a pure memory, a pure will, a pure intention, and a pure feeling. In this way it will go only to honor me, without considering whether any other soul will go or not, and for no other reason; it will not go to feel some sweetness, no, no; not even to show itself or for any other thing, but only, only for my honor and glory."

And after these words she came out of that rapture, when the father confessor arrived for the confession, as if she had been awakened from sleep. And while she confessed, she was out of this rapture. And immediately after, she went back to the rapture, even though she did not resume it until this morning. But she started to

224

analyze what the Word's soul was doing in his Father's bosom at that time.

After Communion this soul spoke to the eternal Father: "Oh Father, please, I still have him like you, God and Man, Man and God *[silence]* Father, you know, love makes me speak in this way. But, please, do not weigh the words, only the affection *[silence]* please, Father, now tell me the workings, the words, the sentences, and the contemplation that this holiest Soul did in your bosom. To this you called me from the very beginning, but me, so far I've had nothing but pain."

ETERNAL FATHER

"My dear daughter, the holy Soul of my Word was in my bosom; although it was united with the Divinity, it was not [united] with the Humanity yet. Nevertheless, it worked, spoke, asked for sentence, and contemplated. And it did workings of admiration, of might, and of wisdom. It generated admiration in the angels, when they wondered to see that holy Soul, previously united with the body, receiving now so much rest and delight in my bosom. They admired the way and the means through which it was led to such a height, and they praised it with a joyful melody. In this manner the angels increased their glory with a new glory, although they were already glorious, since I had created them. But at that point I glorified them with an infinite glory. However, through the vision and admiration of the holy Soul of my Word, their glory increased even more."

SOUL

"So, you believed that man was inferior to you, and he was made superior to you. Of course you couldn't help but admire. I believe it! *[silence]* oh admiration, if I could have it myself, it would increase my glory. Like the angels, even if I were already glorious, I would acquire a greater glory."

MARIA MADDALENA DE' PAZZI

FATHER

"In my bosom this Soul also generated workings of might. Might, in order to confound your adversary. It generated might with might, since it had left you its reign with might, like stairs to climb up to it."

SOUL

"Let us have a great might, yes, since your reign is in our power, and we can obtain it or not, it's up to us. Oh, a great might you have given us, yes, really."

FATHER

"With might it worked to conform the conformed will of the angels, so that they would offer themselves to the human creatures, who would ascend with their veritably noble and glorious spirits. Such a might is this, yes, yes *[silence]* my Word generated a great might down there for you, by annihilating and, so to speak, putting justice to sleep *[silence]* he generated workings of a great wisdom by gazing at your intellect and that of the other creatures; and through his gaze he infused in your intellect such a knowledge of the greatness of his wisdom, that he ended and ends your intellect, since it is limited. Oh, do not you find that he generated a great wisdom, when he glorified so many souls and exalted them to the point that they may become God? Moreover, he does so that God becomes man. Oh, this is also a great wisdom, since nobody can oppose this working, through which God becomes a creature and the creature becomes God; nobody, nobody, no, can oppose it. And also this wisdom from itself *[silence]* he generates a great wisdom when he tolerates that an impurity, a nothingness, a nothing offends a wisdom so full of perfection and considers it [his wisdom] a base thing."

THE DIALOGUES

SOUL

"Tell me, Father, what words did the Word say to you?"

FATHER

"Oh, daughter, what words did he speak? He spoke words of life, because he was Life himself. He spoke words of nourishment, attractive words, consoling words, eternal words, having an eternal conversation in my bosom. Did not you hear them down there? Even though they were all for you? Were they unknown to you? No, they were not known to you, because they can become known to you only by *gratia gratis data [silence]* oh, did not my Word speak words of life, when with such a sweet affection he offered you to me, so that I would attract you to my divinity and would turn you from human creatures into divine ones? *[silence]* do not they sound to you like words of nourishment (but you cannot know, because you could not hear them) the words that the Word said to me before I incarnated him?[44] I provided that he would assume your humanity through Mary, so that later you would be able to receive his divinity. Committing the sin of disobedience, man broke my commandment and thus met his death. Being thrown out of heaven, no more could he live off the tree of life, that I had given to him as his nourishment. It was thus necessary that my Word assume your humanity and become a tree of life for you, so that you could feed on it without ever failing. Being in my bosom with his divinity, the Soul of my Word spoke words of nourishment to you while his body, never divided from his divinity, was in the sepulcher. And, my dear daughter, what kind of words do you think he spoke? What kind? [He spoke] words of such a nourishment that they give life to you, since he has determined to give himself to you as food con-stantly, so that you could receive his divinity in yourselves. His divinity generates a great capacity in you to receive me.[45] In his incarnation he took your humanity, and in his death he gave you his divinity. However, he wanted his body to lie dead in the sepulcher. In so doing, he showed that he intended to leave to you that which, still and forever united with his divinity, he had taken from you; and [he intended] to let his Soul come back to my bosom along with his divinity. However, his Soul never left his humanity, through which he begged and obtained the capacity of his divinity for you, and consequently that of myself."

SOUL

"Oh, eternal Father, in your bosom the Soul of my Word spoke words of such a nourishment, that they give us life and a capacity for you! Yes, I also understand that, when it was in the sepulcher, his Humanity was never divided from his divinity; and that showed that he had left us his Body, along with his divinity, as a food to nourish us. Moreover, I understand that at the same time his Soul was united with his divinity in your bosom; and he still retained the humanity that he had assumed, and he was begging for us the capacity of that divinity, without which we would never be able to obtain a capacity for you *[silence]* oh eternal Father, why do I understand what I do not understand and feel what I do not feel? Tell me, I beg you, what other words did the holy Soul of the Word speak when it was in your bosom?"

FATHER

"Oh my dearest, then he spoke consoling words, praying to me to send you the comforting Spirit, as he had promised when he said: *'Ego rogabo Patrem*, and *Spiritum Paraclitum dabit vobis'*;[46] and he arranged to come with me and my Spirit and support you in your duties *[silence]* he also spoke attractive words, attracting glory from the glory that I am, and then infusing it down to you. You know, when you speak you open your mouth, and when you open your mouth you draw breath in, but when you open your mouth you also exhale that breath. That is what the Soul of my Word did in my bosom. He drew and infused; although he did not speak, he spoke. And without opening his mouth he drew glory from me in order to infuse it into you, because he wanted your joy to be perfect. As he told you when he conversed with you down there, the world will rejoice and you will become sad, but your sadness will turn into joy, and that joy will be the eternal glory I will give you through my Word. The world's gaiety fails soon, but the glory and the content you acquire once will last forever *[silence]* he bestowed eternal words upon you, granting you the above eternity. I mean that my Only Begotten Word spoke eternal words and bestowed eternity upon you. Although you had it [the eternity] before, since I gave to you when I created you eternal as I am, because of sin you met your death, and it was necessary that the eternal Word die on the cross to acquire this eternity for you again."

SOUL

"Oh, eternal Father, how much the holy Soul of your Word bestowed upon us when he was in your bosom! And they were all words, sentences, and workings."

FATHER

"Yes, dear daughter and spouse of *Unigenitis mei,* when he was in my bosom that Soul not only had a conversation, he also had a sentence of great many sentences. Sentence of peace, sentence of union, sentence of supreme generosity, sentence of mercy, sentence of might, sentence of justice, sentence of communication, sentence of love.

"Sentence of peace. Oh, sentence of peace! My dear daughter, this sentence of peace, that the Word did in my bosom, was nothing but the act of uniting man who was so disunited from me, his God, divinity with Humanity, and my Word's divinity and Humanity with the simple man. Isn't this a great sentence of peace? Isn't this other one a great sentence of peace, that is, that I have given my christs the great authority to offer my Word and to take it out of my bosom? At my will, everyone may offer it, but not everyone is allowed to take it out of my bosom. I have decreed that my christs only, only, may take it out of my bosom, and they may also offer it. I have given you, only to you, the authority to offer it. But offer it to me often, reconciling every creature with me through this medium so precious to me.

"Sentence of union. And, my dear daughter, what kind of sentence is this? Sentence without sentence. And what do I communicate? I communicate myself, and I communicate the unity which is in the idea of my essence, every time you offer me my Word's Blood. Your offer of his Blood is so powerful, that with it you can unite what you want. If you want to unite man with God, you can be sure that with that Blood he will be united. If you want to unite God with man, offer that Blood, and God shall unite with you. If you want to unite something, this Blood shall bring about this union. And if the devil could participate in this Blood, it would unite him with me. But because of his great stubbornness he does not want it, and by no means can he be suitable to receive it. And since he can never be suitable for it, this union can never and will never occur.

"Sentence of supreme generosity *[silence]* generosity unequal within myself. Generosity with the blessed souls up here incomprehensible to you *[silence]* generosity with the living souls who are in prison down there, absolutely unimaginable and lovable."

SOUL

"Oh, infinite generosity! Generosity *a[d] destris* and *ad sinistris*. And you are all unimaginable and [are] an immense generosity *[silence] et procidentes adoraverunt liberalitatem unitatis essentie Trinitatis tue dicentes: 'Isti sunt digni accipere unitatem liberalitatis tue, que pro liberalitate creasti eos, et pro inmense liberalitatis tue recreasti eos.'* "[47]

FATHER

"Sentence of mercy. Sentence of mercy is a mercy unknown to you. No, that mercy is not understood. The great mercy my truth showed after he gave his Blood, and after his body was buried, when his Soul came and placed itself in my bosom. And I tell you, this act of placing itself was a great mercy. Try to understand it. You may constantly sing: *'Misericordias Domini in eternum cantabo,'*[48] because at that

230

time it made my bosom forgiving and gentle toward you. Thanks to him not only his Soul, of course, but any soul eager for that sentence of might was able to place itself and rest in my holy bosom.

"Sentence of might, and sentence of wisdom, sentence of peace; peace that had already been given, but it then was taken by that holy Soul. It did so that not only the divinity, but also the Humanity would have that might; and that the soul would have the might that the divinity and the humanity shared. Might, might, might. Where do you participate, even a little bit, in that might, which allows you to work with my Word's might? Did not he say that with his might you would generate more things than he did?"

SOUL

"And what working do you, Father, refer to? I think you mean these extrinsic ones down here, because we are incapable of touching the intrinsic and divine ones. Thus, everything we understand of you and everything we generate, everything is through your communication; and in fact you generate in us, because by ourselves we can do nothing, nothing. And what we can do, we have it from the surface of your might, through which we generate everything we generate."

FATHER

"Sentence of justice. The Word's Soul did also justice in my bosom. And it seems contradictory that, after doing so much justice to you, at that time he wanted to generate a sentence of justice. My dear daughter, listen to me. No, at that time it seemed as if my Word would not generate a sentence of justice, since he had taken it all in himself and had thus used it up entirely. As a consequence, it became so covered up in both of us, that we did not seem just anymore, but rather absolutely merciful. Nevertheless, this justice was not missing; in fact, it had to be exerted with more purity and more perfection. Having expiated every guilt on the cross, the Word could not stand seeing the smallest defect in the creature, a twisted

231

intention, an impure thought, and a vain word, which would not be punished and purged through penitence either in this life or after death. This sentence of justice, generated by the Word's Soul in my bosom, was thus immensely rightful. At that very moment while his body, on which not only that justice, but also the guilt had been carried out, rested in its sepulcher, in my bosom his Soul was preparing the Purgatory to consume the minimum rest of guilt or sin. Indeed, although he had already purged every thing through himself, he still had to carry out this justice in your souls."

SOUL

"Oh eternal Father, *dilexisti iustitiam super benignitatem*, your Prophet says.[49] Although mercy is inherent in you, justice is no less greatly dear to you. But some creatures do mercy, yes, this is good. However, their mercy is done unjustly, since with that excessive mercy they sustain your offense. As a consequence, it is not an actual mercy, but rather an unjust justice *[silence]* But your sentence of justice will be fulfilled at doomsday, when timorous and tremulous each of us will be waiting for the Word to pronounce his last judgment with supreme justice *[silence]* woe, woe betide those who will not have foreseen that day. But how can you foresee it? Only with the conformity and the union with you, by keeping the promises given to you, by fulfilling your commandments, and by being totally abandoned and consumed in you for the salvation and in help of your neighbors. And the more will the soul anticipate and prepare itself for the future things, the more God will prepare those gifts and graces he wants to give to it [the soul]. Great are your judgments: *judicia Dei abissus multa*."[50]

FATHER

"Sentence of consolation. How great and intrinsic was this sentence of consolation that the Word's Soul did in me! This sentence of consolation was unspeakable; it consoled not only the creatures, but the angels as well. Indeed, if the angels could have grieved, they would have grieved intensely for the numerous thrones left vacant because of the fall of the apostate Angels. They saw those beautifully adorned thrones, contemplated by the eternal idea of my essence. It [the sentence of consolation] also consoled the creatures on earth, I mean, those who had some light and knew the greatness of this love *[silence]* the insensitive creatures received this consolation as well. Whence, you see, stones broke up and the sepulchers opened and the veil of the temple tore down, converting everything into a communication of consolation. It was also of great consolation for the souls in limbo, whom he disposed to visit and to take up on himself in order to lead them to those beautiful thrones and thus to exalt them, to beatify them, and to glorify them with such a great exaltation, beatification, and glorification, that neither David, nor any other prophet ever perceived. I tell you, there was consolation even in hell, because my Word visited it and freed so many souls who were there. Now, every time a soul goes down to hell, those who are there suffer from a more intense pain, because by taking out so many of those souls he gave them consolation."

At this point she stood up and went to the desk, as usual, with her face turned to the window. And standing there for quite some time, then she sat down; and after a short while she said, still speaking in the person of the eternal Father: "Sentence of fortitude. Arming all of you like valiant soldiers with his armors, the Soul of the Word, my Only Begotten, gave you his Blood as a vestment and a primary armor, the lance that opened his side as a knife, the cross as a sword, the reed with the sponge as a light spear, the hammer and the pincers as a wield and a buckler, the dice as gloves, the crown of thorns as an armor for the head (I mean, as the helmet), the ropes he was tied up with as a horse, the nails as bridles and adornments, the column as a pavilion, the garden where he prayed and sweated Blood with an immense agony as his sheltered city, the cenacle on the mount Sion as his bed most comfortable to rest *[silence]* see, you need to fight, to rest, and to recreate yourselves.

"Is it not his Blood a strong vestment and the worthiest armor? Yes, of course, the sole mention of it makes the devils shiver. And the soul dressed of that Blood is able to attack its enemies with great courage. And no sword is stronger and sharper than the cross that cut the serpent's head off *[silence]* no knife is more pointed than the lance that opened his holy side and pierced through his divine heart. And by offering this opened wound you pierce not only the creatures' hearts, no, no, but also through my bosom *[silence]* no glove is stronger and fitter than the dice with which (oh incomprehensible mercy and patience!) the glory and the pleasures of heaven were derided and scoffed at. By remembering what had been done with these dice you arm your hands with purity. Your reign was not made with hands, no, as Paul, his beloved, rightly says *[silence]* no shield, no buckler are stronger than the hammer and the pincers. They are so strong that the soul, contemplating the blows that nailed the Word on the cross, is forced to tolerate fierce blows in the name of his love: *'Nos autem gloriari oportet in Cruce Domini nostri Jesu Christi'*[51] *[silence]* no helmet, no armor are stronger than that sharp crown of thorns. The fiercest blow, from anywhere and from anyone, will never be able to overcome it, because who is humble can never be overcome. And who will not humble oneself, seeing my Word crowned with thorns? *[silence]* the reed with the sponge is nothing but a light lance. Ask the hermits, who have made themselves suitable for the intrinsic working of my Word *[silence]* no horse is stronger than the rope which pulled my Word, your only Spouse. Which soul, even worse than an incarnate devil, would not feel moved seeing its sweet Love pulled from place to place? Which soul would not rush to be scoffed at, no, no, to be led to a place of relief and consolation? *Satiabor cum apparuerit gloria tua*[52] *[silence]* no bridle is more suitable than the nails of my Word, which tightened that tightening Love and sometimes make that love so fervent and warm, that could melt the loving soul. Thus, the soul refrains from contemplating the nails which fastened the Word on the cross. In this way it is pulled away from the immensely fervent pain he sustained, because it would harm it *[silence]* no pavilion is more comfortable than the column to which my Word was tied and was struck so cruelly for you. You can resort to it every time you are scared of your enemies; it is extremely strong, because the Word had shed so much Blood on it. And who would not love to stay under its shadow and receive the Word's Blood on him? *[silence]* no city is more sheltered than the garden where my Word prayed and shed his Blood.

Anyone can run to it if he is tempted; and he will find every consolation *[silence]* who feels weak may also come here, and he will be fortified. In that city you are taught to ask for conformity, in which you see the union of the essence of the Trinity who participates in the union you have with each other down there on earth. *Ecce quam bonum* and *quam jocundum habitare fratres in unum.*[53] And as my Word also told you: '*Ubi sunt duo vel tres congregati in nomine meo, Ego sum in medio eorum*'[54] *[silence]* no bed is more comfortable and peaceful than his cenacle where my Word had his last supper with his holy disciples, and he instituted the Sacred Sacrament of his Body and his Blood. There you comprehend and fathom the ineffable gift he gave you at that moment; the sweet words that he said to you, and that give the soul such a peaceful rest. And primarily those [words] of the consecration that are of such a great substance: '*Qui manducat meam carnem* and *bibit meum Sanguinem in me manet et ego in eo.*'[55] Where he also taught you that fraternal devotion."

SOUL

"Now it is the turn of the sentence of communication and of happiness from yourself, God. Communicate to us your liveliness that is incomprehensible, inscrutable, and unfathomable to us."

FATHER

"Sentence that brings the communication of my divinity. In a second this communication allows you to penetrate my bosom; and here the soul is not appeased, no, until it penetrates the essence. And even later it cannot stay there, unless it takes on the other souls and brings them with itself to that bosom, where they rest and dwell together with my Word. There they participate in that liveliness coming from such an intimate communication that, as God can be wherever he wants in a instant, similarly the soul that has acquired that liveliness can be wherever it wants in a moment. If [it wants to be] in my bosom, it can be in my bosom; if in the deepest hell, [it can be] in the deepest hell; if in my might, wisdom, and goodness, it can be there as well; and if in the idea of the essence of the Trinity, it can be there at its will. The Soul of my Word ordered this sentence in my bosom while his Body still rested in the sepulcher.

"The last sentence, sentence of love, compendium of all the sentences the holy Soul of my Word did in my bosom, where it imposed Love, generated *ab eterno*, newly produced, eternally contemplated, painfully consumed, and in which [love] the Word's soul gloriously and joyfully took pleasure. Sentence of love. And what does it mean to utter love? And what is love? Just by saying 'love' the soul should feel content, and should not care about comprehending anything else. And how could my Word express a greater love to you if, after shedding his own Blood and his life for your redemption, he also wished to resurrect for your justification and sanctification? What more? Conversing with you in his glory for forty days, with so much benevolence? This was a sublime love, which amazed even the angels, and the creatures are still astounded. Oh, what a great sentence my Word had!"

SOUL

"Certainly yes, Father, the Word's love for us was and is so great, that it is more able to open us heaven than the devil [is able to open us] hell. [It is] more able to offer and give, than we [are able] to receive and take. Oh, love, so painfully consumed and with so much desire desired, penetrate our frozen hearts!"

FATHER

"My dear daughter, the soul possessed by this love is so beautiful and joyful, because it is adorned with every virtue. Tell me, does not the soul possessed by this love have every virtue? Does not it have humility? Indeed, it is extremely humble, because it loves the source of every humility, my Word, who has been so humble that my Prophet said in his person: '*Ego sum vermis* and *non homo*.'[56] Does not it have charity as well? Oh, his lover is that on whom it has been written: *'Ignis consumens est,*[57] *Deus charitas est, e[t] qui manet in chari-tate in Deo manet et Deus in eo.'*[58] Oh, does not it have mercy? No, I mean, yes, since its Spouse, the Word, is all mercy, and the soul, his Spouse, would give its life a thousand times a day for his love, if it could. Does not it have patience too? Indeed, it is extremely patient; it accepts tribulations as the most precious joys, and it feels more pain when it has no pain and tribulation, than when it has it. The soul that loves is all pure, all admirable, and all well-adorned; and all its glory is in the Crucifix. In his heart of hearts its Spouse thus calls to it saying: *'Veni columba mea, veni formosa mea, surge propera amica mea* and *veni ad me,*[59] *quia amo te,*[60] *quoniam macula non est in te.'*[61] And when it goes to him, it becomes all lustrous and marvelous receiving the splendor of his divinity; and dressed in the nuptial dress of his Blood, surrounded by palms, crowned with doves, it keeps two gentle sheep under its feet; and it hides in my bosom together with my Word by means of this sentence; so great is the love it possesses."

Here she woke up from the rapture and rested the time neces-sary to take some food, and while she was eating she went back to her rapture. And, as usual, after being silent for a while she began to speak these words: "Oh, eternal Word, there is still a big difference. Why do you let one taste it, if then you deprive him of it? If I have ever desired to be united with you, it is now that I desire it. When I pray to him to withdraw, I pray because I'm unable to bear the great abundance of his grace."

And after being without speaking for quite a long time, at once she cheered up immensely, raising her eyes and showing such a beautiful and joyful face that she looked like a heaven, and saying: "Oh, do you see how that Soul feels wonderful in that bosom? If I could only take it a little bit! And what am I saying? You are the eternal, consubstantial Word, one of the three Per-sons. And what else than saying: Word and Truth! *[silence]* oh, eternal Word, oh eternal Father, let us come back to the vocation you called me to, that is, to your contemplation. And what do you contemplate?"

FATHER

"Being in my bosom, the Soul of my Word contemplates and I contemplate him with an admiring contemplation; a contemplation of admiration; a contemplation of love; a contemplation of annihilation, of purity, of peace, of sentence, of pity; a contemplation of generosity, of mercy, of justice; a contemplation of goodness, of wisdom, of might; a contemplation of communication, of truth, of union; a contemplation of eternity, of clarification, of transformation, and of glorification."

And after these words she became quiet, looking in awe, thus showing that she was perceiving something."

SOUL

"But always in the Father's bosom, no, no, I'm not happy, although I can't ascend more. For, you know, to be always in this height then brings about pain, and my past pain makes me understand that it's not convenient to be always there. And then it's not right, because one must fight before one receives the prize. *Non coronabitur misi qui legittime certaverit*[62] *[silence]* then yes, to the saint Fathers in limbo. And then? You know what you want to give me."

And being quiet for quite a while, she tackled what Jesus had mentioned the night before, that is, his promise of giving his heart to her. And having the impression that she was going off the subject concerning the Word's contemplations in his Father's bosom, she said: "Oh, I'm digressing. One moment I discern something of you, and then I enter into myself *[silence]* Word, see, two by two! Like that other one, you know *[silence]* you know why then I would like to go through hell because of so many things; your constant offenses are enough for me."

She meant that because she was receiving his heart, she prayed to Jesus not to give her more than two things to testify to that gift, like when he gave her the heart of the Virgin Mary. In that occasion he told her that, as an attestation of that gift, she would always feel two things within herself: the first would be her immense desire to suffer for his love; the other would be her passionate love for her neighbors, a fervid and constant longing for every creature's salvation, including the infidels. Thus, then she said: "I have seen that much has been fulfilled in one of them."

She meant that great desire for the salvation of every creature. Indeed, since then that desire has been so strong that she always feels like she has been martyred. And being quiet some more, she went back to the previous topic of the Word's contemplations in the Father's bosom. Thus, she said: *"Admirabo admiration ista."*

Here she showed that she was seeing the Word having this first contemplation of admiration. And she began to speak with such a dignity and so quickly that we could not help but stop writing and listen to her, reporting no more than the beginning. Then, being very careful we have been able to write what follows, although we could never relate her words with the dignity and the beautiful manner she spoke and uttered them. For during that rapture she always spoke in the first person and in the person of the eternal Father, as in a dialogue, with her posing questions and the Father giving answers. And he told her so many divine things, that it would be impossible to give a full account of them. We shall attempt, at least, to tell the substance of that little bit that we have understood and retained.

She continued to speak about the sentence of admiration for almost three hours. We were totally amazed by that. When she spoke in the person of the eternal Father she expressed herself with such a dignity, majesty, and with such an impressive voice that inspired a great awe, not because she frightened us, but because she consoled and comforted us. And when she spoke in the first person she expressed herself in a humble way, with a submissive and sweet voice; and she crouched as if she wanted to become a nothingness.

About the first contemplation that the Word's Soul had in the Father's bosom, she began to say: "He contemplates with a contemplation of admiration, his eyes conforming to, or better yet, facing his Father's; both of them are invisible to us. That infinite, unfathomable, and incomprehensible love of equality that makes the Father and the Word share the divine splendor; and that great warmth of love that the Word has toward the creatures; and the splendor of clarification that the Father gives for his bloodshed and his working of redemption; such a great abundance of warmth and splendor brought forth by the mutually admiring contemplation of the Word into the Father, and from the Father into the Word, lets an amazingly copious infusion descend from them to our sightless eyes. Oh, oh, [it is] similar to a liquor, as one would say, of milk and Blood; and in a great flux this infusion flows downwards. By infusing and reinfusing it makes two sources spring forth: one of milk and one of Blood; and it waters the two spouses, the spouse soul and the spouse church, making them fructify two fruits, one of abnegation and the other of comfort *[silence]* contemplation of admiration, yes, that the Word's Soul does in the Father's bosom."

SOUL

"Oh, eternal Father, tell me please, what is that infusion? And what is my Word's contemplation in you, and what is yours, oh Father, in him. How does he contemplate? Please, tell me."

FATHER

"Oh daughter and spouse *Unigeniti Verbi mei,* if you want to understand, pay a great attention to what I am going to tell you. My Word contemplates with an infinite contemplation, incomprehensible and unfathomable to you. And at that moment when his Soul came into my bosom, by gazing at me it was clarified with an infinite clarification. Not that before it was not glorious, because it was always united with me since the moment of his Incarnation. But this clarification had a more specific clarity of glory. I gave it to him because he offered me the triumphant victory that he had won against death and sin, and also because with an ardent and eager love toward every creature he consummated the working of obedience that I had imposed upon him for your redemption. The beauty in his Soul, result of that splendid clarification and of the intense love for the creatures that my Only Begotten constantly showed me, pleased me so deeply that, when

240

his Soul came into my bosom and firmly contemplated my, his Father's, eyes, I was moved to contemplate him. That intense warmth of love and the splendid glory of the divinity producing such an infinite abundance, from the Word's contemplation of me and from mine of him resulted that abundant, copious, admirable infusion that you have seen. Flowing into the spouse soul and into the spouse church, that infusion generated in them those two sources, one of milk and one of Blood, as you would say. That of milk proceeds from my divinity and from my Word who is the purity I tell you about so often; and that of Blood proceeds from the intense love that my humanate Word has for every creature. As if they watered the two spouses, they make them fructify those fruits."

SOUL

"Yes, yes, Father, one of abnegation and one of comfort. But, tell me, please, what does your Word contemplate in your bosom? I, I really don't understand it. Yes, I understand that you, oh eternal Father, was moved to contemplate him by the pleasing love that is between you and the divine Word in the equality of the divinity, and by the love with which the humanate Word had accomplished his redemption and had deeply loved his creatures, and through the pleasing clarification that you gave to his Soul at the moment when he came to rest in your bosom. But I do not understand what the Word actually contemplated in you."

FATHER

"My dear daughter, do you want to know what my Word's Soul contemplate in my bosom? Or better yet, what contemplation did he have in me? He contemplated myself. His holy Soul contemplated the divinity. He contemplated the divinity, his unequalable being. Do you understand now?"

MARIA MADDALENA DE' PAZZI

SOUL

"Yes, oh eternal Father. But I still do not understand that source of milk that, you say, is your purity. I would like to understand a little bit what this purity is. You tell me so much about this purity, but by myself I'm unable to understand it. Another time you told me about it at length. That time I couldn't understand it; now I want to understand it."

FATHER

"Oh daughter and spouse *Unigeniti Verbi mei*, you ask me about such a high and sublime thing that you will never be able to understand it fully. For my purity is such an intrinsic thing that neither you nor others, albeit holy, not even wise and vigorous human beings adorned with every virtue and science, never, never, they will never be able to understand it fully. Notwithstanding, for your satisfaction I shall tell you that little that you are able to understand now. Later, when you are released from this body and come to me, at that point you will understand it as best as you can, even though no one can fully understand it, not even up here, since I, myself, am the sole, the sole one who can perceive it and understand it. This purity is in fact my own being. As I have showed you, that copious and abundant infusion, originated from that source of milk, derived and proceeded from me and from my divine Word. And, although I compare this purity of mine with milk because you are unable to have anything more delicate, stainless, and white, nonetheless it is not milk but my actual and pure being, the divinity. And so it is not a source, although it is called source because I infuse in you my divinity that is my purity. As I told you, my dear daughter, this purity is such an intrinsic and immense thing that no human creature can perceive it and understand it fully, even though thanks to my grace and my pure generosity one may have some knowledge of it, that is, one may attain and acquire a tiny particle of it; someone more and someone less, according to the disposition of each soul, to your intention of becoming similar to me, and to the degree of your participation in my being. I gave you my being when I created you

242

in my own image and likeness, in that pure condition of innocence, in that righteous and original justice that I gave you, in order to take pleasure and enjoyment in you. But when the first man sinned and revolted against me, you lost this innocence and purity along with all the other gifts and graces that I had given you; and you were almost totally deprived of my pure being, in which I had created you in my mind *ab eterno*. Oh my daughter, how happy and how pure was your being at that time! I mean, before the world were, because your being was content and peaceful, only enjoying the essence of the unity of my idea. At that time the purity of your being was so great that it was almost another me through participation. And no created thing, neither the angels, nor the cherubim, nor the seraphim, nor the blessed spirits, nor even your being itself could understand its purity. I, its Creator, was the sole, the sole one who was able to understand it, because I am the source whence this purity derives; and I purify every thing. And, if I purify every thing, all the more purified became what was in me, that is, your being! My dear daughter and spouse of my Only Begotten, its purity was so great that, if the creature had not lost the purity it was created in, not only the celestial beings, but also my Word's Humanity itself, which is not divine per se, albeit united with the divinity, would marvel and remain astounded. But when this innocence was lost, in order to recuperate that purity there was no remedy but to bathe and drown in that second source of Blood coming from the humanate Word, by means of the holy Baptism and of the Sacrament of penance that receive that virtue from the source of Blood. However, the soul cannot regain the purity it had in my idea before the beginning of the world, since now the soul knows its being whereas before it did not and, although it is a sheer nothingness, this knowledge is still something. And even though this knowledge is good, it hinders you from being able to receive my purity, which is so great. Nevertheless, the creature will be capable of attaining a purity that will grant her a complete unity with me, her Father and God. And this union will be so great, that neither a thought, nor a word, nor a deed, nor a glance will ever be able to separate the creature from me, that is, from this union and pleasure of mine. But the creatures do not know my being, and they do not look for it, do not desire it, do not want it; and they go on walking along crooked paths, looking for their being outside of me. Thus, they will never be able to have my purity, since they do not follow my inner draught, through which you make yourselves able to receive the gift of my purity, as much as you can at the moment."

SOUL

"Oh, eternal Father, if I could have your being, I know that I would not keep it for myself, but I would give it to the creatures and would take theirs away from them. And I would do so much to straighten out their intentions and direct them more toward you, so that they would be able to receive in themselves a minimum of your purity."

FATHER

"My dear daughter and spouse of my Only Begotten, I wish only to tell you that, if a soul were so zealous to become able to receive from me a minimum of my purity, if that soul besought me to forgive the devil, provided that he would be willing to repent and to reject his pride, I would forgive him out of love for that soul possessing a minimum of my purity, because that soul would please me immensely. Let me add that I am so delighted to see the soul anxiously wishing to have and to possess my purity that, if it were possible for me to beseech, or better yet, if it were becoming for me to beseech, I would beseech the soul, I would beseech the soul to ask me for that purity, to long for it, and to make itself able to receive that purity within itself, even though to long for that purity, to ask for it, and to want it means to stain it. For that purity is such an intrinsic thing, that by herself the creature can never, never acquire it; she can have it only, only, only from me, the purity's own being, indeed the origin and the source of that purity."

THE DIALOGUES

SOUL

"Oh eternal Father, I don't understand. I don't know what to do in order to obtain this purity. You are so great, and I am such a minimum thing, such a little thing, that I am a nothingness, a nothing. Nonetheless, I would like to have it to please you more. You tell me that one cannot have it without you; that you would like one to desire it; and that to ask for it and to desire it means to stain it *[silence]* listen, I know what I am going to do, and I won't ask you for it. I will go to my Word, and I will tell him to ask for it in my place, because you love him so much that you would never deny it to him. And then I will take some of his Blood and put it before your eyes. In this way I will blind you; and you will not see that I have asked you for it. Oh, if I could come to that throne, I would hide in a corner of the throne close to my Word, and so you wouldn't notice that such a littleness of mine had received your purity. But since I just told you that, you'll know it. But I know very well that in any case you would know it, even if I hadn't told you, because you see and know everything in yourself and from yourself."

FATHER

"Oh daughter and spouse *Unigeniti Verbi mei,* if you want to understand fully now you need to listen very carefully to what I am going to tell you. If you keep your memory firm, your intellect rapt, your will dead, and your affect stupefied, you will see how one can acquire that purity to the extent of one's capability. As I have already told you, when my Word contemplated me and I contemplated him an infusion flew out so copiously that those two sources were born, that of milk and that of Blood. These two sources watered the two spouses, the spouse soul and the spouse church, fructifying in them not only those two fruits I showed you before, that is, abnegation and comfort, but also these two more, one that nourishes and the other that fructifies. Indeed, this watering is so abundant that it makes each spouse generate two more sources in the same way, one of milk and one of Blood. These two sources fecundate them and make them generate many sons. Now, consider how from this fructifying watering

245

derive the two aforementioned sources in the spouse soul and in the spouse church. If one wishes to have the first source, that of milk— which is my purity, as I have already told you—, one must dwell nowhere, neither in heaven, nor on earth, nor in any creature who has being; you cannot dwell in my Word's humanity either, because it is created, although it is glorious thanks to the Deity's union. You can only, only, dwell in my Deity, divine essence and eternal substance; and you must discard any other thing, any other thought, and any other inclination, since any minimum thing could prevent you from attaining this purity and could stain and spoil it, once you have received it."

SOUL

"Oh eternal Father, yes, yes, I understand that, if the soul wishes to be able to have it, it must dwell in nothing, but only in you with a perfect purity. But I would like to know also how the soul can acquire this purity to the extent of its capability. This I do not understand."

FATHER

"Oh daughter and spouse *Unigeniti Verbi mei*, as I told you and I repeat it so that you can keep it in mind, one needs to dwell in nothing, because one acquires this purity by being nothing, by understanding nothing, by knowing nothing, by dwelling in nothing, and by wishing nothing, nothing, nothing. But if I want you to understand, I need to do to you what you said you would do to me, that is, I need to blind you, because this purity sees nothing, knows nothing, is aware of nothing. As I told you at the beginning, it does not know wisdom. It knows neither faith, nor might, nor virtue. It knows neither humility, nor patience, nor any other thing, because you can only acquire it through nothingness, by being nothing, knowing nothing, and wishing nothing, nothing, nothing; and only by following my inner draught can the soul become able to receive this purity within itself, although as long as you are in this mortal life you can never, never possess this purity in its totality; you can only, only receive it from my pure and prompt generosity."

SOUL

"Oh eternal Father, it seems to me that this purity is such an admirable, magnificent, and intrinsic thing, and I see myself so low, frail, and base that, I'm convinced, I would be neither ready nor capable of preserving it in myself. Then I won't ask you for it. Keep it for yourself, since only yourself, through yourself, from yourself, and in yourself can keep it and possess it worthily. I would stain it. You know that, when I'm down there, I'm like the others. I'd like to receive it from you only only when my soul leaves my body; for the time being I do not ask you for it and do not want it, because I would stain it and would be neither ready nor capable of keeping it. Oh, oh, it is something that is too intrinsic and too precious."

FATHER

"Oh daughter and spouse *Unigeniti Verbi mei*, I want to give it to you, not only when you, close to death, come to have me fully, but also one time while you are in this mortal life, provided that you prepare yourself and make yourself worthy to receive it. Pay attention, I want to tell you four more things with which the soul, as long as it is by itself, can acquire this purity, so that you prepare yourself to receive it in a better way. The first is that, if it wants to receive this purity, the soul must be purely dead and indeed as if dazed and beside herself, without any understanding, any knowledge, and any will whatsoever, so that all its understanding, its knowledge, and its will can be in me. And it must lose all its being completely, taking my being, as far as it can. It must have understanding and knowledge of nothing, but, as if it were beside herself and completely dead to herself, it must live only in me, its Creator and God. These are the souls called earthly angels, because of their great purity, since they possess it in the most perfect and supreme manner ever possible to you, pilgrims. *[silence]*

247

"The second thing necessary to acquire this purity is that the soul purify all its thoughts, reflections, and all its feelings and desires, and direct them to me, its God and Creator; and that it let no thought creep into its heart and stain it. Abstaining from any minimum sin, the soul must strive to remove any image and fantasy of these worldly and base things that could separate it from me or could generate some stain in its heart and in its mind. And these are the persons my Word speaks about: *'Beati mundo corde, quoniam ipsi Deum videbunt.'*[63]

"The third thing [necessary] to acquire this purity is bodily cleanness and purity, that is, holy virginity, in which condition I posited you and the other religious. And since you have taken a vow to me, it is better for you to observe it strictly, striving to keep it and protect it like a precious treasure. Through virginity you please me greatly and therefore become able to receive this purity within yourself. Virginity makes you similar to me and, giving you that original pure being, it almost lets you go back to that pristine state of innocence in which I created you. They are really very good, those who do not take virginity into account and do not consider it of great value![64]

"The fourth and last thing is holy humility, which pleases me so much that, if the soul did not have humility, the other three things would not satisfy me in the least. Humbleness is the mother of purity and purity is the mother of humility; humility generates purity and purity generates humility. Humbleness is so precious to me and so useful to the soul that has it, and [it is] so powerful, that it has the faculty of giving purity back to the soul, even if the soul has lost its virginity, [which is] the supreme way to acquire this purity. Nonetheless, even without virginity the soul may attain its purity through humility. In fact, many virgins will be in hell, but no humble soul possessing this purity will be there, because a humble soul may acquire, protect, and keep its purity by means of this humility, and through this humility it may take back its lost purity.

"Oh, let us converse now on the second source, that of Blood, proceeding from the humanate Word, Love itself. One can acquire it with an anxious and dead desire. I and my humanate Word infuse both sources, that of milk and that of

Blood, in the spouse soul and the spouse church. Into the spouse soul that follows my inner and pure draught I first infuse the source of purity through my humanate Word. And then this purity generates in the soul that anxious and dead desire that later leads the soul to the source of my humanate Word. In this source the soul drowns and annihilates itself, so that it tastes nothing but Blood, sees nothing but Blood, wishes and wants nothing but Blood, lives and feeds on nothing but Blood. Into the spouse church I first infuse the source of Blood through its, the church's, dispossession of any form of selfishness, pride, and of any will, and of any counterfeit faith. By drowning and annihilating themselves in the source of Blood, the faithful then reach the source of purity that for lay people is the observance of the law [expressed] in the Gospel and in my commandments whence, as my humanate Word said, they acquire eight beatitudes. From these two sources the spouse soul acquires two things; from the source of purity it obtains the possession of me, its God, and from the source of Blood [it obtains] an anxious and passionate desire to lead souls to me. Do not believe, my dear daughter, that I give to the spouse church more than I give to you because I give eight [things] to the church and only two [things] to you. Do not even dare to think that I do better for the servant than for the son, better for the maidservant than for the spouse, better for the slave than for the friend. No, no, do not even dare to think that. And if you happen to think it, cast this thought off immediately, for you must know that, although I give more to the spouse church than to the spouse soul, the fruit will be the same, actually more copious. Indeed, from the two sources of milk and of Blood that I and my Word have infused in the spouse soul and in the spouse church, I mean, from my purity and from the love my humanate Word has for you two similar sources, as I have already told you, generate in the two spouses, one of milk and one of Blood. The spouse soul generates first one of milk and then one of Blood, and the spouse church generates first that of Blood and then that of milk."

SOUL

"Oh Father, I don't understand how these two sources can generate in the spouse soul. Yes, I understand a little bit that the source of milk can generate in the soul through that purity that you, Father, give to it. I mean, I understand that through the same source of milk proceeding from you a source of milk can generate in it. Oh Father, am I correct?"

FATHER

"Bene intellexisti sponsa Unigeniti Verbi mei."[65]

SOUL

"But, Father, I do not understand the source of Blood. How can it generate in the soul. Please, explain this."

FATHER

"Do you want to know how it can generate, my dear daughter? As I have already told you, it can do it through that anxious and dead desire that the soul acquires when it follows my inner draught by means of the source of Blood that the humanate Word infuses in the soul itself. From this source the soul acquires an anxious and passionate desire for the salvation of its neighbor. The soul in fact uses this source of Blood more for its neighbor, so to speak, than for itself, because through this anxious and passionate desire it leads the creatures to this source of Blood, through which the creatures then betake themselves to me. My dear daughter, did you understand this time?"

SOUL

"Yes, eternal Father."

THE DIALOGUES

FATHER

"Let us examine now the fruit that the source of milk and that of blood generate in the spouse soul and in the spouse church. These sources make them so fertile, that they give birth to several sons. The spouse soul gives birth to many of them either in wisdom or in goodness or in might and justice. And these are from the source of milk. These sons are extremely wise in their might and are so mighty that they can achieve any mighty and great working. In goodness, they are all good, sweet, and gentle sons. In justice, they are just sons in any of their virtue and working; speaking about them my Word said: *"Beati qui exuriunt* and *sitiunt justitiam."* You will generate two of them, that is, of those in goodness and justice. You will generate no child in wisdom and might, but you will generate those of goodness. They will be sons of gentleness, who will draw others toward gentleness with their good example. You will also generate some in justice. These sons will follow my path faithfully. But their quantity and the moment [of their birth] are known only to me. From the source of Blood the soul gives birth to many other sons in mercy, in goodness, in generosity, and in humility.

"In mercy the soul gives birth to sons all full of mercy; speaking about them my Word said: *'Beati misericordes quoniam ipsi misericordiam consequentur.'* In goodness, [it gives birth to] sons without malice and without fraud. In generosity, [it gives birth to] sons that would give away both their properties and their resources out of love for me. And in humility, [it gives birth to] humblest sons, without any ostentation of pride. You will generate sons only in goodness and in generosity. From her sources of Blood and milk the spouse church generates and gives birth to many sons as well. She first gives birth in charity to sweet and affectionate sons. She then generates and gives birth to others that are sons in my generosity. She also generates some others in my fortitude, and they are armed with Blood. Some others in temperance; they are those who follow the path of penance. The spouse church generates many other sons, but it would be too long to say everything about them."

MARIA MADDALENA DE' PAZZI

SOUL

"Oh eternal Father, you told me that there are two more fruits. I remember that you mentioned them to me, but I do not know what they are *[silence]* one of nourishment and the other, but I'm not sure, of comfort. Ah, ah, no, I really don't remember them *[silence]* ah, ah, Father, I don't know if it is a fructifying one."

FATHER

"Yes, my dear daughter and spouse of my Only Begotten, one that nourishes and the other that fructifies. That of nourishment is generated by the spouse soul, and the one that fructifies [is generated] by the spouse church. That of the spouse soul is one of sincerity and its fruits, you must know, are generated, or better yet, proceed from this tree; they are the seven gifts of the Holy Spirit, and they adorn it like the flowers adorn the spring. And the fructifying one, generated by the spouse church, is faith, and its fruits are not only the seven gifts of the Holy Spirit, but also the twelve fruits of the Spirit that adorn them like the lamps in your churches."

And later, keeping quiet for a while, she came out of her rapture between the eighteenth and the nineteenth hour. And staying like this for half an hour, she resumed her rapture.

And going back to the second contemplation, that of admiration, that the Word's soul had done in the Father's bosom, she said: "The second contemplation of the Word's holy soul in the Father's bosom is one of admiration, when that holy soul admires the divinity. And this contemplation generates darts of love in the three divine Persons and a furnace in the creatures, in whose furnaces many sorts of things are being made with a flame of love fire *[silence]* it generates darts of love among the three divine Persons in that equality where they are together. The Word never refrains from giving it, the Father never refrains from infusing and the Holy Spirit from being pleased. And thanks to the Word's gift the soul becomes rich, thanks to the Father's infusion the soul becomes a lake of love, and thanks to the Holy Spirit's pleasure the soul becomes the treasurer of the Holy Trinity. This contemplation of

admiration generates a furnace of purification within us, the creatures, where unpolished vases and fragile, transparent vases are
formed, and also others. There are other furnaces where things for
construction are made, like bricks, lime, and similar ones *[silence]*
the first furnace is a furnace where one bakes bricks for construction, and this is nothing but the union. There is the second one
where one makes some unpolished vases, and this is mercy *[silence]*
the third where one makes those gentle vases is doctrine. Then,
there is also the furnace where one purifies gold, and this is the wisdom in which one does away with any false wisdom and ignorance.

"The third contemplation of the holy Soul in his Father's
bosom is a contemplation of love, a unitive love *[silence]* but, Word,
here one needs to do as you do in yourself, you that are understandable to no one. So, since we cannot understand you, it is better for
us to tell you not to communicate it to us. Yes, yes, Word, you are
too great! *[silence]* oh, who could see and comprehend those beautiful eyes that gaze at us and contemplate us! And you are all incomprehensible *[silence]* and your contemplations are so many that I
leave them all in you, but you know that I will understand them
later in a different moment *[silence]* but, oh my soul, you that take
such a delight in the Word, you must remember that he is in the
sepulcher *[silence]* yes, the Soul must go and glorify the body in the
sepulcher, and in limbo *[silence]* I don't know *[silence]* oh shortness of
time! *[silence]* oh Soul of the Word, please, yes, come back to glorify
the body in the sepulcher *[silence]* oh holy Humanity, you have
received so much glory, so that later you can glorify us; we had to
stay underground, but you wanted to stay in the ground; you
wanted to be placed in the ground to dig us out of the ground
[silence] oh happy enjoyment without enjoyment! *[silence]* oh holy
Soul, when you were reunited (although you were in an identical
union) you took your body back and glorified it with a glory partly
invisible to those blessed souls in limbo, because if they had seen it
they would have been annihilated and nullified. You do so to your
elect; you do not let them enjoy as much as they understand,
because if they enjoyed it they would vanish completely and would
not be able to tolerate such a great sweetness *[silence]* oh Word, in
the Father's bosom you were as Soul. I mean that you were not

totally in this bosom; then you take your body back, and united with that body you descend to those blessed souls in a perfect glory. They have been waiting for you for so long.

"This holy body united with the Soul, and faster than the twinkling of an eye this union occurred where the union of the divinity was. That Soul [was] so pure, that body [was] so chaste *[silence]* and as you glorify your Soul, so you also glorify our souls and lead them into the Father's bosom where he holds a dialogue, whence proceeds an inebriating wine, a seasoning oil, and purifying water *[silence]* the seasoning oil is nothing but the eyes of my Word, nothing but the infusion infused from my Word's eyes, so that his eyes are like two olive trees and are owned only by the doves. Their pupils are branches, which are taken by these doves and brought into the ark of the holy church, where they squeeze these branches and fill it up with that infusion coming from that oil *[silence]* then these little doves go and shake those olives with their beaks, drawing all their juice out and feed on it *[silence]* the wine that gladdens the spouse is squeezed from the vine. The vine is the mouth of the Word, the shoots are the words of the Word, the bunch is the substance of the divinity. The grapes are taken with the lips of desire and are pressed with the teeth of faith; and this is how one draws the juice. And everyone can do that, but only a man who has the image of God can take it, no beast can. For the beast takes the stalk, and it does not draw the substance out of it because it does not comprehend. But those who have faith comprehend very well that the beasts are the infidels who, although they have the image of God, nonetheless do not comprehend because they do not have the light of the true faith *[silence]* this Soul is also a source of nourishing and purging water drawn from the divinity, that is the glorification of the soul. This glorification is like a channel poured by the Word into the soul, and poured back by the soul into the Word; and by this constant and mutual pouring the whole city of Jerusalem is watered. And then it drips here in the world, now on that flower and now on that lily, and on this [flower] and on that rose and flower; now on that tree and now on that plant, and it makes it sprout and fructify, still watering the entire world with its infusion. And then many feed on this water, and the thirsty crows [feed on it] immensely. This soul receives [its] glorification from the divinity, from the Soul of the Word, and from his Humanity. From the divinity it receives a splendor of life, from the Soul an eternal clarity, from the Humanity an innocence of wisdom. This splendor discloses to the soul the book of life that is the humanate Word, in whose divinity and Humanity we all are written, unless we erase ourselves from it *[silence]* the clarity of the Soul makes us follow the Lamb wherever he goes. The innocence of the Humanity makes enjoy the embraces of the spouse. The Soul of the Word combined with the divinity unites with the humanity, I mean, with the body; it assumes the humanity and gives it an unspeakable name, and gives it such a dignity that one can say: *'Domini est terra* and *plenitudo eius,*[66] *Deus Deorum,*[67] *Rex Regum* and *Dominus dominantium';*[68] and it gives it total might both in heaven and on earth; might first given and then possessed *[silence]* the Soul of the Word assumes his Humanity back and gives it such a glorifying and communicating glory, that one can say: *'Gloriosus apparuisti in conspectu Dei.'* The Holy Spirit unites with this body, although it had been always united with it, and gives it a splendor superior to every splendor, that about this Humanity one can say: *'In lumine tuo videbimus lumen.*[69] *Oculi nostri sint semper in humanitatis Verbi'* *[silence]* yes, of course we see splendor in the Humanity: *de vultu tuo procedet omne splendor glorie tue,*[70] so that the Humanity of my Word receives the crown of the essence of the Trinity, the ring of virginity, the garland of the martyrs, the splendor of the apostles, the mirror of the confessors, the book of the doctors, sun and light of every creature *[silence]* oh Humanity, you are who we want *[silence]* who will ever be able to thank you for the gift of your Humanity, because in your Humanity you have exalted ours greatly *[silence]* and if your crown of your essence is our crown of you, Word, if you are the garland of the martyrs and we are your garland. You are the ring of virginity, and we will be the hand holding it as the most precious thing; you are the splendor of the apostles, and we will be the gaiety of the virgins so much loved by you and so much dear to you *[silence]* you, Word, are the book of the doctors and we will be the book in which your gifts and your graces for all your beloved souls will be transcribed. You are the mirror of the confessors and we will be a mirror for you, in which you will gaze at the beauty of the purity you have given to the soul *[silence]* you are a sun warming every creature and, if not with our deeds at least with our ardent desire, we will warm your creatures in some parts. You are the glory of the Angels, and we will be the gaiety of those angels. And what cannot we desire that is not in your Humanity? *[silence]* the gratitude we will express to it will be: '*Calicem salutaris accipiam* and *nomen Domini invocabo.*'"[71]

She awoke from the rapture at the twenty-second hour, and she stayed like this until she said Vespers; then entering a rapture again she said as follows: "Here is the eternal Word *[silence]* the eternal, triumphant Word goes down to limbo to the holy Fathers in order to comfort them (in fact to free them from that prison) and take them to the eternal homeland, where our first Father was, who had been waiting for so long with a pain stronger than the others', and Who saw that all of them were finally there thanks to his love *[silence]* but so, oh eternal Word, it occurs that those who cause evil suffer more than the others, because they have done evil to them. But much worse, woe woe betide those who hinder good and with their example are the cause of everybody else's evil. Ascending with your assumed Humanity, all glorious and triumphant you were recognized by them, because John the Baptist was among them. But the devil did not recognize you, so that limbo became heaven thanks to your visitation, and with not less love you assumed those souls when your divinity assumed your Humanity again. You glorified them at that moment, although they were glorious, but more because of grace than because of glory *[silence]* I dare to say that in this world you glorify the soul with grace as you do in the other [world] with glory, so that it is a greater gift to have grace in this world than to have glory in the other *[silence]* they did not heed the past any longer; they faster gloried in the present in what was going to come."

At this point she rejoiced greatly, showing such a joyful face that she looked jubilant. And after quite a while, she said: "Oh souls, who could ever describe your present joy and content? You are right, because you have the Truth, the Word, and the Only Begotten in yourselves *[silence]* he comes to you with his divinity, his Soul, his Spirit, and his body. With his divinity he will glorify you; with his body he will give you the vision of himself; with his Soul he will give you a perfect fruition; with his Spirit he will glorify you of a glorification of conformity, so that unlike us you will not try to force God *[silence]* the angels will rejoice at your freedom, because you were in a ghastly prison, close to the demons and for some time you were struck by them *[silence]* they remembered no pain; they remembered no sin, and if they did their memory was glorified. With joy they denied their fault. Oh, how much you rejoiced, but your joy should be more enjoyed than understood *[silence]* you are such a great and uncreated God that a soul would become glorious simply by perceiving that you want to get closer to it. But who can ever possess such a copiousness? What can one do? This God of ours is so great, that there are and there could be no possible workings."

After this, she kept rather calm; then she spoke these words: "Please, come here!"

According to what will be said later, we understood that she was calling our Carmelite St. Angel and St. Catherine of Siena so that they would help her recite Compline that she immediately began to recite: *"Jube Donne benedicere."* And she stopped without reciting the benediction, that is, *"Noctem quietam"* etc. Then she said: *"Fratres"* etc., and once the Confiteor;[72] she completed the Compline in this way, reciting every other verse. And her pauses were so long that we always recited what followed; and when she finished it, she showed that those saints wanted to leave, so she said: "Oh, please don't go. You must stay for high things."

And at once she started to invoke the holy Virgin with these words: *"Ora pro nobis sancta Dei Genitrix. Ora pro nobis beate pater Angele. Ora pro nobis beata mater Chatarina."* And she invoked them so that they would help her receive the heart of Jesus properly because the previous night he had promised her that he would give it to her; and seeing that he was there to offer it to her as a gift, she besought Jesus-Love not to render this gift visible; and she said: "Oh my Jesus, please don't let them perceive that."

And at that moment (as she told us later) she made the sign of giving the Virgin's heart to a nun who was there. As one can read in her previous raptures, she had received the Virgin's heart some time before. Then she opened her arms looking like St. Francis when he received the stigmata; and she stretched them slowly showing that she wanted to take the heart Jesus was giving her. Indeed, she drew them back at once and crossed them on her heart. Holding it tight, in the person of Jesus she spoke thus: *"Collocavit cor meum in anima sponse mee."*[73]

She kept silent in that position for a long time without speaking. Then, in the person of the eternal Father she said: *"Sponsa Unigeniti Verbi mei, quid vis ad me petis."*[74]

SOUL

"I do not dare to ask, but I hope that the fact that I do not ask for myself will not offend [your] purity. However, I do ask you to increase good in each of us *[silence]* I offer you these ones in particular," by that meaning a monastery that had besought her to pray for them.

"It seems like you love them. Give them your light. But some of them need to walk without a light because of the abundance of the great light, and some others need the general light along with the particular one. And although I am not in their congregation, nonetheless since I know that you love them as your own creatures, I recommend them to you. I offer you every creature, and for all of them, in every moment, I would suffer the martyrdom and thousand deaths. Oh, happy me if I had this grace!"

I have omitted that, when Jesus gave her his heart, he gave her two signs to testify that she had actually received it, that is, as I have already said, the annihilation and the desire of his honor. After her thanksgiving *"Benedic anima mea Domino,* and *omnia que intra me sunt nomini sancto eius"* and the above offering, she went back to the mystery concerning the time before his resurrection. Thus, turning her discourse to the Virgin with the following words:[75] "Oh Mary, you waited for your Word with a great anxiety. By infinite names you tried to call him! You did not lack faith, not in the least. But you kept waiting like a lioness. Did you lack conformity? Not at all. You called him: '*Surge gloria mea, surge psalterium meum,*[76] your glory, glory of himself and of ourselves. Oh Word, I would like to call you myself, but I would like to be with you and without you, as you like *[silence]* your Glory. Oh Mary, in how many ways did he glorify you? He

glorified you by electing you; he glorified you by making you
mother *[silence]* the Father glorified you by electing you; the Holy
Spirit glorified you by descending into you; the Word glorified you
by living so many months in your holy womb, where you were virgin
and mother. With your mercy you were an example for the creatures, and with your purity you were an example for us, virgins. With
your fecundity you made the world and the sky fecund, and with
your purity you made the Holy Trinity pleased with you *[silence]* but
now, oh Mary, you look forsaken by the Father, despised by the
Word, and abandoned by the Holy Spirit. But, Mary, it was not like
that; you were not forsaken by the Father, you were rather accomplished in your mercy toward your neighbors with an accomplished
will. Were you abandoned by the Holy Spirit? No, no, it followed
you in your journey *[silence]* but, what a sweet and tender journey is
when the body journeys with the Spirit, and the Holy Spirit [jour-
neys] with the body, so that at every step it takes the soul gives birth
to God thousand times, if he could be given birth to, but he cannot
[silence] at every step, so to speak, it takes the soul it gives birth to
God. Every time it moves its feet this soul gives birth to God, and
along the way it converses with this Spirit that is pure pure Love, so
that in every word and thought this soul gives birth to Christ *[silence]*
does it look despised by the Word?[77] No, no, absolutely not. In fact,
he wants to glorify you with an invisible and incomprehensible glorification, that cannot be understood by any creature; and he has
already conceived to visit you in his glory and to console you *[silence]*
Exurge gloria mea, exurge psalterium et citara, exurge psalterium.[78]
Psalterium played so well by Mary's pure and expert hands *[silence]*
you could wait for him with faith, because with faith you had conceived him *[silence] psalterium* like that of David, with ten strings. *In
psalterio decaccordo psallam tibi*[79] *et adorabo ad templum sanctum tuum.
Sanctum meum.* And what did one have to worship, since everybody
had to worship him? *[silence]* in you one had to worship your
Humanity, your divinity, your Father *[silence]* this psaltery had ten
strings, and he stretched them and showed them on the cross,
although they should have been touched and loosened beforehand.
Every creature should look at them and admire them with an anxious desire *[silence]* ten strings. The first two strings are your pierced

and wounded feet. The other two [are] your right and left hands, transfixed by nails. The fifth one [is] your side, that is so large that the spear has divided it into two parts, the side and the heart. And two more in the separation[80] of your holy members *[silence]* now the holy psaltery is complete, with two more strings taken from your holy thorned head, which are a compendium of all the others *[silence]* *in decaccordo psallam tibi [silence] psallam tibi* and *glorificabo*, etc. *[silence]* oh Mary, with the embrace of your Word, you wanted to sing and dance *[silence]* oh Mary, to honor the Father you played this Word of yours when he was a baby and you had it and carried it in your arms. These strings were not formed yet when with so much love you looked for him in the temple *[silence]* you could easily play these strings, but they were not stretched yet, as he stretched them later on the cross *[silence]* and what does one play this psaltery with? Oh, to take nails, and then? It will make a melodious and gentle sound that will content the spouse *[silence]* *In decacordo psallam tibi*, and *adorabo ad templum sanctum tuum*. Mary, you were a temple, and a temple was your Word. You saw yourself in him, and he [saw himself] in the neighbors. You were that beautiful temple where that admirable offering had to be done, though you were not sanctified, no, but immaculate conceived *[silence]* he will confess, narrating his marvelous workings *[silence]* *psallam tibi* and *confitebor nomini tuo* *[silence]* oh Mary, you believed you received it, and not even you could receive it *[silence]* with this sound you bend all the Angelic Spirits, the creatures, and all those who are in heaven and on earth *[silence]* he comes and turns you into a sound, and you turn him into a sound that pierces the intrinsic bosom of the Father, the depths of hell, and into every creature that is sensible."

She stood up showing that she was seeing something wonderful; and after keeping silent for a bit she continued as follows:

"*Vidi thronum Dei, altum* and *elevatum, sedentem in eum Mariam Mater Jesu [silence]* surrounded by various lilies, and held by four angels *[silence]* what glorification could one ever give to Mary for the Word's great vocation, and for such a firm and constant faith? She certainly deserves it *[silence]* with the constant seeing of his sight the Father gazes around among many, and he doesn't find anyone who has a faith like Mary; and he confirms all of them and establishes that they be firm and established in him *[silence]* and as greater were Mary's faith and her awaiting, so greater will be their embraces *[silence]* but looking at her right and at her left, Mary saw and gazed if her sweet Word was appearing. She knew that he had such an infinite power, that all of a sudden, while someone was coming back in tears from the burial, he might appear alive to that person, since he is everywhere and nowhere, so fast is his speed *[silence]* oh when will we enjoy his embraces? *[silence]* oh Mary, one enjoys them. You were really right about the fact that to generate and to nourish with affection and in effect is something different from generating and nourishing only with affection. But you, Mary, had generated him with affection and in effect *[silence]* abiding faith *[silence]* that the strong armed rise soon, so that those armed will be worthless *[silence]* but with falsity they will try to excuse themselves and with falsity they will accuse themselves. Oh Mary, you certainly knew, and with abiding and firm faith you believed. But you wanted to spur on the Apostles who were losing their faith *[silence]* and you were giving thanks to the eternal Father, when your Only Begotten appeared *[silence]* no, they won't deceive you, oh no, Mary! Neither Peter, nor John, nor Magdalen, who wanted to go with the ointments to anoint. But that body was already glorious in limbo. Oh Magdalen, you wanted to go anoint him, believing that his body was in the sepulcher, but I wouldn't have believed it. Well, you really showed you did not remember the words of Truth, who had said that he would resurrect within three days, but you didn't remember it and did not have faith *[silence]* how can it be that she who loved did not believe? *[silence]* but to feel, to see, and to enjoy, I hope it's not more important *[silence]* and, and, John, you that had rested on his chest and had drawn from him those high secrets, high for us down here, but not for God! I can't believe that you didn't have faith, and that along with the others you didn't remember the words that the Master had said! *[silence]* Mary, she lets them go. I wouldn't have let them go. They believed they would find the dead body, and it was not there.

"We are taught that, when the Word has left us and we do not perceive him, almost like dead, we are not supposed to stay, we must rather look for him with a great desire, and with impassioned sighs we must go up to the right side of the eternal Father's bosom; never halting until we find him, never refraining from calling him with the most intrinsic voice, and from sending constant arrows with the crossbow of love; and the Word, like a bird that falls on the ground, lets himself be taken; and his potency makes him impotent *[silence]* the soul indeed must feel content with its being nothing, since the eternal Word lets himself be moved by a sigh and by an intrinsic voice, when this voice is sent with a perfect aim into the Father's bosom, or to his right. Oh, how much more must the soul let itself be moved by the Word's intrinsic draught!

"The Word's love is so great, that it seems more difficult to take it out from the souls in hell than from the Father's bosom. Not because he likes the place of iniquity better than that of enjoyment, no, but in order to show us his pure goodness. And with supreme wisdom he did this to make us know how great is the order of his love. He resolved to ascend down there in order to establish some sort of limit, albeit already present, to their sufferings, even though given their innumerable iniquities and sins they deserved to suffer much more than they did. But in his immense generosity the Lord wanted to establish that limit and order to their sufferings for the future, and also for the present *[silence]* it seems like you enjoy the Father's soul more than his bosom. It's not that his soul is more suitable to you, but you rest better there because your being is all goodness and communication. You draw him to yourself, and when you are in your creature you are in yourself, and by contemplating him you see your own image. You order this order in yourself, in your creatures in heaven, in those on earth that you have created, in the elements, and even in hell this order of yours is ordered *[silence]* oh foolish demons, you wanted to know him, but you lost him because of your pride. He showed you his beauty, but with your horrible eyes you didn't deserve to see it. I don't think you were amazed by his amazing beauty, because you didn't see it, but certainly you feared his might *[silence]* oh happy souls! Although you were not present when the Word shed his Blood, in any case you shared its virtue and adjusted to it and made a vestment of Blood. As soon as you had it, you wouldn't be able to live in that place any longer. So, if the soul made itself able to share that Blood, it would never happen that it weren't saved; and we all receive it, unless we make ourselves unable to. Oh Word, what led you down to earth? Love. What leads us up to heaven? Blood. What led you to us other than your being which is pure communication? What leads us to heaven other than your pains and wounds? Who wouldn't be grateful to him for his infinite blessings? *[silence]* oh Mary, every second must have seemed a year to you while you waited for your Word; and maybe he was somewhere among the devils. Even if he were in the Father's bosom from which you drew him with your humility, you drew him and pulled him into yourself, but when you saw the joy that this Soul shared with the Father in his bosom you wouldn't dare to raise your voice to call him. But when he saw your intrinsic movement, at once the Father sent him with that same speed when he sent him to you for us. Oh, if he does it to us, think if he would have done it to you![81] Love drew him from heaven to earth, and Blood draws us from earth to heaven [silence] Word, oh Word, come to Mary and come to me! Don't stay down there in limbo any longer *[silence] Descendet inferioribus terre, ut educat me in interioribus terre.*[82] If you don't mind, I would like to perceive a little bit the love dialogue that you had when you came from those ministers of justice *[silence]* oh my Word, come, please come! *[silence]* I will perceive what he said to Mary. But I would like to perceive something else inside *[silence]* my Spouse, come *[silence]* when the splendor of his body and the brightness of a splendor more beautiful than anything else."

She indicated that she was seeing Jesus resurrected. "'*Omnes videntes eum mirati sunt in splendore glorie eius*' [silence] where are the wounds? Where the blows, the spit, the abuse, the insults, and the scorn? What is missing to this holy body of yours? *[silence]* oh, you told your workings, and now you told Mary the workings, yes, those that will generate admiration and love in us *[silence]* oh my Spouse and my Word, how beautiful you are! *[silence]* but you wanted to appear to Mary first because she had given birth to you, because she was a Virgin, because she had maintained her faith, because she had waited for you with an anxious desire, and because she had been the humblest one. But does it matter to the soul if it is the first to be visited? Time is so short. *Dies eius sicut umbra pretereunt*[83] *[silence]* yes, it matters because she will be the first to participate in his glory; and this matters a lot *[silence]* first, one must have given birth to you if one wants to be the first to be visited *[silence]* one conceives you through a painful, anxious, and longing pain. Then one gives birth to you through our constant working; through the faith she had maintained. And who wants to ascend to the sublime union with you, must have so much faith that is no faith. God cannot fail to himself. When the soul betakes itself to forget itself and to unite with its lover and creator, it is the first to be confirmed in its faith. And God being a perfect, infinite, immense, and inscrutable goodness that can be perceived only by itself, the more the soul believes in him, the more it participates in his goodness. Oh who wouldn't like to believe a lot in order to unite with you more and more intrinsically? *[silence]* then because she is a Virgin. We must be a virgin not only in our body but also in our having nothing, nothing that may prevent us from being perfectly pure; and our soul will be the first to be consoled and to be visited, and will be the first to enjoy the Word. She [Mary] was the first to be consoled for the humility with which she drew him from heaven out of the Father's bosom; and humility hastens, so to speak, his visitation, since you, you sole principle, cannot help but visit and exalt the soul that keeps a pure humility in itself. She was right when she said: '*Deposuit potentes de sede et exaltavit humiles, respexit Deus humilitatem ancille sue*'[84] *[silence]* oh Word, how beautiful you are! What do you give to the soul that is the first in this communication of yours? Oh, you give it the vision of yourself, your embrace, your fruition, Yourself, and everything that is suitable both in heaven and on earth.

"Oh Word, you are divine! There is no pain, not any more. Your Mother was properly the first to be consoled for her conformity to your will and for her fulfillment of it. So, the soul that wants to be consoled needs to have this conformity of will *[silence]* a father loves his first-born; the Groom loves his bride, and gives her a greater participation in himself. In the same way you let the soul that participates in this conformity of will participate in yourself as the first one, giving it [the soul] the vision of yourself, your fruition, and its glorification."

She came out of this rapture at the seventh hour, and recited the morning prayer. And right when she finished to pray the bell rang for Communion, and it seemed that Jesus was waiting for her.

Let us always praise, extol, and glorify our great victor. Be he blessed to the end of time.

End of the dialogue of the forty hours.

Laus Deo e Virgini.

Dialogue 50
An Ascension Rapture

On Wednesday, June 5, 1585, we wrote down the following conversation concerning two raptures that the blessed soul had had during the previous days. First [we will write about] the vision that took place on the glorious Ascension Day and revolved around the mysteries of that solemnity. And then the second one, which she had last night, when the Father gave her his purity, as he had promised in the rapture of the forty hours. As we have done previously, our transcriptions of these two raptures are based more on the words she pronounced during her visions than on what we learned from our subsequent conversation with her. Indeed, in this case our conversation was very short, just to clarify the unclear points of her vision.

The rapture of the Ascension started in the evening of the previous day at the twenty-fourth hour. She entered it because she was called by the eternal Father, who wanted her to understand first something about himself and then something about the mystery of that solemnity. First of all, [He wanted her to understand] something about himself, concerning the aforementioned probation, as we shall clarify later.

That night she was in the room for the novices with a sister novice. While she was reading the gospel that had been read during the morning mass, she meditated on the following words: *"Pater clarifica Filium tuum."*[1] As we said, all of a sudden she was called by the eternal Father with these words: "Plunge into the blood of my Word, come to the congregation with my Only Begotten your Spouse, with Mary his mother, and with his beloved apostles."

After that call, walking very fast, she left this place and went to the large room. As soon as she got there she was rapt in spirit. And after being silent and engrossed for a long while as usual, she said:

266

"Nocte ista?", by that meaning that she would be in that rapture the whole night, as it actually happened.

And showing that she was in that congregation, she said: "Thriving chorus. All the apostles around *[silence]* oh John, through a mute speech you ask many questions and understand a lot *[silence]* where is Jesus. He is in heaven, for where he is there the angels must be *[silence]* well, when the angels descend *[silence]* oh marvelous multitude, who could possibly count them? From chorus to chorus, from hierarchy to hierarchy. But you don't come down as fast as your brothers and enemies did when they came down there *[silence]* oh, heaven will be empty if you do that; none of you will remain there *[silence]* if all of you are here, please take all of us up there *[silence]* oh, what a great preparation you do for the Word! Oh, what a pleasant shade!"

She sat down and said: "Now I want to contemplate a little bit."

And she stopped for a long time. She said: "But, Word, in order to come to you and do what I am asked to do, I need to listen to the will of the eternal Father, who called me at the beginning."

Then, in the person of the eternal Father she said: "Oh *sponsa Unigeniti mei*, what you perceived in the past, which is present for me, I want you to perceive it again. And I say that, no matter how strong your enemies are, if you persevere you have nothing to fear. And before you enter the lake of lions, I want you to prepare to receive my holy Spirit. Then, with its strength you will start your battle *[silence]* and I tell you and make you understand that you must keep your body like a vessel that you have received from me, and you must be careful not to break it, because you must give it back to me. And you know that a broken vessel is something horrible; it displeases me as if I were broken myself. And your forces will grow insofar as you become aware of your nonbeing. And you will make sure to follow my intrinsic path, and to do everything you can in order to understand it *[silence]* when your enemies arrive like ferocious beasts, do not be dismayed, because I will make them meek, as I did with my servant Daniel and the lions thanks to his purity; since I gave it [purity] to him, I will give it to you as well *[silence]* the spouse of my Word should take pride in what dismays her the most, that is, that now I give it to her and take it away from those who have found their life in it.[2] And even if they came as serpents, you will confound them, since already others have overcome them."

At this point we had the impression that the Father was showing her the place where she would go the day of the holy Spirit; and these were the devils and the innumerable temptations she would undergo, for she seemed to be in a great pain and to be afraid and distressed. And she asked the eternal Father if this suffering would have to be continuous; thus she said: "Then continuous? *[silence]* oh, oh, they want to devour me, right?"

And she raised her skirt up her legs, showing that she wanted to move away from those beasts that wanted to devour her. And after a short silence, she said: "Oh, what are they saying to the Word my Spouse? *[silence]* instead, with your narration I will narrate the truth of your faith *[silence]* oh, they are frightening even where I would have never thought they could be. And what is more necessary than faith? *[silence]* and who could ever penetrate you? But if through this temptation something could be taken away from those infidels (even though I wish their entire infidelity could be taken away from them), I would be more than willing to suffer every temptation against the faith. It is a marvelous thing to take pride in suffering; and it is nothing, but it is still something. But, oh eternal Father, since you know how weak I am, you show me something so that later it is not totally new to me *[silence]* it doesn't look like the angels are here; it looks like hell has been here *[silence]* who will regret having lost his life because of his faith in you, if through faith he has taken away infidelity? *[silence]* its time hasn't come yet, but you let me taste it *[silence]* oh eternal Father, now I'd like to go to your Word, and in this night I'd like to understand what he offered and asked you with these words: '*Clarifica me, Pater, apud temetipsum claritate quam habui priusquam mundus fieret apud te.*'"[3]

She saw Jesus asking his Father for clarification and, after being very engrossed for a long time, said to her Spouse: "Loving Spouse, ask for your spouse what you are asking for yourself *[silence]* who will be able to narrate your love and benignity besides your blood? Your blood. Just by saying and mentioning blood, my heart should melt. But why do I say 'my'? It would be nothing; every,

every heart! *[silence]* the clarification of the Word's humanity, so to speak and to understand, is equal to the divinity because the divinity protected and was united with the humanity. But my soul should observe how the Word, my Spouse, requests this clarification, which is a path that leads us to him. In his request he shows that being he had before the beginning of the world. That beginning of union, that beginning of glorification which is in himself, that beginning without beginning. *In principio erat Verbum [silence]* all your words are your manifestation of a beginning without beginning, but some of them [are your manifestation] in a way that is comprehensible to everybody, and others in a more intrinsic way. And my soul, your spouse, rejoices in this, while it trains itself and knows you, who are eternal, richer, wiser, nobler, in a word better *[silence]* from the way the Word asks for himself his spouse understands what she must ask for herself. She must ask not for the being of the angels, the archangels, the seraphim, the apostles, the martyrs, confessors, or virgins. She must ask for the being she had before the world was *[silence]* but what did I have before the world was? Since I was and was not? *[silence]* what was my being before I was? A nonbeing and a great being, much greater than now, because it was in the idea of your mind. My being was glorious in you because it derived from you, who are glorious in yourself. And although you do not need our glory and have no need for others, nonetheless you are pleased and delighted when we give it to you. And although at the time the soul couldn't give it to you because it was not, you rejoiced and gloried in your love and generosity, through which you kept my being in you. You also gloried in your wisdom, because you had decided in yourself to take this being out of yourself, without leaving yourself without it, and to send it to earth to work so that at least something, a little bit somewhere, would strive to acquire the glory you wanted to give to it when you would unite its soul with you. Thus you also gloried in the glory you wanted to give to it, that you have in yourself and is so great that it doesn't need anything else to glorify every soul. And you also gloried in the glory the soul would give to you when you would glorify it. And when, before the world was, my being was in you, thanks to your glory my being rested in you, was content, and gloried because it enjoyed the essence of the unity of your idea. My being's purity was such that it was almost another God through participation; and no created thing was able to understand it, neither the seraphim, nor the angels, nor the blessed spirits, not even itself, but only its Creator could, because this purity derived from you who are the source of purity and purify everything; and if you purify everything, how purer was what resided in you, I mean, my being. Its copiousness was such that this purity wished never to leave the essence of your idea, because there it found every contentment and delight. For there it enjoyed you who are everything, without whom nothing is; it was copious because it was in you who are an infinite copiousness. Its beauty was such that it admired itself, because it proceeded from you who are beautiful with an infinite beauty. They say about you: '*Speciosus forma pre Filiis hominum.*'[4] But now the soul cannot find and have all the above things in the way it had them before the world was, since before it was in God's mind and now it has a knowledge of its being that it didn't have at that time, although this knowledge is nothing, a nothingness. Even though it is good, this knowledge is an obstacle in comparison with God's great purity. In fact, this knowledge makes us unable to enjoy and perceive God's greatness in the way we enjoyed and perceived it when it [our purity] was in his mind, because at that time we had no knowledge of our being. Of course we shall have it, but in a different way. The soul will be glorified because it will participate in the glory of the Word's divinity and humanity, and it [the soul] will receive as much glory as it is able to contain. If it hadn't lost the innocence in which it had been created, its purity would be such that not only the angels, but the Word's humanity itself, which is not divine even though it is united with his divinity, would admire it and admire itself in it. And although the soul won't have the purity it had before losing its innocence, nonetheless it will have such a great purity that it will unite it with God who is purity itself. Later the soul, recognizing that it is so immensely pure, will look around with its pure and beautiful eyes, here and there, on its left and on its right side, whence its purity proceeds. The soul will see that the Word's Blood has given it [the soul] such a purity, through which the soul unites with God in such a deep manner that neither a thought, nor a word, nor a desire, nor a deed, nor a glance would be able to separate it from its union and enjoyment of God.

"Its copiousness will be the union and love with which the divinity took up and accepted his humanity; through his humanity he brought about the soul's redemption. With the achievements and efforts of the Word the soul acquires its copiousness. Its beauty will be its vision of God, who is so beautiful and precious that the soul, by participating in this beauty, becomes beautiful itself. Will the soul be conceited if it asks for this glorification? I don't mean the glorification of the body, although the body itself will become glorious eventually, but that of the soul. No, the soul won't be conceited, because in asking for this glorification it contemplates God, and its sole goal is to honor God; its intention is to honor God. In fact, God rejoices in the soul's request even faster, because he does not care about any obstacle (even if the soul asked him to become God himself) and would not consider the soul conceited if its beginning and sole, sole goal is to honor him, God *[silence]* honor, honor in heaven, on earth, and in hell. Honor *[silence]* but why don't the creatures correct their intentions? Their workings would be more pleasing to God than those of the angels and every blessed soul, because we work with our free will and they don't *[silence]* oh, why can't I have all my intentions in my hands? I would offer them to you again and again because they would please you and I would correct them better than the spouse does when she adorns herself and puts the crown and the wreath on her head. Oh, if I could I would make them straighter than a column and brighter than the sun! If they were like this, oh how pleasing they would be to you! We should be like the beloved disciple who loves and cares for his neighbor. Never refrain from saying: 'straighten your intention, straighten your intention,' as he said: 'love each other' *[silence]* but the creatures find excuses and claim that they can't straighten their intentions while they are doing their profane and base workings. But I say that intentions don't do workings, but rather workings do intentions. However, this is not an excuse because, even if they were in hell and did the workings of the devil with good intention, they would please God anyway. For this integrity is of such a great value that it turns base workings into magnificent ones, so that with a glimpse of its eye it can acquire a great merit. On the other hand, a magnificent working, done without integrity, becomes base and unpleasant to God."

After keeping quiet for quite a while, she changed her speech and her understanding. She entered the conversation Jesus was having with the Virgin Mary and the apostles. She said:

"*Cor meum* and *caro mea dilataverunt se in colloquium Verbi quod fecit cum Maria Matre sua et discipulis suis[5] [silence] omnia quecumque audivi a Patre meo nota feci vobis[6] [silence]* no, you didn't need to manifest everything the Father had done to you, but you did need to show us that you were good, incomprehensible, omnipotent, and good. However, you didn't need to manifest how the divinity had united with humanity, but rather [you needed to manifest] that you were the Son of God so that we could believe in you and understand that our faith was the right one *[silence]* yes, you needed to leave us your body and blood in food. But you didn't need to leave it with us in such a pleasant and delectable form as food is *[silence]* yes, you needed to leave us the other sacrament, the confession. But you didn't need to leave it with us in such a fast and easy way to acquire, that is, you have authorized each of your christs to take a soul out of hell and send it to heaven with a single word and with the sole act of raising his hand. You absolutely needed to tell us that we had to be vigilant, for we couldn't know the moment of our death; but no, you didn't need to tell us that, but rather [you needed] to teach us the paths and the way of dying safely. *Memorare novissima tua, et in aeternum non peccabis.*[7] You needed, yes, to tell us that you were the way, the truth, and the life. But you did not need to tell us through your faithful servants so early that your ways are beautiful and your path is broad; and that you are the light of your ways and the lamp of your path; and that in comparison with your light the sun and the stars lose their splendor, or better yet they become dark and do not send any light out. You needed to tell us that you were the truth, yes, but you didn't need to show us so many ways and to give us such a copious abundance of your word, proceeding from you, Word *[silence]* oh word of my Word, so few understand you! *[silence]* but, oh Word, you did it so that we could walk more safely through you, infallible truth, and the sole truth of the Father *[silence]* you also needed to tell us that you were the life, but not that you had come to give us life *[silence]* but the spouse must do everything her Spouse does *[silence]* the spouse needs to express her desire of leading souls to you; but she doesn't need to say how content she feels in herself. Of course, she needs to say that she proceeds in truth, but she doesn't need to say that she is intrinsically united with you *[silence]* but for the spouse everything becomes necessary because she sees her Spouse doing it, and [she] is also compelled by charity, so that others as well may follow the same path toward you.

"Yes, since to give substance and gain is fundamental but to give adornments is not necessary, but we give them because they give pleasure, and who gives them is loved more. And if the earthly spouses give adornments to their spouses because they love them, you who love your spouse so much, do you want them to overcome you? And I know that you love them with an infinite love. And since it is so, show me the adornments of your divine heart, that you granted her so that she may know the virtue of your divine heart more profoundly. And what would the use of having a gift be without knowing how to use it and without understanding its worth? It would be a great gift, yes, but if I didn't know its virtue I would be like a blind person who doesn't distinguish between a piece of crystal and a diamond, between a piece of glass and a ruby, or between a bit of earth and a precious stone. Why? Because he is blind and doesn't understand its value. The same thing would happen to me if I didn't understand the adornments of your divine heart. But I want neither the adornments on the right side nor those on the left one. I will leave those on the right side to those who are at home, and [I will leave] the adornments on the left side to those who are still down here. But your spouse will be content with those in the middle, because they participate in both of them.

"One adornment is that virtue that the loving Paul exalts so much, that is, charity, which is so sublime that it binds God. It is able to do everything and creates an invisible Trinity in the church similar to the Holy Trinity because, as the Father is God, the Son is God, the Holy Spirit is God, and the three of them are united and are the same thing, they let this union of the holy church descend upon us by means of the virtue of this charity. For charity unites the soul with God, and one neighbor with another, and in this way a Trinity arises in the church in a way that is invisible to us *[silence]* oh, how great is our God. Who can understand him? But this is what we must glory in; we have such a great and immense God that we cannot understand it.

"Another adornment of your divine heart is justice, which gives everyone what he merits; and this working is between the soul and the devil. And this justice gives God what he deserves, that is, honor; and [it gives] sin the devil because it belongs to him; and [it gives] peace to itself. And there is no bigger peace than a constant duel and war, and there is no bigger war than a constant peace *[silence]* another adornment is love; and this is between the soul and God. Many people say that charity and love are the same thing, and they are wrong. For charity is very different from love, since charity is a bond that binds us and generates in God, whereas love is a compendium of every virtue. Oh love, oh love, so few love you and know you! *[silence]* your heart has these three adornments, and I will give each of them to each of the three Persons of the Holy Trinity; [I will give] love to the Father, justice to the Son who took justice upon himself, charity to the Spirit; charity is indeed a compendium of all the virtues contained in the Holy Spirit *[silence]* but, oh Word, what is the use of these adornments if you don't infuse them in the heart that is in me and in you, and in many other servants of yours? But if it's in you, how can it be in many other servants of yours? Oh, how can this be? You are one God and one heart. And perhaps the creatures are only one; no, no, they are different. And you communicate it to them in different ways, according to how they are able to receive it *[silence]* but please, Word, infuse these gifts."

Jesus infused these three adornments in her and, when she asked him who would be present, she said: "The angels and the apostles no *[silence]* Mary yes, yes *[silence]* but among the saints St. Augustine [will be present], St. Angel, St. Catherine, and Mother Sister Mary *[silence]* we accept one of those virtues through desire, one through will, and the other through language; and Word? [We accept] charity through desire, justice through will, love through language and through your intrinsic and extrinsic word *[silence]* everything is a grace coming from you; *gratis data*, but it is different. It is not different, because its difference does not come from its giver *[silence]* but it is as different as the creature is different from her creator *[silence]* what images do you, Word, deign to give in order to respond to our base intellects and wills? *[silence]* when will the time come, when we are able to cherish you without any image? *[silence]* but we must purify our love. Can we do it in this world? We can *[silence]* in the heart, formed by the soul, love forms a soul with a great alertness, which is charity *[silence]* Word, please do it well; draw a bunch of them, *gratiam pro gratiam;* it is necessary to work [well].

"Word, what conversation do you have with Mary? *[silence]* an adoptive, consoling, and unifying conversation. But, oh Word, you leave Mary separate from you. Yes, you consoled her as far as the body was concerned. But did Mary need consolation? No, because although she remained in her mortal flesh, she conformed to your will so perfectly that she would be still here, if this was your decision. You consoled her so that she could strengthen the apostles' will and attract the virgins. Imagine how few the virgins would have been if she had ascended to heaven with you. John was there, but still *[silence]* oh, what would I be if Mary had not fortified the apostles with the Holy Spirit? How could I possibly know so many high and profound secrets, which she hadn't been able to grant before because she couldn't find where to infuse them? The Word as well refrained from infusing his word because he could not find where to infuse it. And how many times, my Spouse, does she intercede in your graces and gifts? She felt consoled, and whoever contemplates her feels consoled for all his pains, worries, and fears, and overcomes every temptation. Who doesn't know what God is, should apply to Mary. Who doesn't find mercy in God, should apply to Mary. Who doesn't have a conformity of will, should apply to Mary. Who is weak and fails, should apply to Mary who is strong and powerful. Who is in a constant duel, should apply to Mary who is a peaceful sea. Who is suffocated by worldly pleasures, should apply to Mary who is a bitter sea. Who is possessed by the devil, should apply to Mary who is Mother of humility, and nothing sends the devil away more than humility *[silence]* apply to Mary, apply to Mary, apply to Mary! *[silence]* great

and marvelous are the secrets granted by Mary *[silence]* great is our
God *[silence] Fluminis impetus laetificat civitatem Dei, sanctificavit
tabernaculum suum altissimus.*[8] Like a crystal-clear source, the
Word's mouth is sanctifying the sanctified body of Mary *[silence]*
oh Mary, the conversation you had with your Word when he went
and suffered was a conversation of conformity. That [conversa-
tion] of the resurrection was a conversation of joy, and that which
you are having now is a conversation of satisfaction. And what satisfaction is this? Satisfaction because God was a man? Not at all.
Satisfaction because he was glorious? No. Satisfaction because he
was adored by the creatures? Not at all. Satisfaction because he
was at the right of the Father? Exactly. Satisfaction because he
would come and judge all of us? No, no. Oh Mary, what kind of
satisfaction is this? *[silence]* this is the last conversation and you
make it more glorious *[silence]* but, Mary, why were you satisfied?
Because the Word was the Spouse of the virgins and had elected
the virgins for his crown *[silence]* oh, should I be surprised? No,
because you were a virgin yourself, and the Word loved virginity
so much that of course this satisfaction concerned the virgins. For
like the crown manifests that the king is the king, so do the virgins
manifest his power, his wisdom, and his goodness. But the virgins,
and the more virgins, are those who withdraw in religion. These
virgins manifest his power in abandoning everything; they manifest his generosity in abandoning themselves; they manifest his
wisdom in abandoning their parents and the others; they manifest
his worth in abandoning every created thing and want to love and
to listen to their Spouse only, and in so doing they also manifest
his nobility *[silence]* he keeps this crown neither in his hand nor
under his feet, but on his head, which is the noblest part of the
body. The virgins are the internal members of the church's mystical body, and when an internal member is missing the whole body
becomes sick and dies. This doesn't happen when an external
member fails, besides the head because life is there. Oh, how
deeply has the Word loved this virginity! If only one of those virgins were missing, the whole body of the church would become
crippled. But if all of them were missing, faith itself would be
missing, because God became incarnate within you, Virgin, and

has always loved and honored this virginity in himself. When he recreated the human kind he showed it [his love for virginity] in committing every virgin to the Virgin. And when he ascended to heaven, didn't he show it in placing this frail sex among the superior beings and among those who had been granted his power? But he worked in this frail sex more than in the other; indeed, in heaven there are so many [virgins] that have manifested his power, wisdom, and goodness. The virgins and martyrs [have manifested] his power; Catherine first and many others [have manifested] his wisdom. The other Catherine and many others [have manifested] his goodness. But in the primitive church only? No [silence] But if we contemplated your bosom, we would see an infinite number of them living in the substance of your Trinity's idea [silence] the splendor that the Word emanates in electing his virgins attracts the other creatures' heart toward him and unites them with him. And in comparison with the splendor of virginity the light of the sun is dark, because it can never be as bright as virginity [silence] when you went to your passion, Mary became doleful. When you rose again from the dead, she became undoubtful. When you ascended to heaven, she became joyful [silence] in a similar way, when you visit the soul with your afflictions it becomes doleful but not impatient. It does not regret its suffering, but rather [it regrets that] it deserves it. And even if it did not have any pain in itself, it would regret that its neighbors deserve that pain. And even if its neighbors were in the condition of having no pain, it would regret that its being was generated in pain. But not only this: it even regrets that the devil deserves that pain, although the soul never regrets the pain, but only the cause of the deserved pain [silence] Mary was undoubtful about the resurrection. In a similar way the soul is undoubtful thanks to the grace it has received. As the apostle says: '*Omnia possum in eo qui me confortat*';[9] '*et pone me iusta te, et cuiusvis manus pugnet contra me*'[10] [silence] but when it is in heaven and enjoys you, and primarily enjoys you in the Holy sacrament, the soul is neither doleful nor undoubtful, but totally joyful because, as it enjoys you, God, your mute conversing fills it with a perfect joy, joy for your greatness; and it keeps saying: 'Oh great

God, admirable God, communicating God, communicating God, communicating God, great God, great God, great God.'

"You confirm and strengthen them because they had to become the columns of your church. With your wisdom you exhort them, and with your power you confirm and strengthen them *[silence]* with your passion you gave them an example, with your resurrection [you gave them] peace, and with your ascension you grant them happiness because you promise them the gifts of the Holy Spirit, but you also reproached them with their disbelief *[silence]* with your passion you gave them an example, because you wished to show them that your faithful and loving servants must give an example in suffering. In fact, many preach well but do nothing. Instead, we must suffer and avoid making suffer, to be as you want us to be. Oh, blessed and happy are those who suffer for your sake, Word! I shall dare to say that it is better to suffer for you than to have you, because when we have you we can lose you, but if we suffer for your sake you write it in the book of life, where it can't get lost *[silence]* with your resurrection you give him peace, because as soon as you resuscitated peace was made between God and the creature, and between the creature and her neighbor. If the heart has peace, it has heaven, because you are there. This peace does not judge, does not try to offend anyone, and speaks of our neighbors only to honor you. The peaceful and humble heart always contemplates this union *[silence]* with your ascension you save them and satisfy them by promising them the Holy Spirit; you teach them and show them how to receive it; and you tell them that they will accomplish great things in your name; and then you promise yourself, saying that you will be with them until the consummation of the world. No creature can promise a similar thing, because the creature possesses nothing, not even herself. In fact, if I promised myself, you could take myself away from me, but if the creature promises you no one can take you away from the creature because you said that you are the truth *[silence]* you lend everything to us, but you have given yourself to us. You can take myself away from me, my life, but you can't take yourself away from me because you are the truth; and you said that you want to be with me forever *[silence]* oh word, crown of my Word, how few know you, love you, have you."

Then she pronounced her offerings for the sake of every creature. And she came out of this rapture at the eighth hour. She took Communion with the other nuns, and together they recited the office in the choir. Later she had dinner with the others. Toward the end of her meal, feeling drawn, she left the refectory at the ninth hour and went to the oratory of the novices. And at once she was rapt in spirit and was in this condition until the seventeenth hour. As we shall explain later, during that time she showed that she was seeing Jesus ascend to heaven to the Father's right side.

As it usually occurs in her more important raptures, she was drawn by means of a calling, with these words: "Come, my dear dove, come to this multitude. I want you to be in my Father's bosom with me *[silence]* I have taken up my soul and my humanity, united with my divinity, and I have placed it in my Father's bosom *[silence]* the spouse will be in this bosom with her Spouse and will wait for him to send the Holy Spirit.

"Fortify the body, but take the soul wherever you wish *[silence]* oh, all the choruses take the insignia and victories of the Word! *[silence]* thus, your humanity was placed first in the Father's bosom, and then into his right side *[silence]* even though your humanity had not ascended to heaven yet, it was suitable for it to rest in the Father's bosom. The soul rested in it, but the Word *ab aeterno [silence]* the unknown and holy fathers arrive. Mary sees [the Word's] humanity, that had been drawn out of her and formed with her pure blood and nourished with her milk, approach heaven. And then she sees herself at once ascending with him and being on earth *[silence]* and it is very probable that the eternal Father, who infused her soul in his bosom, wishes to reunite both the soul and the body in himself *[silence]* Mary sees the multitude of the angels and the beautiful company of the holy fathers. And could I doubt that with her devoted and beautiful eyes she will gaze at John the Baptist, through whom she was praised and extolled him? *[silence]* many had prophesied and announced the Word, but I think that no one has penetrated his glory with such a sublime generosity and incomprehensibility *[silence]* oh David, why don't you renew your songs, and when you do it you reveal them to us? *[silence]* but being among such a chaste and beautiful company I will not be pleased if he assumes my soul only, not at all. I wouldn't be pleased, because I don't want to be alone; but, please, assume them all and, since not all of them are adequate, I will withdraw a little bit *[silence]* please, assume those your spouses, and assume them in the bosom of your eternal Father *[silence]* and as Mary and the apostles waited for the Holy Spirit at the Supper, we shall wait for him here and be closer to him; and we won't feel bad if he doesn't stay long. Oh Word, how many do you take with you? I know that not all of them are apt to live here but at least don't let them be on earth, but a little bit raised from earth *[silence]* oh Word, how can you assume the souls living in the Father's bosom?"

She answers in the person of the Word, saying:

"Some of them will live in that bosom with affection, since I take them there; and this will be in effect for some time. Some others will live there with their pure breathing into me. These souls will have no sentiment *[silence]* some others will live in that bosom with the pure infusion my humanity will distill when it rests in my Father's bosom, as a spouse does in his garden. But it must leave. And I shall grant them that pure distillation, so that they will be allowed to live there and be ready to receive the Holy Spirit *[silence]* others [will live there] with an anxious and dead desire for God and will taste and feed on the substance of divine essence. And these won't be inferior to the others. Some others will be drawn and tied up by my pure grace, which ties and unites the creatures' hearts to me. And since I am in the Father's bosom and they are united to me, as a consequence through this grace they too will be in this bosom."

At this point she stood up looking upward for quite a while, keeping her arms open and her hands up toward the sky, expressing a great admiration. She looked as if she wanted to go up to the sky herself. And her face was so beautiful and its expression [was] so resplendent that she looked like heaven. She showed such a majesty that for us she resembled Jesus when he ascended to heaven. And this was what she was actually seeing at the moment. Thus she said:

"Oh you, you are leaving *[silence]* oh what a jubilation they will have up there! *[silence]* oh Mary, we, we stay down here *[silence]* oh pure angels, yes, if you are there, I'm there too; and if he is your Lord, he is also my Spouse *[silence]* oh insane love, oh eternal Word, oh infinite wisdom, oh perfect goodness, what did the creature do to you, that you love her so much? You created her in your likeness in order to make her equal to you; not equal to you, no, but rather participant in you who are infallible Truth, infinite mercy, eternal Word. What have you done to this creature? And what do you want from her but love? *[silence]* what is this creature that you love so much? What do you give her? What do you want from her? *[silence]* you love her like yourself; you give her yourself who are everything. And without you she is nothing. From her you want her total will, knowledge, and power; and by giving you this she gives you everything, and she remains a nothingness. She gives you more than you give her because, being infinite you can never end giving yourself, even though you gave yourself infinitely. But given that the creature is finite, she is unable to comprehend you and thus her gift to you is bigger than the present you give to her. Oh infinite wisdom, oh sublime goodness, oh love, love, so few know you, love you, and possess you. Oh incarnate love and humanate Word! It is different and it is the same thing. Oh eternal wisdom, neither loved nor known! Oh ingratitude, you ruin everything; oh selfish love, oh our blindness, cause of every evil! Oh purity, so few know you and desire you! For if one doesn't know something, one can neither love it nor desire it *[silence]* cor mundum crea in me Deus, et spiritum rectum innova in visceribus meis.*"[11]*

And that was the end, at the seventeenth hour sharp.

Now we shall transcribe her rapture about purity, which this blessed soul entered last night at the twenty-third hour and a half. She cried and suffered intensely until the first hour of the morning. And at once she looked very happy, showing a very joyful face, with two resplendent eyes that resembled two stars. And being quiet for a while, then she spoke these first words:

"Now that pure being was making me taste hell; and I had the feeling I was offending him. And now he adorns me, and this is my glory *[silence]* your goodness is admirable and pure; you don't allow us to comprehend the beginning but you allow us to taste the end *[silence]* immense purity, infuse yourself and reinfuse yourself, so that it can be infused and reinfused into you. And if it is possible, please let the other creatures participate in it, because I would be more glorious if others were with me. But it is essential that those who have received your same gifts testify to every gift proceeding from you and all the others [gifts] you have granted me. Let them come now with joy *[silence]* Mary, the pure dawn, will not disdain giving thanks to her perfect humility; the truthful Augustine, the chaste Angel, the loving Catherine and the humble Mary *[silence]* all this purity proceeds from God's pure essence *[silence]* moreover, oh Father, the essence proceeding from you will purify the mind. Word, the essence which is in you will purify will and assume it. The essence proceeding from the Holy Spirit will purify memory and assume it. The unity of the essence of your Trinity will purify and assume the soul; the humanity of the incarnate Word will purify and assume the body *[silence]* And Mary, participating in this purity, will make it communicating for those who can receive it and comprehend it. Thus, the abyssed, dead, and vivifying one understands nothing, seeks nothing but in seeking everything and understanding everything it will live a dead life;[12] and here he will live enlightened, and with a dead light it will lighten the other eager minds, even though they don't know this purity *[silence]* and every cognition excluding this purity will seem a great ignorance to him, and the fact that this purity is unknown will cause a great pain in him *[silence]* will will be totally immersed in the humanate Word, infallible truth. Will will long for more than God, and it will long for nothing but God. It will desire God, and deprive itself of God. It will look at its neighbor, and will quiet down in that purity it knows it is unknown *[silence]* with a sublime barrenness memory will be extremely fecund in the Holy Spirit; thinking and remembering, without thinking and without remembering it will be sorrowful in that purity *[silence]* memory's thought will be about God's being and God's nonbeing. And how can you be and non-be? But the essence of your purity is so great that it creates the humanity of your Word, our being *[silence]* this purity, it loves itself so much because the others neither understand it nor comprehend it, regenerates the ungenerated Word *[silence]* it regenerates the ungenerated [Word], who has neither beginning nor end, the way God himself is. But this purity gives him a beginning and an end, and takes every beginning and every end away from him *[silence]* purity regenerates the ungenerated creature, which is made in the likeness of the Trinity, and a Trinity is made in the creature itself. And this purity unites this Trinity with God's Trinity; and this purity recreates the Trinity *[silence]* this recreated Trinity offers this purity and makes it equal to God's Trinity through participation *[silence]* but what do you accomplish, eternal and uncreated Trinity? Are your workings base because you work with the creature, who is so base? Your workings were eternal and were meant to please yourself *[silence]* you worked and work so that the creatures love you; your workings are about union, and [you] work to accomplish workings of vision and eternal glory *[silence]* you worked when you created spirits who would be able to praise you *[silence]* and the soul's Trinity, when it is absorbed in this purity, fulfills the same workings of God's Trinity *[silence]* so that its working makes it similar to you, my God, through participation and grace *gratis data*, of course *[silence]* the creature is pleased with its being when it is absorbed in this purity. The creature realizes that this purity is so great that she is pleased by that pleasure and thus her working becomes similar to yours. She is pleased with herself and [she is pleased] to be capable of having you. And she is also pleased not to be capable of having you *[silence]* she creates spirits that are capable of praising her and relating to her. And how can she do this? Believe me, my soul; every creature that is capable of this purity, every soul that leads to God creates spirits that praise it. However, they do not praise the soul in its essence, they rather praise God, and their praising God redounds into the soul *[silence]* and this soul, led by the other soul, is capable of this purity and creates other spirits itself *[silence]* she also creates living creatures. But, Word, how can this be? How can the creature recreate creatures that are created by you first? *[silence]* but when a thing has lost the essence of its being, the creature that gives its essence and its being back to that thing is believed to have recreated that thing. Similarly, when a soul has lost this purity, the soul that leads this soul back and helps it regain this purity is believed to have recreated the soul. In this way it gives the soul its essence back, making it capable of receiving this purity *[silence]* who will ever be able to narrate how deeply a creature loves the creature that has recreated her? Who will ever narrate this? Who will ever be capable of the love the creature expressed for her when she recreated her and of the purity she granted her? *[silence]* God fulfills a working of union; and this soul too fulfills a working of union, because in the twinkling of an eye it [this soul] unites all the creatures together and, moreover, unites all the creatures with God himself, but only those that become capable of this union *[silence]* the soul fulfills workings of vision, in which it comprehends God's being; it sees God in God, itself in God, and its neighbor in God *[silence]* it also works by constantly operating eternal and glorious workings *[silence]* glorious because they proceed from you who are the glory of the angels and of every creature *[silence]* eternal because they contemplate you who are eternal and their goal is eternal as well *[silence]* this Trinity generates *ab aeterno*, and the ungenerated Word himself is generated *[silence]* this soul also generates a word similar to the Word and brings his working to its conclusion. And this is your praise, that so few of us discern and tepidly articulate; so few of us love and carefully proffer. In this praise we honor you, joy for our neighbor, justice for the wanderer, mercy for the poor; it begs pity of the souls in purgatory, and in a word it inclines your being toward us *[silence]* the Word told us everything the Father manifested to him; and his praise tells everything the Word has manifested to his elect *[silence]* the Word preached in order to lead the souls back to his Father; and his praise preaches and exhorts in order to lead us back to him. And its preaching and exhorting is in fact praising God *[silence]* the Word shed his blood; and his praise too sheds its blood, and even more plentifully because you, Word, shed it once and in a short period of time, whereas this praise lasts forever. And when it offers your blood, Word, it sheds it and offers its own blood with its love *[silence]* the Word dies and resuscitates; and this praise dies and resuscitates, or better yet, it gives life. This praise dies in itself because it hides in the heart so that the heart works dead, and not alive *[silence]* then it resuscitates with such a vehemence that it fears neither itself, nor the devil, nor God himself, because it has acquired such a deep confidence with him that it does not fear him anymore *[silence]* it ascends to heaven, or better yet, it penetrates heaven *[silence]* and it also penetrates your heart, Word, in the Father's bosom. And here *ascendet oratio sicut incensum in conspectu tuo*[13] *[silence]* it sends, or better yet, infuses the Holy Spirit into those who do not trust themselves *[silence]* this praise judges the Word, and we shall be judged. And who could be a better judge than this praise to you? It will judge those who have uttered it, and it will be much more severe with those who have uttered it because they felt obliged to do it; [it will judge] why they uttered it, and if they comprehended why they didn't practice it. This praise will be the judge *[silence]* and what the Trinity of the soul possesses comes from its participation in the uncreated Trinity. And this participation is a nothing, a nothingness. But then, thanks to its insane love it becomes, so to speak, equal to it *[silence]* and if the soul possesses such a purity, what does it think of? It only thinks of purity, it only desires purity, it only understands purity, it only speaks of purity, it only remembers and glories in purity; it only tastes, wishes, loves, enjoys this purity *[silence]* even the slightest act of will offends this purity *[silence]* to possess a particle of earthly things offends this purity *[silence]* an unfitting and hasty word offends this purity *[silence]* every contemplation of one's own being, which is a nonbeing, restrains this purity *[silence]* this purity abhors every selective love, *etiam* in God *[silence]* this purity despises every emotion, feeling, and imagination outside God *[silence]* this purity is so pure that it wants the soul to have no will, no intellect, no knowledge, for its will, its intellect, its knowledge are all in God *[silence]* it is easier to create the sky and the earth than to possess this purity in oneself *[silence]* for the soul that is dead to itself it is more difficult to turn a leaf than to reject this purity. Happy and glorious is the soul that is dead to itself, because it apprehends this purity at once."

Standing with clasped hands, she showed that she was receiving that purity as a vestment. She spoke the following words: "I take the purity of that who has taken me, and I will not leave it until my soul abandons my body *[silence]* but who will preserve it? No creature that has a knowledge of being *[silence]* but you, Word, must change into my soul and preserve it. And the consoler must confirm it and nourish it."

As she told us later, at this point she saw two columns she had to walk through in order to preserve her purity. One was beautiful and resplendent outside but full of animals and bad things inside. The other was ugly outside and looked struck and beaten. This was Christ's column, which was beautiful inside, but inside it was covered with his humanity, struck and beaten during his passion. She understood that the echo of the beating and of Christ's blood shed over his humanity would prevent the soul from hearing the noises of the devils' temptations. Thus she said:

"Oh yes. First I want the one that looks ugly and beaten and will run away from the one that looks beautiful and polished [silence] because his humanity is its wall and its main wall."

She meant that here her soul cannot be offended by its enemies. Then she continued: "Here I will be like the stonecutter; I will work to support the construction of the militant church and to adorn that which doesn't need to be supported, I mean, the triumphant church [silence] qui retribuam Domino pro omnibus que retribuit mihi?[14] [silence] abandonment in you [silence] what's the major work we will do? To be united with you, Word? No [silence] it seems less important to me than to live a dead life and to tolerate the hell you make us taste here. And does this seem glorious? It seems more important to me, as important as to desire and to aspire to our neighbors' salvation [silence] oh yes, in that dead life we wouldn't see your sight, which gives us pain down here."

And keeping silent for a while as usual, she came out of this rapture at the fourth hour and a half. She was very happy, cheerful, and content.

Selections from

Probation

Probation

Volume One
Excerpts from the "Devil's Temptations"

(pp. 33–34)

She was…distressed and in pain as the result of two terrible visions that were always before the eyes of her mind, that is, the vision of the devils and that of the offenses given to God; and sometimes she saw the devils with her corporeal eyes as well. And what gave her an even deeper pain was the fact that she heard with her ears the horrible screams, howls, and curses that the devil and sometimes also the creatures uttered to offend God. And sometimes these screams invaded her hearing to the point that she had difficulty in understanding us when we spoke to her. This blessed soul suffered a constant martyrdom because of the internal and external pains that never abandoned her. God himself had allowed the devils to afflict her body. Indeed, they often pushed her down the stairs, made her fall down; and other times, like venomous vipers, they wrapped around her flesh, biting her with a great cruelty. She was besieged by all kinds of afflictions, sufferings, torments.

Her internal suffering was constant, whereas the external one occurred from time to time and in particular during the days of solemn and holy celebrations, and also at night when she was going to bed. Sometimes her sufferings kept her up until the fourth or the fifth hour in the morning. And whereas in the past during those days the Lord used to visit her and take her to an excess of mind so

289

that she could taste and perceive profound secrets, on the contrary now she suffered more and more.

Against these temptations she used remedies similar to those that the saints are reported to have used themselves. In particular one day, since she was deeply afflicted and attacked by a temptation against her purity, she did like St. Benedict. She went to the room where we keep firewood and among the brushwood she picked out some thorns and piercing twigs, which she bundled together. Then she went to a secret place where she undressed and, throwing herself on those thorns, she tossed and turned repeatedly. In this way she wanted to mortify her body and conquer the temptation that the devil had instilled in her.

(pp. 73–74)

On Sunday, July 19, after having had her meal, she went to some rooms that we have but we do not use. She went to the most remote one, where she was drawn by Jesus to a great insight into her self and, like St. Augustine in his *Confessions*, she confessed to God all the offenses she knew she had committed to him. When she finished confessing, in our presence she had a big fight with the devil because he is always before her eyes. But during this day he was much more present than usual, and it seemed that like a big beast he attacked her with the intention of devouring her. But she immediately took some big stones that were in that room and, throwing them at him with a great vehemence, she said: "Leave me alone, you, horrible beast, don't come close to me. I tell you, in the name of Jesus, leave me alone." And she repeated these and similar words several times. And it was very moving to look at her because she stepped back—how can I explain this—she tried to hide, as we do when we are very scared. And she did this in a rush. And when she had fought for a while, she turned to Jesus and told him something, and then she went back to send the devil away. And that battle lasted for almost two hours. Then, when she came out of this rapture, she was very tired and exhausted because of her confrontation with the devil.

With regard to this subject, we would like to add that when she came out of this rapture, we asked her if she always sees the devil with her physical sight. She told us that she does not, but she always sees him with the sight of her mind with no respite, as when (like a similitude) a creature sees something with her physical sight, and then that something stays in her mind so clearly that, even if she does not see it concretely, she has the impression that she always sees it. Her vision of the devil is so frequent that he never departs from her eyes because God wants her to suffer in this way.

(pp. 115–17)

One night, at the beginning of her affliction, she entered a rapture for a short period of time and was told by Jesus that her affliction was not natural. He allowed this to happen as a probation because he wanted her body to suffer, like Job, both internally and externally. He had granted the devil the power to make her suffer. And during the days of her affliction, she continued to do her usual exercises. And the devil was so resentful because he was unable to overcome and beat her that when she was going to the Choir for the Mass, for Communion, or to similar places, he made her fall down the stairs. But she did not hurt herself at all. She stood up with renewed energy, against his will heading for that good that she had stood up for. At the beginning of that affliction she suffered many attacks from the devil. Sometimes she felt as if she were being bitten in a cruel way and were falling apart inside, and on the outside as if her members were severed. And after these incidents she felt so drained and exhausted, that for quite a while she could neither move nor be fully alert.

She became extremely weak, both because of the constant fever and because the Lord abandoned her to her natural condition. He wanted us to understand that without his supernatural help no creature can survive by feeding only on bread and water, as she always does. And her weakness was so great that she felt as if she was passing away. And she often said: "I tell you that I am finishing and dying, but you don't believe me." And although he could have given her her strength back without the support of natural resources, he did not want to do it. However he granted her, after she suffered a lot—she had been ill for ten days, during which she only ate a pap with a bit of water—as I said, he granted that, apart from meat, cheese, and eggs, she be able to eat other kinds of food so that she would regain her strength. And when she recovered her health without any physical remedy, she went back to her normal life; that is, again she fed only on bread and water, feeling very eager and satisfied.

...

With his constant temptations, the devil tries his best to take this blessed soul away from the holy and austere life that she has embraced for God's will. The devil puts doubts and fears in her mind so that she thinks that maybe this is not God's will, I mean, what she started doing some months ago, that is, to walk barefooted and to wear only a gown, both in winter and in summer. I mean that for this reason she undergoes intolerable conflicts. In particular, on the eve of St. Ursula's day, the twentieth of the same month [September], the devil appeared to her in the form of two nuns, one dressed in white and the other in gray, and started to talk to her as follows. He told her that God did not like her lifestyle and was rather offended by her behavior and that if she did not change it she would lose God's favor. And he told her many other things that I omit for the sake of brevity. The poor thing felt very oppressed and confused. And she reported all this to the Mother Superior, asking her to pray for her soul. The Mother Superior consoled her and recommended that she pursue the life to which she had devoted herself. The Mother Superior was convinced that that was the devil's deceit because he wanted to take her away from what is good. So, after feeling oppressed for many days for these and other temptations, the eve of the celebration of the glorious Sts. Simon and Jude she was, as usual, rapt in spirit. During this union the Virgin granted her a deep insight into herself and into the gift of the holy religion. And she was in that union for three hours.

(pp. 133–39)

Our blessed soul never desisted from her spiritual exercises even though temptations, afflictions, and depression constantly haunted her. But on January 6, Epiphany, she was rapt in spirit. During that time she complained to Jesus because she feels abandoned by him when she is going through a great temptation and thus later she cannot help but offend him. On this occasion Jesus consoled and supported her greatly.

Since the month of January, she has been tormented by innumerable temptations, and in particular she has felt tempted by the devil with a great temptation of despair. He made her believe that she would not be saved, and thus she did not need to say her offices and practice the holy exercises of our religion because they were of no use, offended Jesus even more, and totally alienated her from him. And she was afflicted by this temptation very often so that she was almost never free from them, and even abstained from our religious exercises for a day or two. Indeed, if we had not cared for her, she would have stayed in her room by herself. And on January 28, walking by a picture of Our Lord crowned with thorns, she was thrown on the floor and rapt in spirit. In this rapture the Lord showed her how she had offended him, and she wept unceasingly, screaming and howling because of the inner knowledge she suddenly had about herself. And she often spoke these words: "I wished I could go to hell, if in this way I would be able to make up for my offenses to you!" And this lasted nearly two hours.

On Sunday, the last day of January 1587, the above soul felt very afflicted by a great temptation, and so she went to the Mother Superior and told her that she could not tolerate it anymore because that temptation tormented her immensely. Our Mother Superior told her that she did not want her to leave from there so that she would be tempted to yield to him. And then she told her [Mother Superior]: "Tie my hands, please." When the Mother Superior tied her hands, the Lord was pleased by this act of humility that, as usual drawing her to him for a short while, he granted her so much grace and fortitude that she was able to overcome the above temptation.

She spent the following week with a new temptation. In this case the devil instilled a vision in her mind, but not only in her mind, since he manifested himself to her in many forms and ways, showing her all the innumerable pleasures and splendor she would have if she rejected our religion. And he never let her rest for a moment. The Lord made her understand that, if she wanted to overcome this temptation, to fool the devil she had to do a simple act; that is, because her good intention would be sufficient, in the name of God she should humbly ask for the habit of our holy religion.

(pp. 156–65)

No one could either describe this soul's exile and pains or communicate them, unless one sees her with his own eyes. I believe, though, that at least one can say—and I am totally sure about it—that her inner suffering and probation, similar to that which the Lord deigns to grant certain chosen creatures (like this blessed soul), can be only perceived by those who experience them; just as God's workings in those souls that love him, since every time a devout soul sees someone offending God she suffers martyrdom; just as this blessed soul of ours who, as we have said several times, constantly sees devils in various forms and manners, as St. Catherine of Siena did. They manifest themselves to her with different temptations, sometimes even in the form of angels of light. However, through the virtue of the holy humility she confounds them and sends them away. In this way she always defeats them.

As a matter of fact, I want to narrate what happened to her last Friday, July 15. Because that night our Mother Superior was going to recite chapter, the devil troubled her immensely and tempted her not to go to it because he knows that, as he confessed to St. Dominic, in the chapter room he loses everything he has gained during the day because of the penance we do in it. So, while we were all in the chapter and a devil was right in front of the chapter's door, she saw out there, in a very large room, a vast multitude of devils, who were trying to persuade her to come out of the chapter. But because they were unable to convince her, they insistently strove to prevent our Mother Superior from speaking so that she wouldn't be able to reprimand the nuns and show them their errors. However, God did not allow them to do this. In the end, when she stood up to go and confess her faults, she saw the devils (so it seemed to her) stirring up a dense smoke like fog because they realized that she did not want to yield to their temptations. And they tempted the nuns in this way so that they would not come in, for some of them felt bored and weary; others [felt] inattentive and lethargic; others were unable to be there with the respect, humbleness, and awe required in that holy room because it represents the day of the final judgment, where we must respond for every little sin and fault. And thus we must keep in mind that it is imperative to watch over our hearts to understand the devil's temptations and illusions.

On Tuesday, July, 19, 1588, because our blessed soul felt haunted and persecuted by the devil with an extremely intense temptation, God, who never abandons his servants, deigned to succor her. What happened was that a nun went to our Mother Superior (who was with her at the moment) to give her a picture of a newly canonized saint (that had been sent to our convent), St. Diego of the Franciscan Order that has really flourished in Spain. As soon as our blessed soul saw it, she knelt down for a sudden feeling of love and stared at it both with her physical and spiritual eyes. And after a while, as usual, she was rapt in spirit, albeit only for a short period of time. In fact, during this probation she is drawn to these excesses of mind not to taste God, but only to understand each time what she is supposed to do to herself and to others. Going back to what I was just saying, she saw the aforementioned saint up in the highest spheres of heaven, and she almost had the impression that his throne was close to that of the glorious father St. Francis. And when she asked him why he found himself in such a high and glorious condition, he answered: "Because when I was down in the world, I did the following: First, I abandoned and despised myself, embraced the cross, the crucifix, and took holy humility as my helmsman and guide." Then she saw that flames came out of his mouth; his hands distilled myrrh; and his eyes, she saw this, made him unique to God, as on earth they had made him honored among men. And because she wished to know why he showed himself to her in that manner, he said that if she listened to his life in a human way she would be able to fathom the things she had just seen, that is, when she received his life, given that they were printing it in Rome right at that moment. Listening to the narration of his virtues, she would be able to understand what the members of his body meant in the vision she had just had.

This happened when the Lord inspired our Mother Superior (how we must believe, given what occurred afterward) to give Sister Maria Maddalena the aforementioned saint as her brother. When she recovered consciousness, our Mother Superior told her about the Lord's inspiration. Accepting it in a gracious and reverential way, she asked her why she had decided to do so in particular. Thus, our Mother Superior said that she believed that the aforementioned saint had walked toward that path and divine calling in a way similar to hers.

After having had dinner with the others and having given thanks to God, our Mother Superior asked all of us to pray to that saint so that he would protect our monastery. And after that prayer, in a rush, Sister Maria Maddalena flew from her place absorbed in a rapture and went to the image of that saint. The Lord had drawn her to show and explain to her the excellence of that place (if in heaven places can be distinguished one from the other) and the supremacy of the glory in store for those who in this world walk along the righteous and profound path of a perfect humility; all of them [are] transformed in the name of Christ crucified, as it occurred to this saint. And God asks our blessed soul to do the same.

St. Francis also showed and explained to her that the Lord had inspired our Mother Superior and that for God's will he himself gave her St. Diego as a brother so that she could follow his steps.

The following Thursday, the eve of St. Mary Magdalen's Day, she started to recite some psalms in the main room with another sister, one psalm for each letter of St. Diego's name. While she was doing so, she was rapt in ecstasy, where the saint was shown to her mind's eyes. He told and explained to her what she had to practice and work at during that time of probation. He gave her many suggestions and advice concerning this issue, and thus she remained in this rapture about two hours.

The morning after St. Mary Magdalen's Day, that is, on July 22, during the Mass the devil tempted and urged her to leave the church, but to overcome this temptation she went to confess it to our Mother Superior, who ordered her not to leave. Then the devil, as he often does, showed her that he was going to harm her in some way, that he would strangle her if she did not obey him. And when our Mother Superior told her that she should not believe him because, as St. Augustine says, he is the father of every lie, our blessed soul became very depressed and all of a sudden was rapt in spirit. She saw her devout St. Diego sending devils away with a cross and a crucifix. And after quite a while she uttered the following words, speaking out loud as she usually does during her raptures: "Oh glorious saint, send them away, all of them, because there are still more." And after a short pause, she showed that they had gone away because she became very happy and her face had a beautiful expression. Totally engrossed, her eyes looked toward the sky.

And she said: "It was quite likely that, since we were celebrating your day, you would let us see you with all the gifts you wanted to dispense to us." She was speaking of St. Mary Magdalen. Then she continued: "And while you are dispensing your gifts to us I will be staying with that saint who manifests himself to us repeatedly, whose throne seems to excel every other saint's in glory, transcending in love every saint's mountains and hills. Oh our frailty, it's so easy to draw you toward the newest and easiest things! In fact, it's not true that he is the highest saint, for many many are superior to him in merit and glory! But to manifest how pleased he is when someone enters His glory and to move His creatures to love Him, the Lord grants him a special glory and makes his creatures believe, so to speak, that he is superior to all the other saints; but this is only a transient glory. But, oh Magdalen, you loved more than him and did more perfect deeds. It is thus suitable that, if one does more good deeds and loves more intensely, one receive more glory and beatitude. But you have received so much of it [glory], that you are known and loved by every creature. Please, Magdalen, continue to dispense your gifts to every spouse. And, my soul, while she is dispensing her gifts, please listen to the sweet songs they are singing in heaven."

At this point she stood up. She was very engrossed and absorbed, as if her spirit were not in her body. And after a while she spoke the following words:

"I hear someone singing: *sub mantu Agni sunt sponse iste.*"[1] Then she added: "The blessed souls love us so much that they sing to the eternal Father the perfection we should have (not that we have) in order to urge him to love us. If we want to join the Father, we need to go through the Word's heart, where we cannot enter unless we abandon ourselves and our will. For it's impossible that the soul that loves itself and maintains its will can join God; for *ubi voluntas ibi mors*, and where selfish love is no virtue and no good can ever be."

Having spoken these words, she looked absorbed like before, listening to what the angels were singing for the Holy Spirit. And after a long while, she said:

"To the holy Spirit they sing the purity and virginity we have solemnly promised in our profession, and not only the general one which is virginity, but [also] that intrinsic purity God requires from us. And I would be content if I just had this purity because it contains every perfection. For pure is the soul that is humble; pure is the soul that has abandoned itself; and pure is the soul that wants nothing, knows nothing, and understands nothing. In a word, purity exclusively, absolutely lies in seeking God's honor and glory, and in enjoying it. Oh, in hell there are so many who are virgins in their soul and in their body, but no one has this purity. And, here on earth there are so many who live with virginity but are against you because they lack that purity, and your union is where this purity is."

She became very absorbed again, in a way as if she were melting down. And later, after a while, she said:

"To the Word they sing their yoke of light. But how will they be able to sing it for those who have broken their holy obedience? They won't be able to find them because, as the Word said, his yoke is easy and light, and those who walk with it walk with a great delight."

Having spoken these words, she stopped as before for a long time. Then she said:

"Will I forget the sweet music they sing for Mary? Oh, this is the most needed one, because the beautiful soprano of God's love is missing. Nobody is singing the counterchant, which is the love they have for each other. Nobody is playing the lyre, since we express no enthusiasm in our homages. Nobody is playing the trombone, for our deeds are inconsiderate and are not enriched with his wise judgment. The organ is not tuned, since a pure and rightful intention is missing. Nobody is playing the trumpet with a fervent and constant prayer, and thus nobody fervently leads and invites people to listen to this music. There is no sign to indicate where we must sing this sweet music, that is, the flag placed over the house where people are going to sing. This sign must be our voluntary imitation of Christ crucified through a simple and contrite life. Oh blessed angels, you love us so deeply that you always gaze at Mary's dwelling! And you wish to sing for us what you sang for Mary; that is, as Mary was a medium between God and the human kind, we should be a medium between God and the human kind through a constant willingness and desire to help every soul and lead her to God *[silence]* oh blessed spirits, by gazing at God you clearly see what he wants from Mary's dwelling! *[silence]* to be removed from the world, to live a dead life in God only longing for God himself, an anxious and constant desire for the souls' salvation, and a simple and contrite attitude in eating and dressing."

After saying these and other things that we have not written down, as she usually does she offered many creatures to the Lord and to St. Mary Magdalen, and after her thanksgiving she came out of her rapture. This vision lasted about three hours.

This soul continues her exile and spiritual isolation and immense suffering of temptations, which are constant and countless. Now the Lord has granted this blessed soul such a strong fortitude and freedom that, as soon as she feels assaulted by some temptation—and they are constant—, but in particular when they assault her in a vehement way, she immediately leaves the place where she is and goes to report this temptation to the Mother Superior. In the past she was not able to do this every time because when she left the place where she was she was unaware of being led somewhere else. God allowed the devil to do this so that she could know herself and us as well, and also [so that she could know] that we can do nothing by ourselves and thus feel compassion toward the others.

But let me go back to what I was saying before. As soon as our blessed soul reports a temptation to the Mother Superior, the Lord deigns to allow her to defeat the devil. He tells her what he told St. Anthony, that is, that only through humility she would be able to escape the world's innumerable snares. Indeed, if the Mother Superior did not inflict some mortification and humiliation upon her, she would never be free. As soon as she has received some form of mortification and humiliation, defeated and confused the devil leaves with all his temptations. However, she is not completely without temptations, but just a bit freer to work. It is important to remember that, when we say that this soul is not free, we do not mean that the Lord deprives her of her free will because this is not the case. He rather hides it from her so that she cannot use it during that time. The same thing happens in the external world, for when something is hidden we cannot make use of it. And this is what the Lord told her when, elevated in spirit, she asked him about this topic.

Volume Two

(pp. 47–86)

On Maundy Thursday, March 26, 1592, after taking communion she was rapt in ecstasy. Looking very engrossed, she spoke only a few words, which concerned the greatness of the Holy Sacrament, the love God shows us through it, and the fruits and effects it produces in the soul. Then she perceived that the gift Jesus had promised her the morning before was that he wanted her to participate in his passion.[1] He had already done this seven years ago, that is, in 1585, as one can see in the book of *The Dialogues*, where it is written everything she did and said during that rapture of the passion. And when she understood this, at once our blessed soul of the Lord besought him not to give her this gift in a way that it would be apparent to us like that other time, when she physically moved from one place to another, made gestures, and acted as Jesus had been forced to do in his passion. By all her acts we had understood all the mysteries of this passion very well. For this reason she said: "Oh my most loving and passionate Spouse, if you deign to give me the great gift of participating in the sufferings of your passion, I beseech you that this be between you and me, and not be visible to the creatures. Let my body suffer as much as you wish but, please, let it stand still without any exterior act," and many other similar words. At last, seeing that the Lord did not deign to grant her that grace, she abode by his will and totally abandoned herself to it. However, she asked him to let her go for a bit. Thus, after a short while she came out of her rapture and stayed out of it until the eighteenth hour.

That day, after the meal, while she was reciting the morning prayer in the oratory of the novices, when she started the Psalm *"Laudate Dominum de coelis"* she entered a rapture.[2] It was indeed the eighteenth hour, when the Lord is believed to have visited His holy Mother. And after keeping quiet for a while, as usual she started to speak.

And her first words were: "Here he is, Abraham, the faithful servant who is looking for a spouse for his son Isaac. He finds her at the spring, and he given to drink by her[3] *[silence]* This is my Spouse that tries to give the entire humankind to his eternal Father. He finds Mary that, by consenting that he suffer the pains of his passion, finds that bride that he wanted to offer to his eternal Father."[4] After a little bit she said: "Mary gave him to drink through her conformity with the divine will that wanted him to suffer *[silence]* Oh, what a sweet spring was this, that let the Word breathe while the anguish of his passion was already starting!"

After these words she left the oratory and went to the scriptorium of the procuratrix that for her was the Virgin's house; and during this passion she went to the same rooms and places where the other time the Lord communicated with her, as one can see in the book of *The Dialogues*, that reports everything she did and said in that rapture of the passion. As we did that time, we shall write the continuation of the present rapture as carefully as we can because it is impossible to write everything we saw. It was indeed amazing to see all her gestures and the external acts of her body expressing both admiration and compassion; through her movements and her words one could easily understand all the mysteries of Jesus' passion and the pains he endured for us during that passion. This soul participated in his pains and partially felt them in her body; and in her mind she meditated and contemplated them and felt pity for Jesus, her Spouse.

Now, getting back to our subject I say that, as soon as she walked into the scriptorium she knelt down, and with great love and compassion she gazed at the holy Virgin. That is what we imagine because she acted like when one gazes at someone with great affection and compassion. And after being preoccupied and engrossed in that way for quite a while, she started to speak; and she spoke sometimes with Jesus, sometimes with the Virgin, and sometimes with herself. She paused between one and the other, which we shall indicate with the spaces that we leave between the words.

And the first words she said, the first words we wrote down, were the following (because at the beginning, when she started to speak, we missed some of her words because only one sister was there, while the others gathered for the Washing of feet, as one usually does on Maundy Thursday), that is: "Now the sun and the moon are united. The sun, in order to make the moon more radiant in this dark night of the passion *[silence]* today the Word examines three excesses with Mary. The first is the excess of love; the second, the excess of passion; the third, the excess of capacity of heavenly things[5] *[silence]* Mary, what will you do? Christ, what will you do? You have always granted grace and melody to her ears, and she has given birth to love for you. And today you examine that sublime excess of passion, but passion of love *[silence]* Three loves made you speak to Mary about this excess of passion. The first was the love you had for Mary because she conformed to your humanity, since she was conceived immaculate and you by virtue of the Holy Spirit.[6] The second was the love you had for your eternal Father. The third was that pure and holy love you had for the angels *[silence]* but why for the love you had for the Angels, unless it was because Mary had a special participation in the purity of the angels above all the elect?

"Mary had three passions. Oh Word, Mary conformed to your will, but she endured a passion coming from the passion that would overflow into your humanity, as you said: *'Spiritus quidem pronptus'*[7] etc.; and this is the first passion. The second passion is that she had a glimpse of your divine greatness; as she saw your divinity, she could not help but withdraw from your humanity. The third passion is a passion of compassion: compassion for the apostles, for Mary Magdalen, and for the entire human kind; and also compassion for the humanity that you drew from her. And in order to take that passion away from her you granted her your glorious resurrection with a splendor that is impossible to narrate *[silence]* and you granted passion to Mary *[silence]* Mary, what did you do when you wanted to keep asking? *[silence]* oh my Word, I imagine that one of the first things you examined with Mary was the ardent charity that, proceeding from your pure being, you had for the entire human kind that had been molded and formed by your pure and holy hands in the likeness of the Father, of you, Son, and together with that of the Holy Spirit. Many would lose this ardent charity of yours *[silence]* the enjoyment of the humanity and the divinity created a bond and tied the human kind to the holy Trinity *[silence]* and here you revealed her your being, which is nothing else but love and charity; and in order to distill the liquor in your soul you couldn't find a more suitable vessel and more appropriate receptacle than Mary. It was appropriate to reveal it to the Angels, because the entire world had to know it.

"Why didn't you lament before your eternal Father that had imposed upon you the burden and the weight of the passion? *[silence]* he didn't lament before his eternal Father for two reasons. One is that he had decided to place the burden of the passion upon his shoulders[8]; the other is that the Word had a perfect equality with the divine being of his eternal Father *[silence]* oh eternal Word, why didn't you have a dialogue with the Holy Spirit from whose virtue your humanity was conceived? *[silence]* why didn't you lament before the three divine Persons, whom you were one of, and instead you lamented before those who were inferior to you? I am not surprised that it wasn't helpful *[silence]* but you didn't lament, you rather narrated.

"After narrating your entire charity, you narrated the internal and external reward you wanted to give to every single creature, according to the fruit she received from this passion *[silence]* I believe that you failed to narrate to him and communicate to him the deification you wanted to give to our souls by means of your passion, because, once we respond to them, all your gifts, all your graces make us gods by participation and, moreover, with the vestment of your Blood your passion is so powerful that we, as Jacob did, are able to deceive your eternal Father. Although he knows us, your Blood, so to speak, blinds him *[silence]* and because of your scourges this vestment of Blood gives out a smell, with which the souls adorn themselves, and in this way he is deceived.

"My Spouse, multiplying your dialogue I imagine that you recounted to him how your scourges, your thorns, your nails had to grant the souls the vision, comprehension, and communication of the Holy Trinity *[silence]* what the vision, comprehension, and communication of the unfathomable Trinity entail, one cannot understand and is not allowed to know *[silence]* and as if delight lacked in heaven, you gave Mary the cognition of how the eternal Father, the angels, and the blessed souls took pleasure from your humanity *[silence]* but reflecting upon the pains you endured at the moment, Mary's heart melted and distilled drops of love *[silence]* I don't want to end my contemplation of the dialogue about the capacity of the highest sky that you narrated to Mary; [that dialogue was also about] the pleasure that the virgins imitating her and your humanity would receive; when they were in heaven they would have to follow you, humanate Lamb nailed to the cross, and when they were down here on earth they would come inebriated and become insane for love, placing in you that love that they could have placed in someone against you *[silence]* and this pleasure must have been quite quite a support and relief, so to speak, to the passion you had to suffer.

"And what shall I say about your wounds? They must have been similar to that rainbow God gave to Noah, signifying that he would never bring the waters of the Deluge upon the earth again. And, Word, your wounds will be like that bow; placed between the eternal Father and the human kind, your wounds will abate our faults and thanks to them he will not be called God of revenge anymore but rather God of mercy and love *[silence]* oh, how joyful Mary must have felt when she saw that the Blood the Word had taken from her would be a stole for all the elect!

"But let's come to what is known and possible to every mind and easy for every imagination, that is, when you narrated her each act and each minimum passion your humanity would suffer. A great compassion generated in Mary when she saw that your delicate, beautiful, and graceful humanity had to die *[silence]* you told her so many compassionate words, so many knives pierced her heart. Affection should stop then! *[silence]* Mary, your powers were like three channels sending those love words to your Son's heart *[silence]* your heart became full of sorrow for your compassion toward your Son, and from your mouth came out words full of compassion."

At this point she knelt down seeing both Jesus and the Virgin Mary kneeling down and feeling disconsolate. Thus she said:

"They felt increasingly sorrowful within themselves and gave forth a rain of tears. They will suffice to refresh each passion of ours, because they are so capable and effective that they will last until the consummation of time *[silence]* even though I would be moved more to tears, who wouldn't smile at that contrast, since one is God and man and the other is the holiest and honest human being who has ever lived both at present and in the future; and nevertheless they are overwhelmed by passion? *[silence]* how can he become prey of passion, if one drop of his grace takes any possible passion away?"

After these words, she started to cry and shake, seeing both Jesus and Mary crying. And then she continued: "The womb of the Mother and the heart of the Son were distressed; he even sends others to begin his passion. In short, everything startles and oppresses my heart more than it lets my mouth narrate *[silence]* oh my God, where shall I see your dignity and your beauty go? *[silence]* and also that one, who is so beautiful, I mean Mary, holy, *pulchra ut luna*,[9] etc? Tears will bathe her eyes and 'squalid' her face[10] *[silence]* Mary, how will you feel? Word, will you be able to leave her who generated you? But love leads you to give a significant sign of love, for which you had come to the world."

At this point she saw the Son asking her Mother for her benediction: "the Son asks his Mother for it and the Mother asks him for it *[silence]* oh Word, you'll give her the benediction that your eternal Father gave your soul when he infused it in that small and well-organized body in Mary's womb *[silence]* and during this benediction he will promise her what God promised to Abraham, that is, that her seed will multiply like the stars in the sky *[silence]* it is through that benediction that you, Word, will give Mary every grace, every gift, and also every benediction that the Father gave to every just man in the Old Testament, along with that that Isaach gave to his son Jacob."

She saw the Virgin almost fainting because of the pain for her Son's departure; and she said:

"Oh Mary, I am not surprised that you almost faint!"

And she stood up saying these words with great compassion: "Mary, please stay."

And all of a sudden, at the twenty-second hour, she left from here and went to a large room, upstairs, still rapt. Indeed, even though during this rapture she moved from one place to another, from the eighteenth hour until the eighteenth hour of Friday she did not come out of it. And so, when she got to that room that for her was the cenacle where Jesus had his last supper, she knelt down and stayed very engrossed and preoccupied for quite a long time. Then she pronounced these words:

"First you had supper, washed our feet, and gave yourself to us." Then she added these other words speaking to Jesus:

"When I see you washing the feet, I want to help you out."

After these words she kept quiet for a while. Then seeing Jesus and the apostles sitting at the table to have supper, she stood up from where she had been on her knees and took some steps and still standing she spoke these words:

"While you were eating the lamb you stood *[silence]* I think I see you eating: end, end, this law must end, and another one must begin. Word, you'll be the lamb, well roasted, and soon you'll be taken and dead on the cross *[silence]* one must eat all of you (like the lamb that symbolized you), because one cannot serve both God and Mammon *[silence]* one must ruminate everything, because one must believe not only in the head of your divinity, but also in the feet of your humanity. Oh, don't I take you all God and all man? *[silence]* bitter was not that rustic lettuce, but rather the comments you heard from those treacherous Jews who dwelled on the legal matters and were unable to move on *[silence]* one must eat in a hurry, and the apostle says we must serve you with a fervent spirit in all our workings *[silence]* oh holy Christ, how different were your thoughts from those of your apostles! While they should be full of compassion, they only think about who is going to be the first one *[silence]* poor apostles! you were flesh like us, but since you were going to unfasten our knots, you would have cut them [our knots] too soon unless you hadn't understood them first *[silence]* if I had been present at that question, I would have answered that [the first would be] that who would love my Spouse the most, and not those who nurtured those thoughts *[silence]* you give them an answer which is both easy and difficult, difficult for the human nature but easy for those who want to overcome the others in the virtue of humility *[silence]* oh my God, you have always shown with acts and words how pleasing is humility to you *[silence]* oh Philip, you came up with an idea on how to feed that multitude, and now you can't find a remedy for those thoughts? And still, you had heard your Master and my Spouse: *'discite a me,'* etc."[11]

When she finished speaking the above words, she saw her beloved Jesus preparing to wash his apostles' feet; thus, as she had said, she went and helped him, crouching in a corner of the room where she saw the apostles sitting. And after kneeling down, she performed those exterior acts as if she were really washing feet, with such a dexterity and care that she instilled a great consolation and admiration into us who were seeing her. And she repeated the same acts twelve times, calling up each of the twelve apostles, as we shall write now. And first she washed St. Peter's feet:

STS. PETER AND ANDREW

"You don't want to be washed. Careful, careful, Peter, that word will become so harsh for you that you won't participate in him."

She said something to almost every apostle so that we could know who she was washing. After St. Peter, she went to St. Andrew, and said:

"Blessed Andrew, you won't dare to say anything."

ST. JOHN

"Oh pure John, you are the beloved *[silence]* I wouldn't like having to find that Judas!"

ST. THOMAS

She didn't say anything to St. Thomas, but she gazed at him with a joyful and delighted face.

ST. JAMES

"You are one of those who wanted to participate in the reign *[silence]* and still you tolerate that God, your Master, washes your feet. But you heard what he said to Peter: 'you do not want to miss that part,' while one tried to stay at his right and the other at his left."[12]

ST. PHILIP

"You are my Philip. I believe that you loved my God with sincerity and purity of heart."

[JUDAS]

When she got to Judas, she became distraught and started to cry and to shake, saying:
"And you will be the one who betrays my Christ."

ST. JAMES

"Oh blessed James, we descend from a cursed one to a blessed one!"

ST. BARTHOLOMEW

"You will let yourself be flayed, not only washed. You had a beautiful face."

ST. MATTHEW

"Ah, you are the one who followed the Lord as soon as he called you."

ST. SIMON

"I want to take more water and pour it on your feet. Oh holy Simon, I have never heard in the Gospel that you spoke or said anything."

ST. THADDAEUS

"Oh yes, you are the twelfth one! *[silence]* you shouldn't have been in that group; your manner doesn't show it."

When she finished to wash and kiss the feet of every apostle, she went to the table, that is, to that place where she had seen Jesus having the supper. And once she got there, she said:

"Oh, here one must do something else, and eat something else *[silence]* Judas will have it as well *[silence]* and still you let them know that one of them will betray you. Oh my Christ, oh my Spouse, oh my life, oh abysm of mercy, oh spring of piety! *[silence]* '*Hoc est enim corpus meum,*' my Christ says[13] *[silence]* as long as he gives it to me! *[silence]* Please, give it to all the spouses of this dwelling place *[silence]* if they open their mouth of affection, you'll give yourself to them with great love; if they don't perceive with their bodily sense, not for us it will be enough you give yourself to them[14] *[silence]* oh benignity, oh humanity of my Christ, you gave it to him too!"

At this point we understood that the Lord administered Holy Communion to her because she recited the Confiteor, "*Domine non sum digna*" etc.,[15] and opened her mouth exactly like when one receives Communion; and she did not speak for quite a while, enjoying his God reciprocally. Then she said to St. John:

"Oh John, what are you going to do?"

And seeing him rest on Jesus' chest, she too bent on that divine chest, and speaking to St. John she said:

"And here you enjoyed. *In principium erat Verbum,* etc. It would be enough for me to enjoy *Verbum caro factum est.*" And keeping quiet for a moment, she added these words: "Oh *altitudo sapientiae* and *scientiae Dei, quam incompreensibilia sunt iudicia eius et investigabiles viae eius.*"[16]

About these words she said so many beautiful, elevated, and divine things so quickly and in such a rush that we could write nothing down; and like St. John the Evangelist, she seemed to be drawing wonderful secrets from that amorous chest. Then, after doing an exterior act with her head, she stood up and began to talk about the Holy Sacrament. And her first words were these:

"In memory of your passion I must do this *[silence]* oh, what memory? oh what memory? Happy souls, they would enjoy the paradise on earth if they had that memory: *Hoc facite in meam comemorationem*[17] *[silence]* and tell them not to drink from the grapes until the Son of man is resurrected from death. You are Life, as you just said: *Ego sum via, veritas et vita*[18] *[silence]* and what kind of wine do we think it is? For us it will be your Blood, even though we won't receive you until you are resurrected. Tonight you can say that to us."

She speaks with Jesus in this manner because she knew that she would not receive Communion until Easter morning, according to the traditional rule of the holy church. She keeps talking, saying:

"But one can't have your Blood yet, not until you are resurrected. What fruits would a soul receive from you, if it hasn't known you before as passionate, dead, buried, and resurrected? *[silence]* what benefit can a soul receive if it doesn't consider that you passed away, were buried, and resurrected for it, without wishing to imitate you? *[silence]* Yes, we must do penance during the time you are dead to us for our sin, until you are resurrected and give us your grace."

She left that place that was the cenacle for her at one o'clock in the morning and went to a room next to it. This room was going to be that house close to the garden where we believe Jesus completed his sermon to the apostles, and in the end, as St. John writes in his Gospel, he recited that beautiful prayer to the eternal Father. The soul dwelt on this prayer saying many beautiful things, but only a few of them we were able to gather as carefully as possible. Raising her eyes and her hands toward the sky without speaking, she started to speak as follows:

"*Sublevatis oculis Jesus in coelum dixit: Pater venit hora clarifica filium tuum,*[19] etc. until those words, *et nunc clarifica me, tu Pater apud temetipsum claritate quam habui priusquam mundus fieret apud te.*[20] While the divine Word, my beloved Spouse, totally inscrutable and incomprehensible to us, and who is comprehensible only to himself, as I said, while he was going to embrace his passion and our redemption *[silence]* being almost in his death agony and recreating me through the excellence of his being and his knowledge, he cries out at his Father: *"clarifica me Pater claritate quam habui priusquam mundus fieret apud te"* *[silence]* oh my humanate Word, you ask him

311

for that clarification that you had before the world came into existence *[silence]* you make me understand that you had three clarifications before the creation of the world *[silence]* you were clarified by being in your Father's bosom and enjoying your divine being, gazing into yourself, you fell in love with your communicative being, and enjoying it you communicated yourself and created those marvelous and pure angelic Spirits so that they would delight in your inscrutable being and those divine enjoyments between the Father and you, and the Holy Spirit, that constantly overflows those divine enjoyments in the Father, in the Word, and in itself *[silence]* and when Lucifer, though he was a noble creature, decided to become similar to you, divine Word consubstantial with the Father, he thought to himself: *"in coelum conscendam super astra Dei exaltabo solium meum sedebo in monte testamenti, in lateribus aquilonis; ascendam super altitudinem nubium similis ero altissimo"*[21] *[silence]* oh eternal Father, you fell in love with your Only Begotten and only Word, the only one who is capable of yourself; and in this act of love, while you were enjoying him in this enjoyment you hurled Lucifer into hell and belched forth an unfathomable clarification to your divine Word, and finally your deity enjoyed the Word's request for incarnation. When the fullness of time came, the Word became incarnate and, after wandering thirty-three years down here among us, my Spouse and your Truth went to his passion and reminded his humanity of this clarification; and he asks you for it saying: *"clarifica me Pater,"* etc. *[silence]* oh my Christ, you are asking for that clarification that you had before the world came into existence. Isn't this but the clarification you received when you were in your Father's bosom, thanks to that condemnation that the Father expressed with you and the Holy Spirit by hurling Lucifer and all his followers into the abyss of hell and manifesting to the other angelic Spirits the consubstantiality, equality, and unity that you, Word, have with the Father and the Holy Spirit? This manifestation (to the extent that you permitted) granted your almighty and divine being to those who humiliated themselves and undertook to venerate you, to love you, and to obey you, enjoying the decision that you, infallible Truth, made to create the human kind and to become incarnate. Humiliating themselves even more, they considered all your working rightful and venerable *[silence]* and for this reason I assume that it is a clarification, because Lucifer rose and wanted to become similar to you; because of you he rose and because of you he fell; you became incarnate and were glorified *[silence]* so, you, divine Word, ask for that clarification that you, divine being, had when you were in your Father's bosom; and you ask to receive it when you return to his right side with your humanity.

"I believe that the second clarification you had before the world came into existence was that your Father enjoyed himself and you, and you enjoyed him and the Holy Spirit, when you decided to create the great machine of the world, in order to create inside of it the human being in his image and likeness. And since you saw everything as if it occurred at that moment, you also knew that you would have to come and live inside of it, by means of that humanity that you would take up *[silence]* and for this reason it was a clarification, thanks to the Father's enjoyment of you, Word, and to the Holy Spirit's communication in every working accomplished by the Holy Trinity in creating not only the creature but also all the things necessary to her. And this clarification was so delightful to you, that it generated an indissoluble clarification in you, Word; and the Holy Spirit took an immense pleasure in your delight, and its love came and supported you when you shed your Blood for our redemption *[silence]* but, oh old and new Truth, how joyful must have been for you the communication that the Holy Spirit did to many of your elect, so that they said to the skies: *'Rorate coeli desuper,'*[22] etc., and to the throne of your deity, asking for you: *'Emitte Agnum Domine, dominatorem terre,'*[23] with that communication that it, the Holy Spirit, had to do to all the just *usque* as *consumationem seculi,*[24] so that they could achieve those divine workings, thanks to the fact that you, being with us in your own virtue, worked as you had told them you would: *'Amen, amen dico vobis qui credit in me opera que ego facio et ipse faciet,'*[25] etc.; and as the just will multiply, so will this clarification be more visible through the breathing in and the breathing out of all the just within your goodness, essence, and deity; and by sprinkling their own blood they will adorn your spouse, the church *[silence]* oh my incarnate Word, you asked for the clarification that you had before the constitution of the world; you asked that one for it, that one who came close to you during your passion[26] *[silence]* and I imagine that it was the pleasure the Holy Trinity took from the communication that the Holy Spirit and your humanity would do to us, your creatures *[silence]* oh, how great is the love you have for the creature, because all the gifts and graces you give her you take them for your clarification. Oh abyss of love, oh infinite, incomparable, and inscrutable love! Oh greatness of love, oh my God of perfect goodness, let me and all the creatures know you, long for you, and love you. For this reason you created us in your image and likeness.

"The third clarification I recall is the one that you, humanate Word, received before the constitution of the world *[silence]* it is the one that the eternal Father gave you in his bosom, his Truth, in a divine and mutual contemplation, in an act of love. The Father took pleasure in your wish to become incarnate in the purest and most immaculate womb that ever existed or would exist, because it was the most suitable place for you, his Only Begotten, and for that divine purity that is contained in the incomprehensible, inscrutable, and eternal Trinity *[silence]* oh, how great was the pleasure the eternal Father took from the incomparable purity he knew your humanity and the inexpressible purity of the woman who would generate and feed you would receive! *[silence]* seeing it reflected in those two mirrors, the Father felt such a great love for his uncreated purity, that he decided to place into our custody, his creatures, those pure angelic spirits so that we keep that purity that he communicated to us and constantly communicates to us in the sacrament of the holy baptism *[silence]* oh, my tender and rosy Spouse, I dare to say that the clarification you are asking the Father for is that clarification you received when in your divinity you enjoyed the purity you knew your humanity would acquire. And now you ask that, even though your humanity is emptied,[27] exposed to afflictions, thorns, nails, cross, and death, your humanity wants to clarify you by having in you the same pleasure that it had before you took on your humanity.[28] And you were so crazy for love, that you intended to ask for that clarification not only for your humanity, but also for every elect, who would share your Blood; and you also asked for purity for us, so that we would be clarified in you."

She left this place at the second hour and accompanied Jesus to the garden. And before entering that room, that she saw as the garden, she indicated that Jesus should leave the apostles here, because she spoke the following words: "*Sedete hic, donec vadam illuc et orem.*"[29]

She spoke these words in the person of Jesus, as she often did in this rapture of the passion. Indeed, she acted and moved in the person of Jesus, as we shall write later. She resumed speaking as herself to Jesus, saying:

"Oh my Christ, what do you tell them? *[silence]* you gazed at them with such an affectionate love, assuring them that, if they fell, they would fall for their salvation, and not like the miserable Judas! *[silence]* in order to share my misery. *Percutiam Pastorem et dispergetur oves.*"[30]

Then, inside that room, she left three apostles with these words:

"Peter, Jacob, and John, you stay here. *Tristis est anima mea usque ad mortem.*"[31]

And moving away from them quite a bit, she prayed and kept silent with her hands up to the sky for about half an hour. Then she started to speak with Jesus:

"In a thrill of love you prayed, sharing with your just all their afflictions, temptations, and persecutions that your elect would suffer until the end of the world *[silence]* in your anguish you obtained a consolation for your elect in their afflictions and temptations *[silence]* how could that communication be obtained if your humanity had not besought it? *[silence]* but you made your elect see their temptations, afflictions, and torments as a glory and [you made them] glory only on their cross and on their suffering. At the same time thousands of just men suffer and you communicate your consolation to all of them, so that it seems like you have only this one or that one. And you communicate all yourself to me, and to this one and to that one as well; and you obtained this in a thrill of love."

Almost at the end of the first hour of prayer, we saw that she suffered and trembled inside herself. And being like this for a while, she spoke these words:

"*Pater si possibile est transeat a me calix iste, veruntamen non sicut ego volo sed sicut tu.*"[32]

After saying this, she stopped praying. Indeed, an hour had gone by. It was the third hour of night and she went to that place where she had left the three apostles. And she told them:

"*Quid dormitis? Sic non potuistis una hora vigilare mecum*[33] *[silence]* Even John, who rested on your chest, is asleep. Oh my Jesus, how will they be able to rest, those whose head is suffering so intensely?"

She leaves them and goes back to her prayer. And after looking very preoccupied for around half an hour, then she started to partake of Jesus' anguishes. So she said:

"Oh anguish, oh anguish! *[silence]* oh what a piteous quiver must have been! Not only piteous, but also painful. Oh, what a painful pity, when my great God and piteous man at once saw that many would not fructify his precious Blood. Nonetheless, he abandoned himself to his sacrifice, although he still prayed that the calice would pass from him; but he saw that many from his people would not fructify *[silence]* what a suffering! And still, if it had been allowed to his soul and humanity, he would have suffered his passion for each of us in particular. Oh holy soul, the divinity was slowly receding, so that it could suffer more pains, anguishes, and torments! *[silence]* oh eternal Word, if we considered the pain we made you suffer, we would embrace hell rather than committing a deadly sin. The eternal communications finished. The amorous gazes finished. In your Father's bosom your deity was leaving you as a man, so that you could suffer many pains and your passion *[silence]* how could the angels not support you in your passion? I would like to have thousand tongues to curse sin, which causes such a great pain to my God. I see his face becoming pale, that beautiful face of his, more beautiful than any man's *[silence]* you suffered in that kitchen garden more than Daniel in the lake of lions *[silence]* you lie on cool herbage and love keeps you warmer than the three children in the furnace *[silence]* oh holy Christ, you were in a kitchen garden and prayed to the Father that generated you and will always generate you. You are loved by him, honored by him, glorified by him, and still he does not respond to you. Oh eternal Father, but you responded to Moses in the desert! You said of your Son: *"Hic est Filius meus dilectus in quo mihi bene complacui, ipsum audite."*[34] You order something that you do not want to do yourself. *Ipsum audite.*[35] *[silence]* he prays for me, and I will pray for him, but I will pray like him: *"Non mea voluntas,"*[36] etc. *[silence]* oh my Christ, before you did say that no matter what we ask in your name we will obtain it, but now you ask and are not answered *[silence]* oh my Christ, eternal Word and my spouse, how could I possibly trust the words you spoke: *"Petite et accipietis, querite et invenietis, pulsate et aperietur vobis,"*[37] if you knock on your Father's ears and he does not hear, and still *dolus non est inventus in ore eius*[38] *[silence]* You asked for a right thing but you were not answered."

After the second hour of prayer, she left and went to the apostles. Looking at them with a benign and compassionate expression, she said:

"Vigilate. And they sleep. *Paratus sum,*[39] etc. It was enough for him to say: *"et si omnes scandalizati fuerint, ego nunquam* will *scandalizabor."*[40] *Simon dormis?*[41] *Vigilate et orate ut non intretis in tentationem. Spiritus quidem prontus est caro autem infirma.*[42]

She resumes her prayer and, after keeping her hands and her eyes toward the sky, she lay down on the floor. She stayed in this way for almost the entire hour, without speaking at all. And during this last hour it was apparent that she suffered a lot, shaking often. Almost at the end of the hour, she stood up and spoke these words:

"Non mea voluntas sed tua fiat."[43]

At this point the angel must have appeared to console her because of the words she spoke in the person of Jesus. Her first words were these:

"Ego te formavi et tu me confortasti[44] *[silence]* True, true. I created you so that in my vision I could enjoy my glory. And now you bring me this cup *[silence]* if I do not suffer for you I suffer for a man, because one of you tempted him, and because of him now I suffer this pain."

When the angel disappeared, she stood up and went to the apostles. She said to them:

"Non potuistis una hora vigilare mecum[45] *[silence] ecce appropinquavit hora ut filius hominis tradetur in manus peccatorum. Surgite,*

317

eamus, ecce appropinquavit qui me tradet."[46] After saying this, she left this place at the fifth hour, and went to a room where she indicated that she was seeing Judas with the soldiers. And she said: "*Quem queritis?*[47] *Ego sum.*"[48] And the soldiers fall down, and she continues as follows: "Where is their power? They fell."

And she questions them again:

"*Quem queritis? Si me queritis sinite hos habire.*[49] [silence] the love he had for them makes me go toward them so that they take me, although I could leave them on the ground [silence] for this reason I abandoned my omnipotence and glory, to take this little lamb and lead it to you. Oh my eternal Father, it is time for me to take the lamb on my shoulders. This is the way to lead to you those who are not united to you [silence] here justice takes place, but I shall use mercy [silence] if my omnipotence did not want to, how could you possibly move your hands and feet to take me? But no, no, my food is to do the Father's will."

She turned to St. Peter and said to him:

"*Mitte gladium tuum in vagina.*[50] Oh Peter, oh Peter, love deceives you, and wisdom does not instruct you! You think you can hinder my Father's will? *An putas quia non possum rogare Patrem meum et exhibebit mihi modo plusquan duodecim legiones Angelorum?*"[51]

At this point she made the gesture of healing her ear.[52] Then with a benign and sweet expression she went up to Judas and greeted him as follows:

"*Amice a quid venisti?*[53] *Juda, osculo Filium hominis tradis?*"[54] Then she turned to the mob: "*Tamquam ad latronem existis, cum gladiis et fustibus comprehendere me?*[55] etc."

After saying these words, we saw that she was taken and tied up with her hands behind her shoulders, because she made a gesture to signify it; and then with great violence and fury she was led to Annas. In other words, she left that place and went to another room that was much more distant. Along the way she suffered a lot, because we saw that once in a while she was wrenched with the ropes behind her back. Hence, she suffered very much. It is important to note that, when she ended this rapture of the passion, we asked her whether, during this vision, she saw who hit, tormented, and tied her up, or whether she felt the pain without seeing anything. She answered that she had the impression to see all the chief priests she was taken to, and all the soldiers who made her suffer Jesus' pains, at least as much as her frailty could tolerate. Now, when she was led to Annas, she showed that she was being questioned about her teaching. Thus, she answered:

"*Ego palam locutus sum mundo. Ego semper docui in sinagoga,*[56] etc."

She showed that she was being slapped:

"*Si male locutus sum, testimonium perhibe de malo. Si autem bene, quid me cedis?*"[57]

She saw Peter denying. She said:

"Readiness of my Peter, where are you? If everybody wants to abandon me, he was the only one who wanted to follow me; and he is the first to deny me *[silence]* he says that he doesn't know me and that he is not a disciple of mine *[silence]* for certainly my holy Christ enumerated and kept in his mind the words of Peter, his beloved disciple, but that night he saw who he had elected prince of his apostles denied him *[silence]* and the beautiful face of my God, *in quem desiderant Angeli perspicere,*[58] *alapas sucepit propter me.*"[59]

She left this place around the sixth hour. While she was accompanying Jesus, her Spouse, to Caiaphas's, along the way she suffered a lot because it was apparent that she was being pulled so vehemently and violently that she was almost dragged on the ground. It looked almost impossible that at each step her sudden jerks did not make her fall down. And sometimes she was pushed back and sometimes pulled forth. To look at her brought about a great devotion and compassion. At the sixth hour she arrived at the chapter house (that for her was Caiaphas's house) and stayed there until the seventh hour and thirty minutes. During this time she clearly shared the sneers, torments, offenses, and insults that Jesus received. By her exterior acts we understood that she was blindfolded, slapped, that her hair was pulled, and other things. And in this place she hardly spoke, as we will show later. Her first words were:

"*Ego sum;*[60] *et videbitis Filium sedente a dextris virtutis Dei,*[61] etc."

After a while she said: "The cock has crowed *[silence] et iuravit [silence]* and I gave him myself only a few hours ago and now he swears that he doesn't know me *[silence]* if they knew that you pry into human heart, they wouldn't say: *Prophetia quis est qui te percussit.*"[62]

As we said, she left this place at the seventh hour and a half. She went to Pilate's, which was in another place. Here she kept silent for quite a while. Then she said:

"*Regnum meum non est de hoc mundo.*[63] Oh humanate Word, your reign is not in this world, but where? Yours is an eternal reign, an immortal reign, in which you have your stall of majesty and glory *[silence]* the angels adore you; the Dominations fear you; the highest Thrones give you a stall; the Virtues praise you; the Principalities invite you; the Cherubim long to glorify and honor you *[silence]* your origin cannot be described, your end cannot be understood because it is eternal. The angel Gabriel, that great champion, said: "*et regni eius non erit finis.*[64] Before being conceived, the world apprehended that your reign was eternal *[silence]* it is eternal, and not like those down here, that are full of misery, calamities, and dishonor. Yours is full of peace, contentment, and infinite joy *[silence]* the beauty of this reign cannot be narrated. John, the beloved apostle, describes it to a certain extent when he says: *Plate et muri eius ex auro purissimo. Zaffiro et smaragdo eius duodecim porte eius, et duodecim columne eius*[65] *[silence]* you lacked the spring that would irrigate this beautiful reign; and you created it *[silence]* oh my Jesus, when will that coronation of thorns take place? Oh, what a pain! *Quid est veritas?*[66] *[silence]* you are not allowed to understand it, but you don't wait for the answer[67] *[silence]* man's power wouldn't have led me to abandon myself to you if I had not deigned to do it *[silence]* Oh my Jesus, who could have ever been able to contemplate you well!"

She was in this place an hour and a half, that is, until the ninth hour. Then she left and went to Herod's; and along the way she suffered as before. And after being in that place, that for her was Herod's house, for quite a while, she made the gesture of asking for the white gown. And she said:

"Do you really think you can deride my Christ? No, no, on the contrary you manifest his purity and innocence, and what he was going to give to his elect. Later his holy Church would praise them singing: "*Candidiores nive, rubicondiores lacte*"[68] etc. *[silence]* it was really true that he was crazy for love and for my salvation."

She was here for a short time. Without coming out of her rapture, she left this place and went back to that room that for her was Pilate's house. Here she made the gesture of being placed with Jesus in the old cistern. Indeed, when the other time the Lord communicated his passion to her, she understood that, as Joseph had been placed by his brothers in that old cistern, so had Jesus been placed in an old cistern in Pilate's house. For that reason, she got into a hole under the staircases; and here she threw herself on the floor, remaining crouched in a very uncomfortable position for more than a half-hour. During this time she prayed and made an offering to the eternal Father in Latin, but her voice was so low that we could not hear anything, only a word here and a word there. The she came out of that hole and went to a room nearby. She stopped here, standing against the wall with her arms folded on her breast. And she stayed there with such a meekness and grace that she could have moved a stone to pity. And after a long while, she started to speak. And her first words were the following:

"They didn't scream so vehemently *Benedictus qui venit*[69] etc., as they do now: *Tolle, tolle, crucifige eum.*[70] Because of these words at Doomsday my God will have to say: *Ite maledicti,*[71] etc. *[silence]* they are right not to want Barabbas, because his blood would not be useful to them at all *[silence]* even in heaven, before you came to us, you were put before[72] Barabbas, even though he was put before you, Word, and sin was put before your justice. Oh, isn't sin so incredibly different from you, as Barabbas was, because you are totally innocent? *[silence]* oh eternal Word, mercy brought you to the Father. Mercy asked the Father to forgive human kind and to grant you to it. You thus became incarnate and were crucified for us. In this way sin died in you, and you satisfied both justice and mercy *[silence]* justice replaced Pilate when he put you before Barabbas; love and mercy was the multitude that did not scream *crucifige*, as the Jews did, but 'mercy, mercy, mercy.' Oh blessed multitude! In this you are different, that they were moved by hatred to scream '*tolle, tolle,*' etc., whereas mercy was only moved by love. The chief priest said that it was expedient that you die for the multitude; and the eternal Father as well told his justice that it was expedient that you die to remove sin, since you were pure and innocent. '*Tolle,*

321

tolle,' etc. But it makes a big difference the fact that ministers drew you to the column and to the cross, whereas here the Holy Spirit drew you into Mary's womb."

She left this place at the eleventh hour and a half and went downstairs. She stood against a column with her hands behind her back and her eyes downcast. She stayed here an hour, hardly saying a word. She continued to keep silent also during the other mysteries of the passion, that is, Jesus' coronation of thorns, his carrying the cross, and his crucifixion. Indeed, by sharing the passion of her sweet love and partaking of his physical afflictions she suffered so intensely that she could not articulate a single word, but she looked engrossed and her face showed a solemn, benign, and joyful mournfulness. And in particular at this point, during the mystery of the column, where we understood that, imitating her spouse Jesus, she was suffering a lot and was feeling the pain of an intense scourging, beating, and whipping. Sometimes she writhed a little, as we would do if we were beaten by someone, but she did it with grace and meekness. After keeping silent for a long while, then she said these words:

"If you changed in order to convert!"

She meant that those soldiers who, lucky them, took turns in beating her because they felt tired, should have converted when they changed position. She understood that there were thirty of them to scourge Jesus at the column, that is, fifteen pairs. We also saw her indicate that they took turns fifteen times during the hour she stayed at the column. When the scourging was finished, she fell to the ground as if she had been untied and let go. And after a bit, she stood up and went back to that place that for her was Pilate's house. Here, after taking a seat, she showed that she was receiving the crown of thorns. And by the movements of her body we saw that she was suffering a great pain. And in this mystery she spoke only a few words. Her first words were:

"I would like to give it back to you when I am placed to the right of my Father. I would like you to be those who will follow me with stoles."

She meant that Jesus would give her the stole of glory in exchange for the scarlet cloak, that the Jews were putting on her.

Then she added: "Like Isaiah the holy Angels now can exclaim: *Quis est iste qui venit de Edon tintibus vestis de Bosdra?*[73] How will they be able to crown with a diadem of thorns that who is crowned with glory? *Gloria et honore coronasti eum Domine.*[74] *Corona aurea super caput eius.*[75]

Now she speaks in the person of Jesus:

"When my humanity is at the right of the Father, I will pierce you for love so that a rain of grace will distill down into you *[silence]* *Egredimini filie Sion,*[76] etc."

And after keeping quiet for a little bit, she went back to that room where she had been before the scourging at the column. And after walking around it she stopped in front of the wall. In this way she showed that Jesus with the crown of thorns and the reed in his hand was shown by Pilate to the people. And she still kept her hands crossed and the hand straight. And such a grace, solemnity, and meekness appeared on her face and in the acts and gestures that she did, that she really represented Jesus for us. And standing in that way for a while, she said these words:

"How wisely without wisdom you called him man: *Ecce Homo!*[77] *[silence]* yes, yes, that man that was going to turn you into gods, that man that became man in order to make man a god. *Et homo factus est? [silence]* that man that later will have the power to judge man."

At this point she left this place and went to a room upstairs. Here she prayed to the Father both in Latin and in Italian. We missed the part in Latin because she spoke so low that we could not understand it. And when she got to this place, her first words were the following:

"Oh eternal Father, while they are making a decision I will offer myself to you, *orabo spiritu, orabo et mente,* but I see very well that they will not partake of the Blood I shed with such an ardent love for them *[silence]* the son of perdition is lost, but I pray for the others because I cannot and must not pray for him *[silence]* oh Father, let those molded by you come with me to my reign. I pray less for the world than for my beloved apostles *[silence]* oh my merciful God, much more decisive than this was the decision you made, divinity in three Persons, to send the Word to become incarnate and to communicate your constant grace to your creature in this pilgrimage and in the glory and fruition of the other life. And this is a decision that won't last an hour or two, since you always renew it. *Ecce nova facio omnia.*[78] And you always make this creature bigger and bigger, because what you accomplish in one you also accomplish it in all the others since every creature has been created from a nothingness."

Now she speaks in the person of Jesus: "I shall not feel upset because of your decisions. When I left myself to you I said 'I desired with desire,' and now I say 'with desire I have desired that that decision will be made about me.'"

At this point she stood up and showed that she was seeing Pilate passing a death sentence against Jesus. And she spoke in the person of her spouse Jesus:

"You do not have the power to make any decision against me, and you would not be able to do it, if this power had not been granted to you from above[79] *[silence]* you, wretch, you pass a sentence against me, and then a sentence will be passed against you *[silence]* you passed a death sentence against the Son of the living God, so that he would carry his cross."

Then she knelt down and said:

"Yes, my God, he passes a sentence against the Son of the living God so that he will take death upon himself, and the death of the cross."

After speaking these words, she kept silent for a long while. During this time, with some scattered words she showed that she was seeing the cross being made. And a bit later she stood up again and signified with her hands and arms that she took up the cross and put it on her shoulders. And it was the thirteenth hour. And she carried it for a half-hour walking back to where she had come from. Along the way she suffered very much because sometimes we saw that she was being pushed forward with such a violence that she almost fell down. And sometimes she did fall down, but she showed that someone forced her to stand up with vehement blows. This was clear by her exterior acts, as we imagined it had been done to Jesus. So eloquent were this soul's gestures. Her face was pale and sorrowful, and she always walked with her eyes downcast. She often sighed howling and shaking with such a great pain and sorrow that she moved us to a great devotion and compassion. Her pain could have moved even a stone to pity. And as far as we are concerned, we had the impression that we were, so to speak, at the time of Jesus' passion because with a great accuracy and precision she did everything that had occurred to Jesus during his passion, according to what the holy gospels say. Along the way she only spoke twice, quoting two sentences from the Bible, that is: *"Sicut ovis ad occisionem ductus est, et dum male tractaretur non aperuit os suum*[80] *[silence] Vere languores nostros ipse tulit et dolores nostros ipse portavit."*[81]

She also made the gesture of being helped by Simon from Cyrene as Jesus was, when he met his mother. It was then that he fell down, and when he turned to the women and said that they should not cry for him, and she herself said the same words turning back slightly:

"Filie Hierusalem nolite flere super me sed super vos ipsas flete, et super filios vestros,[82] *etc."*

Finally, after having carried the cross on her shoulders for half an hour, as we have said above, she went to the oratory of the novices, that for her was the Calvary. It was the fifteenth and thirty minutes. And the rest of the hour, that is, until the sixteenth hour, she prayed to the eternal Father. But her voice was so low that the rare words she uttered were not understandable. We understood something by some broken words that we heard. She prayed in the person of Jesus, offering himself up to the eternal Father for all of humanity; and everything he had accomplished during his pilgrimage of thirty-three years down here among us.[83]

When she finished her prayer, she stood up and indicated that she was being undressed; then she lay down on the floor in a corner of the oratory. After a short pause, she showed that her feet were being pierced by stamping them on the ground, shaking her body violently, sighing and quivering internally. She did this with both hands. It is important to note that, as soon as she made that gesture that her hands or feet were being pierced, the nerves of that member became tense like an old and dry piece of wood. And after staying like this for about fifteen minutes, she stood up and leaned against the wall still keeping her hands and feet as they had been nailed to the cross. She stayed in this position for two hours, from the sixteenth hour until the eighteenth, exactly when she had entered a rapture the previous Thursday. During that time she did not speak at all, except for the seven words that Jesus spoke on the cross, having long pauses between each word.

During these two hours she apparently suffered very much. In this mystery of the passion her face was always very red and burning, whereas when Jesus let her participate in his passion her face was so pale and ashen that she looked dead.[84] At the end of her rapture we asked where this difference came from. She answered saying that last time she did not feel any afflictive pain, but a kind of consumption and discouragement as if she was going to faint. This time, instead, she had suffered much more, because she felt a much more violent and afflictive pain that "if I had continued just a little bit more," she said, "I wouldn't have been able to tolerate it." She also told us: "But since Jesus saw my frailty, he made it three hours shorter, that is, until the twenty-first hour." She suffered through the entire passion, but she anticipated every mystery a little bit, so that at the end the whole passion lasted three hours, that is, from the eighteenth hour until the twenty-first, when Jesus passed away. And indeed, as we have said, she came out of her rapture at the eighteenth hour. She had a hard time recovering from it because she felt so numb and her poor body was so tired, worn out, and exhausted that she could not get over it. And because we wanted her to go rest and relax for a little bit, we did not have order that night. However, as usual her meal was nothing but a bit of bread and water.

And for everything let us praise, honor, and glorify the bestower of every grace, Jesus our Spouse.

Selection from

Revelations
and Knowledge

Revelations and Knowledge

(p. 175)

Rapture with no speech until the twenty-third hour at night.

On the Wednesday of the eighth week of the Holy Spirit, the blessed soul entered a rapture again around the eleventh hour. During this rapture she did not speak at all, although we saw that she was suffering for she looked very sorrowful and engrossed, apart from the moment when, as usual, she receives the Holy Spirit. Indeed, at that point she became very happy and made gestures indicating that she was receiving it. And after a long while she became sorrowful and anguished again as before. As we said, she was in that way until the twenty-third hour at night, when she came out of this rapture and stayed with us a little bit, eating something and reciting her offices.

Notes to Introduction and Text

INTRODUCTION

1. Maria Maddalena de' Pazzi, *Renovatione della Chiesa* (Florence, 1966), p. 167.

2. Fr. Ermanno del S.S. Sacramento, "I manoscritti originali di Santa Maria Maddalena de' Pazzi" in *Ephemerides carmeliticae* 7 (1956): 386. My translation.

3. St. Augustine, *On Christian Doctrine*, 2.1, trans. D.W. Robertson, Jr. (New York: Macmillan, 1958), p. 34.

4. Ibid., 1.22 p. 18.

5. By stressing that the Word, as he is reported in the biblical texts, does not possess the physicality of human language, or of any language for that matter, I intend to put aside the intricate discussion concerning what Nicholas Wolterstorff defines "manifestational revelations" and "nonmanifestational revelations," the former meaning revelations communicated through "a natural sign of the actuality revealed"; the latter refer to revelations "in which the means is not a natural sign of the actuality revealed." Nicholas Wolterstorff, *Divine Discourse: Philosophical Reflections On The Claim That God Speaks* (New York: Oxford University Press, 1995), p. 28. The Word's request to the mystic is neither a *transitive* nor an *intransitive* revelation; that is, it is neither intended nor unintended, neither *manifesting* nor *nonmanifesting*. The Word articulates his request through the mystic's obsession. Maria Maddalena's physical torments perform both the Other's demand and her, the mystic's, attempt to respond to his very demand.

6. Michel De Certeau, *La fable mystique* (Paris: Gallimard, 1982), p. 105.

7. Pier Aldo Rovatti, *Abitare la distanza* (Milan: Feltrinelli, 1994), p. 102.

8. *Sermones super Cantica* 67.5 in *Sancti Bernardi Opera*, ed. Jean Leclercq (Rome: Editiones Cistercienses, 1958), pp. 191–92.

9. In his sermons Meister Eckhart had already underscored that

"God is a word that speaks itself. Wherever God is, he speaks this Word; wherever he is not, he does not speak. God is spoken and unspoken. The Father is a speaking work, and the Son is a speech working…all creatures want to utter God in all their works; they all come as close as they can in uttering him, and yet they cannot utter him…God is above names and above nature." Meister Eckhart, "German Sermon 53" in *The Essential Sermons, Commentaries, Treatises, and Defense*, trans. Edmund Colledge, O.S.A., and Bernard McGinn (New York: Paulist Press, 1981), p. 204.

God, says Meister Eckhart, is a word "that speaks itself" through his Son, the Word. However, Eckhart adds, the divine word is both "spoken and unspoken." What Meister Eckhart means is that God has a twofold relation to language. In order to exist, the Word's being must be "uttered" by the believer. However, man cannot express the Word. The Word is doomed to remain unexpressed.

10. Origen, *Comment. in Joan.* in *Opera Omnia*, Patrologia Greca, ed. DD.Caroli and Calori Vincentii Delarue, vol. 14 (Paris: D'Amboise, 1857), pp. 458–59.

11. Desire as "incompletion, an unfulfillment, an aspiration toward the still Unrealized" is a central aspect of Avicenna's angelology. Henry Corbin, *Avicenna and the Visionary Recital*, trans. Willard R. Trask (Princeton, N.J.: Princeton University Press, 1988), p. 71.

12. Thomas Aquinas, *Summa contra gentiles* in *Opera Omnia*, ed. Roberto Busa (Stuttgart: Friedrich Frommann Verlag, 1980), bk. 4.14, p. 121. See also Josef Pieper, "Ueber Das Innere Wort" in *Sinn und Form* 5 (1995): pp. 706–708.

13. Michel de Certeau, *Il parlare angelico* (Florence: Olschki, 1989), p. 203; Massimo Cacciari, *L'angelo necessario* (Milan: Adelphi, 1994), p. 53.

14. See Jn 1:1 and 1:14.

15. The saint asks God that in this second case her vision of his passion be secret, that is, that she suffer without saying anything (*Probation*, 2:48).

16. In *Sermones super Canticas* 39, pp. 4–6 (*Opera* 2:20–22), Bernard speaks of the devil and "his army." As the Jewish people defeated the army of the Pharaoh, so does the bride/soul defeat the army of the Enemy.

17. In *De Anima*, Aristotle first posits the essential relationship between image, *phantasia*, and word. Although the term *phantasia* has a number of meanings in Aristotle's texts, it is crucial to remember that in *De Anima* "*phantasia* is regarded as a necessary condition of thought ('there is no supposition without it', 427b15)." However, Aristotle also holds that "*phantasiai* are mere after-images of sense-perception, often false ones" (Dorothea Frede, "The Cognitive Role of *Phantasia*" in *Essays On Aristotle's De Anima*, eds. Martha C. Nussbaum and Amélie Oksenberg Rorty [New York: Oxford University Press, 1995], p. 280). If after-images, summoned by a given utterance, "can become mere appearances that drift in and out of our consciousness" (Frede, 285), we may infer that the pauses, inserted by the nuns/editors within the mystic's discourse, aim to dispel/annihilate those very after-images created by the edited text. In *The Dialogues* graphic pauses (dots in the original manuscripts) thus bring about mental, intellectual "pauses."

18. Radically different are the words that the devil yells at Margherita da Cortona (Lavinio, 1247–1297). In *Legenda de vita et miraculis beatae Margaritae de Cortona* we read: "he assaulted her yelling at her that her entire life was nothing but a deception and that her internal sweetnesses did not come from Jesus" ("*in eam repente irruit, et cum impetu dixit eidem, quod tota ejus vita nihil erat aliud quam deceptio, et quod illae non erant suavitates internae ab ipso Jesu,*" See Giovanni Pozzi and Claudio Leonardi, eds. *Scrittrici mistiche italiane* [Genoa: Marietti, 1989], p. 125). The devil and the mystic are two distinct interlocutors. The mystic does not express any doubt about her faith. It is the devil that, out of envy, attacks the woman with his direct, and thus less insidious, language.

19. Origen, *In Lucam Homilia*, Patrologia Greca (PG), ed. D.D. Caroli et Calori Vincentii Delarue, vol.13 (Paris: D'Amboise, 1857), 1808.

20. St. Teresa of Avila, *The Life of Saint Teresa of Avila by Herself*, Chapter 13 (London: Penguin, 1957), p. 89.

21. From Civilidade del Friuli, 1255–1292.

22. Pozzi and Leonardi, *Scrittrici mistiche italiane*, p. 189: "*Item eam quandoque capiebat et levabat et tam vehementer projciebat in terram… semel…erexit se contra eum, et capiens eum projecit sub pedibus suis et ponens pedem super collum ejus, coepit eum verecundis vituperare sermonibus.*"

23. St. Teresa of Avila, *Life*, Chapter 31, p. 223.

24. Michel de Certeau, *The Practice of Everyday Life*, trans. Steven F. Rendall (Berkeley, Calif.: University of California Press, 1984), p. 255.

25. Cf. Frances Bartkowski, *Travelers, Immigrants, Inmates* (Minneapolis: University of Minnesota Press, 1995). Particularly interesting is what Bartkowski says about the close relationship between wonder and shame: "Travel writing, immigrant autobiographies, and also concentration camp memoirs…provide a textual unfolding of the relation between wonder and shame. Each of these narratives forms shows writers differentially placed along this axis. How they are positioned is dependent on their relation to power and language as they move from place to place…" (89). Maria Maddalena shares these two basic feelings when she suddenly senses that she "does not belong there" anymore. She both sees her daily places as a new environment and suffers from the displacement that this feeling entails. Julia Kristeva speaks of the "mourning of the mother-tongue" in a paper concerning the relationship between immigrants and the foreign language of their new country. Kristeva examines how the loss of the mother tongue sometimes brings about physical and emotional ailments. *("En deuil d'une langue?"* in *Deuils. Vivre, c'est perdre*, eds. Nicole Czechowski and Claude Danziger [Paris: Autrement, 1992], pp. 27–36).

26. Maria Maddalena has a similar insight into her "baseness" in *The Forty Days*. On July 22, 1584, the Father had marked her heart with his seal. The same day the mystic has a "marvelous sight" of her nothingness and of her constant offences to the divinity (pp. 248–50).

27. See, for instance: Francesco Guazzo, *Compendium Maleficarum* trans. E.A. Ashwin (London: Rodker, 1929), pp. 98–104; Bartolomeo Sybilla, *Speculum peregrinarum quaestionum* (Florence, 1499), pp. 132–45; Girolamo Menghi, *Compendio dell'arte esorcistica* (Venice, 1605), pp. 41–46.

28. Cf. Jean-Luc Nancy, "Corpus" in *Thinking Bodies*, ed. Julien Flower MacCannel (Stanford, Calif.: Stanford University Press, 1994), pp. 17–31.

29. For an exhaustive study of blood in the Holy Scripture, see the entry "Sang" in *Dictionnaire de Spiritualité*.

30. In 1 Cor 10:16 Saint Paul states that: "The blessing cup that we bless is a communion with the blood of Christ."

31. Bynum reminds us that Catherine of Genoa, an Italian mystic of the fifteenth century, sees blood both as a drink and as cleansing water; blood is water and more than it. Caroline Walker Bynum, *Holy Feast and Holy Fast* (Berkeley Mass.: University of California Press, 1987), p. 185. Maria Maddalena seems to consider water only in its purifying element; she overlooks its other aspects. For instance, in the Bible water is often

connected to the Holy Spirit (Titus 3:5–6), and thus to divine grace. Water also as a divine instrument can bring death (Gn 6, 17; 7, 11–12, 17–24). In Maria Maddalena's raptures blood, much more than water or milk, becomes a complex symbol containing opposite meanings.

32. For instance, Angela of Foligno narrates a similar experience: *"Et tunc vocavit me et dixit mihi quod ego ponerem os meum in plagam lateris sui, et videbatur mihi quod ego viderem et biberem sanguinem eius fluentem recenter ex latere suo, et dabatur mihi intelligere quod in isto mundaret me."* Angela of Foligno, *Complete Works*, ed. Paul Lachance (New York: Paulist Press, 1993), pp. 142–44.

33. Gertrude of Helfta, *Spiritual Exercises*, trans. Gertrud Jaron Lewis and Jack Lewis (Kalamazoo, Mich.: Cistercian Publications,1989), p. 43.

34. Bynum, *Holy Feast*, p. 65.

35. In her poem "Love's Seven Names," the thirteenth-century mystic Hadewijch uses the image of two lovers, God and the soul, kissing each other, as if they were sucking each other's blood:

> "When he takes possession of the loved soul in every way,
> Love drinks in these kisses and tastes them to the end.
> As soon as Love thus touches the soul,
> She eats its flesh and drinks its blood."

Hadewijch, *The Complete Works*, trans. Mother Columba Hart, O.S.B. (New York: Paulist Press, 1980), p. 355.

36. "When they [women] are pregnant, the foetus draws its nourishment from the mother's blood vessels. However, the veins situated in this region [the mother's womb] are so large and long that they can feed the foetus and still accumulate something superfluous. During the time of her pregnancy, the mother's blood, stored in these vessels which are also repositories of food for the foetus, enlarges its vessels to a great degree. Blood overflows, so to speak, from these vessels and thus looks for an area where it can go. It only finds the breast." I refer to the following edition of Galen's texts: Galenus, *Utilité des parties du corps.* in *Oeuvres anatomiques, physiologiques et médicales de Galien*, trans. C. Daremberg (Paris, 1854), p. 111. My translation.

37. The theme of the soul's nothingness plays a crucial role in Marguerite Porete's mysticism. In *The Mirror of Simple Souls* we read: "she [the soul] understands that neither she nor any other understands the nothingness of her horrible sins and faults, compared to what is in the knowledge

of God about them. Such a Soul, says Love, has retained no will, but instead has arrived at and fallen into willing nothing and the certain knowledge of knowing nothing." Marguerite Porete, *The Mirror of Simple Souls*, trans. Ellen L. Babinsky (New York: Paulist Press, 1993), p. 126.

38. For the following see: Bernardo Bellini, Gaetano Codogni, Antonio Mainardi, *Vocabolario Universale della lingua italiana* (Mantua, 1853).

39. "And when she looked at it, the mother felt so happy, that she died." Masuccio Salernitano, *Novellino* (Florence, 1572), 5:4.

40. "He was a blacksmith, who practiced his skill all the time, without observing Sunday, Easter, or any other festivity;" Ibid., 6:1.

41. "One can see that every other game is either a part or a constituent of soccer, and that every game depends on it, whereas it [soccer] does not depend on any other game and it represents the fundamental and general master of every game." Giovanni de' Bardi, *Discorso del Gioco del Calcio* (Florence, 1678), p. 9.

42. In *Le rime* LI 4 ("*Non mi poriano già mai fare ammenda/del lor gran fallo gli occhi miei sed elli/ non s'accecasser, poi la Garisenda/torre miraro co' risguardi belli*"), Dante Alighieri uses the word *risguardo* in the sense of "*torre del bello sguardo, da cui si gode un' ampia vista*" (tower from which one has a beautiful view). This sense of the word *risguardo* is very similar to the French *beauregard*.

43. See Loarte's *Instrutione et avertimenti* 79 and 83, respectively.

44. Origen, *An Explanation to Martyrdom. Prayer and Selected Works*, trans. Rowan A. Grean (New York: Paulist Press, 1979), p. 220.

45. See Alois Haas, "Johannes Tauler" in *Sermo Mysticus*, (Freiburg, 1979), pp. 255–95. See also the interesting introduction to the English translation by Josef Schmidt: Johannes Tauler, *Sermons* (New York: Paulist Press, 1985), pp. 1–34.

46. Haas studies this theme in *Nim Din Selbes War. Studien zur Lehre von der Selbsterkenntnis bei Meister Eckhart, Johannes Tauler and Heinrich Seuse* (Freiburg, 1971), pp. 127–28.

47. Johannes Tauler, *Sermons*, trans. Josef Schmidt (New York: Paulist Press, 1985), p. 47.

48. "In this abandonment the Father communicated himself to me, for the sake of every soul."

49. "God, you tested me and understood me."

50. "In the abandonment I made in you."

51. "In this abandonment he hid my face."

52. " In this abandonment he guarded my heart."

53. "In this abandonment he elevated and enlightened my mind and my will."

54. "In this abandonment he enlightened my eyes."

55. In vision 48 the saint has a similar attitude toward the Word's corpse. In the choir of the chapel, she sets the burial of the Son. As a sort of farewell, she mentions single parts of his body before it is buried.

56. When Maria Maddalena directly uses the term *specchio* ("mirror"), she interprets it according to the mystical tradition. In the *Probation* (I:234), an angel, who had been sent by God to purify her body, engraves three mirrors in her intellect: First is his purity; second is her communication with him; third is the charity of all blessed souls. In *The Forty Days* (124), the saint says that Christ's wounds are mirrors in which creatures can reflect themselves. In the same book, Maria Maddalena compares the eyes of the Virgin Mary to two mirrors in which the creatures can reflect themselves.

When she marries the Word (vision 39 in *The Dialogues*), Maria Maddalena receives a ring that is similar to a mirror. In this mirror the mystic first sees her Spouse resting in his Father's bosom; then she sees him resting in his mother's bosom; later, she perceives the Word's infinite love; finally, she sees Mary's purity and Saint Catherine's and Saint Augustine's generosity (22–25).

57. In another letter (1 Cor 13:12) Paul states: "Now we are seeing a dim reflection in a mirror; but then we shall be seeing face to face."

58. The mirror plays a central role also in Sufism. It is associated with the polished reflection that occurs at mystical union. Michael Sells, *Mystical Languages of Unsaying* (Chicago: University of Chicago Press, 1994), pp. 63–89.

59. Hadewijch, *The Complete Works*, p. 136.

60. Gertrude of Helfta, *The Herald of Divine Love*, trans. Margaret Winkworth (New York: Paulist Press, 1993), p. 210.

61. Porete, *The Mirror of Simple Souls*, p. 69.

62. Although one might interpret the term *spirare* as *respirare* (to breathe), this is not how the saint intends it. In fact, we shall see that she distinguishes between *spirare* and *respirare*. The latter plays a role in establishing divine peace which is "started" by the act of spirare. From a theological standpoint, the presence of three Persons in each other is called circumincession, which is based on John 10:38: "the Father is in me and I am in the Father." In *Summa Theologica*, Ia, q. 42, a. 5, Thomas states that circumincession is founded on three premises: essence, origin, relationship. First, the three divine Persons are identical with regard to nature; second, the Trinity has the same origin. The Father generates the Son by speaking to himself, but his Son is nothing else but his own nature. The Word, generated in the

Spirit, is in the Spirit and the Spirit is in him; third, although the three Persons have different roles, they could not subsist one without the others. See the entry "Circuminsession" in *Dictionnaire de Théologie Catholique*, ed. A. Vacant and E. Mangenot (Paris, 1910).

63. Bernard of Clairvaux, *On the Song of Songs*, trans. Irene Edmonds (Kalamazoo, Mich.: Cistercian Publications, 1980), 74, pp. 5–6.

64. Simone Weil, *On Science, Necessity, and the Love of God*, trans. Richard Rees (London: Oxford University Press, 1968), p. 153.

65. Simone Weil, *Waiting For God*, trans. Emma Craufurd (New York: Harper, 1973), p. 121.

66. Jacques Lacan, *Ecrits*, trans. Alan Sheridan (New York, W.W. Norton), pp. 292–325.

67. Ibid., p. 155.

68. Language springs from a sudden awareness of "being without" or being deprived of own's one soul. "The speaking being," Lacan holds, "spends its time speaking to no purpose" (Lacan, *Ecrits*, p. 157). Instead of saying "to no purpose," it would be more correct to say that the speaking subject spends her time speaking to "a nonpurpose." In his "audition" at Ostia, Augustine describes a similar experience (cf. *Confessions* IX).

69. St. Augustine, *Confessions*, trans. Henry Chadwick, bk. 10.20.29 (New York: Oxford University Press, 1991), pp. 196–97.

70. Hannah Arendt offers an insightful interpretation of this passage in *Love and Saint Augustine* (Chicago: University of Chicago Press, 1996), p. 47.

71. St. Augustine, *Confessions*, bk. 10.21.30, p. 200.

72. Cf. Weil, *Waiting For God*: "God created through love and for love. God did not create anything except love itself, and the means to love. He created love in all its forms. He created beings capable of love from all possible distances. Because no other could do it, he himself went to the greatest possible distance, the infinite distance. This infinite distance between God and God, this supreme tearing apart, this agony beyond all others, this marvel of love, is the crucifixion...This tearing apart, over which supreme love places the bond of supreme union, echoes perpetually across the universe...This the Word of God." (pp. 123–24).

THE FORTY DAYS

1. In some passages of *Forty Days*, Maria Maddalena dictates the content of her visions to her sisters. However, in other cases the nuns take

over and report the mystic's words "live." Thus, the manuscript has a peculiar style, constantly switching from the first to the third person.

2. Ps16:15: "I will be rewarded, I will be rewarded, when your glory shall have appeared."

3. Prv 8:31: "[I was by his side...] delighting to be with the son of men."

4. *The Forty Days*, 116–19. The *thalamus* is the bridal chamber; see Ps 18:6.

5. The mystic "absorbs" Christ's suffering by "sucking" it into her soul.

6. Ps 83:3. "*In Porticum Salomonis*" is not part of this verse: "My heart and my flesh sing for joy to the living God."

7. The editors of the modern edition have erased the last name *Bagnesi* which follows the first name *Maria*.

8. Lk 17:15: "*Et ait illis, desiderio desideravi hoc pascha manducare vobiscum antequam patiar.*" [I have longed to eat this passover with you before I suffer.]

9. In the original this sentence concludes with "*e si fa l'A maiuscola perché s'intenda*" (and we capitalize the *A* in order to make it clear). The transcribers probably mean that by using the capital *a* they signify a pause in the mystic's discourse. However, they are not consistent in their method, in that to indicate a pause sometimes they use a period, sometimes a comma, sometimes a sequence such as "love love Love," the last "Love" with capital *L (A)* signifying that it has been pronounced after a pause. Moreover, "Love" *(Amore)* also means the concept of love whereas "love" *(amore)* is the actual love Christ has for the creatures. The transcribers' rendition of this variety of meanings exclusively through one graphic mark (the capital *L*) renders the reading quite obscure. In our translation we prefer to allude to a silence by simply introducing a period or a semicolon, according to the rhythm of the original sentence.

10. Jn 19:28: "*Postea sciens Iesus quia omnia consummata sunt, ut consummaretur Scriptura, dixit: 'Sitio.'*" [After this, Jesus knew that everything had now been completed, and to fulfil the scripture perfectly he said: "I am thirsty."]

11. The term *beginning* seems to refer both to the beginning of her vision and to the beginning of the creation.

12. I translate in English the mystic's half-Italian, half-Latin expression "*Panem nostro quotidianum.*"

13. Ps 128:3: "Ploughmen have ploughed on my back."

14. Lk 23:15.

15. Jn 15:17. *"Sicut dilexi vos"* is not part of the same biblical sentence.

16. Mal 3:6. The actual verse is *"Ego enim Dominus, et non mutor."*

17. Ps 44:3: "Of all men you are the most handsome."

18. Dn 7:10. The actual biblical source is: *"Millia millium ministrabant ei, et decies millies centena assistebant ei."* [A thousand thousand waited on him,/ ten thousand times ten thousand stood before him.]

19. Ps 99:3: "He made us and we belong to him."

20. Mt 19:27. [Then Peter spoke. "What about us?" he said to him. "We have left everything and followed you."]

21. Ps 103:24: "You arrang[ed] everything wisely."

22. Ps 85:1. The biblical verse is *"Inclina Domine aurem tuam et exaudi me."* [Listen to me, Lord, and answer me.]

23. Ps 132:1: "How good, how delightful it is/for all to live together like brothers."

24. The mystic seems to interpret the term *unum* as the Italian *uno,* that is, "one," "one person," whereas *unum* indicates the unity of a group of brothers under the same divinity.

25. Phil 2, 2:7: *"semetipsum exinanivit forma servi accipiens."* [emptied himself/to assume the condition of a slave].

26. The meaning of this exclamations is not clear. *"Satiati, hora satiati"* could be a past participle and refer to Judas, who feels satisfied because he believes that, by kissing him, he has succeeded in deceiving Jesus. The expression is repeated several times later. It refers to the entire Jewish people and to the soldiers who have executed Jesus. This is why the mystic uses the plural form.

27. The second part of this sentence does not have a first clause, even though it is quite possible to hypothesize something like "And we also understood that she was seeing."

28. Rv 19:16. *Deus Deorum* is not part of the actual verse.

29. Lk 23:3.

30. Jn 18:36.

31. Ps 71:1: "God, give your own justice to the king..."

32. Ps 48:13: "Man when he prospers forfeits intelligence:/he is one with the cattle doomed to slaughter."

33. Ps 90:10: "No disaster can overtake you,/no plague come near your tent."

34. These words are a quotation from the monastic ritual and are pronounced at the moment of the nun's profession of faith: "God puts on me a wreath out of gold."

35. Ps 21:7: "The reproach of men, the outcast of the people."

36. Jn 19:15: "Take him away, take him away; crucify him."

37. *Tolo* means "I take away."

38. The mystic gives a free interpretation of the biblical sentence. *Eum* means "him" (male direct object) and thus cannot mean "it" (sin).

39. Mt 21:9: "Blessed is he who comes in the name of the Lord."

40. Ps 13:3: "There is no one who does good; not even one."

41. Jn 11:50. The correct quotation would be: *"Expedit vobis ut unus moriatur homo pro populo."* [You fail to see that it is better for one man to die for the people.]

42. Ps 22:1.

43. Ps 101:8. The first part of the verse is *"Vigilavi et factus sum…"* [I stay awake, lamenting/like a lone bird on the roof].

44. Phil 2:8. The actual sentence is *"Humiliavit semetipsum factus obediens usque ad mortem."* [Maria Maddalena says: Christ was obedient until death; even the death of the cross.]

45. *Not so far* translates the Italian *"un po' più presso."* The sense of this expression becomes clear if we relate it to the following sentence. Maria Maddalena thinks that the soldiers have pierced the Savior's body stretching it too much, and thus making him suffer even more.

46. Dt 32:11: *"Sicut aquila provocans ad volandos pullos suos, et super eos volitans, expandit alas suas…"* [Like an eagle watching its nest,/hovering over its young,/he spreads out his wings…]

47. Sg 8:6: "Set me like a seal on your heart."

48. The editors of the sole modern edition of Maria Maddalena's visions have clearly misinterpreted this passage. They have erased the second *never* that refers to the sinful creatures *("non fussi ancor nate");* the editors have eliminated the parallelism between the mystic and the human kind, both sinners before God.

THE DIALOGUES

Dialogue 36: Participation in Jesus' Passion

1. The original version is *"e fece questo o quell'altro ratto."* *Altro ratto* must be read as *altro atto* (other act).

2. Jn 3:16: "God loved the world so much that he gave his only Son." What follows is not in Scripture: "And he loved Mary and did not make [things] known about all matters."

3. "And because I was humble, I pleased you."

4. The two Latin sentences seem to express two different subjects. The first is uttered in the name of the Father: "I have chosen her with you"; the second is articulated by the mystic herself, who describes that "you," the Word or the Father, has confirmed the Virgin as the chosen one.

5. Cf. Lk 2:19: "*Maria autem conservabat omnia verba haec, conferens in corde suo.*" Maria Maddalena says: "pondering them in your heart."

6. "Humanate" is the direct, and technical, translation of the Italian *umanato*. Both terms are very rarely used today.

7. 120:4: "*Ecce non dormitavit neque dormiet qui custodit Israel.*" [The guardian of Israel does not doze or sleep.]

8. Ps 74:3: "At the moment I decide I will dispense strict justice."

9. "And those falling prostrate worshiped her and said: She is suitable to receive the right hand of God's power."

10. Ps 109:1: "*Dixit 'Dominus Domino meo: Sede a dextris meis.'*" [The Lord said to my lord, "Sit at my right hand."]

11. "I think thoughts."

12. The meaning of this Latin sentence is that her soul understood the fact that the Word makes his beloved suffer for him so that she can be more joyful in heaven. When the mystic understands this point, she participates in the Word's project.

13. Lk 22:15: "I desired with desire."

14. "The scriptures will be fulfilled."

15. Maria Maddalena means *eructavit cor meum humilitatem*, a variation of *eructavit cor meum verbum bonum*.

16. "[He] established her in the humbleness of rejection."

17. Lk 18:14: "He who humbles himself will be exalted, and he who exalts himself will be humbled."

18. Cf. Jn 13:8: "You shall not wash my feet forever."

19. Jn 13:8: "If I do not wash you, you can have nothing in common with me."

20. "And I accepted his clothes."

21. Instead of *vorrei a te* (I would like to you), I believe that we must read *verrei a te* (I would come to you).

22. "Faith suffices by itself."

23. "So great a sacrament." From the Hymn for Vespers of the Feast of Corpus Christi.

24. Cf. Ps 149:9: "*et miserationes eius super omnia opera sua.*"

25. Ps 110:4–5: "God is merciful and tenderhearted; he provides food for those who fear him."

26. 1 Cor 11:24: "Do this in memory of me."

27. Sg 5:10: "My beloved is fresh and ruddy."

28. Ps 44:3: "Of all men [he is] the most handsome."

29. Ps 72:1: "Chosen from thousands."

30. Ps 44:3: "Your lips are moist with grace."

31. "Open my heart so that it lead the whole creature to communion with your body and your blood."

32. Ps 72:1: "God is indeed good to Israel."

33. Jn 14:6.

34. The literal translation of this clause ("*non sei accettatore di persone*") would be: "you do not accept people."

35. Jn 12:26: "*et ubi sum ego, illic et minister meus erit,*" that is, "Where I am, my minister will be."

36. Phil 2:10: "All beings in the heavens, on earth and in the underworld, should bend the knee at the name of Jesus."

37. Cf. Jn 17:1: "*Pater veni hora, clarifica filium tuum, ut filius tuus clarificet te;*" Jn 17:4: "*Ego te clarificavi super terram.*"

38. "[He] comes from God and goes to God."

39. Ps 36:30: "The mouth of the virtuous man murmurs wisdom."

40. Maria Maddalena blends Italian with Latin. The sentence means: "And [he] placed my soul in the words of my Word."

41. Cf. Jn 16:16: "*Modicum, et iam non videbitis me.*" [In a short time you will no longer see me.]

42. Jn 17:3: "*Haec est autem vita aeterna: Ut cognoscant te, solum Deum verum, et quem misisti Iesum Christum.*"

43. Mt 26:38.

44. Mt 26:41.

45. Mt 26:39.

46. Lk 22:42.

47. Ps 39:13: "My courage is running out."

48. Ps 2:7.

49. Mt 26:50.

50. Mt 5:9: "Happy the peacemakers: they shall be called sons of God."

51. "Who are you looking for?"

52. Cf. Jn 18:4–5.

53. Cf. Mt 26:55: "*In illa hora dixit Iesu turbis: Tamquam ad latronem existis cum gladiis, et fustibus comprehendere me.*" Maria Maddalena: "You came to me as if I were a thief."

54. The mystic has modified the first clause of her sentence.

55. Ps 62:4: "These double-talkers have been in error since their birth."

56. "They followed the wrong path and did not know it."

57. "And they bowed down and praised the Word's hands saying: these are able to receive power in every place of his Father's domination."

58. 1 Cor 4:4: "My conscience does not reproach me at all, but that does not prove that I am acquitted."

59. Cf. Ps 118:135: "*Faciem tuam illumina super servum tuum.*" [Make your face shine upon your servants.]

60. Lam 1:2: "She passes her nights weeping; the tears run down her cheeks."

61. "and the face of the virgin becomes dark."

62. Is 50:6: "I did not cover my face against insult and spittle."

63. Ps 17:27: "With perversion you will pervert."

64. Ps 87:10: "My eyes are worn out with suffering."

65. "And they bowed down and venerated my Spouse's eyes saying: these are able to receive the vision of the divinity in his eternal participation." This sentence has a rather incorrect syntax.

66. The meaning of this sentence is unclear. *Crazy (pazzo)* could refer either to those who want to arrest Christ or to Christ himself, considered "crazy" by his accusers.

67. Ps 24:15: "My eyes are always on God, for he releases my feet from the net."

68. Cf. Ps 40:3: "*Quoniam ipse liberavit me de laqueo venantium, et a verbo aspero.*"

69. Ps 140:3–4: "God, set a guard at my mouth, / a watcher at the gate of my lips. / Let me feel no impulse to do wrong, to share the godlessness of evildoers."

70. Instead of "they condemn it" the original version has "they condemn them." The inconsistency is probably due to a phonetic assimilation ("*con le operatione le condannano*").

71. Ps 118:66: "Teach me good sense and knowledge."

72. Cf. Rom 11:33: "*O altitudo divitiarum sapientiae, et scientiae Dei: quam incomprehensibilia sunt iudicia eius, et investigabiles viae eius!*" Maria Maddalena's Latin sentence probably means: "how rich are the depths of God—how deep his wisdom and knowledge—and how impossible to fathom for all flesh."

73. Sg 1:3.

74. Jn 18:36.

75. Ps 108:17: "[The wretch] hounded the poor, the needy and the brokenhearted to death."

76. "Lands of God, the King."

77. "Truth comes from the Father through me." However, it is possible that the mystic pronounces *per me* in its Italian meaning ("for me").

78. Ps 3:2: "More and more are turning against me."

79. The mystic speaks both as Pilate and as herself.

80. Lk 7:7.

81. Jn 19:6.

82. Maria Maddalena's *impeccabile* ("impeccable") is strictly related to the word *peccato* ("sin"). In this context *impeccable* means both "sinless" and "unable to sin." The latter connotation is Maria Maddalena's.

83. 1 Sm 2:6.

84. Cf. 1 Tm 6:15; Ps 49:1.

85. Ps 128:3: "Sinners have ploughed iniquities on my back."

86. Jn 14:2: "There are many rooms in my Father's house."

87. Ps 72:14: *Et fui flagellatus tota die, et castigatio mea in matutinis.* [I am plagued all the day long and disciplined every morning.]

88. "They gathered and scourged you."

89. Cf. 116:5: "*Considerabam ad dexteram, et videbam: et non erat qui cognosceret me.*"

90. "They scourged your body, so that your members could be consoled." *Fr* instead of *fl* in *flagellaverunt* is a dialectism.

91. Ps 90:11: "He will put you in his angels' charge to guard you wherever you go."

92. "He thus worked for our redemption." This sentence results from an incorrect assimilation of the two clauses of the previous biblical quotation.

93. Ps 26:4.

94. The whole sentence means: "One thing I ask of God, one thing I seek, that I be able to free the body of my Church from its scourges."

95. Cf. Ps 12:2: "*Quamdiu ponam consilia in anima mea, dolorem in corde meo per diem?*" [How much longer must I endure grief in my soul, and sorrow in my heart by day?]

96. Mk 15:19: "They struck his head with a reed."

97. Jn 19:14.

98. Mt 21:9.

99. Jn 19:6.

100. "I told you in the beginning."

101. Cf. Is 53:7: "*Oblatus est quia ipse voluit, et non aperuit os suum: sicut ovis ad occisionem ducetur.*" [Like a lamb taken to the slaughterhouse, he did not open his mouth.]

102. Lk 23:28: "Daughters of Jerusalem, do not weep for me; weep rather for yourself."

103. Cf. Lk 23:34: "*Pater, dimitte illis: non enim sciunt quid faciunt.*" The whole sentence means: "Father, forgive them; they do not what they are doing to your Word, who deigned to share his pain with me."

104. Lk 23:43.

105. Jn 19:26–27.

106. Cf. Mt 27:46: "*Eli, Eli, lamma sabacthani.*"

107. Jn 19:28: "I am thirsty."

108. Lk 23:46.

109. Jn 19:30.

110. Ibid.

Dialogue 39: Marriage to Jesus

1. For a description of this ritual, see *Regola e statuti delle monache di Santa Maria delli Angeli di Fiorenza* (Florence, 1564), 12r.

2. The mystic interprets a verse from Ps 64:3: "*Circumdederunt me doloris mortis: et pericula inferni invenerunt me.*" [Death's cords were tightening round me, the nooses of Sheol; distress and anguish gripped me.]

3. "They turn to vanity and fall into iniquity; they turn to the heights and fall into a deep abyss."

4. "Who curses your name cannot live in your house [*silence*] I consumed their iniquities, and the sorrows of hell tightened round me. His soul descended upon me, and came to you."

5. "And I abandoned myself to your generosity."

6. Ps 89:12: "The slanderer not hold his own on earth."

7. Ps 52:4. The actual verses are: "*Omnes declinaverunt, simul inutiles facti sunt:/non est qui faciat bonum, non est usque ad unum.*" [All have turned aside,/all alike are tainted/There is not one good man left,/not a single one.]

8. Cf. Ps 35:4: "*Noluit intelligere ut bene ageret.*" Maria Maddalena combines two clauses in the past in Latin with a quotation from a psalm that she has adopted to the syntax of the previous clauses. This sentence

means: "Everybody has rejected you, and has not known you, and does not want to understand what he needs to realize the good."

9. Ps 48:15: "Death will devour them."

10. Ps 68:28: "Charge them with crime after crime."

11. 2 Tm 2:5: "*Non coronatur nisi legitime certaverit.*" [He cannot win any crown unless he has truly fought.]

12. Cf. Ps 95:1: "*Cantate Domino canticum novum.*"

13. Ps 46:2.

14. Jn 1:14.

15. Ps 82:1: "*Ecce quam bonum, et quam iucundum habitare fratres in unum.*" [How good, how delightful it is for all to live together like brothers.]

16. "He married me with the sweet kindness and generosity of his love, in union with the holy Trinity."

17. Gal 2:20: "*Vivo autem, iam non ego: vivit vero in me Christus.*"

18. Ps 44:2.

19. Sg 4:12.

20. Ps 15:1: "*Conserva me Domine, quoniam speravi in te.*"

21. The whole sentence, quotation plus clause in Latin, means: "Look after me, God, because my innocence regenerated me in your blood."

22. Cf. Is 6:1: "*Vidi Dominum sedentem super solium excelsum et elevatum.*" [I saw the Lord seated on a high throne.]

Dialogue 43: The Regeneration of the Church

1. Ex 3:14. The whole sentence means: "I live but I do not live in myself; my flesh lives in the Word and in the blood of the union of my Spouse."

2. "And he took me out of the shadow of death and took my soul to the breadth of human regeneration."

3. Jn 14:15.

4. From the Preface to the Roman Mass.

5. Whip or scourge used for religious penance.

6. Phil 2:10: "In the heavens, on earth and in the underworld, should bend the knee at the name of Jesus."

7. I offer to my Spouse his chosen [spouses].

8. "The desire for your souls consumes me."

9. Ps 21:7: "I am more a worm than a man."

10. Lk 21:19: "Your endurance will win you your lives."

11. Mt 5:6.

12. "Lord, look after me, because my soul burned longing for [your] souls."

13. "My Word, I placed myself in that desire he himself had in his humanity." Instead of "*collocavit*" I read "*collocavi*."

14. "I guarded the desire that my Word gave me, because if he does not find any capability in me, at least he will find that desire."

15. Ps 136:8: "A blessing on him who takes and dashes their babies against the rocks."

16. Ps 113:1.

17. Ps 136:1.

18. Ps 116:5.

19. "I looked on on my right side and saw, and no one was able to satiate the desire of my soul."

20. Ps 128:3.

21. "They have ploughed on my back a desire for the salvation of every believer in my Word."

22. "When I was a young girl I was pleasing to the Most High." From a Responsory for Matins of Feasts of the Blessed Virgins.

23. Cf. Am 6:13: "*[C]onvertistis in amaritudinem iudicium, et fructum iustitiae in absinthium.*" Maria Maddalena means: "Turn it into a foreign and bitter vine."

24. "In a future day iniquity will be dissolved." Antiphon from Lauds of the Vigil of the Nativity.

25. The mystic may mean: "I saw that his spouse's soul saw itself being taken away from your enemies."

26. "and some of your Christs being enlightened."

27. Sg 2:6: "His right hand will embrace me."

28. "We aspire to the salvation of every believer's soul."

29. 1 Jn 2:1.

30. "Everything for everything, and everything in this itself."

31. Ps 113:4: "The mountains skipped like rams, and like lambs, the hills."

32. Ps 118:25: "Down in the dust I lie prostrate: revive me as your word has guaranteed."

33. Cf. 1 Jn 1:8.

34. 2 Tm 2:5: "He cannot win any crown unless he has truly fought."

35. Ps 79:15: "Look down from heaven and see."

36. Ps 13:2–3: "All have turned aside; there is no one good man left."

37. Ps 83:11: "I have chosen to be a castaway in your house."

38. Ps 41:2. The whole sentence means: "As a doe longs for running streams, so longs my soul for your generosity in the communication of your spouse to every believer."

39. Maria Maddalena probably refers to Queen Elizabeth of England. Jezebel, princess of Tyre, was a fervent worshiper of Baal and Asherah (1 Kgs 16:31–33; 18:4, 19:1–2). The name *Jezebel* is often used as a derogatory epithet for a woman.

40. Ps 67:1: "Let God arise, let his enemies be scattered, let those who hate him flee before him."

41. Ps 120:4: "The guardian of Israel does not doze or sleep."

42. The sentence probably means: "All those who love him give me joy."

43. Cf. Sg 1:3: "*Oleum effusum nomen tuum.*"

44. "They preferred to be cursed and their curse reaches them; they rejected blessedness and their blessing withdraws from them."

45. "In hell there is no redemption." An Antiphon from Matins of the Office of the Dead.

46. Cf. Is 6:1: "*[V]idi Dominum sedentem super solium excelsum* get *elevatum.*"

47. Ps 113:1: "Glorify your name."

48. Ps 98:7: "He talked to them in the pillar of the cloud."

49. "And the just will rejoice when he sees justice."

50. Cf. Mt 13:42: "*Et mittent eos in caminum ignis.*" Maria Maddalena means: "If they don't want to, he will throw them into the blazing furnace."

51. "By means of your spouse, great signs and prodigies occurred in the union of your Divinity."

52. "I saw Mary sitting on a small vessel."

53. Eccl 24:14–15: "From eternity, in the beginning, he created me, and for eternity I shall remain. I ministered before him in the holy tabernacle."

54. Instead of *conformavit* I read *conformavi*: "I conformed my will to the eternal Father's and to the Word's, whom I nourished and generated in my womb."

55. "Three children worshiped her."

56. "Twelve young girls worshiped her; thirty-three seniors proceeded her."

57. It is not clear what the mystic means with this sentence.

58. "I saw his spouse lie on her Spouse's chest and enjoy [it] and feel consoled."

59. Is 60:6: "Everyone in Sheba will come, bringing gold and incense and singing the praise of God."

60. Ps 63:8: "Man will draw near the deep heart and God will be exalted."

61. Ps 41:8: "Deep is calling to deep as your cataracts roar."

62. Ps 50:12.

63. Ps 144:19: "Let him make the will of those who fear him."

Dialogue 44: On the Humanity of the Word

1. Ps 30:2; Ps 70:1: "In you, God, I hoped; never let me be disgraced."

2. Ps 33:4: "Proclaim with me the greatness of God, and together let us extoll his name."

3. "And he tested me through his enemy."

4. Ps 117:14: "My strength and my praise, God."

5. Ps 33:2.

6. Ps 67:1: "Let God arise, and let his enemies be scattered."

7. Ps 118:25: "Down in the dust my soul lies prostrate: revive me as your word has guaranteed."

8. Ps 33:1: "I will bless God at all times, his praise shall be on my lips continually."

9. "I saw the Spirit moving from the Father and assisting the Word's humanity. And he himself granted him to us."

10. Ps 50:14: "Give me again the joy of your salvation, and strengthen me with your chief spirit."

11. Ps 59:7: "In union with your blood, so that your beloved will be rescued."

12. "He judges everything."

13. "I saw a throne in the sky and the Spirit moving down on earth and surrounding it."

14. The Italian *per* ("for") has a number of connotations. In this passage *per* means "for," "through," and "in name of." These different meanings are present in each segment of the mystic's monologue.

15. Ps 67:29. The whole sentence means: "Confirm what has been done through the generosity of your blood."

16. Cf. Ps 74:11: "*Et omnia cornua peccatorum confringam, et exaltabuntur cornua iusti.*" ["I will cut off the horns of the sinners and raise the horns of the virtuous."]

17. Mt 3:17.

18. Lk 11:20: "If it is through the finger of God that I cast out demons."

19. Ps 118:131: "I opened my mouth and drew the Spirit."

20. Ps 50:17: "God, open my lips and my mouth will speak out your praise."

21. Mt 28:20.

22. "He whom heaven could not contain you have carried in your lap." Responsary from Matins of Feasts of Blessed Virgin.

23. "Christ our God, the Sun of Justice." From the Offertory of Saturday Mass of Blessed Virgin.

24. Ps 17:27.

25. Cf. Jn 13:15: "*Exemplum enim dedi vobis, ut quemadmodum ego feci vobis, ita et vos faciatis.*"

26. Jn 15:5: "I am the vine, you are the branches. Whoever remains in me, with me in him, bears fruit in plenty."

27. The Italian verb *[ri]mane* (remains) echoes the previous Latin *manet*.

28. Ps 103:15.

29. Mt 26:38.

30. Lk 22:42.

31. Mt 26:39.

32. Cf. Heb 10:17: "*peccatorum et iniquitatum eorum iam non recordabor amplius.*"

33. Rom 5:3.

34. Jn 18:36.

35. Cf. Jn 1:47: "*Ecce vere Israelita, in quo dolus non est.*"

36. Cf. Ps 98:7: "*In columna nubis loquebatur ad eos.*" ["He talked with them in the pillar of cloud."]

37. "She is beautiful among the daughters of Jerusalem." Antiphon from Lauds of Office for Virgins.

38. Sg 2:13–14: "Come then, my love, my lovely one, come. My dove, hiding the clefts of the rock, in the coverts of the cliff."

39. Mt 25:34.

40. Ps 138:8: "If I climb the heavens, you are there, there too, if I lie in hell. If I flew to the point of sunrise, or westward across the sea, your hand would still be guiding me, your right hand holding me."

41. Sg 1:12: "My beloved is a sachet of myrrh lying between my breasts."

42. Ps 101:8.

43. "And he took me to his cave."

44. Ps 123:7: "[L]ike a bird escaped from the fowler's net."

Dialogue 45: An Inner Test

1. Mt 26:39: "[she] fell on her face."

2. Ps 39:13: "My heart has abandoned me."

3. The mystic means to say: "Then the Word's blood raised me."

4. "The Word abandoned me."

5. Cf. Ps 80:8: "*Probavi te apud aquam contradictionis.*"

6. "The Word was pleased by his spouse's annihilation."

7. Is 38:15: "I will reflect on you through all my years in the bitterness of my soul."

8. "And he plunged me in the depth of the sea."

9. Cf. Ps 81:8: "*Surge Domine in requiem tuam, tu et arca sanctificationis tuae.*"

10. Ps 142:7: "For the sake of your blood don't hide your face from me."

11. "Alleviate the crimes of your people." Response for Nones from Office for Season of Advent.

12. "I shall narrate my Word's qualit[ies], which are beauty, miracles, wisdom, science, power, eternity, impassability, union, and communication."

13. Ps 2:8: "Ask and I will give you the nations for your heritage."

14. Ps 48:5: "I turn my attention to a proverb."

15. Ps 44:3.

16. Cf. Ps 30:12–13: "*Qui videbant me, foras fugerunt a me: oblivioni datus sum, tamquam mortus a corde.*" [Those who see me in the street hurry past me; I am forgotten, as good as dead in their hearts.]

17. Cf. Phil 1:23: "*Desiderium habens dissolvi, et esse cum Christo.*"

18. Ps 77:36.

19. 2 Cor 11:26.

20. Ps 146:5.

21. "And his wisdom satiated me."

22. 1 Cor 4:10: "Here we are, fools for the sake of Christ, while you are the learned men in Christ."

23. Lk 12:49.

24. Jn 6:58–59.

25. "I have found nothing by myself."

26. Ps 139:12.

27. Mt 19:19; 22:39.

28. 1 Cor 6:20: "You are not your own property."

29. Cf. 2 Jn 1:5: *Et nunc rogo te domina, non tamquam mandatum novum scribens tibi, sed quod habuimus ab initio, ut diligamus alterutrum.*

30. Mt 5:6: "Happy those who hunger and thirst for justice."

31. Mt 5:7.

32. Ps 10:8.

33. Ps 23:1: "To God belong earth and all it holds, the world and all who live in it."

34. Ps 32:9: "He spoke, and it was created."

35. Dt 32:39: "It is I who deal death and life; when I have struck it is I who heal."

36. Cf. Mt 24:42: *"Vigilate ergo, quia nescitis qua hora Dominus vester venturus sit."*

37. Prv 8:31.

38. "I shall speak in parables."

39. Cf. Jn 1:3: *"Omnia per ipsum facta sunt."* [Through him all things came to be.]

40. Vespers Hymn for Feast of Corpus Christi.

41. Jn 3:16.

42. Cf. Jn 3:17: *"ut salvetur mundus per ipsum."*

43. Ps 110:4.

44. "Because purity is God and [he] loved purity."

45. Ps 132:1.

46. Ps 36:25: "I never saw a virtuous man deserted or his descendants forced to beg their bread."

47. Heb 9:11.

48. Jn 15:15.

49. Ps 36:16: "The little the virtuous possesses outweighs all the wealth of the wicked."

50. Cf. Sg 2:3: *"Sub umbra illius, quem desideraveram, sedi: et fructus eius dulcis gutturi meo."*

51. Cf. Is 6:1: *"Vidi Dominum sedentem super solium excelsum et elevatum."*

52. "Oh, all of you, admire those who love him in the communication of his majesty and goodness."

53. Cf. Ps 118:60: *"Paratus sum, et non sum turbatus: ut custodiam mandata tua."* Maria Maddalena means: "Free me from those who slander, so that I be able to preserve your commandments."

54. Is 40:1.

55. "Console, console that who did not deny his spouse's desire, in the communication of his elect."

56. Cf. Ps 29:7: *"Ego autem dixi in abundantia mea: Non movebor in aeternum."* Maria Maddalena's sentence means: "I said to you: 'Nothing can ever shake me.'"

57. Cf. Ps 118:57: *"Portio mea, Domine, dixi custodire legem tuam."* Maria Maddalena means: "You are my portion; I said I will keep your law."

58. Ps 130:1: "God, my heart has no lofty ambitions, my eyes do not look to high."

Dialogue 48: Jesus' Forty Hours in the Tomb

1. As the mystic will clarify later, although the Savior's body rests in the sepulcher for forty hours, his soul visits a number of "places."

2. "Father, I offer you for every creature the blood that the Only Begotten Son shed for the human redemption."

3. "Give me my Son and Spouse who was my consolation and in this hour is my affliction. He consoled me and made me sad."

4. "Whom the heavens cannot contain you carried in your lap." Responsory from Matins of Feasts of Blessed Virgin.

5. "Have faith, my daughter."

6. The transcribers refer to "dialogue" 46, in which the mystic held a long conversation with the Father. In that occasion, Maria Maddalena articulated two voices, the Father's and her own. *Dialogue* 46 revolves around the Father's role within the Trinity (*The Dialogue*, 2: 195–262).

7. Ps 110:4.

8. Ps 144:9: "His tenderness embraces all his creatures."

9. Mt 16:18: "You are Peter and upon this rock I will build my Church."

10. Mt 26:31: "I will strike the Shepherd and the sheep will be scattered."

11. "I saw the Word's soul place its spirit in the essence of the divinity, the powers of his ideas, for the sake of our souls."

12. "I shall guard everything in myself, and shall give my spirit."

13. "I shall not answer, and shall continue to speak to you in him [the Word]." Once again, the mystic contaminates Latin with Italian (*continuo loquor*).

14. This sentence does not have a main clause.

15. The transcribers mean: "what we have just mentioned according to what she indicated at that point."

16. "And he took me to a great and elevated place."

17. "I saw the Word's soul rest, place [himself], and expand in the Father's bosom."

18. "He placed their souls in hell and they lose the glory that the Word had prepared for them."

19. "And he killed each of them and placed them in the darkness and in the shadow of death."

20. "Because of the angels' pride he confounded the angelic nature, and because of the humility of the Word he exalted our humanity."

21. "And placed them in hell."

22. "And elevated our humanity through their confusion."

23. "It will no longer be known."

24. "I saw in him my glorification and that of every creature."

25. "Stand up, [he] rested and walked."

26. "And I didn't know it."

27. The second clause does not have a verb.

28. The parenthesis probably mean that the transcribers have added this clause.

29. "And two thousand million adorned the face of the Groom, the Lamb, and he placed thousands of thousand on his throne."

30. Cf Ps 118:135: "*Faciem tuam illumina super servum tuum.*"

31. Ps 47:2. The second part of the verse is: "*in civitate Dei nostri, in monte sancto eius.*"

32. "And an infinite crowd went against its God; and they did not want to understand his words; and he placed their souls in the abyss."

33. Wis 5:5.

34. Gal 2:20.

35. Ps 19:6: "In the evening, a spell of tears; in the morning, shouts of joy."

36. Phil 4:13: "There is nothing I cannot master with the help of that who gives me strength."

37. Cf. Ps 138:6: "*Confortata est, et non potero ad eam.*"

38. Lam 1:12: "All you who pass this way, look and see: is any sorrow like the sorrow that afflicts me?"

39. Ps 138:8: "If I ascend to heaven, you are there; if I descend to hell, you are present."

40. 2 Cor 12:3.

41. Ps 33:2.

42. Cf. Ps 20:3: "*Desiderium cordis eius tribuisti ei: et voluntate labiorum eius non fraudasti eum.*"

43. Cf. Ps 125:6: "*Venientes autem venient cum exultatione, portantes manipulos suos.*" [Those who come come with joy, bearing their sheaves.]

44. Parenthesis may signify that the transcribers have inserted these words later.

45. The Italian word *capacità* means both "capacity" and "capability." *Capacity* is closer to the meaning present in the mystic's discourse.

46. Jn 14:16: "I shall ask the Father to give you the Spirit of truth."

47. "They are worthy to receive the unity of your liberality, because you created them thanks to your liberality, and thanks to your immense liberality you recreated them."

48. Ps 88:2.

49. Cf. Ps 51:5: "*Dilexisti malitiam super benignitatem.*"

50. Cf. Ps 35:7: "*iudicia tua abyssus multa.*"

51. Cf. Gal 6:14: "*Mihi autem absit gloriari, nisi in cruce Domini nostri Iesu Christi: per quem mihi mundus crucifixus est, et ego mundo.*" [As for me, the only thing I can boast about is the cross of our Lord Jesus Christ, through whom the world is crucified to me, and I to the world.]

52. Ps 16:15.

53. Ps 132:1.

54. Mt 18:20.

55. Jn 4:55–57.

56. Ps 21:7.

57. Dt 4:24: "He is a consuming fire."

58. 1 Jn 4:8: "God is love and anyone who lives in love lives in God."

59. Cf. Sg 2:10: "*Surge, propera amica mea, columba mea, formosa mea, et veni.*" [Come then, my love, my dove, my lovely one, come.]

60. Jn 21:17.

61. Sg 4:7: "No stain is in you."

62. 2 Tm 2:5.

63. Mt 5:8: "Happy the pure in heart; they shall see God."

64. The Father's sentence is ironic and scornful at the same time.

65. "You understood correctly, spouse of my Only Begotten."

66. Ps 23:1.

67. Ps 49:1.

68. Rv 19:16.

69. Ps 35:10.

70. "From your face proceeds every splendor of your glory."

71. Ps 115:13: "I will take up the calice of salvation, invoking the name of God."

72. These prayers are all part of the Office for Compline.

73. "I have placed my heart in the soul of my spouse."

74. "Spouse of my Only Begotten, ask me what you wish."

75. This sentence does not have a main clause.

76. Cf. Ps 56:9: "*Exurge gloria mea, exurge psalterium et cithara: exurgam diluculo.*" [Awake, my muse, awake, lyre and harp, I mean to wake the Dawn!]

77. It is apparent that, whereas at the beginning of this section the Saint had addressed the Virgin, now she merges Mary with the "perfect soul" of her previous discourse.

78. Ps 56:9.

79. Ps 143:9: "I have made a song for you to be played on the ten-string lyre."

80. The manuscript reports *disiuntion*e, a term that does not exist in Italian.

81. The sentence's ambiguity is present in the original.

82. "He will descend to the depths of the earth and will lead me into the depths of the earth."

83. Ps 143:4: "His days, as fugitive as shadows."

84. Lk 1:52 and 48: "He put down the might from their seat and exalted the humble; he looked upon the humility of his handmaid."

Dialogue 50: An Ascension Rapture

1. Jn 17:1.

2. The meaning and the syntax of this sentence is obscure. The mystic probably means that "what dismayed" the spouse has been taken away from those people who have been enlightened through their dismay and thus do not need "it" any longer.

3. Jn 17:5: "Father, is time to glorify me with that glory I had with you before even the world was."

4. Ps 44:2: "Of all men you are the most handsome."

5. "My heart and my flesh expanded during the conversation between the Word and his mother Mary and his disciples."

6. Jn 15:15: "I have made known to you everything I have heard from my Father."

7. Eccl 7:40: "In everything you do, remember your end, and you will never sin."

8. Ps 45:4: "There is a river whose streams refresh the city of God, and it sanctifies the dwelling of the Most High."

9. Phil 4:13: "There is nothing I cannot master with the help of that who gives me strength."

10. Jb 17:3: "Set me alongside you, and let any man's hand fight against me."

11. Ps 50:11: "God, create a clean heart in me, put into me a constant spirit."

12. The mystic coins the verb *to abyss* (to throw into the abyss) and the past participle *abyssed (abissato)*. The thirteenth-century mystic, Angela da Foligno, also used this term.

13. Cf. Ps 115:2: "*Dirigatur oratio mea sicut incensum in conspectu tuo*." [Prayer rises like incense before you.]

14. Ps 115:12: "What return can I make to God for all his goodness to me?"

PROBATION
Volume One: Excerpts from the "Devil's Temptations"

1. "These spouses are under the Lamb's mantel."

Volume Two

1. In her previous rapture, the Word had "plunged" her in his bleeding side twice in order to purify her with his blood. The Word told her that, after this purification, she would be apt to receive a unique "gift." (p. 47)

2. Ps 148:1.

3. The auxiliary verb is missing in this sentence.

4. Although the syntax of this sentence seems to mean that Mary found the bride for the Word, the mystic in fact intends to say that when he found Mary, the Word found his bride.

5. The Italian "capacity" means both "capability" and "capacity."

In this passage the mystic refers more to the "capacity" of the human soul to receive the Word's gifts.

6. In this first section the Saint's discourse tends to be both elliptical and convoluted. The omission of parts of a sentence does not result exclusively from the mystic's colloquial style. Even in the original version this sentence is truncated.

7. Mt 26:41: "*Spiritus quidem promptus est, caro autem infirma.*"

8. The subject of the sentence is the Father. "His shoulders" are the Son's. However, the sentence does not clarify why the Son did not complain with the Father.

9. Sg 6:9: "*Quae est ista, quae progreditur quasi aurora consurgens, pulchra ut luna, electa ut sol, terribilis ut castrorum acies ordinata?*" [Who is this arising like the dawn,/fair as the moon,/resplendent as the sun,/terrible as an army with banners?]

10. The mystic coins a neologism *squallidare* from the adjective *squallido*, whence the neologism *to squalid*.

11. Mt 11:29: "*Discite a me, quia mitis sum, et humilis corde.*"

12. The sense of this sentence is unclear. The mystic seems to allude to the fact that the disciples had already planned to hold a certain position in God's reign.

13. Mt 26:26; Mk 14:22; Jn 22:19.

14. The Italian version ("*non da noi a basta gli dia te stesso*") is an erroneous transcription. The meaning is incomplete.

15. Cf. Mt 8:8: "*Domine non sum dignus ut intres sub tectum meum.*"

16. Rom 11:33. The actual sentence is: "*Oh altitudo divitiarum sapientiae, et scientiae Dei: quam incomprehensibilia sunt iudicia eius, et investigabiles viae eius!*" [How rich are the depths of God—how deep his wisdom and knowledge—and how impossible to penetrate his motives or understand his methods!]

17. Lk 22:19; 1 Cor 11:24–25.

18. Jn 14:6.

19. Jn 17:1.

20. Jn 17:5. The last clause of this quotation is: "*priusquam mundus esset, apud te.*"

21. Satan's words express his pride. He believes he will be able to ascend beyond God's starts and will place his throne there. In this way, he will become similar to God.

22. Is 46:8: "*Rorate caeli desuper, et nubes pluant iustum*" [Send victory like a dew, you heavens, and let the clouds rain down justice.]

23. Is 16:1.

24. Mt 28:20.

25. Jn 14:12: "Amen, amen, I say to you, the one who believes in me will do the works that I do."

26. "That one" (tale) is the Holy Spirit.

27. The mystic uses the term *esinanita*. This is really a Latinized form from *exinare*.

28. The syntax of this sentence is quite convoluted. The first clause "and now you ask that" is replaced with "your humanity wants."

29. Mt 26:36: "Stay here while I go there to pray."

30. Mt 26:31: "I shall strike the shepherd and the sheep of the flock will be scattered."

31. Mt 26:38: "My soul is sad, even unto death."

32. Mt 26:39: "Father, if it be possible, let this chalice pass me by; but not as I will, but as you will."

33. Mt 26:40: "You had not the strength to keep awake with one hour."

34. Mt 17:5.

35. "Listen to him."

36. Lk 22:42.

37. Mt 7:7.

38. 1 Pt 2:22: "There had been no perjury in his mouth."

39. Lk 22:33: "I am ready."

40. Mt 26:33: "If all are scandalized, I will never be scandalized."

41. Mk 14:37.

42. Mt 26:41: "Watch and pray that you are not tempted. the spirit is willing, but the flesh is weak."

43. Lk 22:42.

44. This sentence is another case in which the mystic merges Italian and Latin. Although the sentence has a Latin "sound," it is closer to Italian. The first clause could be Latin, whereas the second one is clearly Italian: "I formed you and you consoled me."

45. Mt 22:40.

46. Mt 22:45–46.

47. Jn 18:4.

48. Jn 18:5.

49. Jn 18:8: "If I am the one you are looking for, let these others go."

50. Jn 18:11: "Put your sword back in its scabbard."

51. Mt 26:53: "Do you think I cannot appeal to my Father who would promptly send more than twelve legions of angels to my defense?"

52. The mystic here imitates Christ's action in healing the ear of the servant wounded by Peter (see Lk 22:51).

53. Mt 26:50: "My friend, why did you come here?"

54. Lk 22:48: "Judas, do you betray the Son of man with a kiss?"

55. Mt 26:55: Have you come here to arrest me with swords and clubs, as though I were a thief?"

56. Jn 18:20: "I have spoken openly for all the world to hear; I have always taught in the synagogue."

57. Jn 18:23: "If there is something wrong in what I said, point it out; but if there is no offense in it, why do you strike me?"

58. 1 Pt 1:12.

59. "He received strokes because of me.

60. Mk 14:62.

61. Mt 26:64: "You will see the Son seated on the right hand of God's power."

62. Mt 26:68: "Play the prophet, Christ. Who hit you then?"

63. Jn 18:36.

64. Lk 1:33.

65. Cf. Rv 21:18–21: "Its squares and streets are from purest gold. sapphire and emerald are its twelve gates and its twelve columns."

66. Jn 18:38.

67. In this long passage the pronoun *you* seems to refer to a different subject. It is either the humanate Word, or his reign, or the creature.

68. Lam, 4:7: "Wither than snow; more gleaming than milk."

69. Mt 21:9.

70. Jn 19:15.

71. Cf. Mt 25:41: *Discedite a me maledicti in ignem aeternum, qui paratus est diabolo, et angelis eius*."

72. The mystic uses the verb *proporre* in its double meaning of "considering someone more important than someone else" and "offering/suggesting." For both cases I use the verb "to put before."

73. Is 63:1: "Who is this coming from Edom, from Bozrah in garments stained with crimson?"

74. Ps 8:6: "Lord, you have crowned him with glory and honor."

75. Cf. Rv 14:14.

76. Sg 3:11.

77. Jn 19:5.

78. Rv 21:5: "Behold, I make all things new."

79. Cf. Jn 19:11.

80. Is 53:7: "Like a lamb that is led to the slaughterhouse, harshly dealt with, he never opened his mouth."

81. Is 53:4: "Ours were the sufferings he bore."

82. Lk 23:28: "Daughters of Jerusalem, do not weep for me; weep rather for yourself and for your children."

83. The second clause of this sentence is connected with the first one if one considers that "along with" is missing from the text. The Word offered his Father himself and everything he had done in his life.

84. The transcribers refer to the *dialogue* 48, during which the mystic had experienced the death and resurrection of the Word.

Bibliography

PRIMARY SOURCES

Androtio, Fulvio. *Meditatione della vita e morte del nostro Salvatore Gesù Cristo*. Milan, 1579.

Angela of Foligno. *Complete Works*. Ed. Paul Lachance. New York: Paulist Press, 1993.

Augustine. *On Christian Doctrine*. Trans. D. W. Robertson, Jr. New York: Macmillan, 1958.

———. *Confessions*. Trans. Henry Chadwick. New York: Oxford University Press, 1991.

Bardi, Giovanni de'. *Discorso del Gioco del Calcio*. Florence, 1678.

Bernard of Clairvaux. *On the Songs of Songs*. Trans. Irene Edmonds. Kalamazoo MI: Cistercian Publications, 1980.

Gagliardi, Antonio. *Compendio della perfetione cristiana*. Venice, 1572.

Galenus. *Utilité des parties du corps. Oeuvres anatomiques, physiologiques et médicales de Galien*. Trans. C. Daremberg. Paris: J. B. Baillière, 1854.

Gertrude of Helfta. *Spiritual Exercises*. Trans. Gertrud Jaron Lewis and Jack Lewis. Kalamazoo, MI: Cistercian Publications, 1989.

———. *The Herald of Divine Love*. Trans. Margaret Winkworth. New York: Paulist Press, 1993.

Granata, Luigi. *Della introdutione al simbolo della fede*. Venice, 1587.

Hadewijch. *The Complete Works*. Trans. Mother Columbia Hart, O.S.B. New York: Paulist Press, 1980.

Loarte, Gaspare. *Instrutione et avertimenti per medi are la passione di Cristo nostro redentore, con alcune meditationi intorno ad esse*. Rome, 1571.

Meister Eckhart. *The Essential Sermons, Commentaries, Treatises, and Defense*. Trans. Edmund Colledge, O.S.A. and Bernard McGinn. New York: Paulist Press, 1981.

———. *Teacher and Preacher*. Trans. Bernard Mc Ginn. New York: Paulist Press, 1986.

BIBLIOGRAPHY

Origen. *In Lucam Homilia. Opera Omnia*, Patrologia Graeca. Ed. DD.Caroli and Calori Vincentii Delarue. vol. 13, Paris: D'Amboise, 1857.

——. *Comment. in Joan. Opera Omnia*, Patrologia Graeca. vol. 14, Paris: D'Amboise, 1857.

——. *An explanation to Martyrdom. Prayer and Selected Works.* Trans. Rowan A. Greek. New York, 1979.

Pazzi, Maria Maddalena de'. *Tutte le Opere.* 7 vols. Eds. Bruno Nardini, Bruno Visentin, Carlo Catena, Giulio Agresti. Florence: Nardini, 1960–66.

Porete, Marguerite. *The Mirror of Simple Souls.* Trans. Ellen L. Babinsky. New York: Paulist Press, 1993.

Tauler, Johannes. *Sermons.* Trans. Josef Schmidt. New York: Paulist Press, 1985.

Theresa of Avila. *The Life of Saint Teresa of Avila by Herself.* London: Penquin, 1957.

Thomas Aquinas. *Summa contra gentiles.* In *Opera Omnia.* Ed. Roberto Busa. Stuttgart: Friedrich Frommann Verlag, 1980.

SECONDARY SOURCES

Arendt, Hannah. *Love and Saint Augustine.* Chicago: University of Chicago Press, 1996.

Bartkowski, Frances. *Travelers, Immigrants, Inmates.* Minneapolis: University of Minnesota Press, 1995.

Bellini, Bernardo and Gaetano Codogni, Antonio Mainardi. *Vocabolario Universale della lingua italiana.* Mantua, 1853.

Bynum, Caroline Walker. *Holy Feast and Holy Fast.* Berkeley: University of California Press, 1987.

Catena, Carmelo C. *Santa Maria Maddalena de' Pazzi carmelitana; orientamenti spirituali ed ambiente in cui visse.* Rome: Institutum Carmelitanum, 1966.

Certeau, Michel de. *La fable mystique.* Paris: Gallimard, 1982.

——. *The Practice of Everyday Life.* Trans. Steven F. Rendall. Berkeley: University of California Press, 1984.

Corbin, Henry. *Avicenna and the Visionary Recital.* Trans. Willard R. Trask. Princeton, NJ: Princeton University Press, 1988.

Dinzelbacher, Peter. *Vision und Visionsliteratur im Mittelalter.* Stuttgart: Hiersemann, 1981.

Ermanno del S.S. Sacramento. "I manoscritti originali di Santa Maria Maddalena de' Pazzi." *Ephemerides carmeliticae* 7, 1956. 336–99.

Frede, Dorothea. "The Cognitive Role of *Phantasia*." *Essays on Aristotle's De Anima*. Eds. Martha C. Nussbaum and Amélie Oksenberg Rorty. New York: Oxford University Press, 1995.

Guazzo, Francesco. *Compendium Maleficarum*. Trans. E.A. Ashwin London: Rodker, 1929.

Haas, Alois. *Nim Din Selbes War. Studien zur Lehre von der Selbsterkenntnis bei Meister Eckhart, Johannes Tauler and Heinrich Seuse*. Freiburg: Schweiz Universitäts verlag, 1971.

———. *Sermo Mysticus. Studien zu Theologie und Sprache der Deutschen Mystik*. Freiburg: Schweiz Universitäts verlag, 1979.

Héritier-Augé, Françoise. "Semen and Blood. Some Ancient Theories Concerning Their Genesis and Relationship." *Fragments for a History of the Human Body. Part three*. Ed. Michel Feher. New York: Zone, 1989. 159–75.

Kristeva, Julia. "En deuil d'une langue?" *Deuils. Vivre, c'est perdre*. Eds. Nicole Czechowski and Claude Danziger. Paris: Autrement, 1992. 27–36.

Lacan, Jacques. *Ecrits*. Trans. Alan Sheridan. New York: W.W. Norton, 1977.

Maggi, Armando. "The Voice and the Silences of Maria Maddalena de' Pazzi." *Annali d'italianistica*, 13 (1995): 257–81.

———. "Blood as Language in the Visions of Maria Maddalena de' Pazzi." *Rivista di letterature moderne e comparate*, 48 (1995): 219–34.

———. "Performing/Annihilating the Word: Body as Erasure in the Visions of a Florentine Mystic." *TDR. The Drama Review*, 41 (Winter 1997): 110–27.

McGinn, Bernard. *The Foundations of Mysticism. Origins to the Fifth Century*, New York: Crossroad, 1992.

———. "Donne mistiche ed autorità esoterica nel XIV secolo." *Poteri carismatici e informali: chiesa e società medioevali*. Palermo: Sellerio, 1992.

———. *The Growth of Mysticism*. New York: Crossroad, 1994.

Menghi, Girolamo. *Compendio dell'arte esorcistica*. Venice, 1605.

Nancy, Jean-Luc. "Corpus," in *Thinking Bodies*, Ed. Julien Flower Mac-Cannel. Stanford, CA: Stanford University Press, 1994.

Pieper, Josef. "Ueber Das Innere Wort." *Sinn und Form*, 5, 1995. 706–708.

Pozzi, Giovanni. *Le parole dell'estasi*. Milan, 1984.

BIBLIOGRAPHY

————. "L'identico del diverso in Santa Maddalena de' Pazzi." *Freiburger Zeitschrift für Philosophie und Theologie*, 33, 1986. 46–68.

————, and Claudio Leonardi, Eds. *Scrittrici mistiche italiane*. Genoa: Marietti, 1989.

Quint, Joseph. "Mystik und Sprache." *Altdeutsche und Altniederländische Mystik*. Freiberg: Schweiz Universitäts verlag, 1964.

Rovatti, Pier Aldo. *Abitare la distanza*. Milan: Feltrinelli, 1994.

Salernitano, Masuccio. *Novellino*. Florence, 1572.

Secondin, Bruno. *Santa Maria Maddalena de'Pazzi. Esperienza e dottrina*. Rome: Institutum Carmelitanum, 1974.

Sybilla, Bartolomeo. *Speculum peregrinarum quaestionum*. Florence, 1499.

Vacant, A., and Mangenot, E. Eds. *Dictionnaire de Théologie Catholique*. Paris: Letouzey et Ané, 1910.

Walz, A. M. "Tauler im italienischen Sprachraum." *Johannes Tauler, ein Deutscher Mystiker*. Essen, 1961.

Weil, Simone. *On Science, Necessity, and the Love of God*. Trans. Richard Rees. London: Oxford University Press, 1968.

————. *Waiting For God*. Trans. Emma Craufurd. New York: Harper, 1973.

Wolterstorff, Nicholas. *Divine Discourse. Philosophical Reflections on the Claim That God Speaks*. New York: Oxford University Press, 1995.

Index

References in **Boldface** are to Introductory material.

INDEX

22, 25; love, 44, 45, 46;
suffering, 52; text, 97–286;
Word, 14, 16, 17, 18–21,
24, 26
Diego, St., 295, 296–97

Enemy. *See* Devils
Ermanno del S.S. Sacramento, 10
Eternity, 192–93

Forty Days (De' Pazzi), 10; anxious
love, 49–50; inner senses,
35; text, 59–94
Francis, St., 138, 295–96

Gertrude of Helfta, 30, 38–39

Hadewijch, 38
Happiness, 51–53
Humility, 248

Imperturbability, 193–95
Inner senses, 35

James, St., 308–9
Jesus Christ: Ascension, 266–86;
marriage to, 124–34; Passion,
64, 77, 90, 97–123, 306–11,
325–26; in tomb, 202–65
John, St., 310, 311; Passion,
77, 78, 104, 308; Word,
16–17, 67, 73, 105
Judas, 79–80, 110, 170

Lacan, Jacques, 47
Leonardi, Claudio, 5
Loarte, Gaspar, 8, 34
Love, 26, 43–51, 59–72; anxious
love, 45, 46–47, 48, 49–50;

dead love, 45, 46; separate
love, 45

Maria Maddalena de' Pazzi, St. *See*
St. De' Pazzi, Maria
Maddalena, St.
Mariani, Gaetano, 1
Mary, 51, 129–30, 131, 138, 141,
154, 156–58, 170, 257–61,
263–65, 274–77, 279–82;
Passion of Christ, 98–102,
203–22; peace, 40, 41–42
Mary Magdalen, St., 98, 204, 208,
297, 299, 303
Matthew, St., 309
Milk, 31–33, 248–51
Miracles, 183–84
Mirror of Simple Souls (Porete), 39

Nardini, Francesco, 8
Neumann, John, St., 1

Obedience, 62, 68
On Christian Doctrine (Augustine),
12
On the Song of Songs (Bernard), 15,
43
Origen, 15, 22, 34–35

Parole dell' etasi, Le (Pozzi and
Leonardi), 5
Passion, 64, 77, 90, 97–123,
306–11, 325–26
Paul, St., 34, 38, 130, 174
Pazzi, Maria Maddalena, de', St.
See De' Pazzi, Maria
Maddalena, St.
Peter, St., 78, 82, 111, 113, 308,
318, 319; contemplation, 35;

Other Volumes in This Series

Other Volumes in This Series

Other Volumes in This Series